DESIGNING SOCIAL SERVICE MARKETS

RISK, REGULATION AND RENT-SEEKING

DESIGNING SOCIAL SERVICE MARKETS

RISK, REGULATION AND RENT-SEEKING

EDITED BY GABRIELLE MEAGHER,
ADAM STEBBING AND DIANA PERCHE

Australian
National
University

ANU PRESS

Australian
National
University

ANU PRESS

Published by ANU Press
The Australian National University
Canberra ACT 2600, Australia
Email: anupress@anu.edu.au

Available to download for free at press.anu.edu.au

ISBN (print): 9781760465315
ISBN (online): 9781760465322

WorldCat (print): 1343931525
WorldCat (online): 1343931378

DOI: 10.22459/DSSM.2022

Cover design and layout by ANU Press

This book is published under the aegis of the Social Sciences Editorial Board of ANU Press.

ACADEMY OF
THE SOCIAL SCIENCES
IN AUSTRALIA

Contents

Abbreviations

ACCC	Australian Competition and Consumer Commission
ACECQA	Australian Children's Education and Care Quality Authority
ACFI	Aged Care Funding Instrument
ACTU	Australian Council of Trade Unions
AIRC	Australian Industrial Relations Commission
ALP	Australian Labor Party
ANAO	Australian National Audit Office
ATSIC	Aboriginal and Torres Strait Islander Commission
AUST	Allied Unions Superannuation Trust
BUS	Builders Unions Superannuation Fund
CCS	Child Care Subsidy
CDEP	Community Development Employment Projects
CDP	Community Development Program
COAG	Council of Australian Governments
CRA	Commonwealth Rental Assistance
CSHA	Commonwealth–State Housing Agreement
DAA	Department of Aboriginal Affairs
DEWR	Department of Employment and Workplace Relations
DIAC	Department of Immigration and Citizenship
DILGEA	Department of Immigration, Local Government and Ethnic Affairs
DIMA	Department of Immigration and Multicultural Affairs

DIMIA	Department of Immigration and Multicultural and Indigenous Affairs
DPO	disabled people's organisation
DSS	Department of Social Services
ECEC	early childhood education and care
FOFA	Future of Financial Advice
FPO	for-profit organisation
GFC	Global Financial Crisis
HSP	Humanitarian Settlement Program
HSS	Humanitarian Settlement Services
IHSS	Integrated Humanitarian Settlement Strategy
IOM	International Organization for Migration
ISC	Insurance and Superannuation Commission
JSA	Job Services Australia
KPI	key performance indicator
LLLB	Living Longer, Living Better policy
LUCRF	Labour Union Cooperative Retirement Fund
NAHA	National Affordable Housing Agreement
NCCS	National Child Care Strategy
NCOA	National Commission of Audit
NDIA	National Disability Insurance Agency
NDIS	National Disability Insurance Scheme
NDS	National Disability Services
NGO	non-government organisation
NPO	non-profit organisation
NQF	National Quality Framework
NQS	National Quality Standard
NSW	New South Wales
NTER	Northern Territory Emergency Response
OECD	Organisation for Economic Co-operation and Development
OSSA	*Occupational Superannuation Standards Act 1987*

PM&C	Department of the Prime Minister and Cabinet
PPP	public–private partnership
RAC	residential aged care
RJCP	Remote Jobs and Communities Program
ROMAMPAS	Review of Migrant and Multicultural Programs and Services
RSE	Registrable Superannuation Entity
SHA	State Housing Authority
SHI	Social Housing Initiative
SHP	Special Humanitarian Program
SIS	Superannuation Industry Supervision
SMSF	self-managed super fund
UK	United Kingdom
UN	United Nations
VET	vocational education and training

List of figures

List of tables

Acknowledgements

Several of the chapters in this collection began as contributions to a workshop sponsored through the generative and generous program for such events funded by the Academy of the Social Sciences in Australia. We would like to thank the Academy of Social Sciences for its support. The workshop was co-convened by Gabrielle Meagher and two very generative and generous fellows of the academy, Valerie Braithwaite and Mark Considine, both of whom have made towering contributions to the study of public policy, marketisation and regulation. We would like to thank Val, Mark and all the participants in the workshop for two very informative and engaging days.

We would also like to express our gratitude to Frank Bongiorno, Jenny Stewart and the Social Sciences Editorial Board of ANU Press for their support for and confidence in the book. We thank the two anonymous reviewers who gave us thoughtful and very helpful advice for improvements, to which we have done our best to respond.

In addition to the expert knowledge and deep insights that readers will find in their chapters, the authors have made contributions visible only to us as editors: they have been responsive and patient, which we appreciate enormously.

Gabrielle Meagher, Adam Stebbing and Diana Perche
March 2022

Contributors

Dr Elizabeth Adamson is a Research Fellow at the Social Policy Research Centre at the University of New South Wales. Elizabeth's research interests cross broad comparative care and family policy, including early childhood education and care, the social and political economy of formal and informal care, and gender, migration and care.

Dr Richard Baldwin was a senior lecturer and director of Health Service Management in the Faculty of Health at the University of Technology Sydney. Richard's research focuses on residential aged care policy in Australia.

Dr Megan Blaxland is a Senior Research Fellow at the Social Policy Research Centre at the University of New South Wales. Megan's research on family policy focuses on early childhood education and care, particularly family day care, and practices that facilitate service access for low-income families.

Natasha Cortis is Associate Professor at the Social Policy Research Centre at the University of New South Wales. Natasha's work explores the organisation, delivery and evaluation of human services, focusing on funding and workforce issues in community services, and women's employment and economic security.

Dr Bob Davidson is an Honorary Research Fellow in Sociology in the School of Social Sciences at Macquarie University and has extensive experience as a senior government official, private consultant and researcher. Bob's research and consultancy work are centred on the intersection of economics, social policy and organisational theory, with a particular focus on the provision of human services, human service markets and service providers, especially in aged care.

Dr Adèle Garnier is Associate Professor in the Department of Geography, Université Laval, Canada, and Honorary Senior Lecturer in the School of Social Sciences, Macquarie University. Adèle's research investigates the interplay of regulatory levels (local to global) in migration and refugee policy.

Gabrielle Meagher is Professor Emerita in the School of Social Sciences at Macquarie University and Adjunct Professor in the Department of Social Work, Stockholm University. Gabrielle's research investigates political, economic and social dimensions of the marketisation of social services in Australia and Sweden.

Dr Diana Perche is Senior Lecturer in Social Research and Policy at the University of New South Wales. Diana's research focuses on the participation of First Nations people in Australian politics and policymaking, and the ways in which governments use evidence and ideology to design public policy affecting or targeting Indigenous people in Australia.

Dallas Rogers is Associate Professor in the Sydney School of Architecture, Design and Planning at the University of Sydney. Dallas has a broad interest in housing, land, real estate and urban development.

Kristian Ruming is Professor of Geography and Planning at Macquarie University. An urban and economic geographer, Kristian has conducted research on the management and redevelopment of social housing estates, affordable housing provision, urban regeneration and community participation and activism in urban planning and development.

Dr Pranita Shrestha is a Postdoctoral Research Associate at the Sydney School of Architecture, Design and Planning, at the University of Sydney. Pranita's research is centred on issues of social justice, specifically related to informal urbanism, public and affordable housing and gentrification and displacement.

Dr Adam Stebbing is Lecturer in Sociology at Macquarie University in Sydney. Adam's research focuses on the growing importance of 'welfare by other means' for Australian social policy.

Dr Georgia van Toorn is a Postdoctoral Fellow at the ARC Centre of Excellence for Automated Decision-Making and Society, University of New South Wales. Georgia's research program comprises a series of projects investigating the neoliberal restructuring of social welfare regimes through the prisms of disability, work and technology.

Dr Laura Wynne is a researcher living and working on Dharawal land in New South Wales, whose work has focused on sustainability and justice in Australian cities. Laura's research has examined transitions to sustainable urban futures in relation to food, transport and development, as well as on justice and equity issues relating to urban renewal and public housing.

Foreword

The past 40 years have seen theories of privatisation and marketisation dominate government decision-making. The public narrative has been to portray everyone as a winner. Private service providers would be welcomed into the market to give universal coverage and diversity of choice to consumers. Consumers would steer the market towards quality by choosing the best service providers, which in turn would profit and prosper and outperform their competitors. The theory was simple and captured the imagination of both the right and the left sides of Australian politics.

Hopes—possibly blind hopes—were unrealistically raised for better social services for everyone. We failed collectively to anticipate the dire consequences of discounting the values of care and compassion for fellow humans. Tragic stories have emerged of markets in which atrocious harms have been incentivised rather than the anticipated quality services. The past decade has seen a rollout of Australian government royal commissions that have brought to light market failures of this kind: Institutional Responses to Child Sexual Abuse (2013–17), Detention and Protection of Children in the Northern Territory (2016–17), Aged Care Quality and Safety (2018–21) and Violence, Abuse, Neglect and Exploitation of People with Disability (2019–). There have also been many government inquiries critical of the delivery of a range of social services in both the government and the private spheres.

This collection traces the historical ascendancy of the marketisation of social services in Australia. The book does not rail against marketisation but calls for a more open-minded and dispassionate analysis of the conditions under which markets will offer benefits and the conditions under which governments are best equipped to meet the needs of people. It does this through meticulously documented historical case studies of policy developments within seven domains important in the everyday lives of Australians: child care, housing, employment programs, superannuation, aged care, disability services and refugee settlement services. All have encountered serious obstacles to delivering the equitable, diversified, high-quality and efficient services that are in the public interest.

The collection strikingly demonstrates how the various pathways governments chose to marketise social services were peppered with potholes. Private providers looked for profitable ventures. Care-giving without adequate profit margins was not an attractive investment. It was up to government to help create the profit margin. And, as for quality, what did that mean anyhow? To free marketeers, regulation of quality was anathema. Quality was to be created—and so it was through advertising, public relations and communication departments that grew to prominence in private providers and government departments alike. Citizens had to wade through spin and hype and complex tables of government statistics to find the truth. But truth often revealed itself belatedly with disappointment, a sense of abandonment and sometimes tragedy.

This is not to suggest that successive governments did not recognise market failures and did not try to contain or correct them. Chapters detail the 'patches' that were applied to address emerging problems. The right and left sides of politics tweaked their policies in different ways to address problems. Parties of the right designed policy to benefit providers while parties of the left sought to empower consumers. The more important point is that, decade after decade, market thinking has increasingly become entrenched in government policy and in the public's imagination. At the same time, as the case studies in this book reveal, policies were being revised at a frenetic pace. Policies were not working as expected.

This book reminds us that we need to better understand the place of markets alongside the provision of government services in particular social service contexts. The balance we have struck over the past 40 years has not worked as well as expected. Furthermore, getting the balance right is not a job of policy design 'by template' or by generalist public servants or consultants. Rather, balancing private and public provision with consumer needs requires the guidance of experienced and sector-wise people, with the public interest foremost in their minds, who can pre-empt problems and develop contingency plans in readiness for when obstacles arise. Implicit in the discussions in the following chapters is a picture of too many policymakers and stakeholders who are ideologically trapped and bereft of a deep understanding of the needs and lives of the people for whom social services exist.

With each chapter of this book, we see the growth of not only markets and the private provision of social services, but also the power of private interests. Across different domains of marketisation, consumer power was no match for corporate power; the regulatory state was incapacitated as deregulation ideology was spun and enacted; and evidence of market failures was supplanted with determined ignorance, misinformation and communications of denial of undue harm. Trapped by free-market ideology, successive governments proved incapable of standing up to opportunistic rent-seeking and of supporting professionally committed staff who continued to perform their duties responsibly and diligently in the face of poorly designed policies.

As private providers increasingly dominate service delivery markets, governments become increasingly dependent on them. Their place at the decision-making table is guaranteed; they are too big to be ignored. This power is wielded to ensure that market-failure 'patches' developed by government do not break out of the ideological bubble within which policy has been designed and, therefore, do not intrude on private sector profitability. Quality standards and their enforcement continue as a point of contention among social service providers, as do contract transparency and performance accountability. The chapters also provide glimpses of governments privileging some private providers over others, encouraging consolidation, risking domination and losing perspective on how the mission of governments to serve their people is different from the mission of corporations to make a profit. Arguably most alarming of all is the cumulation of stories in these chapters of taxpayers' money being funnelled into a system where expenditure on quality service delivery is reduced by expenditure directed to achieving greater influence over policy development as well as competitive advantage in the court of public opinion.

The twenty-first century has illuminated the complexities of us living with one another in an interconnected world. Extreme climatic events, pandemics and militarisation globally have unsettled populations and exposed governments that are better on rhetoric than on orchestrating actions to keep their citizens safe. These stories—both of success and of failure—are yet to be told. This book challenges us to think more critically about how our world works and should work. We are invited to see greyness, to be wary of singular theoretical visions of the future and to accept that ideology is about values and always needs to be tempered by data, rigorous analysis and contestation. Our insights will be richer and our understanding more profound through reflecting on the case studies of social service provision presented in this book. Lessons learnt can collectively elevate the public interest to a higher level of consideration and serve future generations more humanely, equitably, effectively and efficiently.

Valerie Braithwaite, FASSA
December 2021

Introduction: Designing markets in the Australian social service system

Gabrielle Meagher, Diana Perche
and Adam Stebbing

In Australia, as in many other countries, governments on both the left and the right are increasingly designing markets to deliver publicly subsidised social services.[1] For services including child care, aged care and support for people with disabilities, various market instruments including contracting, competition and consumer choice have been introduced to organise provision. Market instruments, particularly contracts with providers external to the public sector, are also used to organise services offered to less-visible social groups, such as prisoners, asylum-seekers and children living in out-of-home care. And across all social services, from aged care to prisons, marketisation has expanded the reach of private businesses in service delivery.

Policymakers argue that market designs for the delivery of services such as child care, aged care and disability support benefit consumers, who gain increased choice, higher-quality services and more diverse and innovative providers. This case could hardly have been put more explicitly than in a 2015 budget factsheet on the Liberal–National Coalition government's aged care reform:

---

1   We use the term 'social services', but it is interchangeable with other commonly used terms—including 'human services', 'welfare services' and 'community services'—which other researchers, including contributors to this volume, variously employ.

The Government's Aged Care Agenda will progressively move aged care from a welfare-style system to one that empowers older Australians to choose their own care services, through a market-based system …

Importantly, there will be increased competition, leading to enhanced quality and innovation in service delivery, and reduced regulation and red tape for providers. These changes are a key step in moving to a less regulated, more consumer-driven and market-based aged care system. (DSS 2015: 1)

Proponents of market designs across all social services argue that, in addition to these advantages, they will benefit citizens in their role as 'taxpayers', because they drive lower costs.[2]

How much faith in markets for social services is warranted?

Clearly, Australian policymakers have put great faith in market mechanisms, invoking this faith in support of extending contracts, competition and choice to more and more service areas over more than three decades (Cahill and Toner 2018; Lyons 1995, 1998; Meagher and Goodwin 2015). Yet significant problems have emerged that might be expected to challenge the depth of this faith. Many of these problems are predictable, arising from what economists call 'market imperfections' related to the way market participants respond to the structure of incentives and the availability of information (Blank 2000). These problems, while common in markets in general, are more likely in social services, not least because these are aimed at meeting the development, support and care needs of people, many of whom have limited capacity as consumers (Davidson 2009: 47). The attributes, operation and characteristic failures of social service markets are well established (Blank 2000; Davidson 2009, 2011, 2018; Gingrich 2011) and we discuss some of them briefly in the next section. In this section, we briefly survey some Australian evidence that the marketisation of social services has too often resulted in poorer service quality, especially for more vulnerable people, and wasted resources.

---

2   See, for example, the terms of reference framed by then treasurer Scott Morrison for the Productivity Commission's study report *Introducing Competition and Informed User Choice into Human Services: Identifying sectors for reform* (2016: iv–vi).

We begin by presenting some vignettes of experiences of marketised social services from the service user's perspective (see Box 1). Drawn from the lives of mostly middle-class Australians, the vignettes do not point to unusual or extreme problems. Rather, they give a sense, at the outset of the book, of the day-to-day difficulties many people have in navigating social service markets and receiving services within them.

Box 1 Vignettes capturing service users' experiences of marketised social services

Choice and competition in the NDIS?

Margot is the full-time carer for her husband, Gerard, who, at 63 years of age, has been diagnosed as in the advanced stages of early onset dementia. Gerard's condition has deteriorated rapidly; he can no longer be left alone at night as he is at risk of injury due to increasing disorientation. His individualised budget with the National Disability Insurance Scheme (NDIS) has recently been increased to cover the cost of a carer to keep him safe at night while Margot sleeps. Holding power of attorney for Gerard, Margot is responsible for finding a suitable carer service. However, her around-the-clock caring responsibilities leave little time to find and research suitable carer services, let alone to find comparable information about the range of services offered and reliable indicators of their quality. After a few months with little success in navigating the system, Margot learns she can use funds from Gerard's individualised budget for a care coordinator to assist. The care coordinator is not aware of any suitable carer services with staff availability, so she asks for a recommendation from a colleague. As the recommended carer service can take Gerard on as a client immediately, they are employed within the week.

Active consumers in residential aged care?

Daniel is hopeful he has finally found appropriate residential aged care for his father, Reginald, who is 87 years old. Reginald requires around-the-clock care and has osteoporosis, so is at risk of major injury if he falls. Reginald had been living in a retirement village and moved temporarily to the nursing home on the premises. But, other than for a short respite period, there were no permanent spaces available. Daniel found his father's choices were limited. Reginald moved to a second, more affordable facility closer to where Daniel lived that was run by a large charity and had a space available. It had a nice website and positive testimonials, but Daniel soon became worried about staffing levels, the cleanliness of facilities and the quality of the food. Daniel then found a spot at a third facility that was new, expensive and even boasted it had a chef on the premises. Yet, Reginald complained about a lack of privacy as other clients could enter his room at any time because there were no latches on doors, and he had items stolen. Staff often took a long time to respond to calls, too. Unable to rely on price signals or available information about service quality, Daniel resorted to 'trial and error'. He recently received a call back from a residential facility after being on a waiting list for 12 months. He hopes this fourth service will meet his father's needs.

Choice and supply in the childcare market?

Yen and Ollie searched for suitable child care for their six-month-old twin boys. As they both needed to work on Mondays and Tuesdays, Yen and Ollie were after two days of child care a week, preferably in a service in their Melbourne suburb or close by. They contacted two services that were highly recommended by their friends; neither had places available and both had very long waiting lists. Yen and Ollie then contacted a third service with a good reputation that did not have places available, but they were able to put their sons on the waiting list. Four weeks after putting their sons' names down, Yen received a call from the service, which had one place available on the requested days. The service would not hold the place until two became available. As Yen and Ollie did not want to separate their twins, or have the hassle of dropping off and picking up their children at multiple services, they declined the place and kept looking. Eventually, they were able to find two places at a local childcare service that had a mixed reputation.

Buying knowledge to navigate the aged care market

Susan's mother, Anne, was in hospital for the third time in a few months with respiratory problems and early stage dementia. This time, the geriatric specialist and the social worker in the hospital decided Anne could not be discharged to return home. Instead, the family would need to find a place in a residential aged care facility, urgently. The hospital told Susan if the family could not find a place themselves, Anne would be discharged to the first available facility on their list—on the other side of Sydney—with no room for negotiation. The hospital provided Susan with a list of local residential facilities, but there was no information on what each one was like or whether there was a likely vacancy. Susan spent hours ringing for appointments, waiting for phone calls to be returned and visiting aged care centres. Very few had vacancies, and none seemed acceptable for her mother, who was very unhappy about not returning to her own home. The rules around government-subsidised places, entry charges and the 'extra services' were confusing. Susan knew she would also need to arrange to sell Anne's retirement village unit to cover the entry fee to secure a place, which would cost more than $700,000. Susan was feeling desperate when a friend recommended she hire a consultant to help her navigate the aged care market. The consultant knew all the local residential facilities and kept track of where places were becoming available. She helped Susan to find a suitable place for her mother and to fill out the paperwork to secure it. The consultant charged a non-refundable fee for her initial assessment and meetings with the family, and a second flat fee for the search. It was an unexpected expense of a few thousand dollars at a difficult time.

Employment assistance or compliance reporting? Priorities in the CDP

Mick waited with the other Community Development Program (CDP) participants in the yard outside the CDP building on the edge of town for his name to be marked off. He knew if he was not marked off correctly by the contracted service provider, he would risk being breached by Centrelink and losing his unemployment benefits. The so-called work-like activities he would be undertaking this week were, however, hardly worth showing up for. The participants had been promised training in mechanics, but the provider could not raise the funds for the equipment, so instead, they were back to gardening and keeping the town tidy. The women were given craft to do—like children. It was the same thing, five days a week. He wished he could take some time off so he could visit family up north. He had been to the office of the employment services agency the previous day for his regular meeting with his case manager. As usual, she had not offered any advice about finding jobs in the local area; she was just interested in keeping his record updated in the computer system. She was not from the local area, was on a working holiday visa and did not know much about the local people. The provider for whom she works is based hundreds of kilometres away, in the big city. The people from the agency do not seem to care much about the people in Mick's community; they just worry about reporting who attends the work activities each day so they receive their activity fee from the government. Mick cannot see how things will ever get better for him and his family.

Failures in social service markets take their toll on the lives of the people these services are meant to develop, support and care for. Some failures are relatively pervasive, occurring during the conduct of business as usual. Other failures occur less often but are no less the result of the design of the markets in which they happen. A few examples serve to illustrate.

One set of problems arises when authorities tasked with overseeing quality in social service markets do not identify, appropriately sanction or remedy poor-quality services. Monitoring and oversight are essential when governments delegate delivery of social services to external providers and research has shown that marketisation and private sector provision increase the need for effective regulation (Braithwaite et al. 2007). If oversight is weak, poor quality can become business as usual. In social service markets, regulatory oversight is prone to weakness if private providers exert influence over its terms, if supervising authorities are under-resourced and because of the low political salience of most affected consumer groups. To a greater or lesser extent, these weaknesses are evident in the various Australian social service markets.

Australian governments had provided disability support services both directly and by outsourcing them to mostly non-government providers before the introduction, in 2013, of the National Disability Insurance Scheme (NDIS). This scheme—the origins of which are the subject of Georgia van Toorn's Chapter 5 in this volume—has further marketised disability support. The hope of the scheme's designers is that marketisation will solve many of the problems of previous arrangements, including inefficiency, rigidity and lack of choice for people with disabilities. Accordingly, scheme 'participants' are assigned an individual budget, which they can use to purchase supports approved in their plan in markets for relevant goods and services. Using language very like that cited above in relation to aged care marketisation, the National Disability Insurance Agency (NDIA) declares in its 'market position statements' that 'a core part' of its role is 'to facilitate a vibrant and competitive supply of services in order to maximise the potential benefits, choice and control for people with disabilities' (NDIA 2016: 17).[3] The design of the NDIS includes 'lower barriers to entry' to the market and opening supply to 'for-profit and other new entrants from adjacent markets, digital disruptors, mainstream and offshore organisations' (NDIA 2016: 17). In 2016, the market position statements estimated massive growth would occur in the coming three years in both the number of disabled people accessing the NDIS (up by 70 per cent) and the number of workers required to support them (up by more than 90 per cent).

The relatively liberal market design of the NDIS, its very ambitious growth targets and the high proportion of vulnerable people among participants[4] create demanding conditions for quality oversight. Yet the agencies and systems required to undertake oversight were not in place when the scheme started and have only recently become fully operational. A quality framework was not released until 2017, after the scheme's state-by-state rollout began in mid-2016, and a dedicated authority, the NDIS Quality and Safeguards Commission (NDIS Commission), was not established until mid-2018. Only in mid-2019 were 'acceptable checks' made mandatory for workers providing 'NDIS supports

---

3   We quote the NSW 'market position statement' here; the NDIA created one for each jurisdiction, each containing these programmatic statements.
4   According to our analysis of data on the primary diagnosis of NDIS participants for December 2019, 35 per cent have an intellectual disability or other diagnosis causing cognitive impairment, 30 per cent have autism and 9 per cent have a major mental illness. Other participants have mainly physical or sensory impairments. (Available from: data.ndis.gov.au/media/2156/download).

and services on behalf of a registered NDIS provider to people with disability' (NDIS Commission n.d.), and a nationally consistent worker screening program was fully implemented only in mid-2020. The NDIS Commission became operational nationally on 1 December 2020.

Early evidence emerging from the NDIS Commission suggests quality problems in the NDIS have been significant, although enforcement actions have been few. In the 18 months to December 2019, the commission received almost 67,000 reports of the use of inappropriate restraints, more than 1,800 reports of abuse and more than 1,000 reports of neglect under its mandatory incident reporting requirements. Nearly 5,000 further complaints were also made (SCALC 2020a). Across the same period, the commission 'took compliance and enforcement action against 17 individuals and seven providers' (SCALC 2020b).

In a pattern well documented in aged care (see below; see also Braithwaite et al. 2007), a major scandal in 2020 prompted media and public criticism of the NDIS Commission, and the government responded by tightening regulation. Ms Ann-Marie Smith died apparently as a result of extreme neglect, despite being in full-time care under the NDIS (Henriques-Gomes 2020b). An inquiry soon revealed that the care worker assigned to assist Ms Smith had not been screened by her employer until after Ms Smith's death (Henriques-Gomes 2020a), despite the employer attesting on its website that all its workers were screened and security checked, had 'strong moral values and personal integrity' and 'a firm understanding of … their duty of care'.[5] Within weeks, the government announced expanded powers for the NDIS Commission to 'ban unsuitable providers and workers from working with … NDIS participants' (Robert 2020).

Meanwhile, following concerns expressed over many years by people with disabilities and their families, the Royal Commission into Violence, Abuse, Neglect and Exploitation of People with Disability was established in April 2019. The commission's wider terms of reference include the quality and safety of services and supports for disabled people, and the efficacy of the NDIS Commission will no doubt come under further scrutiny. Emerging evidence of the efficacy of oversight from disability workers' perspectives suggests some provider organisations prioritise profit over service quality and their reporting obligations, leaving their staff

5   The Internet Archive is the source of a version of the page that pre-dates the death of Ms Smith (available from: web.archive.org/web/20200602101317/integritycare.com.au/about-us/).

with too few resources to provide good care and too little time to engage with complex and often cumbersome reporting systems (Cortis and van Toorn 2022).

In care for older people, marketisation is more longstanding than in support for people with disabilities. Aged care services have been provided by public, non-profit and for-profit organisations in a 'mixed economy' since the 1960s, with governments subsidising and managing a growing system with various instruments since then (see Chapter 6, this volume). However, market rhetoric and deliberate market design have become increasingly prominent in the policies of governments of both major parties since the 1990s. In residential care, the Howard Coalition government's *Aged Care Act 1997* deregulated key aspects of funding and introduced user-pays principles, both of which made the sector more attractive to for-profit providers, including large corporations. Marketisation intensified with the wave of reforms legislated under the Labor Party, following the Productivity Commission's inquiry 'Caring for Older Australians' in 2010–11, and expanded beyond residential care. Support for older people living in their own homes was provided almost entirely by public and non-profit organisations until one of the two major programs, the Home Care Packages Program (HCPP), was reorganised around market-inflected ideas of consumer choice in 2016. Since then, the share of for-profit providers has grown from 13 to 36 per cent, and international franchise companies and gig-economy platforms have moved in (Meagher 2021).

Media reports year after year have also documented community concerns, particularly about the quality of residential care for older people (for example, Blumer 2018; Casben 2019; Connolly 2014, 2017, 2019; Day 2015; Ford 2018; Keane 2019; Lane 2016; O'Neill 2013; Opie 2019; Squires 2010; Strachan 2014). Researchers and public inquiries have found widespread inappropriate use of physical and/or chemical constraints (Royal Commission into Aged Care Quality and Safety 2019; Westbury et al. 2019) and a high prevalence of malnutrition (Kellet et al. 2015) in nursing homes, both of which undermine older people's health and wellbeing and shorten their lives. Further evidence of poor—even declining—quality of care is the increased incidence between 2000 and 2013 of premature death from causes such as falls, choking and suicide (Ibrahim et al. 2018). Despite these evidently sustained problems, the statutory regulator has typically found little to fault. In 2017, the year for which the most up-to-date consolidated data are available, more than 95 per cent of audited facilities met all 44 of the quality standards prevailing at that time, and more than 98 per cent were reaccredited for the maximum period (AACQA 2017: 48).[6]

Across the decades, policymakers have responded to media scandals about poor-quality aged care by setting up inquiries and reorganising regulatory agencies. In 2017 alone, the federal government initiated three reviews into nursing home quality and the efficacy of its oversight.[7] However, media reports of serious problems in many facilities continued to appear— ultimately leading to the establishment of the Royal Commission into Aged Care Quality and Safety in 2018, along with a new agency for the oversight of quality, the Aged Care Quality and Safety Commission. Despite the new oversight agency and the royal commission in progress, in July 2019, yet another major adverse event—this one very intimately related to marketisation—prompted yet another inquiry. Conflict between a private 'approved provider' of residential care services and the company it had subcontracted to manage delivery of those services resulted in the evacuation, without warning, of 69 residents of two nursing homes within the Earle Haven Retirement Village on Queensland's Gold Coast. The inquiry into the incident made yet further recommendations for how the aged care market should be managed by public authorities (Department of Health 2019).

Since the Earle Haven incident, the Covid-19 pandemic has struck, and nursing homes have again been much in the news. In the first wave of the pandemic, Australia avoided the cataclysmic, widespread failure of nursing homes to manage exposure and care of their residents seen in Europe and the United States. However, this was mostly luck: there were relatively

---

6   Equivalent data are not published in this format in the agency's final annual report, for 2017–18. From 1 January 2019, the Aged Care Quality and Safety Commission (ACQSC) replaced the AACQA and the aged care complaints commissioner, and on 1 January 2020, the ACQSC took over other regulatory functions formerly held by the Department of Health. At the same time, the accreditation standards and auditing and reporting procedures changed.

7   In May 2017, the minister for aged care commissioned a review of national aged care quality regulatory processes in response to abuses at the Oakden facility in South Australia (Carnell and Paterson 2017). In June, the Senate referred the matter of 'the effectiveness of the aged care quality assessment and accreditation framework for protecting residents from abuse and poor practices, and ensuring proper clinical and medical care standards are maintained and practised' to its Community Affairs References Committee (SCARC 2019: ix). In December, the minister for health referred the matter of the quality of care in residential aged care facilities to the House of Representatives Standing Committee on Health, Aged Care and Sport (2018). In August 2022, the new ALP government brought forward the scheduled review of ACQSC in the light of its apparent failings during the pandemic.

few cases and little community transmission in Australia overall. Where the coronavirus took hold in two Sydney nursing homes, it cut a terrible swathe. One managed better, losing six residents (Alexander 2020). In the other, more than 70 staff and residents were infected with Covid-19 and 17 residents died (Patty 2020).

A second wave of infections occurred from mid-June to mid-September 2020 in Victoria—this time, driven by relatively widespread community transmission. During this outbreak, Victoria recorded more than two-thirds of all cases in Australia and nursing homes were affected on a scale commensurate with that of the outbreak itself. Approximately 2,000 people living in nursing homes in Melbourne were infected, 1,600 of them in large outbreaks at 10 private facilities. More than 600 of these people died. Nursing home residents represented less than 10 per cent of all infections recorded in Victoria, but 80 per cent of the people who died.[8] Notably, public nursing homes fared better; only three older people contracted Covid-19 and none died. Experts put this down to state government mandates for high nurse–resident ratios (Handley 2020).

During 2021, most older people in nursing homes were vaccinated and sporadic outbreaks caused a further 220 or so deaths across the year. However, the emergence of the highly infectious Omicron variant late in that year caused a second major spike in deaths in nursing homes in early 2022. Outbreaks occurred in thousands of homes, and nearly 2,500 older residents died during the first seven months of 2022.[9] Delays to third- and fourth-dose vaccinations and infections among thousands of staff exacerbated the already very strained conditions in the sector.

---

8   Authors' calculations based on Victorian and Commonwealth government data available on 20 September 2020. For nursing home infections and deaths, see 'COVID-19 cases in aged care services—Residential care' (available from: www.health.gov.au/resources/covid-19-cases-in-aged-care-services-residential-care). For data on specific nursing home outbreaks, see DHHS (2020). For data on the pandemic in Australia, including information for each state, see the Health Alert 'Coronavirus (COVID-19) case numbers and statistics' (available from: www.health.gov.au/news/health-alerts/novel-coronavirus-2019-ncov-health-alert/coronavirus-covid-19-current-situation-and-case-numbers). An updated analysis of data available to 6 August 2021 reveals that 677 older people living in residential care had died with Covid-19—all in private facilities. Of these deaths, 57 per cent were in for-profit homes and 43 per cent in non-profit homes. (Authors' calculations based on Commonwealth Government data, available from: www.health.gov.au/sites/default/files/documents/2021/08/covid-19-outbreaks-in-australian-residential-aged-care-facilities-6-august-2021_0.pdf.)
9   These data are derived from the Department of Health's weekly reports on 'Covid-19 outbreaks in Australian residential aged care facilities' (available from: www.health.gov.au/resources/collections/covid-19-outbreaks-in-australian-residential-aged-care-facilities).

The catastrophic failures of care in nursing homes exposed to the pandemic pointed to systematic problems with the nursing home market, arising from how the regulations that underpin the market are specified and how they are implemented and enforced. A critical problem is that, even before the pandemic, more than half of all Australian aged care residents (58 per cent) lived in facilities with unacceptably low staffing levels and almost all (99 per cent) lived in facilities with suboptimal staffing levels (Eagar et al. 2020: 508). Further, the share of skilled staff has fallen precipitously during a time when the share of for-profit providers has been growing. Between 2003 and 2016, the share of non-professional personal care workers increased from 57 to 72 per cent (Meagher et al. 2019: 13), during which time the share of places in for-profit ownership increased from 29 to 38 per cent. The relationship between these trends is complex, but the design of the market for residential care has driven them both (see Chapter 6, this volume). And, despite overwhelming international evidence that mandated staffing ratios can drive care quality, providers' lobby organisations have vociferously opposed the introduction of such a regulatory requirement and appear to have captured the regulators (Connolly 2020).

Another set of problems in conducting 'business as usual' in social service markets are transaction costs (Davidson 2009). These arise as all the groups involved—governments, providers and people using services— navigate the market and find themselves variously searching for and negotiating with transaction partners and monitoring and enforcing the exchanges they enter. Of course, most market interactions incur transaction costs, but these costs are generally higher for transactions involving services (which are intangible, interpersonal and often labour intensive), and even higher for social services, which meet the needs of vulnerable social groups (Davidson 2009: 44–49). Thus, in designing and engaging in social service markets, governments, for example, need to establish and operate systems for specifying and managing contracts, licensing or accrediting providers, distributing payments and monitoring and oversight of contract compliance and service quality.

Providers also need organisational infrastructure to engage with funding and monitoring systems, and a satellite market of consultants offers them assistance, for a fee. Providers often also devote considerable resources to marketing their services to their 'customers', particularly in markets where people needing services are expected to choose a provider. These various activities incur extra costs that represent significant 'leakages' of both public and private money; they are not part of service delivery and are only present because the market design requires providers to compete for custom. These leakages often more than offset any hoped-for efficiency gains that may be generated by markets (Davidson 2018).

Consumer choice models also incur search costs for people who need services, as they spend time and perhaps money seeking information about providers and the quality of the services they offer—information that may be incomplete, complex or irrelevant to their concerns and interests, as several of the vignettes presented in Box 1 show. Consumers may also be required to negotiate the content, price and quality of services even when these are subsidised.[10] Markets in which consumers choose a provider usually offer a portable subsidy or 'quasi-voucher' (Lyons 1995); in other words, people can change provider if they are not satisfied. This approach assumes consumers' potential or actual choices to 'exit' will drive providers to improve or go out of business. If consumer exit is the means of market discipline, the cost of monitoring the quality of services at least partly falls to consumers also.

Another evident problem with social service marketisation is that not all people using services are equally subject to the kinds of problems we have been discussing. Those who have the social and economic resources to navigate service markets are typically best placed to benefit from them. Sometimes transaction costs appear to be the major driver of inequality. In disability services, vulnerable groups, including people with intellectual disabilities and older carers, have difficulty navigating the NDIS's processes, and are less likely to receive funded supports than other participants with similar needs, while males and people with higher incomes are more likely to have their needs met (Mavromaras et al. 2018). In home care for older people, the new consumer choice model of allocating services has led to fewer people accessing services as they face

---

10   See, for example, guidance to older people and their families on the 'My Aged Care' website (www.myagedcare.gov.au), which sets out four steps for accessing aged care services: 'Step 1: Learn about the different types of care'; 'Step 2: Get assessed for aged care services'; 'Step 3: Find a provider in your area that suits your needs'; 'Step 4: Manage your services'. Further information on Step 3 states: 'Once you've chosen your preferred provider, they will offer you an agreement before you start to receive services', and agreements cover 'your care plan', 'your services' and 'your fees'. 'Your services' include: 'The exact care and services that will be provided to meet your care needs. It will also cover who will provide the services, when they will be delivered, and how often' (available from: www.myagedcare.gov.au/how-set-your-new-service).

increasing responsibility for finding, choosing, negotiating and managing the service package. Those who did access services were more likely to be relatively advantaged (Jorgensen et al. 2020).

Inequality in social service markets is driven not only by differences in the resources people have for navigating them, but also by market designs that give private providers more latitude to decide what services they offer, where they offer them and to whom. This tendency is exacerbated when private providers can top up publicly subsidised services for those consumers who want and are able to pay more. In child care, for example, which operates with a consumer choice model and without geographical service planning or fee regulation (see Chapter 4, this volume), the quality of services is higher in less-disadvantaged areas. Quality data collected by the Australian Children's Education and Care Quality Authority (ACECQA 2019: 34) show the share of centre-based services that exceed the National Quality Standards is higher in the least-disadvantaged areas of Australia (37 per cent) than in the most-disadvantaged areas (28 per cent).

In education, private schools can choose where they locate, the fees they charge and, within the constraints of mandated curriculum requirements, the kind of educational experience they offer. Critically, they are also able to select students, through both the level of fees they set and other formal and informal selection criteria and processes. With these design features in place, school choice policies have driven socioeconomic segregation, resulting in stark divergences in achievement among advantaged and disadvantaged students (Smith et al. 2019). The individual and social costs of inequality in education are high. Declining performance among the most disadvantaged students has been estimated to cost Australia's economy tens of billions of dollars (Hetherington 2018).

Weak regulation enabling poor service quality, high transaction costs and provider latitude driving inequality are at the business-as-usual end of social service market problems. At the other end—but no less related to the rules and incentives of specific market designs—are problems of unscrupulous behaviour, including fraud, and organisational instability. Again, some examples give the flavour:

- In *job placement services*, 'rorting' scandals have been repeatedly reported since the first outsourcing contracts were struck more than two decades ago, despite several redesigns to prevent provider abuses (and to tighten compliance requirements on jobseekers) (ABC News 2002; Besser 2011, 2013, 2015; Karp 2019; Morton 2017).

- In *residential aged care*, one of the largest corporate providers, Bupa, was fined $6 million and ordered to compensate residents of 20 of its nursing homes in 2020, after the company charged them often thousands of dollars each annually over several years for additional services they did not receive (ACCC 2020).

- In *family day care services for children*, after funding rules were relaxed in 2006, the share of for-profit providers increased rapidly, and fraudulent practice also became a problem, as Natasha Cortis, Megan Blaxland and Elizabeth Adamson show in Chapter 1 of this volume.

- In *vocational education and training* (VET), similar problems emerged when—again—funding rules were relaxed, in 2012. With the aim of growing participation in VET, the federal government paid fees up front to providers, while students incurred a corresponding debt to the Commonwealth.[11] New private providers flooded the market, attracted by the opportunity of essentially unregulated fees underpinned by the public purse. As the dissenting report by Labor senators to the Coalition government–led 'red tape committee' on private education put it: 'Experience has repeatedly shown that rent-seeking, and access to government funding in VET with limited regulation, has led to extreme outbreaks of malfeasance by unscrupulous private, profit seeking providers' (Select Committee on Red Tape 2018: 25). The Australian National Audit Office found that average tuition fees more than tripled between 2009 and 2015, and fees for ostensibly the same course varied widely (ANAO 2016: 29n.27). Until the practice was banned, some providers used inappropriate inducements to recruit students who were ill prepared for study, and many offered inadequate education and training. Many students never graduated, despite acquiring a debt (Senate Education and Employment References Committee 2015).

- In *disability services*, as the NDIS is being rolled out nationwide, reports of fraud are growing (Henriques-Gomes 2019; Topsfield and Millar 2021), and the more lurid cases involving seizure of gold bullion, luxury cars and properties have been splashed across the media (Cormack 2019; Reddie 2021).

---

11   The new rules mirrored those offered in university education, despite most other aspects of university functioning being much more tightly regulated.

- In *immigration detention services*, poor contract design and weak oversight have put the people detained at risk and enabled significant cost blowouts in favour of the large corporations that have gained the contracts to provide them. As Adèle Garnier shows in Chapter 2, waste and mistreatment can occur because governments do not properly use market instruments, such as competitive tendering and careful regulatory monitoring.

There have also been some major corporate collapses in the Australian childcare and VET markets.[12] The most well-known case was the massive publicly listed childcare business ABC Learning, which crashed in late 2008 (Sumsion 2012). In 2015, VET company Vocation Limited collapsed, just two years after listing on the stock exchange (Danckert and Preiss 2015). Another of the largest private VET providers, Global Intellectual Holdings, went into liquidation in 2016 (Cook et al. 2016; Taylor and Branley 2016). Others have since closed—or been closed by the regulatory authorities, following the unscrupulous practices discussed above—stranding students in the middle of their training (Bagshaw and Mitchell 2017; Taylor and Branley 2017).

Such problems in social service markets often create considerable disruption and uncertainty for the people receiving the services even when they are not more directly harmed. Market and regulatory failures are also costly for the community. The government contributed $56 million to maintain operations in ABC Learning's childcare centres until a new owner was found (Sumsion 2012). Various amendments to VET funding policy were introduced from 2015 to address the perverse incentives in the market, but major fiscal damage had been done. In 2019 alone, the government forgave more than $490 million in debts incurred by VET students who were enrolled by unscrupulous providers (Tomazin 2019), and several thousand students have since had complaints dealt with by the Commonwealth Ombudsman.[13] Enforcement actions against providers

---

12 In the United Kingdom, there have also been some disruptive corporate collapses, including the nursing home chains Southern Cross, which held about 750 homes, in 2011, and private equity–owned Four Seasons, which held 322 homes, in 2019. In early 2018, Carillion, another massive government contractor, collapsed. Carillion was involved in a wide range of public services and public infrastructure, from managing contracts for school dinners to building hospitals and motorways under the 'private finance initiative'. A few months after Carillion's crash, the UK National Audit Office estimated the cost to the British public purse would be £148 million—an estimate later exceeded (Inman 2018).
13 For quarterly reports, see the Commonwealth Ombudsman's website: www.ombudsman.gov.au/publications/industry/vet-student-loans.

by the Australian Competition and Consumer Commission (ACCC) or the sector-specific regulatory authorities are also costly to conduct, when they occur.

Ultimately, the costs of navigating and operating social service markets fall on the people using the services or on the community, through public financing. These costs remain mostly unmeasured. Just as important, but also very difficult to measure, are the losses to the Australian community when poor-quality providers and/or complacent regulation lead to poor-quality services that fall below the threshold acted on by oversight authorities. The community loses directly, by paying for services that are not delivered to the expected level, and indirectly, through the ramifying social impact of substandard education, care and rehabilitation.

Of course, nonmarket provision of social services also incurs costs, can be inequitably distributed and has characteristic problems. And markets can offer important benefits to consumers—if they are designed to do so. But, in the light of the problems outlined above, it is also important to note the lack of evidence that Australians demanded market reform of social services or the (ideologically) related privatisations of public institutions and infrastructure (Meagher and Wilson 2015). Marketisation and privatisation of social services have been elite projects and their benefits for most people remain unproven.

Analysing social service markets

Failures in social service markets are often attributed to 'bad apple' providers, with which others should not be lumped.[14] The 'bad apple' explanation might be more plausible—and unbending faith in market solutions more reasonably maintained—if problems were relatively rare and isolated or if they decreased over time, as early wrinkles in market design were ironed out and choice and competition drove improvements for consumers, as proponents predicted. However, it seems problems persist, emerging in sector after sector, as market designs are developed and rolled out. Thus, a more systemic investigation and critique are warranted.

---

14   For example, industry association Leading Age Services Australia used this argument in its submission to the Senate inquiry into the effectiveness of the aged care quality assessment and accreditation framework (SCARC 2019), claiming: 'The aged care sector is working tirelessly to deliver high quality care but one "bad apple" can taint the reputation of the entire industry' (Leading Age Services Australia 2017: 5).

Complementing two recent volumes, *Wrong Way: How privatisation and economic reform backfired* (Cahill and Toner 2018) and *Markets, Rights and Power in Australian Social Policy* (Meagher and Goodwin 2015), which offer such an analysis, this volume includes a further set of original Australian case studies, along with an argument for the vital role of the public sector within social service markets to mitigate the predictable problems to which they give rise.

Faith in markets is typically grounded in ideological commitments to small government. From this ideological position, markets are assumed to be largely self-constituting and self-regulating arrangements in which self-interested, rational individuals and firms exchange goods and services (for a classic statement, see Friedman and Friedman 1990). Competition between firms promotes the efficient use of resources and consumer choice promotes—indeed expresses—individual autonomy. Aside from a handful of tasks, not the least of which is enforcing contracts and property rights, government 'intervention' is mostly a fetter on both efficiency and autonomy.

This world view finds technical expression in neoclassical economics and policy expression in New Public Management, which marries faith in markets with faith in private corporations to propose solutions to putative problems of public bureaucracy (Hood 1991). It is perhaps most frequently called 'neoliberalism' by its critics, who argue that its rise to prominence in recent decades has led to the encroachment of markets and market models on public policy and across social life more generally. Contributors to this volume work with the overlapping and complementary concepts of neoliberalism, marketisation and financialisation to come to a more refined view of how overextended faith in markets has transformed social services in this country.

Understanding neoliberalism, marketisation and financialisation

Despite widespread agreement that neoliberalism is reshaping social institutions, it is 'an oft-invoked but ill-defined concept in the social sciences' (Mudge 2008: 703). Several framings of the concept can be found in the research literature: it is variously the hegemonic ideology of our times (Harvey 2005); a (rightwing) political project that reorders state institutions to market logics (Wacquant 2012); a form of rationality encroaching on everyday life (Brown 2015); and the latest phase of contemporary capitalism (Fox Piven 2015). One approach in response to the many and varied usages of neoliberalism has been to emphasise the links between neoliberal ideas and governance. Yeatman (2018: 21) states that 'neoliberal governance has been driven by a political philosophy that centres on making a competition market order the basis of social organisation'. Another approach has been to frame neoliberalism as essentially 'flexible, adaptive and renewable' (Redden 2019: 713). Researchers working with this concept, however framed, have contributed penetrating insights about recent change in economic and social life, including in social services (Cahill and Toner 2018). Accordingly, several contributions to this volume work with the concept of neoliberalism in shaping their analyses of the broader context in which marketising policies have emerged.

Other contributions work in a more directed way with the related term 'marketisation', which focuses on how states 'craft' (Vogel 2018) the variety of existing markets. This approach understands marketisation as action by the state that reconfigures the policy architecture of the state itself and/or builds new institutions that imbue market logics. Markets have two central attributes: the use of competitive mechanisms to allocate services and products, and the use of incentives (particularly financial and material) to influence the behaviour of consumers and producers (Gingrich 2011: 7). Economists and social policy analysts recognise that markets for social services, like other markets, involve competition and the use of incentives to influence behaviour. However, as noted above, researchers have also shown that social service markets differ from markets for many consumer goods in important ways that do not conform to the basic assumptions of the economic theory of competitive markets (see, for example, Davidson 2009, 2011).

Gingrich (2011: 8–9) provides a handy list of characteristic problems or risks in social service markets—'externalities, multiple principals, information asymmetries and incomplete contracts'—and summarises their implications (see also Blank 2000; Davidson 2009, 2011). Social service markets often have 'positive externalities' because they deliver benefits for society as well as for the individuals receiving them.[15] If individuals alone bear the cost, they may be unwilling or unable to pay enough for the social benefit to be realised, leading to undersupply.

---

15   Negative externalities occur when not all the costs of production are included in the price of a good or service; pollution is the most commonly used example.

This justifies public (collective) financing. The problem of multiple principals occurs when governments finance social services to enable positive externalities to be realised but pay private providers to deliver the services. To whom (which principal) does a provider answer: the government funding the service or the person receiving it? Information asymmetries can occur between service providers and users. Private providers—doctors, social workers, teachers, nursing home operators—can know more about their quality and cost. This puts those purchasing services, whether service users or the government, at a disadvantage in choosing a provider in the market and in assessing whether they are getting what they are paying for. Service users can know more about their further likely need for services, or choose not to disclose important information, thereby putting private insurers at a disadvantage. And contracts for social services are almost always 'incomplete' because it is very difficult, if not impossible, to specify and measure every aspect of the service to be delivered. This means different contract designs can create different arrays of costs and benefits for parties to them—including benefiting providers at the expense of service users and public funders.

Another concept mobilised in some contributions is financialisation. As Adam Stebbing explains in more detail in Chapter 4, on superannuation, financialisation is the process by which financial ways of thinking and acting are integrated into how institutions—from governments to businesses to households—operate (Bryan and Rafferty 2018: 9; van der Zwan 2014). The goal of financial ways of thinking is to quantify, in dollar terms, the potential risks and returns for the available options in a situation. As more and more social processes and interactions are drawn into these calculations, thereby coming to resemble assets and liabilities or profits and losses, they become distanced from their primary uses. Thus, as Laura Wynne, Kristian Ruming, Pranita Shrestha and Dallas Rogers show in Chapter 7, housing has increasingly become positioned as an asset that generates a financial return, with profound implications for the idea of universal access to secure shelter that social housing ideally represents.

Overall, Gingrich concludes that these problems create a complex set of trade-offs for governments in designing and regulating social service markets. They must decide 'how they shape individual and collective responsibility for allocating services (the allocation dimension) and how they structure control over production (the production dimension)' (Gingrich 2011: 9). In other words, there are inherent risks in social service markets, which can be mitigated or exacerbated, depending on how government financing and regulation are designed. Several of the risks position service users or government funders on the downside, with opportunities for rent-seeking by providers a particular challenge. Risks often arise because of conflicts of interest, and many of the examples of problems in social service markets set out in the previous section were caused by private providers taking opportunities to pursue their own interests over those of the people using their services and the collective interest intrinsic in public funding.

Markets as social institutions

To reiterate: governments *necessarily* design markets, including social service markets. They bring these markets into being with actions that support and/or constitute market actors, define the products to be exchanged, construct social arenas and the rules for market exchange, promote for-profit provision and encourage consumer choice and competition (Vogel 2018: 15). Thus, social service marketisation involves complex institutional changes and has variable results depending on the specifics of market design. These features make historical institutionalism an ideal approach to understanding marketisation. Historical institutionalism is a set of interdisciplinary approaches that understand institutional change over the long term to be often more consequential than specific policy choices at a point in time, because institutions can become 'embedded' and impact subsequent developments through intended or unintended 'feedback effects' (Pierson 2004: 15). Feedback effects impose constraints that impede—or confer resources that promote—certain actions. These effects emerge from many sources, including existing state and market institutions, political interests and other policy actors and/or political ideas, and vary with historical and political context (Hacker 2004: 244).

This way of thinking enables us to differentiate between the impact of earlier policy settings and dynamics and new market models on the design and operation of social service markets. When designing social service markets, governments must negotiate political processes that require compromises to be made and work with the structures of existing policies and social service sectors. Although these circumstances are to some extent unique to each social service sector at the time of reform, previous work has highlighted that the cumulative impact of incremental changes to existing policies can be as transformative as (or lead to more) radical revision in the long run (Streeck and Thelen 2005: 19). In fact, as Teles

(2013) observes of the United States, market-oriented policy changes have typically resulted in increasing complexity because they often build on rather than replace existing policies and structures. The importance of both contextual factors and increasing complexity underpins our decision to analyse the design of social service market institutions separately using a historical institutionalist approach.

By recognising markets as social institutions, we see existing markets as social arenas of exchange that, as noted above, use competitive mechanisms to allocate goods, services and information (Fligstein and Dauter 2007: 107; Gingrich 2011: 8). Market exchanges involve the complex interplay of businesses, organisations, suppliers, workers, consumers and the state (Fligstein and Dauter 2007: 107), and it is the governance of these exchanges through legislation, regulation, practices and norms that shapes the capacities and opportunities of the actors engaged in them (Vogel 2007: 26).

We have been emphasising the point that markets are *designed* social institutions and, to avoid confusion, a brief clarification of our use of the term 'design' is warranted. Scholars such as Jane Gingrich use the term 'market design' in research framed, like ours, within a historical institutionalist approach. However, there is a somewhat narrower and more technical concept of 'policy design' in public policy research, in which it is defined as 'the deliberate and conscious attempt to define policy goals and connect them to instruments or tools expected to realise those objectives' (Howlett et al. 2015). Many scholars working with this idea of policy design treat policymaking as primarily a matter of pragmatic problem-solving and see research on design as a means to improve policy effectiveness (Howlett 2018).

Other more critical scholars working on policy design have challenged the technocratic focus on problem-solving, instrument selection and policy effectiveness. They argue that public policy instruments are not simply neutral tools sitting, equally available, awaiting selection in a proverbial toolbox. Rather, these instruments are 'bearers of values, fuelled by one interpretation of the social' among several (Lascoumes and Le Galès 2007: 4). Policy designs are used to frame different groups in society as 'deserving' or 'undeserving', 'winners' or 'losers', and can establish degenerative dynamics that place vulnerable or marginalised people in a position of self-perpetuating disadvantage (Schneider and Ingram 1997). This emphasis on values and politics, and on the impact of the choice of instruments on the relationship between the government and the governed (Lascoumes and Le Galès 2007; Schneider and Ingram 1997), aligns more closely with our approach. Thus, while we are indeed interested in policymakers' goals and the instruments they use to achieve them, we examine the question of market design using a more expansive and critical palette.

Examining Australian social service markets

The complex and diverse history of marketisation in Australian social policy points to the need to examine specific social service markets, to capture how and for whom they work. Contributions to this volume take up this task from a range of disciplines in the social sciences, with some chapters working with more explicitly theoretical framings, and others more empirically grounded.

In Chapter 1, Natasha Cortis, Megan Blaxland and Elizabeth Adams empirically chart the policy changes that led for-profit providers to expand their foothold in the Australian family day care sector and assess the impact of this development. Family day care offers children formal, regulated and government-subsidised early education and care in small groups in the homes of individual educators. Each home-based educator is formally self-employed. However, educators are required to be attached to a coordination unit, which offers support for their educational programming and practice, regulatory compliance and administration. Family day care was established in the 1970s on a non-profit model. It operated on this basis, with little change, for a quarter of a century. A mixed model was introduced in the 1990s, but it was not until the past decade that changes in policy, funding and regulation reorganised family day care around market principles, resulting in very high involvement of for-profit providers. The chapter uses national regulatory data to assess how the dominance of for-profit providers has affected the sector's potential to deliver quality services to children. The authors find that reshaping family day care around a market model has exacerbated the fragility of high-quality practice. In 2018, only 27 per cent of for-profit family day care providers were meeting the National Quality Standard for early childhood education and care services. For-profits performed notably worse than public and non-profit providers against each of the seven National Quality Areas, and many did not meet standards in any quality area. The chapter concludes by considering measures to better ensure children receive quality education and care from all family day care services.

In Chapter 2, Adèle Garnier examines marketisation in refugee settlement services—a niche policy sector that has not yet been studied in the context of marketisation. She uses an expansive definition of refugee settlement that takes in not only specialised, refugee-focused support services for humanitarian migrants in the community but also the punitive and controversial onshore and offshore immigration detention centres that hold asylum-seekers. The result is a fascinating contrast: both types of service have been marketised, but in different ways, with quite different results. During the years of the Howard Coalition (1996–2007) and Rudd and Gillard Labor (2007–13) governments, supportive settlement services for resettled refugees and asylum-seekers in the community continued to be delivered by the non-government organisations that had long done so. However, these organisations now competed for contracts, as part of the general marketisation trend during that period, under arrangements focused on value for money, performance supervision and, increasingly, risk assessment and the development of a quality assurance framework. Evaluators found that implementation of this approach largely succeeded on its own terms. By contrast, immigration detention management and services were outsourced to for-profit corporations, often on hastily struck contracts with unclear performance objectives, resulting in considerable cost inflation and limited government accountability. Following the re-election of the Coalition in 2013, the design of supportive services increasingly emphasised refugees' self-reliance, while the costs of immigration detention ballooned, and poor government accountability worsened. Detainees subjected to Australia's punitive asylum laws also suffered, and continue to suffer, from lack of oversight of hugely resourced for-profit corporations.

In Chapter 3, Diana Perche examines employment services in remote Indigenous communities in Australia. The chapter documents the risks of marketisation in policy environments that afford limited oversight and control, through a case study of the Community Development Program (CDP). The CDP was introduced by the Coalition government in 2015 as a new 'work for the dole' scheme for more than 1,000 communities across Australia, predominantly affecting Aboriginal and Torres Strait Islander people. In line with the broader push for contestability and streamlining of

Indigenous service delivery under the Coalition government's Indigenous Advancement Strategy, CDP providers are selected by competitive tender. Measured against the goals and ideals of a market-based program, the CDP suffers from several design flaws. With one provider per region, there is a lack of alternative providers. Further, decision-makers are becoming disconnected from affected communities, as some of the non-profit Aboriginal community–controlled providers that had previously offered these services are replaced with for-profit companies. Some for-profit companies have taken over several regions, benefiting from economies of scale but delivering poorly tailored services from long distances. There is also poor government oversight of the quality of services, partly because of the design of the performance monitoring system. Performance criteria create perverse incentives for service providers because they focus on processing and reporting tasks rather than meaningful service provision or engagement with the needs of unemployed people. Because Indigenous people's participation in the CDP is mandatory and compliance is directly linked to Centrelink payments, service providers make decisions about participants' livelihoods. This means the negative impacts of these problems are profound.

In Chapter 4, Adam Stebbing examines how changing policy on retirement incomes has increasingly exposed Australians to the risks and inequalities generated by marketisation and financialisation. The chapter charts how private superannuation has been transformed from an exclusive occupational benefit for about one-third of the workforce in the 1970s to a mandatory private retirement savings vehicle now held by members of almost every Australian household. As private super has become a major source of lifetime savings, particularly for younger generations, the promise of a healthy and secure retirement has become increasingly entangled with financial markets, with their associated risks of volatility and failure. At the same time, existing inequalities between individuals are compounded, as superannuation savings are tied to earnings. Meanwhile, broader social inequality is exacerbated by the vast sums lost to tax concessions for superannuation, which are largely enjoyed by high-income earners. While the age pension exists to pool collectively the risks of old age, the financialisation of retirement incomes remains partial. Nevertheless, the rising importance of superannuation to retirement income policy has transferred the risks to households without increasing those borne by employers or the financial sector.

In Chapter 5, Georgia van Toorn investigates the genesis of the NDIS, which is one of the largest, most costly and rapidly implemented social policy reforms in Australia's history. The chapter explores how the NDIS came to take the shape it has, drawing on interviews that reveal the behind-the-scenes advocacy that shaped the Labor government's thinking as it developed the scheme. At the core of the design of the NDIS is individualised funding, and the chapter documents the role of transnational advocacy networks in facilitating the spread of this key market-aligned idea. The linking of disability rights advocacy to a market reform agenda emphasising consumer sovereignty, cost containment and market primacy helped build consensus and support for the scheme among disparate groups. However, the resulting market design has blunted the emancipatory potential of increased 'choice' for disabled people. One reason is that, as the market was introduced, state governments closed or privatised their publicly provided disability services. This has left some very vulnerable people without access to services either because they do not qualify for the new scheme or because there is no provider of last resort in the market.

In Chapter 6, Gabrielle Meagher and Richard Baldwin examine the evolution of the market for residential aged care over more than half a century. Although mostly publicly funded, most nursing homes are privately owned by non-profit and for-profit organisations. Over time, the balance of power between government funders, private providers of different kinds and older people as residents has shifted back and forth as governments have sought to manage the nursing home market and providers have sought to control their own operations and make money. The focus of the chapter is how successive policies have promoted or suppressed the growth of for-profit provision, since the weight of evidence is that the average quality in for-profit nursing homes is lower than in non-profit and public nursing homes. The chapter shows that, before 1997, there were partisan differences in the approach to for-profit provision and policy differences in the treatment of non-profit and for-profit providers. Although increasingly cost-conscious as time went on, Coalition governments sought to defend and promote the private sector, while Labor sought to improve access to care for disadvantaged groups, to control rent-seeking by for-profit providers and to increase care quality by growing the non-profit sector. Since 1997, under the apparently bipartisan market principle of competitive neutrality, all providers have operated under the same market rules, and governments of both colours have increased the depth of marketisation of residential care in some dimensions. By examining the relationship between market design and ownership of residential care over time, the analysis aims to help identify risks with the current direction of residential aged care policy.

In Chapter 7, Laura Wynne, Kristian Ruming, Pranita Shrestha and Dallas Rogers examine how federal and state governments have increasingly looked to the private sector to fund, construct and manage social housing stock. Historically, state governments constructed and managed public housing, with Commonwealth funding through periodically negotiated arrangements, such as the Commonwealth–State Housing Agreement and, more recently, the National Affordable Housing Agreement. However, in recent decades, the private and not-for-profit sectors have become central to social housing delivery and management as housing policies have marketised and financialised the sector. Taking the case of New South Wales, the chapter shows how the construction of new housing stock has come to be delivered through partnerships with private sector developers, primarily through the large-scale regeneration of existing public housing estates. Meanwhile, management of social housing tenancies has increasingly been delegated to not-for-profit community housing providers, which have also gained a role in funding and constructing new stock. Both these shifts have resulted in new finance, governance and tenancy management configurations and have seen the state step back from the direct delivery of social housing as a vital social service for citizens looking for secure and affordable housing.

In Chapter 8, Adam Stebbing examines another aspect of the Australian market for early childhood education and care (ECEC): how these services are funded. In recent decades, the radical marketisation of the sector has coincided with its rapid expansion, driven by the increased labour force participation of women and the growth of generous public subsidies for private provision. The proportion of children using ECEC has increased considerably over recent decades, which is one measure of success. However, inefficiency, inequity, poor accessibility for some groups and variable quality are evident, with public subsidies contributing to these problems by placing few limits on the rent-seeking behaviour of for-profit providers. The chapter charts the evolution of public subsidies for child care, highlighting the political choices behind the designs of the various policy instruments (tax expenditures, cash benefits and rebates) governments have used. The chapter shows that each of these instruments affects the behaviour of providers in different ways, tending to increase or decrease rent-seeking and price inflation, and to increase or decrease the extent to which ECEC is accessible to lower-income families.

In Chapter 9, Bob Davidson begins by recognising that marketisation has often been counterproductive in achieving the key goals of social services, as also shown in other contributions to the volume. However, the chapter goes beyond criticising existing social service markets. Instead, it makes the case that the limited and strategic use of market mechanisms can consistently improve social services and, more specifically, a public provider represents a powerful policy instrument that can make social service markets work better than they do with private providers only. Davidson articulates the benefits of public providers at the individual and systemic levels and offers a set of operating principles for public providers to ensure they can achieve their potential in enhancing market operations and outcomes. The core of the chapter sets out how a well-functioning public provider can improve a social service market, by providing high-quality and efficient services to a significant proportion of people; by acting as a provider of last resort for people and regions poorly or not serviced by private providers; and by setting sectoral norms that other providers must follow to remain competitive. In these ways, a public provider can both limit the exercise of market power by other providers and use its own market power in the public interest, acting as a powerful countervailing force to others' poor behaviour. Benefits can include more stable, accessible and equally distributed services of higher average quality, increased efficiency, reduced total cost of services and facilitation of other goals of marketisation, such as choice, innovation and diversity. The challenges in maintaining, re-establishing or establishing such exemplary providers are not inconsiderable—but nor are the risks of not doing so, as attested by the ongoing royal commissions and myriad audit reports and evaluations cited in this volume.

We began our work with our contributors in early 2018. Since then, the social service system—like everything—has been shaken by the Covid-19 pandemic. Most chapters address directly in an epilogue the impact of the pandemic on the social policy subsystem they analyse. In the context of the pandemic, and the challenges revealed in their research, all contributors consider 'where to now'.

The volume's Conclusion reflects on the assembled findings of the collection in the light of international research and points to aspects of marketisation in Australia that are yet to be critically assessed. We also consider how the Covid-19 pandemic has affected thinking about marketisation and its ongoing implementation. On one hand, the pandemic has revealed the fragility of market encroachment into health care and social services, resulting in calls for its reversal in rich democracies around the world, including by Anthony Albanese (2020), now Australian prime minister. On the other hand, it has also provided fertile ground for rent-seeking by private interests and its economic consequences reinvigorated calls by the private sector for tax cuts and deregulation in the name of the 'post-Covid recovery'—calls that fell on open ears in Australia's former Coalition government (Coorey 2020).

References

ABC News. (2002). More than 100 fraud probes underway into job providers. *ABC News*, 5 June. Retrieved via Dow Jones Factiva.

Albanese, A. (2020). Australia beyond the coronavirus: Vision statement 6. Address to Federal Labor Caucus, 11 May, Canberra. Available from: anthonyalbanese. com.au/anthony-albanese-speech-australia-beyond-the-coronavirus-canberra-monday-11-may-2020.

Alexander, H. (2020). 'No one knows where it came from': Inside Australia's first COVID-19 cluster. *Sydney Morning Herald*, 10 May. Available from: www.smh. com.au/national/nsw/no-one-knows-where-it-came-from-inside-australia-s-first-covid-19-cluster-20200506-p54qdy.html.

Australian Aged Care Quality Agency (AACQA). (2017). *Annual Report 2016–2017*. Canberra: Australian Aged Care Quality Agency. Available from: www. agedcarequality.gov.au/sites/default/files/media/aacqa_annual_report_2017-18.pdf.

Australian Children's Education and Care Quality Authority (ACECQA). (2019). *NQF Annual Performance Report: National Quality Framework*. December. Sydney: ACECQA. Available from: www.acecqa.gov.au/media/28821.

Australian Competition and Consumer Commission (ACCC). (2020). Court orders $6m in penalties against Bupa and compensation for consumers. Media release, 12 May, Canberra. Available from: www.accc.gov.au/media-release/ court-orders-6m-in-penalties-against-bupa-and-compensation-for-consumers.

Australian National Audit Office (ANAO). (2016). *Administration of the VET FEE-HELP Scheme*. The Auditor-General ANAO Report No. 31 of 2016–17. Canberra: ANAO. Available from: www.anao.gov.au/work/performance-audit/ administration-vet-fee-help-scheme.

Bagshaw, E. & Mitchell, G. (2017). Sage Institute of Fitness staff made redundant as company ceases trade. *Sydney Morning Herald*, 8 March.

Besser, L. (2011). False claims boost chance of survival in jobs game. *Sydney Morning Herald*, 19 December.

Besser, L. (2013). Job seeker funding still open to fraud, despite fee reforms. *Sydney Morning Herald*, 22 April.

Besser, L. (2015). The jobs game. *4 Corners*, [ABC TV], 23 February. Available from: www.abc.net.au/4corners/the-jobs-game/6247206.

Bibby, P. (2014). Nursing home did not check Roger Dean's CV before Quakers Hill fire: Inquest. *Sydney Morning Herald*, 8 September. Available from: www.smh.com.au/national/nsw/nursing-home-did-not-check-roger-deans-cv-before-quakers-hill-fire-inquest-20140908-10e1dd.html.

Blank, R.M. (2000). When can public policy makers rely on private markets? The effective provision of social services. *The Economic Journal*, *110*(462): C34–C49. doi.org/10.1111/1468-0297.00519.

Blumer, C. (2018). Would you eat this? The real food inside aged care facilities in Australia. *ABC News*, 18 September. Available from: www.abc.net.au/news/2018-09-17/food-in-aged-care/10212880?nw=0.

Braithwaite, J., Makkai, T. & Braithwaite, V.A. (2007). *Regulating Aged Care: Ritualism and the new pyramid*. Cheltenham, UK: Edward Elgar Publishing. doi.org/10.4337/9781847206855.

Brown, W. (2015). *Undoing the Demos: Neoliberalism's stealth revolution*. New York, NY: Zone Books. doi.org/10.2307/j.ctt17kk9p8.

Bryan, D. & Rafferty, M. (2018). *Risking Together: How finance is dominating everyday life in Australia*. Sydney: Sydney University Press. doi.org/10.2307/j.ctv175nt.

Cahill, D. & Toner, P. (eds). (2018). *Wrong Way: How privatisation and economic reform backfired*. Melbourne: La Trobe University Press.

Carnell, K. & Paterson, R. (2017). *Review of National Aged Care Quality Regulatory Processes: Report*. October. Canberra: Department of Health. Available from: www.health.gov.au/sites/default/files/review-of-national-aged-care-quality-regulatory-processes-report.pdf.

Casben, L. (2019). Aged care worker Prakash Paudyal jailed over assault of dementia patient. *ABC News*, 23 January. Available from: www.abc.net.au/news/2019-01-23/aged-care-worker-sentenced-for-assault-of-elderly-man/10743004.

Connolly, A. (2014). Death in a five star nursing home. *Background Briefing*, [ABC Radio National], 21 September. Available from: www.abc.net.au/radionational/programs/backgroundbriefing/5753372.

Connolly, A. (2017). Families say loved ones mistreated and neglected in Opal Aged Care homes. *7.30*, [ABC TV], 2 August. Available from: www.abc.net.au/7.30/families-say-loved-ones-mistreated-and-neglected/8768652.

Connolly, A. (2019). Bupa's aged care homes failing standards across Australia. *7.30*, [ABC TV], 12 September. Available from: www.abc.net.au/7.30/bupas-aged-care-homes-failing-standards-across/11507866.

Connolly, A. (2020). Why the government blocked a law forcing nursing homes to reveal staff and food budgets. *ABC News*, 10 February. Available from: www.abc.net.au/news/2020-02-09/federal-government-blocked-law-nursing-homes-reveal-finances/11943380.

Cook, H., Jacks, T. & Danckert, S. (2016). College collapses creates chaos for students. *The Age*, [Melbourne], 11 February. Available from: www.theage.com.au/national/victoria/college-collapses-creates-chaos-for-students-20160211-gmrtlk.html.

Coorey, P. (2020). PM's pro-business growth agenda. *Australian Financial Review*, 16 April.

Cormack, L. (2019). Luxury cars and property of alleged NDIS fraudsters frozen by court. *Sydney Morning Herald*, 24 July. Available from: www.smh.com.au/national/nsw/luxury-cars-and-property-of-alleged-ndis-fraudsters-frozen-by-court-20190722-p529iz.html.

Cortis, N. & van Toorn, G. (2022). Safeguarding in Australia's new disability markets: Frontline workers' perspectives. *Critical Social Policy*, *42*(2): 197–219. doi.org/10.1177/02610183211020693.

Danckert, S. & Preiss, B. (2015). Up to 12,000 students in limbo after Vocation collapse. *Sydney Morning Herald*, 26 November. Available from: www.smh.com.au/business/banking-and-finance/up-to-12000-students-in-limbo-after-vocation-collapse-20151126-gl8xfw.html.

Davidson, B. (2009). For-profit organisations in managed markets for human services. In D. King & G. Meagher (eds), *Paid Care in Australia: Politics, profits, practices* (pp. 43–79). Sydney: Sydney University Press. doi.org/10.30722/sup.9781920899295.

Davidson, B. (2011). Contestability in human services markets. *Journal of Australian Political Economy, 68*: 213–39.

Davidson, B. (2018). The marketisation of aged care in Australia. In D. Cahill & P. Toner (eds), *Wrong Way: How privatisation and economic reform backfired* (pp. 101–16). Melbourne: La Trobe University Press.

Day, L. (2015). Aged care claims of neglect and intimidation with families barred from seeing parents. *7.30*, [ABC TV], 8 October. Available from: www.abc. net.au/7.30/aged-care-claims-of-neglect-and-intimidation-with/6839260.

Department of Health. (2019). *Inquiry into Events at Earle Haven.* Report, 11 November. Canberra: Department of Health. Available from: www.health. gov.au/resources/publications/inquiry-into-events-at-earle-haven.

Department of Health. (2021). COVID-19 outbreaks in Australian residential aged care facilities: National snapshot—As at 8:00am on 6 August 2021. Canberra: Australian Government. Available from: www.health.gov.au/sites/default/files/ documents/2021/08/covid-19-outbreaks-in-australian-residential-aged-care-facilities-6-august-2021_0.pdf.

Department of Health and Human Services (DHHS). (2020). Coronavirus update for Victoria—19 September 2020. Media release, 19 September, State Government of Victoria, Melbourne. Available from: www.dhhs.vic.gov.au/ coronavirus-update-Victoria-19-September-2020.

Department of Social Services (DSS). (2015). 2015 Budget fact sheet: More choice and better care for older Australians. *2015–16 Budget.* Canberra: DSS. Available from: www.dss.gov.au/about-the-department/publications-articles/ corporate-publications/budget-and-additional-estimates-statements/more-choice-and-better-care-for-older-australians.

Eagar, K., Westera, A. & Kobel, C. (2020). Australian residential aged care is understaffed. *The Medical Journal of Australia, 212*(11): 507–8.e1. doi.org/ 10.5694/mja2.50615.

Fligstein, N. & Dauter, L. (2007). The sociology of markets. *Annual Review of Sociology, 33*: 105–28. doi.org/10.1146/annurev.soc.33.040406.131736.

Ford, M. (2018). Sydney aged care worker avoids jail for assault on dementia patient. *ABC News*, 20 September. Available from: www.abc.net.au/news/2018-09-20/sydney-nursing-home-dana-grey-assault-sentencing/10285024.

Fox Piven, F. (2015). Neoliberalism and the welfare state: Plenary Lecture, UK Social Policy Association Annual Conference, 8th July 2014. *Journal of International and Comparative Social Policy, 31*(1): 2–9. doi.org/10.1080/21699763.2014. 1001665.

Friedman, M. & Friedman, R. (1990). *Free to Choose: A personal statement.* New York, NY: Houghton Mifflin Harcourt.

Gingrich, J.R. (2011). *Making Markets in the Welfare State: The politics of varying market reforms.* Cambridge, UK: Cambridge University Press. doi.org/10.1017/CBO9780511791529.

Hacker, J. (2004). Privatizing risk without privatizing the welfare state: The hidden politics of social policy retrenchment in the United States. *American Political Science Review,* 98(2): 243–60. doi.org/10.1017/S0003055404001121.

Handley, E. (2020). Why are there are [sic] more COVID-19 cases in private aged care than the public sector? *ABC News,* 1 August. Available from: www.abc.net.au/news/2020-08-01/why-more-covid-19-cases-in-private-aged-care-than-public-sector/12503212.

Harvey, D. (2005). *A Brief History of Neoliberalism.* Oxford, UK: Oxford University Press. doi.org/10.1093/oso/9780199283262.001.0001.

Henriques-Gomes, L. (2019). NDIS fraud allegations surge as 25 operators kicked off scheme. *The Guardian,* [Australia], 27 June. Available from: www.theguardian.com/australia-news/2019/jun/26/ndis-allegations-surge-as-25-operators-kicked-off-scheme.

Henriques-Gomes, L. (2020a). Former judge to investigate death of Adelaide woman Ann Marie Smith in full-time care. *The Guardian,* [Australia], 26 May. Available from: www.theguardian.com/australia-news/2020/may/26/former-judge-to-investigate-death-of-adelaide-woman-ann-marie-smith-in-full-time-care.

Henriques-Gomes, L. (2020b). NDIS providers used unauthorised restraints more than 65,000 times, watchdog reports. *The Guardian,* [Australia], 27 May. Available from: www.theguardian.com/australia-news/2020/may/27/ndis-providers-used-unauthorised-restraints-more-than-65000-times-watchdog-reports.

Hetherington, D. (2018). *What price the gap? Education and inequality in Australia.* Issues Paper, April. Sydney: Public Education Foundation. Available from: publiceducationfoundation.org.au/wp-content/uploads/2018/04/Issues-Paper_What-Price-The-Gap.pdf.

Hood, C. (1991). A public management for all seasons? *Public Administration,* 69(1): 3–19. doi.org/10.1111/j.1467-9299.1991.tb00779.x.

House of Representatives Standing Committee on Health, Aged Care and Sport. (2018). *Report on the Inquiry into the Quality of Care in Residential Aged Care Facilities in Australia*. October. Canberra: Parliament of Australia. Available from: www.aph.gov.au/Parliamentary_Business/Committees/House/Health_Aged_Care_and_Sport/AgedCareFacilities/Report.

Howlett, M. (2018). The criteria for effective policy design: Character and context in policy instrument choice. *Journal of Asian Public Policy, 11*(3): 245–66. doi.org/10.1080/17516234.2017.1412284.

Howlett, M., Mukherjee, I. & Woo, J.J. (2015). From tools to toolkits in policy design studies: The new design orientation towards policy formulation research. *Policy & Politics, 43*(2): 291–311. doi.org/10.1332/147084414X13992869 118596.

Ibrahim, J.E., Ranson, D.L. & Bugeja, L. (2018). Premature deaths of nursing home residents: An epidemiological analysis. *The Medical Journal of Australia, 208*(3): 143. doi.org/10.5694/mja16.00873.

Inman, P. (2018). Carillion taxpayer bill likely to top £150m. *The Guardian*, 26 September. Available from: www.theguardian.com/business/2018/sep/25/carillion-collapse-likely-cost-taxpayers-more-than-150m-unite.

Jorgensen, M., Siette, J., Georgiou, A. & Westbrook, J.I. (2020). The effect of home care package allocation reforms on service uptake, use and cessation at a large Australian aged care provider. *Australasian Journal on Ageing, 39*(2): e210–e214. doi.org/10.1111/ajag.12764.

Karp, P. (2019). Job seekers allegedly offered cash to lie by private employment service providers. *The Guardian*, [Australia], 16 February. Available from: www.theguardian.com/australia-news/2019/feb/16/job-seekers-allegedly-offered-cash-to-lie-by-private-employment-service-providers.

Keane, D. (2019). Christmas meal 'slop' prompts outrage after being served to Adelaide nursing home residents. *ABC News*, 26 December. Available from: www.abc.net.au/news/2019-12-26/nursing-home-condemned-for-christmas-mash-and-baked-beans/11827694.

Kellett, J., Kyle, G., Itsiopoulos, C., Naunton, M. & Bacon, R. (2015). Malnutrition prevalence in aged care residents: A pilot study. *Topics in Clinical Nutrition, 30*(3): 276–80. doi.org/10.1097/TIN.0000000000000042.

Lane, S. (2016). Secret camera captures nursing home 'suffocation'. *7.30*, [ABC TV], 25 July. Available from: www.abc.net.au/7.30/secret-camera-captures-nursing-home-suffocation/7659690.

Lascoumes, P. & Le Galès, P. (2007). Understanding public policy through its instruments: From the nature of instruments to the sociology of public policy instrumentation. *Governance, 20*(1): 1–21. doi.org/10.1111/j.1468-0491.2007. 00342.x.

Leading Age Services Australia. (2017). *Effectiveness of the Aged Care Quality Assessment and Accreditation Framework for Protecting Residents from Abuse and Poor Practices, and Ensuring Proper Clinical and Medical Care Standards are Maintained and Practised: Submission 4.* Submission to Senate Inquiry. Canberra: Leading Age Services Australia. Available from: www.aph.gov.au/ DocumentStore.ashx?id=777d6a6a-1ba7-4467-9c23-b3f0c49f6a52&subId= 514833.

Lyons, M. (1995). The development of quasi-vouchers in Australia's community services. *Policy & Politics, 23*(2): 127–39. doi.org/10.1332/0305573957824 53509.

Lyons, M. (1998). The impact of managerialism on social policy: The case of social services. *Public Productivity & Management Review, 21*(4): 419–32. doi.org/10.2307/3380549.

Mavromaras, K., Moskos, M., Mahuteau, S. & Isherwood, L. (2018). *Evaluation of the NDIS: Final report.* Adelaide: National Institute of Labour Studies, Flinders University. Available from: www.dss.gov.au/sites/default/files/documents/04_ 2018/ndis_evaluation_consolidated_report_april_2018.pdf.

Meagher, G. (2021). A genealogy of aged care. *ARENA*, June. Available from: arena.org.au/a-genealogy-of-aged-care/.

Meagher, G. & Goodwin, S. (eds). (2015). *Markets, Rights and Power in Australian Social Policy.* Sydney: Sydney University Press. doi.org/10.30722/sup.9781920 899950.

Meagher, G. & Wilson, S. (2015). The politics of market encroachment: Policymaker rationales and voter responses. In G. Meagher & S. Goodwin (eds), *Markets, Rights and Power in Australian Social Policy* (pp. 29–96). Sydney: Sydney University Press. doi.org/10.30722/sup.9781920899950.

Meagher, G., Cortis, N., Charlesworth, S. & Taylor, W. (2019). *Meeting the Social and Emotional Support Needs of Older People Using Aged Care Services.* Sydney: Macquarie University, University of New South Wales & RMIT University. Available from: www.unsworks.unsw.edu.au/primo-explore/fulldisplay?vid= UNSWORKS&docid=unsworks_modsunsworks_61775&context=L.

Morton, R. (2017). Failing jobs sites branded 'a mess'. *The Australian*, 31 October.

Mudge, S.L. (2008). What is neo-liberalism? *Socio-Economic Review, 6*(4): 703–31. doi.org/10.1093/ser/mwn016.

National Disability Insurance Agency (NDIA). (2016). *Market Position Statement New South Wales*. March. Geelong, Vic.: NDIA. Available from: web.archive. org/web/20190311215412/www.ndis.gov.au/media/369/download.

NDIS Quality and Safeguards Commission (NDIS Commission). (n.d.). *Worker Screening Requirements*. Canberra: Commonwealth of Australia. Available from: www.ndiscommission.gov.au/workers/worker-screening-workers.

O'Neill, M. (2013). Aged care crisis. *Lateline*, [ABC TV], 15 July. Available from: www.abc.net.au/lateline/aged-care-crisis/4822054.

Opie, R. (2019). Adelaide aged care worker found guilty of assaulting elderly woman with dementia. *ABC News*, 27 February. Available from: www.abc. net.au/news/2019-02-27/aged-care-worker-found-guilty-of-assaulting-elderly-resident/10853240.

Patty, A. (2020). More medical experts needed on aged care boards and executives. *Sydney Morning Herald*, 1 June.

Pierson, P. (2004). *Politics in Time: History, institutions, and social analysis*. Princeton, NJ: Princeton University Press. doi.org/10.1515/9781400841080.

Productivity Commission. (2016). *Introducing Competition and Informed User Choice into Human Services: Identifying sectors for reform*. Canberra: Productivity Commission.

Redden, G. (2019). John Howard's investor state: Neoliberalism and the rise of inequality in Australia. *Critical Sociology*, 45(4–5): 713–28. doi.org/10.1177/0896920517745117.

Reddie, M. (2021). Six charged over alleged NDIS fraud scheme after raids across Western Sydney. *ABC News*, 22 April. Available from: www.abc.net.au/news/2021-04-22/six-charged-over-alleged-ndis-fraud-scheme/100087086.

Robert, S. (2020). New banning powers strengthen protections for NDIS participants. Media release, The Hon. Stuart Robert MP, Minister for the National Disability Insurance Scheme, 8 June, Canberra. Available from: web.archive.org/web/20200920005326/ministers.dss.gov.au/media-releases/5876.

Royal Commission into Aged Care Quality and Safety. (2019). *Interim Report: Neglect*. Canberra: Commonwealth of Australia. Available from: agedcare.royalcommission.gov.au/publications/interim-report.

Schneider, A.L. & Ingram, H. (1997). *Policy Design for Democracy*. Lawrence, KS: University Press of Kansas.

Select Committee on Red Tape. (2018). *The Effect of Red Tape on Private Education: Interim report—Dissenting report by Labor Senators*. Canberra: Parliament of Australia. Available from: www.aph.gov.au/Parliamentary_Business/Committees/Senate/Red_Tape/PrivateEducation/Interim%20Report/d01.

Senate Community Affairs Legislation Committee (SCALC). (2020a). Answer to Question on Notice: Social Services Portfolio—NDIS Quality and Safeguards Commission. Reference No.: QSC SQ20-000002, Hearing of 5 March. Canberra: Parliament of Australia.

Senate Community Affairs Legislation Committee (SCALC). (2020b). Answer to Question on Notice: Social Services Portfolio—NDIS Quality and Safeguards Commission. Question Reference No.: QSC SQ20-000003, Hearing of 5 March. Canberra: Parliament of Australia.

Senate Community Affairs References Committee (SCARC). (2019). *Effectiveness of the Aged Care Quality Assessment and Accreditation Framework for Protecting Residents from Abuse and Poor Practices, and Ensuring Proper Clinical and Medical Care Standards are Maintained and Practised*. Canberra: Parliament of Australia. Available from: www.aph.gov.au/Parliamentary_Business/Committees/Senate/Community_Affairs/AgedCareQuality.

Senate Education and Employment References Committee. (2015). *Final Report: The operation, regulation and funding of private vocational education and training (VET) providers in Australia*. Canberra: Commonwealth of Australia. Available from: www.aph.gov.au/Parliamentary_Business/Committees/Senate/Education_and_Employment/vocationaled/Final_Report.

Smith, C., Parr, N. & Muhidin, S. (2019). Mapping schools' NAPLAN results: A spatial inequality of school outcomes in Australia. *Geographical Research*, 57(2): 133–50. doi.org/10.1111/1745-5871.12317.

Squires, R. (2010). Aged-care residents in living hell. *The Sunday Telegraph*, [Sydney], 30 May. Available from: www.dailytelegraph.com.au/aged-care-residents-in-living-hell/news-story/8e3d9604f81108bf0ed6ae3d7c51687b.

Strachan, J. (2014). Anger at quality of Canberra nursing home food, hygiene. *The Canberra Times*, 13 September. Available from: www.canberratimes.com.au/story/6078644/anger-at-quality-of-canberra-nursing-home-food-hygiene/.

Streeck, W. & Thelen, K. (2005). Introduction: Institutional change in advanced political economies. In W. Streeck & K. Thelen (eds), *Beyond Continuity: Institutional change in advanced political economies* (pp. 1–39). Oxford, UK: Oxford University Press.

Sumsion, J. (2012). ABC Learning and Australian early education and care: A retrospective ethical audit of a radical experiment. In E. Lloyd & H. Penn (eds), *Childcare Markets Local and Global: Can they deliver an equitable service?* (pp. 209–25). Bristol, UK: Policy Press.

Taylor, J. & Branley, A. (2016). Collapsed training college owners had long-term plan to escape sector, paid themselves $20m. *7.30*, [ABC TV], 14 March. Available from: www.abc.net.au/news/2016-03-14/collapsed-training-college-owners-always-planned-to-cut-and-run/7239372.

Taylor, J. & Branley, A. (2017). Evocca College to close more training campuses in Queensland, Victoria. *7.30*, [ABC TV], 24 February. Available from: www.abc.net.au/news/2017-02-24/evocca-college-to-close-more-campuses-in-victoria-queensland/8298156.

Teles, S.M. (2013). Kludgeocracy in America. *National Affairs, 17*: 97–114.

Tomazin, F. (2019). Morrison government wipes $500 million in dodgy debt from students. *Sydney Morning Herald*, 1 December. Available from: www.smh.com.au/education/morrison-government-wipes-500-million-in-dodgy-debt-from-students-20191130-p53fnk.html.

Topsfield, J. & Millar, R. (2021). NDIS rorters on notice as government cracks down on 'despicable' fraud. *Sydney Morning Herald*, 31 July. Available from: www.smh.com.au/national/ndis-rorters-on-notice-as-government-cracks-down-on-despicable-fraud-20210729-p58e2g.html.

van der Zwan, N. (2014). Making sense of financialization. *Socio-Economic Review, 12*(1): 99–129. doi.org/10.1093/ser/mwt020.

Vogel, S. (2007). Why freer markets need more rules. In M.K. Landy, M.A. Levin & M. Shapiro (eds), *Creating Competitive Markets: The politics of regulatory reform* (pp. 25–42). Washington, DC: Brookings Institution Press.

Vogel, S. (2018). *Marketcraft: How governments make markets work.* Oxford, UK: Oxford University Press. doi.org/10.1093/oso/9780190699857.001.0001.

Wacquant, L. (2012). Three steps to a historical anthropology of actually existing neoliberalism. *Social Anthropology, 20*(1): 66–79. doi.org/10.1111/j.1469-8676.2011.00189.x.

Westbury, J., Gee, P., Ling, T., Kitsos, A. & Peterson, G. (2019). More action needed: Psychotropic prescribing in Australian residential aged care. *Australian & New Zealand Journal of Psychiatry, 53*(2): 136–47. doi.org/10.1177/0004867418758919.

Yeatman, A. (2018). Gender, social policy and the idea of the welfare state. In S. Shaver (ed.), *Handbook on Gender and Social Policy* (pp. 21–36). Cheltenham, UK: Edward Elgar Publishing. doi.org/10.4337/9781785367168.

1

Quality and marketised care: The case of family day care

Natasha Cortis, Megan Blaxland
and Elizabeth Adamson

Introduction

This chapter examines market-based arrangements in family day care, a system that provides children with formal, regulated and government-subsidised early education and care (ECEC) in the homes of individual educators.[1] Our focus is on family day care coordination—the unique and long-running model of coregulation at the heart of Australia's system. 'Coordination units' are government-approved intermediaries within family day care services that support home-based educators with regulatory compliance, administration and educational programming and practice. Initially the domain of community-based providers, family day care coordination has operated as a mixed market since the 1990s. However, changes in policy, funding and regulation over recent decades reoriented services around market principles and enabled for-profit providers to quickly dominate the sector.

---

1   Family day care educators are also known as family day carers or 'childminders' in the United Kingdom. In Australia, as part of a move towards professionalising the sector (Cook et al. 2013), all childcare workers, including those in family day care, are referred to by the term 'educators' if they work directly with children to provide early education and care.

The chapter is concerned with two sets of associated issues: first, we chart the policy developments that led for-profit providers to gain and expand their foothold in family day care; and second, we assess how the dominance of for-profit provision impacted on the sector's capacity to deliver high-quality services to children. As family day care is less familiar than centre-based ECEC, we first outline its distinctive characteristics and contribution, focusing on the role of coordination units, which aim to promote compliance and mitigate the safety and quality risks associated with services delivered by individuals in their homes. Next, we identify the main phases along family day care's pathway to a market model. We outline the arrangements established to promote competition and expand supply in the context of low barriers to entry and show how these led to very high levels of for-profit provision and problems of noncompliance and underservicing, which required significant government effort to address. Finally, we use Australia's official benchmark for quality in ECEC, the National Quality Standard (NQS), to assess the impact of these developments and take stock of patterns of performance among different types of services operating in family day care's mixed market.

Our inquiry recognises that while there are compelling moral arguments against providing early education and care on a for-profit basis, for-profit provision may not be universally incompatible with decent quality. This perspective is based on research evidence about the contribution of public, non-profit and for-profit providers in child care and other social services that has shown service ownership can have mixed, context-dependent effects (Meagher and Cortis 2009). In addition, our previous work documenting family day care practice demonstrated how Australia's model of family day care has enabled for-profit as well as government and non-profit providers to develop exemplary models of leadership and practice, and to provide safe and innovative services that enable flourishing among children, families and educators with diverse sets of needs (Blaxland et al. 2016).

However, while for-profit services may have potential to deliver quality services, the national quality data explored in this chapter attest to systemic underperformance among family day care coordination units that operate on a for-profit basis. For-profit providers are less likely than others to meet the NQS overall, and for-profits dominate among the services deemed to require urgent regulatory intervention. Furthermore, while underperformance of for-profits is also evident in centre-based contexts such as long day care, it is more pronounced in family day care. We show that, while poor-quality for-profit provision grew very quickly after 2010, policy changes and increased enforcement and compliance action by government subsequently reduced the number of underperforming for-profits. Despite this reduction, the problem of poor-quality family day care endures. The analysis raises questions about the appropriateness of market arrangements in family day care and underlines the need to make the quality of services for children the paramount priority of system design and regulation.

Family day care in Australia: A distinctive model of coregulation

Family day care is significant in the provision of children's services in Australia, although it is used by fewer children than long day care or outside school hours care. In 2018, it was accessed by about 162,000 children aged under 12, or 13 per cent of children using approved care (PC 2019: Table 3A.16). Families and educators value the model for offering a personalised approach to education and care, with small groups and home-like environments considered ideal for enabling strong relationships to thrive (Blaxland et al. 2016; Davis et al. 2012). The opportunity to develop close relationships with a single educator is felt to be especially suitable for those who find centre-based settings intimidating or impersonal, such as babies and children with higher care needs, whose requirement for one-on-one support might not be so readily accommodated in centre-based settings (Stratigos et al. 2014). Family day care is also valued for its flexibility in meeting the needs of shift workers and families in sparsely populated communities where there are too few children to maintain long day care centres or preschools (Baxter et al. 2016). Family day care offers flexibility to the overall system of ECEC provision. As establishment costs are low, family day care can help the system rapidly respond to changes in local demand, while traditionally offering more affordable options for families.

Family day care has often been misconstrued as an extension of 'mothering' (Camilleri and Kennedy 1994: 39), but in Australia, it has operated as part of the regulated ECEC system for decades. Since the first community-based schemes were established in the 1970s, coordination units have played a coregulatory role. These units consist of small professional teams of coordinators qualified at diploma level or above[2] who work to support, monitor and train family day care educators. Educators are required to be attached to a coordination unit to access government childcare subsidies, and this has acted as an incentive for people offering home-based care to join the regulated family day care system. As a result, unregulated paid childminding in educators' homes remains relatively uncommon in Australia.[3] The role of coordination units in upholding standards of quality, safety and accountability has meant Australian family day care is considered relatively well regulated by international standards (Blaxland and Adamson 2017).

Family day care services retain considerable flexibility in the ways their coordination units support educators and resource their activities. Typically, services contract educators[4] and levy fees on them and/or families, although some may receive financial or in-kind support from an auspicing agency such as a local council or non-profit organisation. Services are approved by state or territory regulators on the basis that they will ensure educators are adequately monitored and supported, but their detailed tasks are not prescribed. Accordingly, services determine their own processes of monitoring, supporting and training educators, such that the regulatory approach to family day care has been described as 'outcomes-based' (Education Council 2014: 64).

Usually, coordination units link families to educators, manage enrolments and administer and process government subsidies. Coordination units are also expected to monitor educators' homes to ensure safety, to facilitate access to professional development and to help inform and mentor educators to assist with planning and documenting educational programs (Corr et al. 2014). Coordinators help educators monitor child wellbeing and development, provide strategies for supporting children with additional needs and sometimes link children and families to local health and other services and supports when concerns arise (Blaxland et al. 2016). They often

2   Coordinators are required to be qualified to diploma level (or working towards a diploma-level qualification). By contrast, family day care educators must have (or be actively working towards) a Certificate III education and care qualification, or above.

3   There is, however, an unregulated market for nannies and au pairs, though unlike family day care, nannies and au pairs typically work in families' homes and do not attract childcare subsidies (Berg and Meagher 2018).

4   Educators may be employed, as in South Australia where many are employed by the state government's family day care service. However, contracting is standard; family day care educators are almost universally self-employed and set their own fees. For further discussion of family day care workers' employment arrangements, see Delaney et al. (2018).

help educators' families understand the nature of the work, provide practical resources such as equipment and toy libraries and organise play sessions to bring together groups of educators and the children for whom they care. Well-performing coordinators act as bridges between educators otherwise working alone, providing them with workplace companionship and support and enhancing their health and wellbeing (Corr et al. 2014). Providing essential supports to what is otherwise difficult and risky work, coordination units make it possible for the family day care system to deliver acceptable standards of quality care to children.

Marketisation in family day care

Over the past decade, family day care services have been reshaped around a competitive, self-financing model.[5] As for centre-based care (Brennan 2007), for-profit family day care provision has offered governments a source of additional capacity and enabled childcare system expansion. However, market-based dynamics in family day care played out in different ways than in long day care, which saw the rapid growth and collapse of what was the world's largest listed long day care provider, ABC Learning, in 2008 (Brennan 2007; Sumsion 2012). Rather than growing commercial involvement in direct provision of services to children, the growth of for-profit provision of family day care occurred among the coordination units operating as small businesses regulating networks of educators.

Here, we chart the distinctive set of arrangements through which family day care coordination became a highly competitive market dominated by a myriad of new for-profit providers. Our account shows that whereas public and government concerns about the growth of for-profit provision in centre-based ECEC focused on levels of market dominance by a small number of providers and the risk of corporate collapse, concerns about for-profits in family day care related primarily to cases of unscrupulous activity, poor quality and fraud among small businesses (Ley 2014; Worthington et al. 2017). We outline these developments by identifying five phases through which a mix of intersecting, overlapping dynamics have shaped family day care around a market model. These are summarised in Figure 1.1.

---

5   This has broadly followed a policy logic applied across ECEC. For family day care policy to follow in the footsteps of long day care is common in Australia, where home-based care typically appears to be an afterthought in the policy process or subsumed in ECEC policy.

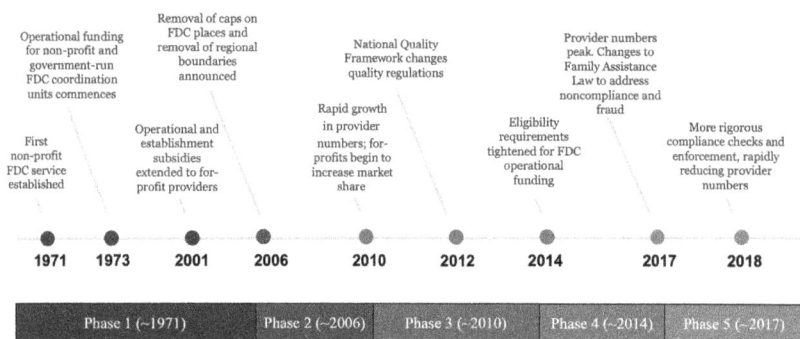

Figure 1.1 Timeline of key milestones in the marketisation of family day care (FDC)

Source: Based on authors' research.

Phase 1: Relative stability in a mixed market

Family day care was established as a non-profit model and operated on this basis, with little change, for a quarter of a century. In 1971, the Brotherhood of St Laurence set up what is recognised as the first service in Australia, after which a series of community-based pilots was undertaken to develop ways to provide flexible care for working parents. Government funds were essential to establishing the model.

The Australian Government first undertook to fund centre-based child care in the *Child Care Act 1972*, which laid the groundwork for funding family day care services. From 1974, non-profit and government-run coordination units were eligible for operational funding under the Commonwealth's Children's Services Program, which supported the establishment of formal, regulated, subsidised home-based care as an ECEC option (Brennan 1998; Jones 1987: 90; Tohme and Darley 2013). Early iterations of operational funding arrangements involved a standard formula that directed Commonwealth support to help meet the costs of administration and regulatory support provided by the coordination units. The rate of financial support increased through the 1980s, in recognition of growing regulatory demands (Jones 1987). Widespread access to operational funding was not significantly tightened until 2014. While information about the numbers and types of providers is not available for the early decades of the program, the number of family day care places is reported to have grown in the 1970s and 1980s (McIntosh and Phillips 2002). Information available from the 1990s shows the number of family day care services remained steady throughout the 1990s and early 2000s and did not start to grow until later (Figure 1.2).

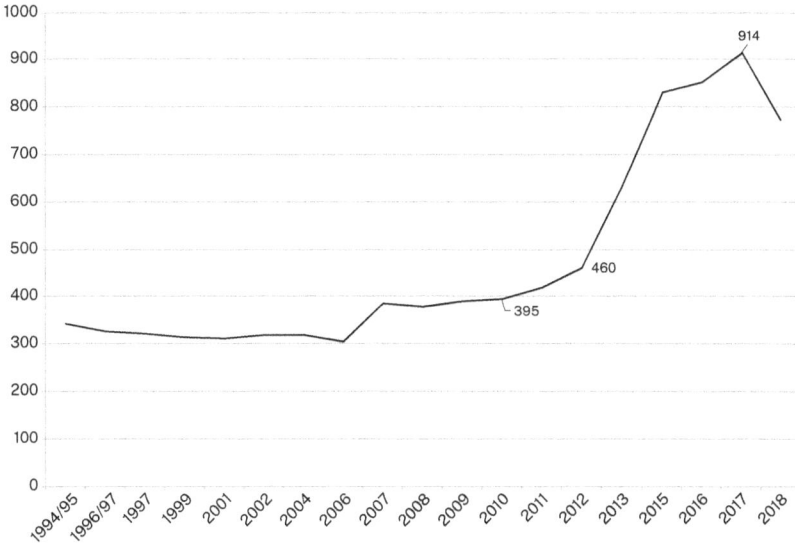

Figure 1.2 Number of family day care services, 1994–2018
Note: These figures include a small but unspecified number of in-home care services, which are routinely counted with family day care in departmental reporting.
Sources: DEEWR (2008, 2011a, 2011b, 2012, 2013, 2014, 2015, 2016, 2017, 2018); FACS (1999, 2000, 2001, 2003, 2005).

Changes in government subsidy rules for family day care lagged behind those for centre-based child care. For example, whereas operational subsidies were extended to for-profit long day care services under Labor in 1991, it was not until 2001, under the Howard Coalition government, that for-profit family day care services became eligible for operational and establishment assistance (AIHW 2003). Further, while an early move of the Howard government was to promote a demand-driven system by removing direct federal support to childcare centres and redirecting subsidies to parents in 1996–97 (Brennan 1998; Meagher 2007), in family day care, although parents could also access fee subsidies, operational funding to coordination units was maintained. Despite having access to operate in family day care, it appears that few for-profits took up opportunities to establish services and access subsidies at this time, and the family day care sector remained relatively unchanged for many years. For-profit providers retained a small market share. Unlike in long day care, where for-profit operators controlled three-quarters of childcare places from 2004, only one in 20 family day care coordination units was for-profit at that time (Meagher 2007).

From 2004, support for coordination units came via the Australian Government's Community Support Program, which was designed to help childcare services establish themselves and operate, especially in rural and remote communities or areas of market failure. Family day care services were able to access funds at specific hourly rates per place. These were more generous than the fixed annual amounts available to long day care and outside school hours care. All family day care services were also able to access an extra component of the program to assist with expenses incurred in supporting and monitoring compliance across their networks of educators. Changes to funding arrangements did not appear to immediately expand supply or attract new providers because the number of places for children was capped.

Phase 2: Promoting competition, system expansion and choice

In 2006, the Coalition Government announced it would remove caps on family day care places to expand supply and provide more choices for families (Tohme and Darley 2013). This policy development followed principles introduced for centre-based services, with the federal government justifying the changes to bring family day care into line with arrangements already in place for long day care (Brough 2006). Later, the removal of caps was criticised by the Australian National Audit Office, for both being poorly targeted and for facilitating a stream of unchecked government spending (ANAO 2012).

While it removed the cap on places, the federal government also removed the regional boundaries that had previously restricted coordination units to operating in defined local areas (Tohme and Darley 2013). Local boundaries had acted to constrain competition by limiting the reach of a coordination unit and the size of each unit's network. Lifting geographic restrictions enabled family day care services to contract educators operating at some distance from their service and expanded the scale at which units could operate. Thus, the geographic coverage of services was now allowed to overlap, which enhanced the prospects for competition for educators and families. This created opportunities for services to reduce fees but still make profits by supporting larger numbers of educators remotely, and by thinning the supports provided.

Unlike for centre-based care, for family day care, government approvals do not specify maximum numbers of places per service. Further, the activities of family day care coordinators were never closely specified by the government. This enabled rapid growth, with providers able to profit through economies of scale or underservicing, without regulatory oversight (Education Council 2017: 61). Reporting of data on the number of educators attached to each unit was not routinely required, making it difficult to clearly assess the effects of lifting the boundaries. Nonetheless, a dramatic expansion in the numbers of services is evident.

Phase 3: Rapid growth of for-profit provision

For reasons that are still unclear, family day care's phase of rapid growth did not occur immediately after 2006.[6] Rather, it happened from 2010, with the number of services more than doubling, from 395 in September that year to 914 in 2017 (see Figure 1.2). Access to operational and establishment funding and other government subsidies, which seemed to assure ongoing viability to new providers, contributed to this growth, coupled with the absence of regulation of the number of educators serviced by each unit. Access to apparently 'easy funding' from the Commonwealth may have enabled new market entrants to quickly dominate family day care. State and territory regulators, who retained responsibility for approving new services, failed to stem the trend. Transformation of the sector was rapid. In 2014, more than 80 per cent of family day care services had been operating for less than three years (PC 2014: 351–52). These new entrants were primarily privately run small businesses. In 2012, the Gillard Labor government introduced the National Quality Framework (NQF) for ECEC, which required family day care coordinators and educators to obtain specified educational qualifications. At least initially, the NQF did not appear to constrain new entrants, who may have been somewhat naive as to the significant resources and commitment required to meet standards and perform properly all aspects of their coregulatory role.

---

6   Family day care is a very under-researched element of the Australian early childhood sector. Despite extensive investigation and discussions with family day care professionals, the authors were not able to determine why this expansion was slow to start. We speculate that it took some time for the business opportunity that family day care offered to be discovered.

47

The large number of for-profit providers among new players is evident in NQS data, which are part of the NQF and include information about each service's date of approval (see Figure 1.3).[7] Corroborating the trends evident in Figure 1.2, there was massive growth in new service approvals between 2012 and 2015. When analysed by provider type, the surge was driven by approvals of new for-profits after 2010, and more quickly after 2012. For-profits made up 42 per cent of new approvals in 2011, but this rose to 59 per cent in 2012 and more than 90 per cent of those approved between 2013 and 2016. In 2013, 295 new services were approved. These services dramatically swelled a sector that, as shown in Figure 1.2, had numbered 460 in September 2012 and doubled in the years that followed.

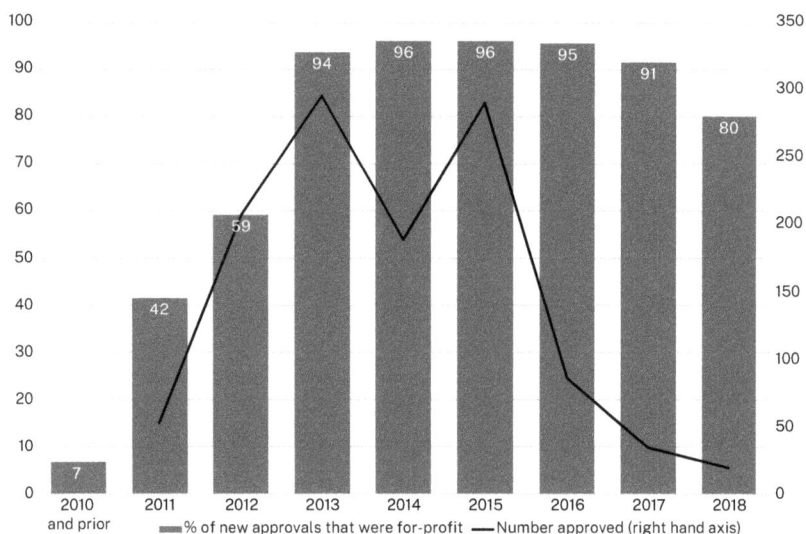

Figure 1.3 Composition of newly approved family day care services

Note: Data for approvals in 2012 and earlier were drawn from the detailed dataset for services, as of Q3 2013. For each year from 2013, the number of services approved is based on Q4 in that year. In and before 2015, small numbers of services did not state their provider type but were manually recoded.

Source: Authors' calculations based on NQS detailed dataset for Q3 2013 to Q3 2017 (ACECQA 2018).

---

7   These approvals reflect approval by regulatory authorities in the states and territories and Commonwealth approval to receive federal subsidies.

Phase 4: Policy reform to contain rising costs

The rapid growth of family day care raised several challenges for government to address, particularly the rising costs of subsidies to services. As the number of services approved by state and territory regulatory authorities escalated, Commonwealth spending on the operational subsidies accessed by coordination units rose. In 2012, the ANAO released a review of the Community Support Program that was critical of its poor targeting to areas of need. It found family day care services were receiving $191,000 per service, on average, which represented 71 per cent of total program funding, and most funding was accessed by family day care providers in major cities, which was considered poorly aligned with the original program objectives of supporting access and provision in areas of market failure (ANAO 2012: 16, 31).

In response, the Abbott Coalition government announced changes aimed at stemming sector growth and containing spending. First, new rules dramatically restricted family day care's access to operational support. From April 2014, tight eligibility requirements for operational funding were introduced, which removed the ability of most services to draw on government funding to cover coordination costs. Eligibility was restricted to circumstances in which there was just one service in the most disadvantaged urban areas or in regional, rural and remote areas. In announcing the changes, the then assistant minister for education, Sussan Ley, framed the development once again in terms of bringing funding for family day care into line with that for long day care. She explained that, while exempting family day care services from the stricter criteria applying to centres had helped support family day care as a viable childcare model, the government was now refocusing financial support on provision in regional, remote and disadvantaged areas (Ley 2014). Budget papers indicated the tighter criteria would provide savings of $157.1 million over three years (Hockey and Cormann 2014: 81).

Figures 1.2 and 1.3 indicate that after operational funding was curtailed, service approvals and overall sectoral growth slowed. The total number of newly approved services dropped sharply after 2015, as reforms to contain costs and unscrupulous practices took effect. However, for-profits continued to make up almost all new approvals, albeit in smaller numbers than a few years earlier. In 2018, after growth in approvals slowed, private for-profit providers were operating 71 per cent of family day care services (see Table 1.1), compared with 65 per cent of long day care and 48 per cent of outside school hours care.

Table 1.1 Proportion of for-profit, government and non-profit ECEC services, 2018 (per cent)

	Private for-profit	Government[a]	Non-profit community-managed[b]	Other non-profit[c]	Total
Family day care (n = 756)	71	12	10	7	100
Long day care (n = 7,455)	65	5	13	17	100
Outside school hours care (n = 5,286)	48	11	20	21	100
Preschool (n = 3,934)	15	26	42	17	100
All (n = 15,763)[d]	47	13	27	13	100

[a] Includes government schools.

[b] Non-profit community-managed refers to those managed by a parent association or cooperative.

[c] This category also includes services operated by independent and Catholic schools, school councils or school boards.

[d] 'All' is not the sum of family day care, long day care, preschool and outside school hours care, as some centre-based services may provide more than one service type.

Note: Counts are of services, not providers.

Source: NQS detailed quarterly dataset (ACECQA 2018).

Phase 5: Addressing underservicing and fraud

As most services had relied heavily on the Community Support Program until 2014, removal of access to funding meant services needed to quickly shift their resource base to fund activities through levies on educators and families. Many services found this to be very difficult as the timing converged with the NQF reforms introduced under Labor. Discussed in more detail in the next section, these changes included new ratios that reduced the numbers of children for whom an educator could care, qualification requirements for educators and coordinators and requirements for educators to document children's learning (DEEWR 2009; Sumsion et al. 2009). In the months that followed the announcement of changes in 2014, many long-running services were unsure how they would fund their activities and remain viable, and flagged plans to change the way they supported educators and their fee structures (Cortis et al. 2014).

Concerns emerged, following the sector's rapid growth, that new for-profit providers were offering coordination services to educators for very low or no fees and delivering minimal support, contributing to a downward quality spiral. Price-based competition was felt acutely by council-run and non-profit providers wanting to maintain a high-quality service but needing to charge educators and families accordingly. Several family day care providers and peak bodies raised concerns that the combined effects of the changes to the regulatory environment associated with the NQF and Community Support Program risked limiting the flexibility of family day care business models and reducing the viability and sustainability of high-quality services (Education Council 2017).

Around the same time, evidence was also growing of serious problems with noncompliance among some for-profit providers. Even after changes to limit operational funding, services were reportedly able to attract up to $200 per child per week in government fee subsidies based on fraudulent enrolment of children who were not in their care (Worthington et al. 2017). Some appeared to be taking advantage of a loophole in childcare subsidy arrangements whereby educators would claim fee subsidies for caring for each other's children, when in fact they each just cared for their own children.

In 2017, the Family Assistance Law was changed to limit this practice. Educators could no longer receive subsidies for their own children to attend family day care on the same day they provided family day care for other children. Additional responses were to establish more frequent compliance checks, suspend fraudulent providers' access to further subsidies, establish a public register of enforcement actions and publicise crackdowns on 'dodgy operators'. In the minister's words, the aim was to ensure that funding flowing into the sector would not be 'stolen by rorters and shonks' (Birmingham 2018).

Further regulatory reform in 2018 included more detailed registers and checks on family day care educators and service providers. It was noticed that noncompliant family day care services often had very high numbers of educators (Education Council 2017). In efforts to ensure family day care services were operating with staffing levels that would allow them to realistically support a network of educators, in 2018, the Education and Care Services National Law was changed to require state and territory governments to set coordinator to educator ratios (most commonly, these were 1:20) and to cap the number of educators at services. In addition, as part of the new Child Care Package in July 2018, family day care services were required for the first time to lodge contact details for each educator.[8] While these changes, combined with increased enforcement action by regulatory authorities, likely went some way towards closing loopholes and increasing public scrutiny of noncompliant services, the changes did not preclude services subject to enforcement actions from later establishing new family day care services or from moving into other market-based service systems where demand-driven approaches underpin opportunities for profit, such as the NDIS (Begley 2018).

Assessing quality across the mixed market

Changes in the structure of the family day care market, and the dominance of for-profit provision, can be assessed using data collected as part of the NQF. Introduced in 2012, the NQF requires long day care, family day care and outside school hours care services to meet nationally consistent standards (ACECQA 2019b). Assessments and ratings against the NQS were introduced as part of a suite of Labor government–initiated reforms that also sought to improve quality, safety and children's outcomes through changes to ratios and staff qualification requirements. The system was developed under the auspices of the Council of Australian Governments and involved extensive consultation with state regulatory authorities, the early childhood sector and its peak bodies. As well as driving performance improvement, publicly available ratings were intended to make quality more visible to families to assist them to exercise choice.

The NQS brought the Australian early childhood sector closer to international benchmarks for quality early education and care (Pascoe and Brennan 2017). Independent evaluation found the NQS assessment and rating instrument had 'very high internal reliability' and was 'fit for purpose' (Rothman et al. 2012: ii). Shortly after implementation, a national consultation confirmed it continued to have broad support and had introduced a focus on continuous improvement, strengthened the focus on outcomes for children and provided national consistency in

---

8   The effectiveness of these efforts is not yet apparent and requires closer analysis. However, as indicated in our Epilogue, they do appear to have helped reduce the number of poor-quality family day care providers in operation.

quality standards (Woolcott Research 2014). However, some claimed the NQS appeared more tailored to long day care than to either family day care or outside school hours care (Woolcott Research 2014: 5). Others took issue with deeming 'minimum standards' to be 'good enough' for children and suggested the prospects for a robust quality framework were undermined by overreliance on for-profit provision (Fenech et al. 2012). Notwithstanding, the NQS is now well established as a national benchmark.

Assessment involves state and territory regulatory authorities visiting services to rate their performance in seven broad areas and their subareas. The seven quality areas—treated as equal in importance for assessment purposes—are:

1. educational program and practice
2. children's health and safety
3. physical environment
4. staffing arrangements
5. relationships with children
6. collaborative partnerships with families and communities
7. governance and leadership.[9]

An overall rating of 'Meeting the National Quality Standard' reflects quality education and care in all seven quality areas. Authorities can also rate services as 'Exceeding the National Quality Standard' if they achieve standards beyond requirements in four of seven areas. 'Working towards the National Quality Standard' indicates that, while the service provides a safe education and care program, one or more areas have been identified for improvement and the next assessment will be scheduled sooner than if the NQS was met. 'Significant improvement required' indicates the service does not meet one or more quality areas or does not comply with relevant legislation, giving rise to significant risk to the safety, health and wellbeing of children. This requires regulatory authorities to take immediate action; services must quickly comply or lose the ability to operate. Finally, services with very high quality can apply for an 'excellent' rating, which can only be achieved via application and reflects exceptional education and care, sector leadership and commitment to continual improvement.

---

9   See the National Quality Standard (available from: www.acecqa.gov.au/nqf/national-quality-standard).

Quality in family day care and centre-based care

Early information indicated family day care was performing well compared with other service types in all but two areas: educational programming and the physical environment (Rothman et al. 2012). Subsequent data call this apparent success into question, perhaps due to the changes in the structure of the sector after 2012. Indeed, data from the second quarter of 2018 show only slightly more than one-quarter of for-profit family day care services had an overall rating of at least 'meeting' the NQS or higher (27 per cent; see Figure 1.4). By contrast, 87 per cent of government services were rated as at least meeting the standard (in family day care, most government providers are local governments),[10] while 75 per cent of community-managed non-profits and 80 per cent of other non-profits met the standard overall. Most often, services failed to meet standards relating to educational programs and practice, the physical environment and governance and leadership.

Poorer quality among for-profits is of course not unique to family day care; Figure 1.4 confirms for-profit long day care services and preschools are also less likely to meet the NQS. However, in family day care, for-profit providers perform comparatively worse against the standards than they do in other ECEC service types. Three-quarters of long day care for-profits met the standards overall, compared with 92 per cent of government and 85 per cent or higher for each type of non-profit, demonstrating a narrower 'provider gap' than in family day care, in which a much lower proportion meets the standard. In outside school hours care, by contrast, provider type appears to have little association with quality, for reasons that have not been explored.

Advocates have suggested that family day care performance against these measures may reflect assessors' poor understanding of the uniqueness of family day care compared with centre-based services (Woolcott Research 2014). On this reasoning, lack of specialised assessment for family day care might explain some of the sector's poorer performance in recent assessments compared with long day care (Family Day Care Australia 2018). Indeed, whereas assessments for long day care take place at each centre, for family day care, the ratings process requires assessors to visit the coordination unit and four randomly selected educators. For large services, this could represent a

---

10   Local council providers are not distinguished from state and territory providers in the dataset; however, the provider name indicates the majority in the category 'State/Territory and Local Government Managed' are councils. Another category, 'State/Territory Government Schools', captures another area of state and territory provision, but these do not provide family day care.

very small proportion of ECEC provision within their operations. As such, ratings may not capture the variability of quality across a family day care service, especially for those supporting very large numbers of educators. However, assessor capacity and assessment method cannot explain the wide gap in quality by provider type within the family day care system.

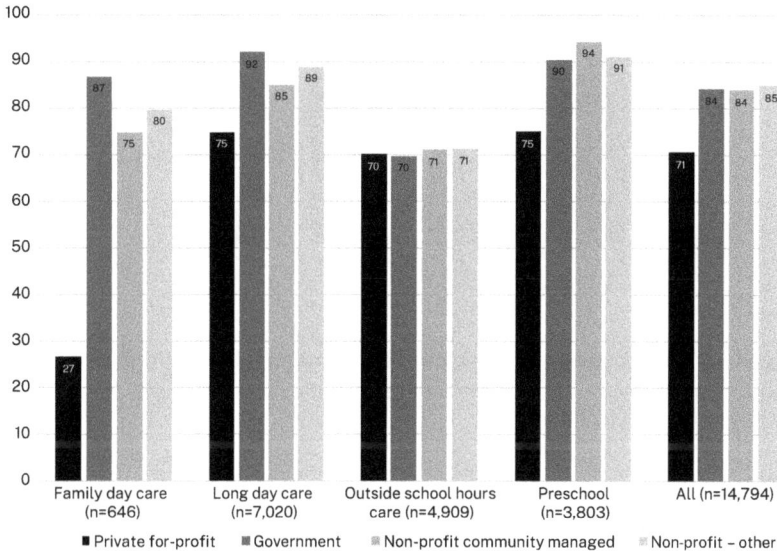

Figure 1.4 Proportion of ECEC services with an overall rating of at least meeting the NQS, by provider type, Q2 2018

Note: 'Government' includes government schools; 'Non-profit community-managed' includes those run by parent associations and cooperatives; 'Other non-profit' includes independent and Catholic schools and services auspiced by school councils or boards.

Source: Detailed dataset for Q2 2018 (ACECQA 2018).

Ratings by provider type in family day care

Figure 1.5 shows overall ratings for family day care in the second quarter of 2018. Public providers achieved the highest standards, although more than one in eight (13 per cent) publicly provided services also failed to meet the NQS. For-profits were more likely to be rated in the lower quality categories ('Working towards' or 'Significant improvement required') and were much less likely than other types of family day care services to achieve ratings of meeting the NQS or above. Further, the only providers that fell into the 'Significant improvement required' category were for-profits. Correspondingly, for-profit family day care providers dominate the Australian Government's register of enforcement actions (see, for example, DET 2019).

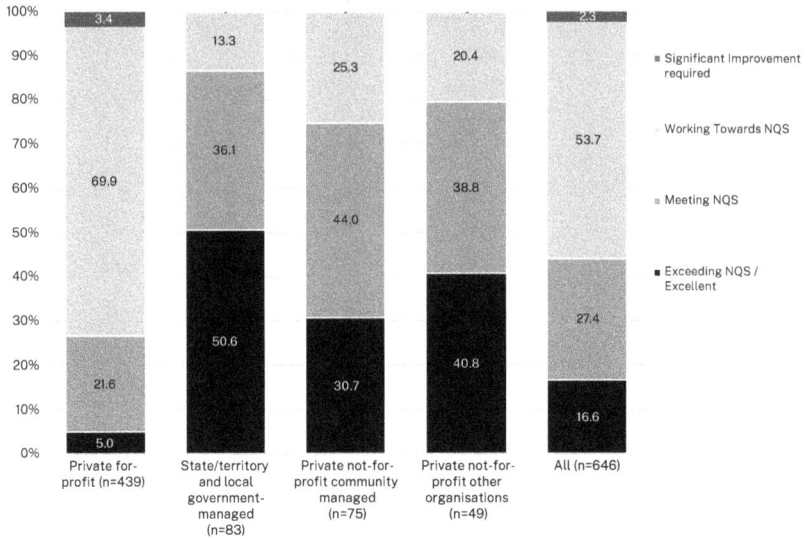

Figure 1.5 Overall quality rating, family day care, by provider type, 2018

Source: Detailed dataset for Q2 2018 (ACECQA 2018), based on the 646 services with a quality rating in that quarter.

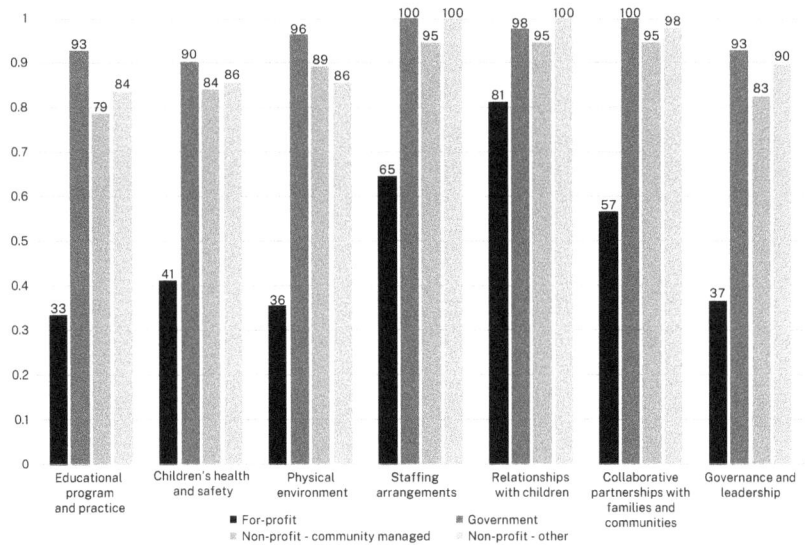

Figure 1.6 Proportion of family day care providers that met each quality area

Source: Detailed dataset for Q2 2018 (ACECQA 2018), based on the 646 services with a quality rating in that quarter.

A closer look at each of the seven quality domains attests to the underperformance of for-profit family day care services (Figure 1.6). Relationships with children (Quality Area 5) appear to be a relatively strong area for family day care. This standard was met by 86 per cent of providers and the gap between for-profits and others was relatively narrow. In terms of educational program and practice, physical environment and governance and leadership,[11] for-profit providers achieved much lower ratings relative to other providers.

In addition to being less likely to meet the NQS overall and performing worse on each of the seven quality areas, high proportions of for-profit family day care services have failed to meet national standards in multiple quality areas. Table 1.2 shows that, in 2018, most government and non-profit services met standards in each quality area. Where these failed, they were more likely to fail in one or two areas only. By contrast, two-thirds of for-profit providers did not meet quality standards in three or more of the seven quality areas, compared with only 5 per cent of government-run services and 15 per cent of non-profits. Of the 200 services that did not meet five or more quality areas, almost all were for-profits. One in eight (12 per cent) for-profit providers did not meet standards in any of the seven quality areas, while no non-profits or government services failed on all seven measures.

As this evidence shows, meeting quality standards has been a challenge in family day care. While at the aggregate level family day care seems to exhibit systemic problems against the quality standards, this breakdown by provider type has shown quality outcomes across the sector are driven by sector composition—namely, the dominance of poorly performing for-profit providers. There are, nonetheless, some poor-performing public and non-profit services and some high-quality services that are operated on a for-profit basis. Indeed, there were 22 for-profits among the 107 services that were rated as 'Exceeding National Quality Standard' or 'Excellent'. NQS data are not sufficiently detailed to demonstrate the common characteristics of these high-performing services. The possibility for some for-profits to meet and exceed high standards acts as a reminder that family day care has the potential to operate effectively as a mixed market in which diverse models of provision can thrive. But while for-profit provision does not necessarily preclude high quality, the NQS

---

11 'Governance and leadership' includes standards relating to organisational cultures fostering professional learning, internal administrative systems and commitment to continuous improvement.

provides the clearest indication yet of the way policy changes that enabled dominance by for-profits have also resulted in lower overall levels of quality for children.

Table 1.2 Proportion of family day care services with unmet quality areas, by provider type, 2018 (per cent)

	For-profit (n = 439)	Government (n = 83)	Non-profit community-managed (n = 75)	Other non-profit (n = 49)	All (n = 646)
All quality areas met	27	87	75	80	44
1 or more unmet quality areas	73	13	25	20	56
2 or more unmet quality areas	71	8	21	20	53
3 or more unmet quality areas	65	5	15	14	48
4 or more unmet quality areas	58	4	9	2	41
5 or more unmet quality areas	45	0	7	0	31
6 or more unmet quality areas	27	0	4	0	18
7 unmet quality areas	12	0	0	0	8

Note: Proportions reported are cumulative percentages.
Source: Detailed dataset for Q2 2018 (ACECQA 2018), based on the 646 services with a quality rating in that quarter.

Conclusion

This chapter has charted the main changes that have reshaped family day care around a market model in recent years, revealing the alarmingly low standards of service provision that have emerged after a period of significant growth and change in the provider mix. For family day care coordination, poor quality is particularly concerning, given the role of these units as coregulators and conduits between government and educators, and in providing practical support and oversight to educators who otherwise work alone with children. National data have shown that after a phase of market expansion, low proportions of for-profit providers met the

NQS. The very large proportion of for-profit services underperforming in multiple domains indicates the provider mix that emerged in this period enabled standards to deteriorate to unacceptable levels across the sector, limiting families' ability to choose high-quality services.

The development of these arrangements reflects a 'quality blindness' in ECEC policy and reform, which is characterised by acceptance of variable quality and the failure of regulatory authorities to manage approvals and funding arrangements in ways that promote quality in the period we examined. The funding and regulatory strategies that were in place in a period of rapid growth were not designed to balance market dynamics with the need for a quality, sustainable sector. First, removing regional boundaries and caps on child enrolments, while offering blanket government support, led to a massive expansion of for-profit family day care services. The subsequent withdrawal of operational funding provided an incentive for profit-seeking services to cut quality. Policy and funding reform failed to differentiate between high-quality services and low-quality profiteers, enabling patterns of sectoral growth that were heavily distorted towards poorer-quality services.

The capacity to correct this was initially left to the choices made by educators in selecting their coordination unit and by parents selecting educators attached to better-quality providers. However, choice is unlikely to correct the market. Family day care educators typically receive very low incomes and may choose to attach themselves to the cheapest family day care service available, even if these do not provide comprehensive professional development or other supports for quality. Families can access information about quality through the NQS, but public reporting of quality standards does not appear to deter choice of lower-performing services. When asked to rank factors that shape their childcare decisions, parents rank quality ratings at the bottom, below considerations of location, cost, educators and the general 'feel' of the service (ACECQA 2017: 62).

In contrast, our discussion of family day care's development demonstrates the impact that decisive government intervention can have on the composition and nature of family day care provision. Enforcement action to curb fraudulent practice has had a positive effect and many unscrupulous family day care services closed as a result (DET 2019). While addressing fraud has no doubt resulted in the closure of poor-quality services, not all such services are also noncompliant with regulations. Further government action is needed with regards to quality, and with repeated failure to meet national standards. At present, only those services considered to pose a significant risk to the safety, health and wellbeing of children, and rated as 'Significant improvement required', face potential closure as a result of poor quality. Stricter action could also address poor quality among services persistently rated as 'Working towards' the NQS but which fail to improve. Indeed, while the NQS is built on an ethos of continuous improvement, this appears to be largely aspirational. Although those rated as 'Working towards' standards are prioritised for reassessment, improvement against the standards has not been required, enabling services to repeatedly—perhaps even perpetually—perform below the NQS.

As family day care receives too little research or policy attention, there is a strong risk the poor quality delivered by so many services could continue to go unaddressed. This is particularly concerning when government commitment to continuing the National Partnership Agreement on the National Quality Agenda for Early Childhood Education and Care has been in question (Early Childhood Australia 2018) and influential conservative lobbyists have called for reductions in the staffing and qualification requirements in the NQF (Joseph 2018). Moreover, the coregulatory role of coordination units can only be effective if those units genuinely understand and are committed and resourced to perform that function. If market incentives push some services to reduce costs by reducing the level of service they provide to educators, the model cannot remain effective and, in this scenario, incentives to achieve a high NQS rating would appear insufficient.

Evidence from case studies with family day care services that do provide high-quality education and care demonstrates the importance of service leadership (Blaxland et al. 2016). High-quality family day care services start with a commitment to quality that affects all aspects of their work, from selecting the most experienced and well-trained educators to high levels of supervision, mentorship and professional development, and to a lack of tolerance of noncompliance and poor-quality education and care. Continuous quality improvement is most likely in family day care services where the unit is led by experienced staff focused on improving quality. For this reason, high-quality leadership is a fundamental underpinning of good-quality practice and should be required and fostered in coordination units. One response would be to set higher standards for leadership, especially among new services and those that are not meeting quality standards, along with additional training, qualification requirements, mentoring or leadership support as a basis for instilling better practices throughout family day care networks.

In some ways, our findings of poor-quality for-profit provision are unsurprising, as there is some empirical research from centre-based settings suggesting for-profits may divert resources from service delivery, skimp on learning programs and staff ratios, and underservice (Meagher and Cortis 2009; Brogaard and Petersen 2021). This chapter suggests that although much reform has been justified in terms of bringing funding and regulation of family day care into line with other areas of early education and care, the strong differentials in performance by provider type suggest for-profit provision may be especially inappropriate for family day care coordination. This may reflect the newness of many providers or the fact the types of profit-based providers emerging are particularly poorly suited to a coregulatory role. In any case, our research provides additional insight into the ways market-based reforms have unfolded in Australia and the implications of making quality considerations too low a priority in the process of system expansion. In the context of low barriers to entry and standards that are difficult to enforce, change can occur very rapidly in this area of ECEC. Quality cannot be a second-order concern. Coordination units should be required to demonstrate commitment to quality and real improvement, regardless of their ownership. By taking tougher action in response to repeated poor quality, the NQS could be used to place quality at the forefront of all family day care provision.

Epilogue

Since preparing this chapter, significant progress has been made in stemming the growth of for-profit family day care provision and addressing the quality issues that became evident in preceding years. Unlike the number of centre-based services (which continued to grow), the number of family day care services has decreased significantly since 2017, as has the number of children using family day care (DESE 2020). The contraction of family day care initially evident in 2018 (Figure 1.2) has effectively returned service numbers to 2012 levels: by the end of the 2019–20 financial year, just 507 NQF-approved family day care services were operating, after reaching more than 900 in 2017 (ACECQA 2020: 5). Moreover, for-profits' share of family day care fell from 71 per cent in 2018 to 61 per cent in 2020 (ACECQA 2020: 4). At the same time, half of all family day care services that had been assessed were at least meeting the NQS overall—up from 44 per cent in 2018. ACECQA (2020: 19) noted improvements in children's health and safety (Quality Area Two), which it considered 'the first and most important objective under the Education and Care Services National Law'. For this quality area, two-thirds of services met the standards—'the highest proportion for more than four years' (ACECQA 2020: 19).

While the family day care sector has again experienced massive transformation, these changes have not fully addressed the problems of quality that emerged over the past decade. Those for-profits still in operation have continued to perform worse relative to other provider types. In the second quarter of 2020, only 35 per cent of for-profits with a quality rating met the NQS, compared with more than two-thirds of non-profit and government services.[12] Developments nonetheless underline the effectiveness of committed state action to tackle the quality problems associated with the rapid growth of poor-quality providers. Reducing for-profits' market share appears to have played a major role in improving quality across the sector. While a more comprehensive account of the drivers of change is warranted, the composition of the family day care market appears to have changed, at least in part because of improved attention to service quality in policy and regulation. In particular, the introduction of coordinator-to-educator ratios and enhanced reporting requirements is likely to have reduced the attractiveness of family day care to services motivated by profit.

Concerted efforts by authorities to identify and address fraudulent and noncompliant services have been essential in turning the sector around. The *Report on Government Services 2021* records the number of confirmed breaches—that is, instances of a regulatory authority finding a provider, supervisor or educator failed to abide by relevant legislation, regulations or conditions. There were just less than 300 confirmed breaches per 100 family day care services in both 2017–18 and 2018–19, but this increased to a staggering 690 breaches per 100 services in 2019–20 (PC 2021:

---

12   Authors' calculations, NQS time-series data for Q2 2020 from the ACECQA's *NQF Snapshots* (available from: www.acccqa.gov.au/nqf/snapshots).

Table 3A.33).[13] While this may reflect some changes in how breaches in family day care are counted, it nonetheless reflects the massive increase in regulatory attention to identify and address quality problems. Further, these data attest to the huge ongoing task of addressing problems in the sector to stabilise provision at decent standards of quality.

The dramatic changes in the structure and quality of Australia's family day care system evident after 2017 could not have been achieved if such matters were left to the choices of individual educators and families in a marketised system. Choice does not offer a plausible mechanism for maintaining or improving standards of quality. It was not until policymakers and regulatory authorities took more strongly interventionist actions that the challenges that too quickly emerged under a market-based approach began to turn around. Deliberate policy and government intervention appears to be both deterring and removing unscrupulous and poor-quality performers and garnering stronger commitment to quality practices across the system. Yet quality risks remain. The dominance of for-profit provision continues to constrain the prospects for quality and will require ongoing policy and regulatory attention in coming years.

References

Australian Children's Education & Care Quality Authority (ACECQA). (2017). *National Partnership Annual Performance Report: National quality agenda— December 2017.* Sydney: ACECQA. Available from: www.acecqa.gov.au/ sites/default/files/2018-02/NationalPartnershipAnnualPerformance.pdf.

Australian Children's Education & Care Quality Authority (ACECQA). (2018). *National Partnership Annual Performance Report: National quality agenda— December 2018.* Sydney: ACECQA. Available from: www.acecqa.gov.au/ sites/default/files/2018-12/NationalPartnershipAnnualPerformanceReport 2018.PDF.

Australian Children's Education & Care Quality Authority (ACECQA). (2019a). *NQF Annual Performance Report: National quality framework—December 2019.* Sydney: ACECQA. Available from: www.acecqa.gov.au/sites/default/files/ 2019-12/NQF-Annual-Performance-Report-2019.pdf.

---

13   By contrast, the numbers of breaches for long day care were 182 per 100 services, and 92 per 100 for outside school hours services (PC 2021: Table 3A.33). The most common breaches related to protecting children from harm and hazards; supervising children; emergency and evacuation procedures; and upkeep of premises, furniture and equipment (ACECQA 2019a: 15).

Australian Children's Education & Care Quality Authority (ACECQA). (2019b). What is the NQF? [Online.] Sydney: ACECQA. Available from: www.acecqa.gov.au/nqf/about.

Australian Children's Education & Care Quality Authority (ACECQA). (2020). *NQF Annual Performance Report: National quality framework—December 2020*. Sydney: ACECQA. Available from: www.acecqa.gov.au/sites/default/files/2021-02/NQF-Annual-Performance-Report2020.pdf.

Australian Institute of Health and Welfare (AIHW). (2003). *Australia's Welfare 2003*. Canberra: AIHW.

Australian National Audit Office (ANAO). (2012). *Improving Access to Child Care: The Community Support Program*. The Auditor-General Audit Report No. 7 2012–13. Canberra: ANAO. Available from: www.anao.gov.au/sites/default/files/201213%20Audit%20Report%20No%207.pdf.

Baxter, J., Hand, K. & Sweid, R. (2016). *Flexible Child Care and Australian Parents' Work and Care Decision-Making*. Research Report No. 37. Melbourne: Australian Institute of Family Studies. Available from: aifs.gov.au/sites/default/files/publication-documents/rr37-flexible-child-care.pdf.

Begley, P. (2018). 'Shamed' out of day care, companies set their sights on NDIS billions. *Sydney Morning Herald*, 29 June. Available from: www.smh.com.au/national/nsw/shamed-out-of-day-care-companies-set-their-sights-on-ndis-billions-20180629-p4zoj1.html.

Berg, L. & Meagher, G. (2018). *Cultural Exchange or Cheap Housekeeper? Findings of a national survey of au pairs in Australia*. Sydney: Migrant Worker Justice Initiative. Available from: www.mwji.org/s/UTS0001-Au-Pairs-in-Australia-Report_final.pdf.

Birmingham, S. (2018). Crackdown on dodgy family day care providers continues. Media release, Senator the Hon. Simon Birmingham, Minister for Education and Training, 3 April, Canberra. Available from: ministers.dese.gov.au/birmingham/crackdown-dodgy-family-day-care-providers-continues.

Blaxland, M. & Adamson, E. (2017). *Comparative Perspectives on Family Day Care: Structure, regulation, and research gaps*. SPRC Report 06/17. Sydney: Social Policy Research Centre, University of New South Wales. doi.org/10.4225/53/590152eadb59f.

Blaxland, M., Adamson, E. & Cortis, N. (2016). *Perspectives on Quality in Australian Family Day Care*. SPRC Report 01/16. Sydney: Social Policy Research Centre, University of New South Wales. Available from: unsworks.unsw.edu.au/fapi/datastream/unsworks:38896/bin859fb350-8189-4ec9-bd14-5a2d698e34b6?view=true&xy=01.

Brennan, D. (1998). *The Politics of Australian Child Care: Philanthropy to feminism and beyond*. 2nd edn. Melbourne: Cambridge University Press. doi.org/10.1017/CBO9780511597091.

Brennan, D. (2007). The ABC of child care politics. *Australian Journal of Social Issues*, *42*(2): 213–25. doi.org/10.1002/j.1839-4655.2007.tb00050.x.

Brogaard, L. & Petersen, O. (2021). Privatization of public services: A systematic review of quality differences between public and private daycare providers. *International Journal of Public Administration*, *45*(10): 794–806. doi.org/10.1080/01900692.2021.1909619.

Brough, M. (2006). 2006–07 Budget: More child care places in Australia. Media release, The Hon. Mal Brough MP, Minister for Families, Community Services and Indigenous Affairs, 9 May, Canberra. Available from: formerministers.dss.gov.au/3446/budget06_more_child_care/.

Camilleri, P. & Kennedy, R. (1994). Educational issues for family day care: Results of a South Australian survey. *Australian Journal of Early Childhood*, *19*(3): 39–44.

Cook, K., Davis, E., Williamson, L., Harrison, L. & Sims, M. (2013). Discourses of professionalism in family day care. *Contemporary Issues in Early Childhood*, *14*(2): 112–26. doi.org/10.2304/ciec.2013.14.2.112.

Corr, L., Davis, E., Cook, K., Mackinnon, A., Sims, M. & Herrman, H. (2014). Information-seeking in family day care: Access, quality and personal cost. *European Early Childhood Education Research Journal*, *22*(5): 698–710. doi.org/10.1080/1350293X.2014.969083.

Corr, L., Davis, E., Cook, K., Waters, E. & LaMontagne, A. (2014). Fair relationships and policies to support family day care educators' mental health: A qualitative study. *BMC Public Health*, *14*: 1214. doi.org/10.1186/1471-2458-14-1214.

Cortis, N., Blaxland, M., Brennan, D. & Adamson, E. (2014). *Family Day Care at the Crossroads: Quality and sustainability in uncertain times*. SPRC Report 24/2014. Sydney: Social Policy Research Centre, University of New South Wales. Available from: www.unsw.edu.au/content/dam/pdfs/unsw-adobe-websites/arts-design-architecture/ada-faculty/sprc/2021-06-Family-Day-Care-at-the-crossroads-2014.pdf.

Davis, E., Freeman, R., Doherty, G., Karlsson, M., Everiss, E., Couch, J., Foote, L., Murray, P., Modigliani, K., Owen, S., Griffin, S., Friendly, M., McDonald, G., Bohanna, I., Corr, L., Smyth, L., Morkeseth, E.I., Morreaunet, S., Ogi, M., Fukukawa, S. & Hinke-Rahnau, J. (2012). An international perspective on regulated family day care systems. *Australasian Journal of Early Childhood*, *37*(4): 127–37. doi.org/10.1177/183693911203700418.

Delaney, A., Ng, Y. & Venugopal, V. (2018). Comparing Australian garment and childcare homeworkers' experience of regulation and representation. *Economic and Labour Relations Review*, *29*(3): 346–64. doi.org/10.1177/ 1035304618781661.

Department of Education, Employment and Workplace Relations (DEEWR). (2008). *2006 Australian Government Census of Child Care Services*. Canberra: Commonwealth of Australia. Available from: www.dss.gov.au/sites/default/ files/documents/05_2015/2006_australian_government_census_of_child_ care_services.pdf.

Department of Education, Employment and Workplace Relations (DEEWR). (2009). *Belonging, Being and Becoming: The early years learning framework for Australia*. Canberra: Commonwealth of Australia. Available from: www.dese. gov.au/child-care-package/resources/belonging-being-becoming-early-years-learning-framework-australia.

Department of Education, Employment and Workplace Relations (DEEWR). (2011a). *Child Care Update: June quarter 2010*. Canberra: Commonwealth of Australia. Available from: www.dese.gov.au/key-official-documents-about-early-childhood/resources/child-care-update-june-quarter-2010-0.

Department of Education, Employment and Workplace Relations (DEEWR). (2011b). *Child Care Update: December quarter 2010*. Canberra: Commonwealth of Australia. Available from: www.dese.gov.au/key-official-documents-about-early-childhood/resources/child-care-update-december-quarter-2010.

Department of Education, Employment and Workplace Relations (DEEWR). (2012). *Child Care Update: September quarter 2011*. Canberra: Commonwealth of Australia. Available from: www.dese.gov.au/download/782/child-care-update-september-quarter-2011/430/document/docx.

Department of Education, Employment and Workplace Relations (DEEWR). (2013). *Child Care Update: September quarter 2012*. Canberra: Commonwealth of Australia. Available from: www.dese.gov.au/download/1353/child-care-update-september-quarter-2012/19101/document/docx.

Department of Education, Employment and Workplace Relations (DEEWR). (2014). *Child Care Update: September quarter 2013*. Canberra: Commonwealth of Australia. Available from: www.dese.gov.au/key-official-documents-about-early-childhood/resources/child-care-and-early-learning-summary-september-quarter-2013-0.

Department of Education, Employment and Workplace Relations (DEEWR). (2015). *Child Care Update: September quarter 2014*. Canberra: Commonwealth of Australia. Available from: www.dese.gov.au/key-official-documents-about-early-childhood/resources/early-childhood-and-child-care-summary-september-quarter-2014.

Department of Education, Employment and Workplace Relations (DEEWR). (2016). *Child Care Update: September quarter 2015*. Canberra: Commonwealth of Australia. Available from: www.dese.gov.au/key-official-documents-about-early-childhood/resources/early-childhood-and-child-care-summary-september-quarter-2015.

Department of Education, Employment and Workplace Relations (DEEWR). (2017). *Child Care Update: September quarter 2016*. Canberra: Commonwealth of Australia. Available from: www.dese.gov.au/key-official-documents-about-early-childhood/resources/early-childhood-and-child-care-summary-september-quarter-2016.

Department of Education, Employment and Workplace Relations (DEEWR). (2018). *Child Care Update: September quarter 2017*. Canberra: Commonwealth of Australia. Available from: www.dese.gov.au/key-official-documents-about-early-childhood/resources/early-childhood-and-child-care-summary-report-september-quarter-2017.

Department of Education, Skills and Employment (DESE). (2020). *Child Care in Australia Report: March quarter 2020*. Canberra: Commonwealth of Australia. Available from: www.dese.gov.au/key-official-documents-about-early-childhood/early-childhood-and-child-care-reports/child-care-australia/child-care-australia-report-march-quarter-2020.

Department of Education and Training (DET). (2019). *Child Care Enforcement Action Register: 2018–2019 first quarter*. Canberra: Commonwealth of Australia. Available from: www.dese.gov.au/child-care-enforcement-action-register/resources/child-care-enforcement-action-2018-2019-first-quarter.

Department of Family and Community Services (FACS). (1999). *1997 Census of Child Care Services and 1996 Census of Child Care Services*. Canberra: Commonwealth Child Care Program. Available from: www.dss.gov.au/our-responsibilities/families-and-children/publications-articles/1997-census-of-child-care-services-and-1996-census-of-child-care-services.

Department of Family and Community Services (FACS). (2000). *1999 Census of Child Care Services: Commonwealth child care support*. Canberra: Commonwealth of Australia. Available from: www.dss.gov.au/sites/default/files/documents/05_2015/1999_census_of_child_care_services.pdf.

Department of Family and Community Services (FACS). (2001). 2001 Family day care services: Census tables. In *2001 Commonwealth Census of Child Care Services*. Canberra: Commonwealth of Australia. Available from: www.dese. gov.au/download/742/2001-family-day-care-services-census-tables/380/ document/pdf.

Department of Family and Community Services (FACS). (2003). *2002 Census of Child Care Services*. Canberra: Commonwealth of Australia. Available from: www.dss.gov.au/sites/default/files/documents/05_2015/2002_census_of_child_care_services.pdf.

Department of Family and Community Services (FACS). (2005). *2004 Census of Child Care Services*. Canberra: Commonwealth of Australia. Available from: www.dese.gov.au/download/745/2004-census-child-care-services/383/ document/pdf.

Early Childhood Australia. (2018). Budget cuts put young children and quality of care at risk. Media release, 15 May, Early Childhood Australia, Canberra. Available from: www.earlychildhoodaustralia.org.au/wp-content/ uploads/2018/05/Budget-cuts-put-children-and-quality-of-care-at-risk1.pdf.

Education Council. (2014). *Regulation Impact Statement for Proposed Options for Changes to the National Quality Framework*. COAG Consultation Regulatory Impact Statement, November 2014. Melbourne: Education Council. Available from: www.acecqa.gov.au/sites/default/files/acecqa/files/Reports/ COAGReviewConsultationRegulationImpactStatement.pdf.

Education Council. (2017). *Decision Regulation Impact Statement for Changes to the National Quality Framework*. January. Melbourne: Education Services Australia. Available from: web.archive.org/web/20210313095309/www. educationcouncil.edu.au/site/DefaultSite/filesystem/documents/Reports%20 and%20publications/Final%20NQF%20DRIS%20January%202017.pdf.

Family Day Care Australia. (2018). *Family Day Care Sector Profile, December 2018*. Gosford, NSW: Family Day Care Australia. Available from: uploads.prod01. sydney.platformos.com/instances/97/assets/public-pdf/Representing-You/ Sector-Profile/FDCA_SectorProfileDec18_online.pdf?updated=1585626543.

Fenech, M., Giugni, M. & Bown, K. (2012). A critical analysis of the 'national quality framework': Mobilising for a vision for children beyond minimum standards. *Australasian Journal of Early Childhood, 37*(4): 5–14. doi.org/ 10.1177/183693911203700402.

Hockey, J. & Cormann, M. (2014). *Budget 2014–15: Budget measures*. Budget Paper No. 2. Canberra: Commonwealth of Australia. Available from: archive. budget.gov.au/2014-15/bp2/BP2_consolidated.pdf.

Jones, A. (1987). Tensions in community care policy: The case of family day care. In P. Saunders & A. Jamrozik (eds), *Community Services in a Changing Economic and Social Environment* (pp. 87–106). Social Welfare Research Centre Reports and Proceedings. Sydney: University of New South Wales.

Joseph, E. (2018). *Why childcare is not affordable.* CIS Research Report 37, August. Sydney: The Centre for Independent Studies. Available from: www.cis.org.au/app/uploads/2018/08/rr37.pdf.

Ley, S. (2014). Tighter rules to stop child care payment rorting. Media release, The Hon. Sussan Ley MP, Assistant Minister for Education, 4 December, Canberra. Available from: ministers.dese.gov.au/archive-ley/tighter-rules-stop-child-care-payment-rorting.

McIntosh, G. & Phillips, J. (2002). *Commonwealth support for childcare.* Parliamentary Library E-Brief, 26 April [updated 6 July]. Canberra: Parliament of Australia. Available from: www.aph.gov.au/About_Parliament/Parliamentary _Departments/Parliamentary_Library/Publications_Archive/archive/childcaresupport.

Meagher, G. (2007). Contested, corporatised and confused? Australian attitudes to child care. In E. Hill, B. Pocock & A. Elliott (eds), *Kids Count: Better early childhood education and care in Australia* (pp. 137–53). Sydney: Sydney University Press. doi.org/10.30722/sup.9781920898700.

Meagher, G. & Cortis, N. (2009). The political economy of for-profit paid care: Theory and evidence. In D. King & G. Meagher (eds), *Paid Care in Australia: Politics, profits, practices* (pp. 13–42). Sydney: Sydney University Press. doi.org/10.30722/sup.9781920899295.

Pascoe, S. & Brennan, D. (2017). *Lifting Our Game: Report of the review to achieve educational excellence in Australian schools through early childhood interventions.* Melbourne: State Government of Victoria. Available from: www.education.vic.gov.au/Documents/about/research/LiftingOurGame.PDF.

Productivity Commission (PC). (2014). *Childcare and Early Childhood Learning.* Inquiry Report Vol. 2, No. 73, 31 October. Canberra: Productivity Commission. Available from: www.pc.gov.au/inquiries/completed/childcare/report/childcare-volume2.pdf.

Productivity Commission (PC). (2019). Early childhood education and care. In *Report on Government Services 2019* (Part B, Ch. 3). Canberra: Productivity Commission. Available from: www.pc.gov.au/research/ongoing/report-on-government-services/2019/child-care-education-and-training/early-childhood-education-and-care.

Productivity Commission (PC). (2021). Early childhood education and care. In *Report on Government Services 2021* (Part B, Section 3). Canberra: Productivity Commission. Available from: www.pc.gov.au/research/ongoing/report-on-government-services/2021/child-care-education-and-training/early-childhood-education-and-care/.

Rothman, S., Kelly, D., Raban, B., Tobin, M., Cook, J., O'Malley, K., Ozolins, C. & Bramich, M. (2012). *Evaluation of the Assessment and Rating Process under the National Quality Standard for Early Childhood Education and Care and School Age Care*. Report for the Standing Council on School Education and Early Childhood, November. Melbourne: Australian Council for Educational Research. Available from: research.acer.edu.au/cgi/viewcontent.cgi?article=1013&context=early_childhood_misc.

Stratigos, T., Bradley, B. & Sumsion, J. (2014). Infants, family day care and the politics of belonging. *International Journal of Early Childhood*, *46*(2): 171–86. doi.org/10.1007/s13158-014-0110-0.

Sumsion, J. (2012). ABC Learning and Australian early education and care: A retrospective ethical audit of a radical experiment. In E. Lloyd & H. Penn (eds), *Childcare Markets: Can they deliver an equitable service?* (pp. 209–25). Bristol, UK: Policy Press. doi.org/10.2307/j.ctt9qgxq1.17.

Sumsion, J., Barnes, S., Cheeseman, S., Harrison, L., Kennedy, A. & Stonehouse, A. (2009). Insider perspectives on developing belonging, being and becoming: The early years learning framework for Australia. *Australasian Journal of Early Childhood*, *34*(4): 4–13. doi.org/10.1177/183693910903400402.

Tohme, S. & Darley, A. (2013). Family day care Australia. *Every Child*, *19*(3): 30–31. Available from: search.informit.org/doi/10.3316/informit.65482 1064941798.

Woolcott Research. (2014). *Summary of Findings from the 2014 National Quality Framework Review Consultation Process*. October. Sydney: Woolcott Research and Engagement. Available from: web.archive.org/web/20150304053527/http:/www.woolcott.com.au/NQFReview/Summary%20of%20Findings%20for%20the%202014%20NQF%20Review%20consultation%20process.pdf.

Worthington, E., Rubinsztein-Dunlop, S. & Kleinig, X. (2017). NSW Education Department warned federal government about 'fraudulent and criminal behaviour' in the family day care system. *7.30*, [ABC TV], 3 April. Available from: www.abc.net.au/news/2017-04-03/commonwealth-warned-of-fraudulent-family-day-care-claims-foi/8411050.

2

The development and significance of marketisation in refugee settlement services

Adèle Garnier

Introduction

Refugees flee their countries of origin out of fear of persecution. Recognition of their need for safety is the main reason Australia admits refugees. Due to the circumstances of their immigration journey, many refugees require more intensive settlement support than other categories of newcomers to thrive in their host society.

That said, there is no widely accepted definition of 'refugee settlement services'. This chapter focuses on early, dedicated federal government settlement services provided to refugees when they first arrive in Australia or are intercepted en route to Australia with the aim to apply for asylum.[1] This encompasses early specialised settlement services for refugees and services provided to asylum-seekers in the community and in Australia's onshore and offshore immigration detention centres. Defined as such, the provision of dedicated refugee settlement services in Australia is a niche

---

1   Definitions of the terms 'refugee' and 'asylum-seeker' are given in the next section. This chapter recognises the significance of subnational refugee settlement support. To trace marketisation dynamics over time in the short space of the chapter, however, the subnational level is not discussed.

policy sector. Since the 1970s, the sector has established itself alongside broader settlement services for newcomers and mainstream welfare services, such as employment support services. The focus of the chapter is narrow enough to allow tracing of specific marketisation dynamics in refugee services–related developments; it is also broad enough to highlight similarities and differences in early service provision to refugees, on one hand, and asylum-seekers, on the other.

Delivery of settlement services to refugees and asylum-seekers in the community is dominated by not-for-profit agencies. Services provided to asylum-seekers in Australia's onshore and offshore immigration detention centres are delivered mostly by for-profit providers. Since the 1990s, management and delivery of refugee settlement services have entailed key elements of marketisation such as accrual budget programming, competitive tendering of service provision and a focus on refugees' self-reliance. This reflects broader marketisation dynamics in the provision of welfare services in Australia (Considine 2003; Mendes 2017) and in immigrant settlement services internationally (Shields et al. 2016; Martin 2017). Yet, this chapter adds nuance to existing research, as it argues that marketisation has been more thoroughgoing in specialised settlement services to refugees than in services provided to detained asylum-seekers, and marketisation has not resolved issues that have characterised refugee settlement service provision since the 1970s. Evaluations consider refugee settlement services deliver value for money and have developed a relatively robust quality assurance framework and risk-management procedure. This is not the case for services in immigration detention centres—in addition to them being punitive and highly politically contentious. This indicates limits to the implementation of marketisation and points to an array of market failures.

This line of argument will be pursued as follows. The next section gives an overview of Australia's humanitarian program. An overview is then provided of the emergence of refugee settlement services as a niche public policy sector before the expansion of marketisation in the field. This historical context helps identify issues primarily related to marketisation and issues that were prevalent before marketisation expanded. Against this background, the entrenchment of marketisation in refugee settlement services is then highlighted, as part of Australia's larger move towards the use of market instruments in social service provision under the Liberal–National government of John Howard, which continued under the Labor governments of Kevin Rudd and Julia Gillard. Contracting arrangements focused on value for money, performance supervision and, increasingly, risk assessment and the development of a quality assurance framework—elements that evaluators found had been largely implemented. By contrast, contracting arrangements for immigration detention services were often made in haste, with unclear performance objectives and, as implemented, featured considerable cost inflation and limited government accountability. The next section focuses on developments since 2013, following the re-election of a Liberal–National Coalition government. During this period, there was an emphasis on refugees' self-reliance, further cost inflation in immigration detention services and government shirking of public accountability. A summary of findings points to the unevenness of marketisation. The Epilogue provides a brief account of current prospects for refugee settlement in light of the Covid-19 pandemic, highlights future research areas, suggests policy changes and considers the chapter's implications for the role of the state in social services.

Australia's humanitarian program

Australia has welcomed more than 920,000 humanitarian immigrants since the end of World War II (DHA 2022: 33). Many came because authorities found their fear of persecution met the refugee definition in Article 1 of the United Nations 1951 Convention Relating to the Status of Refugees: having crossed an international border and being in well-founded fear of persecution because of one's race, nationality, political opinion, religion or membership of a particular social group.[2] Australia has also admitted many others on humanitarian grounds not explicitly stated in the 1951 convention.

Most humanitarian entrants have come to Australia through resettlement—that is, following selection by the Australian Government of eligible humanitarian entrants already living outside their countries of origin.[3] Australia's resettlement intake has fluctuated over time: it increased in the late 1940s and early 1950s (with the resettlement of displaced persons from Europe); from the mid-1970s to the mid-1980s (most prominently

---

2   Originally this definition only applied to persons who had become refugees because of events related to World War II. Geographical and time limits were removed in the 1967 Protocol to the Refugee Convention. Australia ratified the 1951 convention in 1954 and the 1967 protocol in 1973.
3   On Australia's refugee resettlement selection procedures, see Cellini (2018).

in response to the Indochinese refugee crisis); in the early to mid-1990s (with the arrival of refugees from the former Yugoslavia); and in 2015–17 (with the resettlement of Syrian and Iraqi refugees) (see, for example, Kunz 1988; Neumann 2015; Higgins 2017; Carr 2018; Collins et al. 2018). At other times, and since 2017 (excluding the pandemic-related decline in 2020–2021 and 2021–2022), the country's resettlement intake has varied between 10,000 and 14,000 people.[4]

In addition to the resettlement program, Australia admits a small proportion of refugees following an application for humanitarian protection (an asylum claim) on Australian territory. A person who has submitted an asylum claim is an asylum-seeker. Due to the country's geographic isolation, the number of asylum claims in Australia, compared with other rich countries, is small. Yet, asylum has been a politically contentious issue for decades. The number of asylum claims reached an all-time high in the aftermath of the 1989 repression by Chinese authorities of protests in Tiananmen Square and the decision of Labor Prime Minister Bob Hawke not to send Chinese nationals present in Australia back to the People's Republic of China. However, the arrival of people claiming asylum after a maritime journey to Australia has proven more politically salient as numbers rose sharply in 1999–2001 and 2009–12 (Garnier and Cox 2012; Garnier 2014). A recent significant increase in asylum claims made on Australian territory by individuals legally arriving on other visas started becoming contentious in 2019 (Snape 2019). Between July 2019 and June 2020, the Australian Government granted 11,521 'offshore protection visas' to resettled refugees and special humanitarian visa-holders and 1,650 onshore protection visas to asylum claimants (DHA 2020a: 1; 2020b).

Over time, government control of the humanitarian intake has increased, including efforts to deter asylum claimants, and this has been a bipartisan trend. The decision to determine a yearly intake for refugees was taken in 1977 by the Liberal–Country party Coalition government of Malcolm Fraser. Fraser's immigration minister Michael Mackellar cautioned against community sponsorship of large groups of Indochinese 'boatpeople' and insisted on the need for the Australian Government to control the intake (Price 1981). In 1981, the Fraser government also established the Special Humanitarian Program (SHP) for people in refugee-like situations

---

4   See details on the size and composition of Australia's humanitarian program, including all resettlement categories, since financial year 2011–12 in Refugee Council of Australia (2021: 4).

who did not meet the refugee definition of the 1951 UN convention, to replace visa categories targeting specific populations such as Soviet Jews and Timorese fleeing their countries of origin (Jupp 2002: 187). From 1992 under the Labor government of Paul Keating, immigration detention was imposed on asylum claimants who entered Australia without a visa (Garnier and Cox 2012). In 1996, the Liberal–National Coalition government of John Howard introduced a de facto cap on the humanitarian intake by officially subtracting an SHP visa for each person granted refugee status after an asylum claim in Australia (Nicholls 1998). Measures preventing asylum claimants entering Australia without a visa were adopted under Prime Minister Howard, and continued under the Labor governments of Julia Gillard and Kevin Rudd. From 2001 to 2007, and again after 2012, asylum-seekers without a visa intercepted at sea were sent to offshore detention facilities on Nauru and Manus Island (Papua New Guinea). Marr and Wilkinson (2004) argue the so-called Pacific Solution was introduced primarily to sway votes as the Howard government faced a difficult election campaign in 2001, yet the scheme was never entirely abolished when Rudd came to power when Labor won the 2007 federal election. Former asylum claimants' access to permanent residency has become increasingly difficult and includes a ban on the resettlement in Australia of asylum-seekers intercepted at sea after 2013 (Garnier 2018).

Emergence of refugee settlement services as a niche public policy sector

Refugee settlement support started in the 1930s and was considered the sole responsibility of volunteer agencies (Jupp 1994: 32). The considerable expansion of refugee admission after World War II with the arrival of displaced persons from Europe led to the development in 1945 of a government-funded refugee settlement policy under the purview of the Department of Immigration that Jupp (1994: 35) labels 'authoritarian and paternalistic'. The Commonwealth Government funded housing, catering and basic English tuition in former military camps such as Bonegilla in Victoria;[5] refugees were admitted to Australia because they had agreed to be employed for two years in designated jobs, often in remote locations

---

5   As the arrival of displaced persons started to decline in the early 1950s, camps such as Bonegilla housed assisted migrants (Sluga 1998, quoted in Jupp 1994: 34).

(Kunz 1988). Once refugees went to live in the community, they had access to mainstream welfare assistance as well as settlement support provided by charities coordinated by Commonwealth-funded Good Neighbourhood Councils (Martin 1965; ROMAMPAS 1978: 73–74). Religious charities dominated service provision. Between 1952 and 1977, the Australian Council of Churches' Refugee and Migrant Services sponsored individual refugees for resettlement in Australia and had the discretion to assess their needs and provide settlement assistance (Jupp 1994: 71).

The importance of expanding newcomer settlement support was recognised by the Commonwealth Government from the late 1960s. In 1968, the Liberal–Country party government of John Gorton established the Grant to Community Agencies scheme (often referred to as grant-in-aid). The grant-in-aid scheme allowed charities to apply for funding for migrant-focused welfare workers (Cox 1987: 226 ff.). For decades, however, this did not mean a considerable expansion of specialised refugee settlement services.

Recognition of a need for more support to newcomers was part of the establishment of Australia's multicultural policy. The Whitlam Labor government deemed the Department of Immigration unable to embody the ideological shift from the White Australia policy to multiculturalism. The department was abolished in 1972, with immigrant settlement responsibilities reallocated to other departments, including Labour and Education (ROMAMPAS Committee 1986: 32). The first Liberal–Country party Coalition government of Malcolm Fraser re-established the Department of Immigration as the Department of Immigration and Ethnic Affairs in 1975 and commissioned a review of existing migrant services and programs in 1977. The resulting Review of Migrant and Multicultural Programs and Services (ROMAMPAS) adopted four principles: equal opportunity; recognition of other cultures; services to migrants should primarily be provided by mainstream services, while recognising the need for specialised services to ensure 'equality of access and provision'; and clients' participation and self-help should be encouraged 'with a view to helping migrants to become self-reliant quickly' (ROMAMPAS 1978: 4). The review recommended the abolition of Good Neighbourhood Councils and a redirection of their funding to 'ethnic groups' as service providers, with the Department of Immigration and Ethnic Affairs' migrant services units to focus on research, coordination and support for community development rather than direct casework (ROMAMPAS

1978: 71). The 1978 review also recommended the collection of more data on migrants' participation in settlement programs (ROMAMPAS 1978: 121)

Over the following years, successive governments implemented many of the recommendations of the 1978 review. Figure 2.1 captures major policy changes and changes of government since the 1970s. Commonwealth funding for migrant services considerably expanded and a few refugee-specific settlement programs were established. These included material assistance to refugee-supporting volunteer agencies, small loans to help refugees establish themselves in private accommodation, a program of care for refugee minors whose costs were shared between the Commonwealth and the states, and the Community Refugee Settlement Scheme (ROMAMPAS Committee 1986: 123). Established in 1979 as an element of Australia's response to the Indochinese refugee crisis, the Community Refugee Settlement Scheme allowed voluntary agencies as well as individuals to support the settlement of refugees who were not, on arrival, housed in Commonwealth-funded migrant hostels (Hirsch et al. 2019: 110–13). However, the selection of refugees for resettlement under this scheme was controlled by the Commonwealth, in contrast to the church-based refugee sponsorship mentioned above. Hence, by the mid-1980s, several specific services for refugees had been established but they were fragmented. The bulk of refugee settlement support was delivered through broadly newcomer-focused settlement services as well as mainstream welfare services.

The 1988 review by the Committee to Advise on Australia's Immigration Policies, commissioned by the Labor government of Bob Hawke and chaired by Stephen FitzGerald, recommended Australia's immigration policy focus on migrants' economic value and self-reliance to increase the 'added value' of immigration for Australia. Yet the FitzGerald Review recommended the government maintain publicly funded, freely accessible settlement services for refugees and humanitarian entrants, who were the most vulnerable newcomers. However, the review considered the appropriate settlement period for newcomers was two years, rather than the previous five or more years.[6] The review also recognised the need for better coordination of targeted settlement services. The government acted on this recommendation by adopting the National Integrated Settlement

---

6   Compare the ROMAMPAS Committee (1986: 9) with the Committee to Advise on Australia's Immigration Policies (1988: xi–xvi); and see Cox (1996: 10).

Strategy in 1991 and establishing settlement plans in each territory and state (Cox 1996: 11–12) to improve linkages between settlement and mainstream services. However, there were no specifically refugee-focused initiatives as part of this strategy. At the time, the government feared that singling out refugees was politically sensitive but would also limit the flexibility of service delivery (Jupp 1994: 44). Thus, not all recommendations of the FitzGerald Review were implemented.

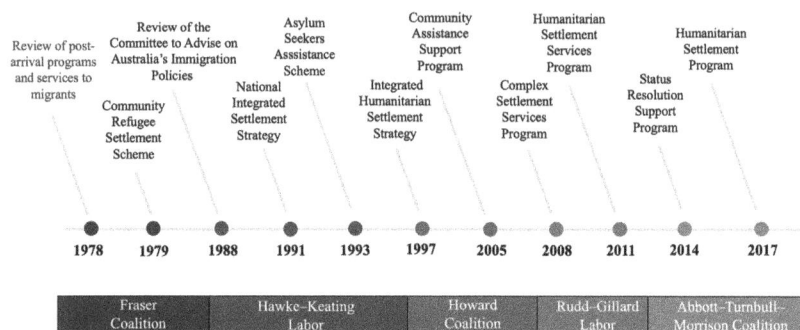

Figure 2.1 Timeline of policy development in refugee settlement services since the 1970s

Note: The figure captures major policy developments only. For more detailed chronologies, see York (2003) and Paxton (2020).

Source: Based on author's research.

Jupp estimated that, by 1994, refugees were the recipients of one-third of the expenditure for migrant-specific services of what was now the Department of Immigration, Local Government and Ethnic Affairs (DILGEA). Mainstream welfare services did not provide a dollar estimate of refugee-related expenditures (Jupp 1994: 46, 49). Refugee-specific expenditures declined between the 1983–84 and 1991–92 financial years, from $24.2 million to $9.4 million, largely due to DILGEA's withdrawal from the provision of hostel accommodation. Immigration officials assisted refugees in finding private accommodation, though it was noted at the time that an increasing proportion of refugees resorted to public housing due to being unable to purchase a home (Jupp 1994: 64–65). Jupp (1994: 77) observed the lack of evaluations of refugee settlement programs and thus the inability to assess whether refugees' needs were met by 'modest' existing expenditure, or whether this limited spending was due to 'the budgetary imperatives of hard-pressed public agencies'.

One type of settlement expenditure did increase in the late 1980s and early 1990s: the budget devoted to asylum-seekers. In part, this was due to far larger numbers of asylum claimants in Australia during this period. Individual claimants without means of support sought emergency assistance from charities. Eventually, the Asylum Seeker Assistance Scheme was introduced, in 1993, with a budget of $20.7 million—more than double DILGEA's budget for refugee-specific settlement assistance in the financial year 1991–92 (Jupp 1994: 12, 46). A further increase in expenditure on asylum-seekers was incurred by the policy of mandatory detention of all non-citizens arriving without a visa from 1994. Figure 2.2 captures the development of immigration detention and changes of government since 1992. Legislated in 1992, mandatory detention was introduced in response to the increase, from late 1988, of asylum claimants who arrived in Australia by boat without a visa. Detention centres were funded by DILGEA and managed by a Commonwealth agency, the Australian Protective Services. Services were delivered by government workers (welfare, education), private professionals (health, religious services) and community groups (involvement in educational and recreational activities) (Joint Standing Committee on Migration 1994: 164–66). Then, as now, refugee advocates denounced the detention of asylum-seekers as a breach of international refugee law,[7] but also as more expensive than residence in the community. In 1994, the bipartisan parliamentary Joint Standing Committee on Migration (1994: 46) disputed this claim, arguing that refugee advocates did not provide a comprehensive costing of community settlement. The committee estimated the cost of detention at the immigration detention centres in Port Hedland, Western Australia, and Westbridge in New South Wales for the financial year 1992–93 at $5.31 million and $1.96 million, respectively (Joint Standing Committee on Migration 1994: 43). The committee responded to the concerns of community groups regarding the limits of service provision in immigration detention centres with mention of the complexity of service delivery in a detention setting, and supported the establishment of an Immigration Detention Centre Advisory Committee including representatives of relevant governmental agencies (the Department of Immigration, Australian Protective Services) and 'detention centre residents, community based service providers and local community services' (Joint Standing Committee on Migration 1994: 193).

---

7   Article 31 of the 1951 Refugee Convention prohibits the imposition by host states of penalties on refugees who flee a territory in which they are threatened and make themselves known to authorities of host states.

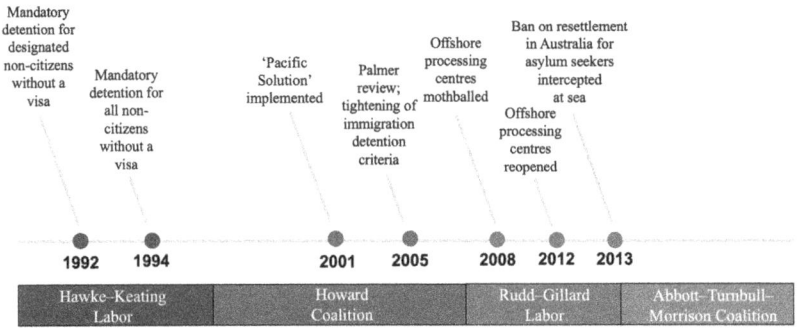

Figure 2.2 Timeline of major policy developments in immigration detention and asylum-seekers since 1992

Note: The figure captures major policy developments only. For more detailed chronologies, see York (2003) and Paxton (2020).

Source: Based on author's research.

By the mid-1990s, refugee settlement services were a niche public policy sector that had experienced little marketisation. Policy reviews had identified the need for more coordination between service providers. Whereas the need for some specialised early settlement services for humanitarian newcomers was recognised, governments argued that most settlement and welfare services to refugees should occur through mainstream service providers.

Mandatory detention for non-citizens arriving on Australia's shores by boat and claiming asylum was introduced in 1992 and expanded to all non-citizens entering Australia without a visa in 1994. Refugee advocates, early on, argued against cost inflation in detention centres, yet the government considered it could not be established that community detention would be cheaper. Overall, expenditure on asylum-seekers and detention services surpassed expenditure on refugee-specific services, while data for total expenditure on welfare and settlement services accessed by refugees are not available.

Marketisation: Establishment and entrenchment

John Howard's Liberal–National government, which came to power in 1996, oversaw a considerable expansion of marketisation in the structure of the public sector and the management of service delivery (Goodwin and Phillips 2015). The Howard government introduced New Public Management methods across the Australian Public Service, including the adoption of accrual budgeting. Government departments had to plan annual budget targets for specific outputs. Services already provided by third parties were put out to competitive tender, as were other services so far provided directly by the Commonwealth. Refugee settlement policies were caught up in this transformation of public administration.

A new model of refugee settlement support was introduced from 1997: the Integrated Humanitarian Settlement Strategy (IHSS). According to the first detailed evaluation, the IHSS sought to reduce the potential long-term dependency of refugees on welfare services, to respect refugees' dignity and to help achieve self-reliance by focusing on initial settlement support, with six months the time frame of reference (Urbis Keys Young 2003: 5). The evaluation, however, describes the 'major innovation' of the IHSS as services being 'competitively tendered and contracted. The IHSS marked the first implementation of the purchaser/provider model of service delivery in humanitarian settlement services' (Urbis Keys Young 2003: 5).

The IHSS superseded existing early arrival programs, including the Community Refugee Settlement Scheme that had provided funding to volunteer groups supporting privately sponsored refugees (Hirsch et al. 2019: 109). The IHSS included on-arrival assistance, accommodation support, provision of household goods, information on the availability of health services, including referrals to torture and trauma counselling, and connection to volunteer groups supporting community participation. Eligibility for the range of IHSS services depended on the visa category of humanitarian arrivals. Resettled refugees were eligible to access all services, SHP visa entrants only to health assessment and referrals and household goods, and refugees on temporary protection visas only to health assessments and referrals (Urbis Keys Young 2003: 6).

As part of the contracting process, the renamed Department of Immigration and Multicultural and Indigenous Affairs (DIMIA) identified services to be provided, their standards and geographical location of delivery. DIMIA invited organisations to tender and contracts were awarded to providers offering the best value for money. The only services not included in the tendering process were health assessments and referrals. Prices for services (calculated in terms of units of service delivered) were negotiated by DIMIA in each individual contract, with yearly revision.

Contract payments were quarterly, three months ahead of the service delivery (Urbis Keys Young 2003: 8–9; DIMIA 2003: 170). The contracts included a suite of reporting requirements, including a monthly report on the number of people provided with services, quarterly meetings with DIMIA contract managers and qualitative reports at midyear (based on client and provider surveys) and at the end of the year (including an audited financial statement and a comprehensive qualitative report on service provision) (DIMIA 2003: 305).

Evaluations noted the reluctance of contracted service providers to transition from a grants-based funding model to the compliance-oriented model of the IHSS but also praised the increasing professionalisation of service delivery. The latter model caused tensions with volunteer groups, who felt their role had been degraded (DIMIA 2003: 187). A key delivery issue was the lack of flexibility of budgeting in the face of variations in client intake, but also in client profile. A sudden and significant reduction of clients could mean a service provider would struggle to offer services over time. To address the problem, an element of core funding was introduced in 2002 (Urbis Keys Young 2003: 31–32). Evaluations also noted the contract model might disadvantage small service providers with limited administrative capacity but also more limited ability than larger service providers to negotiate the pricing of services (Urbis Keys Young 2003: 33–35).

The original IHSS contract, due to expire in 2003, was extended until 2005. The new tender aimed to reduce the number of service providers by focusing on contract regions and to expand eligibility for SHP visa-holders. The new IHSS contracts were awarded to 16 service providers, in contrast to the 39 under the previous contract (cf. DIMA 2004: 129; DIAC 2009: 177); service provision was further amended with the introduction of the Complex Case Support program in 2008. The Complex Case Support program provided intense settlement support to refugees with complex needs who could be referred to the program within two years of arriving in Australia (Spinks 2009).[8]

Various aspects of contract management were delegated to private consulting firms (see DIAC 2007: 75). No evaluation of the reformed IHSS was publicly released; however, the annual reports of DIMIA, and

---

8   By 2015, Complex Case Support eligibility had been extended to five years after arrival (EY 2015: 12).

the renamed Department of Immigration and Citizenship (DIAC), noted that finding affordable long-term accommodation was a major challenge for IHSS service providers (see, for example, DIAC 2009: 213).

Under the first Labor government of Kevin Rudd, this challenge became more acute with the increased arrival to Australia by boat of refugees as asylum claimants from 2009. IHSS services had been designed for vulnerable families resettled from overseas whereas many of the former 'boatpeople' were adult single men released from domestic immigration detention centres (DIAC 2010: 195). Under the Labor government of Julia Gillard, the Humanitarian Settlement Services (HSS) program replaced the IHSS, in 2011. The change followed a tender process starting in 2010. The HSS slightly increased the number of contract regions (from 20 to 23) and service providers (from 16 to 18) (Richmond 2011: 6; EY 2015: 8). The HSS adopted a more needs-based, client-centred approach in which caseworkers determined the suite of settlement services most appropriate to clients from among those similar to what was covered by the IHSS (on-arrival information, assistance with finding accommodation, linkages to health and welfare services, linkages with community). Whereas the assessment of health needs under the IHSS was excluded from competitive tendering, the HSS tender included this (EY 2015: 102). Following the identification and review of a particular case of mismanagement in the NSW Hunter region, an independent review of the HSS was commissioned shortly after the program was introduced and released less than a year later (Richmond 2011).

In contrast to service eligibility under the IHSS, HSS eligibility was not a function of visa categories and was determined instead by caseworkers. All categories of refugees as well as asylum-seekers living in the community were eligible for the HSS. The time frame for service provision was six to 12 months rather than six months under the IHSS (DIAC 2011: 227; Richmond 2011: 6). Potentially, the HSS was thus more inclusive than the IHSS as one's visa category did not determine access to services and there was an acknowledgement that many clients required intensive settlement support beyond six months.

As part of the tendering process, potential HSS service providers were identified via stakeholder discussions, although the Richmond Review did not mention which stakeholders were represented (Richmond 2011: 31). A risk assessment was made regarding the potentially preferred service providers of DIAC (Richmond 2011: 31). However, all awarded contracts were identical and individual discussions of potential risks did not result in individual performance requirements to address these (Richmond 2011: 31). On the part of the service provider, performance management included entering data into a central database, monthly invoices, quarterly meetings with DIAC contract managers, a six-monthly report including a summary of performance on all key performance indicators (KPIs), an annual report, a risk-management plan and a quality assurance strategy (Richmond 2011: 49, 109).

A subsequent review found the HSS and Complex Case Support were delivered effectively, with a high level of satisfaction among service providers. Yet, the review noted the high administrative burden of the program and the strong focus of KPIs on outputs rather than settlement outcomes (EY 2015: 46 ff.). In 2011, the Richmond Review had noted a discrepancy between the intended target clients of the HSS (vulnerable refugees requiring intensive on-arrival support) and a significant proportion of actual clients—namely, asylum-seekers living in the community. Contract obligations meant the HSS lacked the flexibility to deal with the fluctuation in client numbers that resulted from releases from immigration detention (Richmond 2011: 29, 113, 117). By 2015, asylum-seekers were no longer eligible for the HSS.

This exclusion from settlement services can be understood as the continuation of the deterrence approach targeting asylum-seekers. As mentioned in section one, the number of asylum-seekers coming by boat to Australia increased significantly from 1999, resulting in the expansion of the onshore immigration detention network and the opening of offshore processing facilities on Nauru and Manus Island (Papua New Guinea) in 2001.

The Howard government had entered a contract with an intergovernmental non-profit organisation, the International Organization for Migration (IOM), to manage the offshore processing facilities.[9] The IOM managed the offshore centres until they were mothballed (but not formally closed) by the Rudd Labor government in 2008, as there had been almost no arrivals of asylum claimants by boat in Australian territorial waters since 2005. Globally, the number of asylum-seekers decreased in 2004–07 (UNHCR 2020). The onshore immigration detention centres were managed by

---

9   The IOM is a non-profit international organisation, yet it relies almost entirely on project-based funding from its member states (Pécoud 2020: 13).

a succession of private companies (see ANAO 2004, 2006). In both cases, service provision to individuals was subcontracted to a variety of providers. The detention of unlawful non-citizens was not only legal but mandatory on Australian territory and the private companies managing the immigration detention centres otherwise ran regular prisons. The design of contracts was marked by the haste with which successive governments wanted to conclude them (Senate Select Committee for an Inquiry into a Certain Maritime Incident 2002; Taylor 2005). Because offshore processing centres were not on Australian territory and involved foreign governments, Australian oversight of the IOM contract was more limited than over contract management of onshore immigration detention facilities. In relation to the latter, the Australian National Audit Office (ANAO) undertook extensive evaluations of contract management relating to service provision and repeatedly noted the escalation of costs as well as limited departmental oversight (ANAO 2004, 2006). In addition, mismanagement scandals resulted in several high-profile inquiries, including one into the mistreatment of a permanent resident and one into the mistreatment of an Australian citizen (Palmer 2005; Commonwealth Ombudsman 2005). These scandals forced the Howard government to endorse what was originally a Private Member's Bill by Liberal backbencher and longstanding advocate for multiculturalism Petro Georgiou aiming to restrict the use of mandatory detention.

By 2012, the resurging numbers of asylum-seekers arriving by boat had again become politically salient. In response, the Gillard Labor government—under considerable pressure from the Coalition opposition—reopened offshore processing centres but also significantly increased the annual resettlement intake for 2013 (Garnier 2014). Asylum-seekers were transferred to Nauru and Manus Island detention centres before contracts with service providers had been finalised. The main service provision contract was won by Transfield, a company that provided garrison services to the Australian Defence Force. Transfield was selected on the basis that it provided best value for money; the IOM declined to tender (McPhail et al. 2016: 961 ff.). IOM staff previously involved in the management of the Nauru offshore processing centre interviewed in 2007[10] noted they were personally appalled by the situation and astonished at the lack of concern by Australian citizens. Perhaps such concerns made their way to IOM management.

---

10   Author's interview with former manager of IOM detention centre, Canberra, 2007.

Once again, the limited availability of data makes it impossible to precisely gauge public expenditure on refugee settlement services. The total cost of settlement services administered by DIAC, as well as the cost of offshore management of asylum-seekers, is reported in the department's annual reports. There are no continuous data on the cost of specialised refugee settlement services nor on the cost of the detention of asylum-seekers specifically. Expenditure on specific settlement programs is publicly available when program evaluations have been published. What the available data show is that DIAC's expenditure on the offshore management of asylum-seekers routinely dwarfs its settlement expenditure. In addition, expenditures on settlement routinely remain below planned levels whereas expenditures for the offshore management of asylum-seekers are above those planned. For instance, according to DIAC's 2012–13 annual report, the administered costs of offshore management of asylum-seekers were $1.8 billion (a figure above planned expenditure) and of settlement services almost $368 million (a figure below planned expenditure). An evaluation of the HSS in 2015 mentioned that running the program had cost $283 million between April 2011 and December 2014 to deliver services to 55,187 clients (EY 2015: 78). Average expenditure was found to be higher in regional locations (with smaller caseloads) than in metropolitan areas (EY 2015: 80) and to be higher for resettled refugee visa-holders than for special humanitarian visa-holders (who are generally supported by family members) and former asylum-seekers (81).

By 2013, marketisation was pervasive in refugee settlement services, as it was, more generally, in broader settlement services and many mainstream welfare services such as employment support (Considine et al. 2011). The Department of Immigration closely monitored the application of market principles to refugee settlement services, and this was associated with a significant administrative burden. Lack of flexibility in contracting arrangements also meant service providers (most of them not-for-profits) struggled to provide what they considered to be adequate service when client intake fluctuated, and when client profiles changed. Yet service providers lauded the professionalisation of service delivery (Roumeliotis and Paschadilisi-Silas 2013) and some flexibility was added to service delivery with the client-centred approach of the HSS. Also, DIAC sought to broaden the evidence base on refugee settlement outcomes by commissioning a large-scale longitudinal study of humanitarian entrants, called Building a New Life in Australia, in 2012 (Edwards et al. 2018).

Governmental oversight of the far more costly provision of services to asylum-seekers in offshore processing centres, and to asylum-seekers detained in domestic immigration detention centres, was considerably more limited. Arguably, this increased the potential for rent-seeking by detention service providers, most of which were for-profit entities. Weak governmental oversight also increased the risk for asylum-seekers. As was mentioned in the previous section, evidence that immigration detention was more costly than the alternatives had already been asserted by many observers before marketisation in the sector.

Increasingly contentious marketisation

Since the arrival in power of the Liberal–National Coalition of Tony Abbott in 2013, the discrepancy between the focus on value for money in the provision of early settlement services to refugees and asylum-seekers living in the community, on the one hand, and cost inflation in service provision to detained asylum-seekers, on the other, has increased. This has become increasingly contentious. One possible explanation is the significant growth in the number of resettled refugees and asylum-seekers living in the community in Australia since 2013 as opposed to the decline in numbers of asylum-seekers held in onshore and offshore detention, as documented above. However, the Coalition's broader austerity and border security policies are also likely to have played a part, in the context of increasing criticism of marketised welfare services relevant to long-term refugee settlement, such as employment support (see, for instance, Senate Education and Employment References Committee 2019; and, specifically on refugees and employment support services, Refugee Council of Australia 2017).

Reports have stressed the need for better-funded, more flexible, client-centred refugee settlement services in light of the long-term benefits for refugees, but also the long-term public savings made possible by better labour market integration (CPD 2017; Shergold et al. 2019). In parallel, numerous inquiries by public and private entities have highlighted the considerable economic, but also human and strategic, costs of asylum-seekers' detention (ANAO 2016; Save the Children and UNICEF 2016; ASRC et al. 2019) as well as deficiencies in contract management (McPhail et al. 2016; ANAO 2017). Many of these reports, as well as journalistic investigations, noted governmental efforts to reduce public accountability. This was most blatant with the inclusion of nondisclosure agreements in contracts relating to service provision in offshore detention centres (Maylea and Hirsh 2018), but also the considerable delay in the release of a report from a government inquiry into refugee settlement outcomes (Davidson 2019b).

There were significant changes of government machinery over this period. From 2013 to 2019, the Department of Social Services (DSS, formerly known as the Department of Families, Housing, Community Services and Indigenous Affairs) took charge of the settlement services portfolio, and thus administered the HSS. Oversight of immigration and asylum-seeker services remained with the Department of Immigration and Border Protection, which became the Department of Home Affairs in 2017. The settlement services portfolio returned to the Department of Home Affairs in 2019 (Karp 2019; ANAO 2019). Karp (2019) notes that some settlement service providers were worried about their affiliation with a department now dominated by a focus on border security, while others considered departmental affiliation did not matter much to service delivery.

A pattern emerged in the admission of refugees of shifting costs on to the community with the introduction of a community sponsorship program. The program started as the Community Proposal Pilot in 2013 under the Gillard Labor government and became the Community Support Program under the Turnbull Coalition government in 2016 (Hirsch et al. 2019). Eligibility criteria for the program focus on refugees being able to achieve self-sufficiency within 12 months, which means having a job offer, being of working age and demonstrating a functional level of English. The Turnbull government described the program as 'revenue-raising' as the sponsors were required to pay an array of fees covering more than just expected resettlement costs, while program participants did not have access to short-term resettlement services (Hirsch et al. 2019). The program was not designed to bring more refugees to Australia, as private sponsorship spots are part of, and not an addition to, Australia's annual refugee intake. Though the number of refugees admitted through this program (a few hundred) is comparatively small, this community-funded program comes alongside the expansion of humanitarian admissions through the SHP category. SHP eligibility requires family connections to Australia, which are expected to play a crucial role in newcomers' early settlement. Most Syrian and Iraqi refugees admitted in 2015–16 arrived on SHP visas (DHA 2019: 7; Refugee Council of Australia 2020).

Policies were also adopted to reduce the cost of service provision to asylum-seekers in Australia. As mentioned in the previous section, asylum-seekers released from detention on protection visas became ineligible for the HSS in 2015. In 2014, the asylum-seekers assistance program that had existed since 1992, as well as the Community Assistance Support program first introduced in 2005, were replaced with the Status Resolution Support Services program—a system with six bands of support depending on individual circumstances (Okhovat 2018: 10). The quality of support decreased overall. The Australian Red Cross, which had been the main service provider for decades, was replaced with other providers. In 2015, the prohibition on employment that had been imposed on asylum-seekers intercepted at sea and living in the community was lifted. However, claimants were often granted very short visas (as little as a week), which made it very difficult to find an employer willing to provide work (Okhovat 2018: 12). The importance of job-readiness is also greater in the Humanitarian Settlement Program (HSP), which replaced the Humanitarian Settlement Support program in 2017, than in its predecessor (author's interviews with service providers in New South Wales, 2018; ANAO 2019).

The government also aimed for economies of scale in service delivery in the new HSP contracts. The number of service providers declined to five and contract regions to 11 (ANAO 2019). At least in one case, a comparatively small service provider was replaced with a larger organisation considered more likely to deliver value for money (author's interviews with service providers in New South Wales, 2018).

The ANAO released a review of the HSP's contract management and performance in December 2019. The program was said to have cost more than $120 million a year (ANAO 2019: 7), although it did not provide more detailed financial data; the ANAO noted that publicly available data on the HSP were very scarce (p. 47). The report noted there were 17,112 clients in the program in 2018–19 (ANAO 2019: 14), thus the average annual cost per client was slightly more than $7,000. HSP contracts were considered 'largely well designed but contract management has only been partially effective' (ANAO 2019: 7). The engagement of service providers was evaluated as strong[11] and risk assessment adequate, however,

---

11 Contrary to earlier evaluations of refugee settlement programs (EY 2015; Richmond 2011; Urbis Key Young 2003), the ANAO evaluation does not refer to assessment of the effectiveness of the HSP by providers themselves.

performance reporting was lacking as KPIs—notably, employment—were not tracked (ANAO 2019: 9). The ANAO noted deficiencies with the information systems developed to report on performance and that improvements were required. The Department of Home Affairs agreed with all recommendations (ANAO 2019: 6).

A review of refugee settlement outcomes with a broader ambit was commissioned by Prime Minister Scott Morrison in December 2018 and scheduled for release in February 2019; however, the review panel's report was kept confidential for several months. Elements of the review were released in the media following freedom-of-information requests. Once released in November 2019, the review was lauded by refugee advocacy groups for its emphasis on the need for better coordination of refugee settlement services, and especially better provision of refugee employment support (Shergold et al. 2019; Refugee Council of Australia 2019). The Morrison Coalition government accepted most of the review's recommendations in full, apart from the recommendation to profoundly transform refugee employment support, which it considered should remain primarily located with mainstream employment services (Australian Government 2019).

The most controversial aspect of settlement service contracting during this period remained service delivery to asylum-seekers in Australia's offshore processing centres. Following revelations by whistleblowers about the mistreatment of asylum-seekers in this context, the Commonwealth Government expanded nondisclosure provisions in contracts that could result in legal proceedings against whistleblowers (Maylea and Hirsch 2018). Contracts continued to be allocated under conditions that only allowed restricted tendering with limited reporting requirements (McPhail et al. 2016). In February 2019, an *Australian Financial Review* investigation revealed the awarding by the Morrison government of service delivery contracts to provide garrison services in the Manus Island facility for asylum-seekers (excluding food and medical care) worth $423 million to a barely known service provider hosted in a tax haven following 'emergency' restricted tenders (Grigg et al. 2019a, 2019b; Davidson 2019a). To put the size of contracts in perspective, the not-for-profit services provider with the biggest government contracts in refugee and immigrant services, Settlement Services International, has been awarded more than $948 million for refugee and asylum-seeker settlement support since 2012. This sum covers 5 contracts, of which 4 were open tenders and 1 a prequalified tender. Paladin Holdings and Paladin Solutions, the for-profit service provider that was under investigation for its operations in Papua New Guinea, were awarded more than $532 million for for just two contracts for garrison services for the Manus Island transit processing centres, both limited (that is, not open tenders), since 2012.[12] A broader investigation by the ANAO (2020: 9) of the procurement of offshore garrison support and welfare contracts noted that the Department of Home Affairs 'did not demonstrate the achievement of value for money for the PNG [Papua New Guinea] procurements'.

The Australian Parliament's research services, the UN Children's Fund (UNICEF) and not-for-profits have noted that estimating the total cost of the onshore and offshore detention of asylum-seekers is arduous given the fragmentation of data as well as government secrecy. Immigration detention costs, including services, blew out to $9.6 billion between 2013 and 2016 and would amount to $9 billion between 2016 and 2020—a cost of $573,000 per person per annum in offshore detention (ASRC et al. 2019: 8; see also Save the Children and UNICEF 2016; Spinks et al. 2013). This contrasts with the previously mentioned average cost of $7,000 per client of the early, specialised refugee settlement program, the HSP.

Summary

This chapter has traced the development of marketisation in the provision of specialised settlement services to refugees and asylum-seekers in Australia. It has identified trends that pre-existed the deployment of marketisation, especially the dominance of non-government service providers; the residual nature of specialised settlement services, as it has always been argued by Commonwealth authorities that refugee settlement should primarily be supported by mainstream welfare services; and constant demands for stronger policy collaboration within the 'refugee settlement policy niche' and between specialised and mainstream services. The persistence of these trends over time points to institutional path dependence and limits to the transformative effect of marketisation.

---

12 Sums are own calculations using contract data current on 5 August 2022. The figures cover contracts awarded to Settlement Services International by the Department of Social Services and the Department of Home Affairs for refugee settlement and asylum-seeker support only (see www.tenders.gov.au/Search/KeywordSearch?keyword=settlement+services+international), and contracts awarded to Paladin Holdings and Paladin Solutions by the Department of Home Affairs to provide support in the Manus Island Refugee Transit Centre (see www.tenders.gov.au/Search/KeywordSearch?keyword=paladin+solutions and www.tenders.gov.au/Search/KeywordSearch?keyword=paladin+holdings).

Another longstanding issue that pre-existed marketisation is the considerable financial and human cost of detaining asylum-seekers. Regardless, Coalition and Labor governments have stressed the importance of maintaining mandatory immigration detention for all people without a valid visa as a deterrent to future arrivals. Many have argued that governments consider the political cost of policy change to be too high (Garnier and Cox 2012; Hirsch 2017). Measured against the principles of marketisation, one can argue the implementation of marketisation in the detention of asylum-seekers is not thorough even though service provision is dominated by for-profit service providers. It is characterised by restricted tendering, contract allocation to inexperienced service providers, frequently deficient contract drafting and poor governmental contract oversight. This points to various facets of market failure (see also Taylor 2005; McPhail et al. 2016). First, market mechanisms are unable to work as intended in the emergency-like context in which management contracts for offshore facilities are awarded. Restricted tendering results in oligopoly in this sector. Second, contract management at a distance in the context of offshore processing does not lend itself to well-functioning oversight as it creates obstacles to proper 'performance reporting'. Last, Commonwealth regulations have themselves incentivised market failure with the proliferation of nondisclosure agreements regarding service provision. In such a context, risk management is highly likely to fail and the risk of opportunistic rent-seeking by providers is increased.

By contrast, it can be argued that the provision of early, specialised settlement services to refugees is thoroughly marketised even though service provision is dominated by not-for-profit service providers. Service provision contracts are put to competitive tender, mechanisms of contract drafting, oversight and risk management have been developed that are considered consistent with good or even best practice, and procedures are in place to regularly assess compliance of service delivery with program targets. Overall, the quality of service delivery is deemed adequate to high by service providers, clients and evaluators. Several recognised problems of marketisation have been identified, such as a strong focus on measurable outputs instead of program outcomes; a compliance-driven lack of flexibility in service delivery in the face of rapidly evolving client profiles; the administrative burden of reporting requirements; and a reluctance to pilot new programs.

Perhaps counterintuitively, the uneven implementation of marketisation that this chapter has identified points to stronger marketisation in service delivery areas dominated by not-for-profit providers and weaker marketisation in areas dominated by for-profit providers.

Epilogue

The Covid-19 pandemic has significantly impacted refugee settlement services in Australia, yet it does not seem to have had an impact on offshore service provision. The number of refugees who have been able to enter Australia since the closure of international borders has considerably declined. Between July 2020 and June 2021, 4,558 refugees were granted a resettlement visa (though most were unable to travel to Australia during that period) and 1,389 asylum claimants were granted protection (DHA 2022: 33, RCOA 2021).

Since the HSP is a fee-for-services program, fewer refugee arrivals mean fewer clients and hence fewer government payments. Not-for-profit settlement agencies such as Settlement Services International have responded by laying off staff (Dehen 2021). Settlement agencies thus had reduced staff when international borders opened again in December 2021, and as Afghans fleeing the Taliban's return to power and Ukrainians fleeing the Russian invasion were admitted in Australia via special programs (RCOA 2022: 6). This contrasts with continuing high costs for services in offshore asylum-seeker facilities. An investigation by *The Guardian* revealed that Canstruct, a company contracted to deliver services to asylum-seekers on Nauru in 2014, was still being paid hundreds of millions of dollars in 2021 even though the number of asylum-seekers on the island had considerably decreased. As of August 2022, the company's contract for its activities on Nauru was worth more than $1.8 billion.[13] In May 2021, it was also revealed that Applus, a company contracted to deliver settlement services on Manus Island in 2017, had 'overbilled' the Australian Government for staff expenses (McKenzie and Baker 2021). Refugee advocates have pleaded with the Albanese Labor government elected in 2022 to adopt a more generous refugee policy beyond symbolic gestures (Boochani 2022). Advocates and settlement providers have also

---

13 See www.tenders.gov.au/Cn/Show/ba1f752d-8177-44d3-9aa3-49e7439a3fce.

called on the new government to use the upcoming re-tendering process of the HSP to redesign refugee settlement as a more holistic, person-centered and flexible model (RCOA 2022: 2).

It can thus be argued that the pandemic has exacerbated pre-existing dynamics. Future research could investigate to what extent such dynamics are prevalent in other social service markets characterised by strong heterogeneity of service provision and delivery actors. Comparative, qualitative research could also investigate how these diverse service providers understand their roles and mission. In longitudinal perspective, the human and financial impacts of market failure on refugees first confronted with immigration detention as detained asylum-seekers and eventually becoming clients of Australia's settlement services, and of other (more or less) marketised welfare services, also warrant further investigation.

In terms of policy, Australia should end its offshore processing. This would not only incur considerable savings but also put an end to inhumane policies. Failing this, the accountability of for-profit service providers should be considerably increased. By contrast, settlement services in Australia, which have demonstrated flexibility in response to government requirements as well as cost-effectiveness, should be provided with untied funding to ensure continuity of operations in times of considerable fluctuation in refugee arrivals such as during the current pandemic, but also to allow for flexible policy design and implementation.

Overall, this chapter's findings point to the co-opting of non-profit services in the marketisation of social services and the lack of ability (or willingness) of the state to respond to for-profit corporations' market failures in this sector. Much stronger public regulation and implementation control appear warranted to ensure that not only are adequate services delivered to particularly vulnerable people, but also taxpayer money is not wasted. It appears such change is only possible if there is a strong political commitment and election-swaying public demand for it—bearing in mind the recipients of refugee settlement services described in this chapter are not (yet) Australian citizens and thus cannot vote.

References

Asylum Seeker Resource Centre (ASRC), Save the Children and GetUp! (2019). *At What Cost? The human and economic cost of Australia's offshore detention policies 2019*. Sydney: GetUp!. Available from: cdn.getup.org.au/2710-1912_At_What_Cost_report.pdf.

Australian Government. (2019). *Australian Government's Response to Recommendations in the Report: Investing in Refugees, Investing in Australia— The findings of a review into integration, employment and settlement outcomes for refugees and humanitarian entrants in Australia*. November. Canberra: Commonwealth of Australia. Available from: www.homeaffairs.gov.au/reports-and-pubs/files/review-integration-employment-settlement-outcomes-refugees-humanitarian-entrants-government-response.pdf.

Australian National Audit Office (ANAO). (1998). *The Management of Boat People*. Auditor-General Report No. 32 of 1997–98, Performance Audit Report, 17 February. Canberra: ANAO. Available from: www.anao.gov.au/sites/default/files/ANAO_Report_1997-98_32.pdf.

Australian National Audit Office (ANAO). (2004). *Management of Detention Centres Contracts—Part A*. Auditor-General Report No. 54 of 2003–04, Performance Audit Report. Canberra: ANAO. Available from: www.anao.gov.au/sites/default/files/ANAO_Report_2003-2004_54.pdf.

Australian National Audit Office (ANAO). (2006). *Management of the Tender Process for the Detention Services Contract*. Auditor-General Report No. 32 of 2005–06, Performance Audit Report. Canberra: ANAO. Available from: www.anao.gov.au/work/performance-audit/management-tender-process-detention-services-contract.

Australian National Audit Office (ANAO). (2016). *Offshore Processing Centres in Nauru and Papua New Guinea: Procurement of garrison support and welfare services*. Auditor-General Report No. 16 of 2016–17, Performance Audit Report. Canberra: ANAO. Available from: www.anao.gov.au/work/performance-audit/offshore-processing-centres-nauru-and-papua-new-guinea-procurement.

Australian National Audit Office (ANAO). (2017). *Offshore Processing Centres in Nauru and Papua New Guinea: Contract management of garrison support and welfare services*. Auditor-General Report No. 32 of 2016–17, Performance Audit Report. Canberra: ANAO. Available from: www.anao.gov.au/work/performance-audit/offshore-processing-centres-nauru-and-papua-new-guinea-contract-management.

Australian National Audit Office (ANAO). (2019). *Delivery of the Humanitarian Settlement Program*. Auditor-General Report No. 17 of 2019–20, Performance Audit Report. Canberra: ANAO. Available from: www.anao.gov.au/work/ performance-audit/delivery-the-humanitarian-settlement-program.

Australian National Audit Office (ANAO). (2020). *Procurement of Garrison Support and Welfare Services*. Auditor-General Report No. 37 of 2019–20, Performance Audit Report. Canberra: ANAO. Available from: www.anao.gov.au/work/ performance-audit/procurement-garrison-support-and-welfare-services.

Boochani, B. (2022). We pretend there has been change under Labor but hundreds of refugees are still in detention. *The Guardian* (Australia), 27 July. Available from: www.theguardian.com/commentisfree/2022/jul/27/we-pretend-there-has-been-change-under-labor-but-hundreds-of-refugees-are-still-in-detention.

Carr, R. (2018). *Generosity and Refugees: The Kosovars in exile*. Brill's Specials in Modern History, Vol. 2. Leiden, Netherlands: Brill. doi.org/10.1163/ 9789004344129.

Cellini, A. (2018). Annex: Current refugee resettlement program profiles. In A. Garnier, L.L. Jubilut and K.B. Sandvik (eds), *Refugee Resettlement: Power, politics and humanitarian governance* (pp. 253–304). New York, NY: Berghahn Books. doi.org/10.2307/j.ctvw04brz.16.

Centre for Policy Development (CPD). (2017). *Settling Better: Reforming refugee employment and settlement services*. Sydney: CPD. Available from: cpd.org.au/ 2017/02/settlingbetter/.

Collins, J., Reid, C., Groutsis, D., Watson, K., Kaabel, A. & Hughes, S. (2018). *Settlement Experiences of Recently Arrived Refugees from Syria, Iraq and Afghanistan in Queensland in 2018: Full report*. Report #1. Sydney: University of Technology Sydney. Available from: www.uts.edu.au/sites/default/files/ 2019-07/QLD%202018%20Full%20Report%20%5BFormatted%5D.pdf.

Committee to Advise on Australia's Immigration Policies. (1988). *Immigration: A commitment to Australia*. Canberra: AGPS.

Committee of Review of Migrant and Multicultural Programs and Services (ROMAMPAS Committee). (1986). *Don't Settle for Less: Report of the Committee for stage 1 of the Review of Migrant and Multicultural Programs and Services*. August. Canberra: Commonwealth of Australia.

Commonwealth Ombudsman. (2005). *Inquiry into the Circumstances of the Vivian Alvarez Matter*. Report 3, 2005. Canberra: Commonwealth Ombudsman.

Considine, M. (2003). Governance and competition: The role of non-profit organisations in the delivery of public services. *Australian Journal of Political Science, 38*(1): 63–77. doi.org/10.1080/1036114032000056251.

Considine, M., Lewis, J. & O'Sullivan, S. (2011). Quasi-markets and service delivery flexibility following a decade of employment assistance reform in Australia. *Journal of Social Policy, 40*(4): 811–33. doi.org/10.1017/S0047279411000213.

Cox, D. (1987). *Immigration and Welfare: An Australian perspective.* New York, NY: Prentice Hall.

Cox, D. (1996). *Understanding Australian Settlement Services.* Canberra: AGPS.

Davidson, H. (2019a). Paladin contract for Manus Island should be cancelled, PNG's new PM says. *The Guardian*, [Australia], 25 June. Available from: www.theguardian.com/australia-news/2019/jun/25/paladin-contract-for-manus-island-should-be-cancelled-pngs-new-pm-says.

Davidson, H. (2019b). Coalition blocking release of major review into refugee resettlement. *The Guardian*, [Australia], 25 September. Available from: www.theguardian.com/australia-news/2019/sep/25/coalition-blocking-release-of-major-review-into-refugee-resettlement.

Dehen, O. (2021). By the time refugees can enter Australia again, some support groups will have fewer staff. *SBS News*, 22 June. Available from: www.sbs.com.au/news/by-the-time-refugees-can-enter-australia-again-some-support-groups-will-have-fewer-staff.

Department of Home Affairs (DHA). (2019). *Australia's humanitarian program 2019–20*. Discussion Paper. Canberra: Commonwealth of Australia. Available from: www.homeaffairs.gov.au/reports-and-pubs/files/2019-20-discussion-paper.pdf.

Department of Home Affairs (DHA). (2020a). *Australia's Offshore Humanitarian Program: 2019–2020*. Canberra: Commonwealth of Australia. Available from: www.homeaffairs.gov.au/research-and-stats/files/australia-offshore-humanitarian-program-2019-20.pdf.

Department of Home Affairs (DHA). (2020b). *Onshore Humanitarian Program 2019–20*. Canberra: Commonwealth of Australia. Available from: www.homeaffairs.gov.au/research-and-stats/files/ohp-june-20.pdf.

Department of Home Affairs (DHA). (2022). *The Administration of the Immigration and Citizenship Programs*. Canberra: Commonwealth of Australia. Available from: immi.homeaffairs.gov.au/programs-subsite/files/administration-immigration-program-8th-edition.pdf.

Department of Immigration and Citizenship (DIAC). (2007) *Annual Report 2006–07.* Canberra: Commonwealth of Australia.

Department of Immigration and Citizenship (DIAC). (2009) *Annual Report 2008–09.* Canberra: Commonwealth of Australia.

Department of Immigration and Citizenship (DIAC). (2010). *Annual Report 2009–10.* Canberra: Commonwealth of Australia.

Department of Immigration and Citizenship (DIAC). (2011). *Annual Report 2010–11.* Canberra: Commonwealth of Australia.

Department of Immigration and Citizenship (DIAC). (2013). *Annual Report 2012–13.* Canberra: Commonwealth of Australia.

Department of Immigration and Multicultural Affairs (DIMA). (2004). *Annual Report 2003–04.* Canberra: Commonwealth of Australia.

Department of Immigration and Multicultural and Indigenous Affairs (DIMIA). (2003). *Report of the Review of Settlement Services for Migrants and Humanitarian Entrants.* Canberra: Commonwealth of Australia.

Edwards, B., Smart, D., De Maio, J., Silbert, M. & Jenkinson, R. (2018). Cohort profile: Building a New Life in Australia (BNLA)—The longitudinal study of humanitarian migrants. *International Journal of Epidemiology*, *47*(1): 20–20h. doi.org/10.1093/ije/dyx218.

Ernst & Young (EY). (2015). *Evaluation of the Humanitarian Settlement Services and Complex Case Support Programs.* Report prepared for the Australian Government Department of Social Services, June 2015. Melbourne: EY Australia. Available from: refugeehealthnetwork.org.au/wp-content/uploads/DSS_2015_Evaluation-of-the-HSS-and-CCS-programmes.pdf.

Garnier, A. (2014). Migration management or humanitarian governance: The UNHCR's 'resettlement expansionism' and its impact on policy-making in the EU and Australia. *Journal of Ethnic and Migration Studies*, 40(6): 942–59. doi.org/10.1080/1369183X.2013.855075.

Garnier, A. (2018). Responsibility-shifting and the global refugee regime. In M. Middell (ed.), *Routledge Handbook of Transregional Studies* (pp. 400–7). London: Routledge. doi.org/10.4324/9780429438233.

Garnier, A. & Cox, L. (2012). Twenty years of mandatory detention: The anatomy of a failed policy. Paper presented at Australian Political Studies Association Conference, University of Tasmania, Hobart, 24 & 26 September.

Goodwin, S. & Phillips, M. (2015). The marketisation of human services and the expansion of the not-for-profit sector. In G. Meagher & S. Goodwin (eds), *Markets, Rights and Power in Australian Social Policy* (pp. 97–114). Sydney: Sydney University Press. Available from: open.sydneyuniversitypress. com.au/9781920899950/mrp-the-marketisation-of-human-services-and-the-expansion-of-the-not-for-profit-sector.html#Chapter3.

Grigg, A., Shapiro, J. & Murray, L. (2019a). Cashing in on refugees, duo make $20 million a month at Manus Island. *Australian Financial Review*, 10 February. Available from: www.afr.com/policy/foreign-affairs/cashing-in-on-refugees-duo-make-20-million-a-month-at-manus-island-20190210-h1b2e5.

Grigg, A., Shapiro, J. & Murray, L. (2019b). Home Affairs demanded Paladin CEO quit, then paid it another $109m. *Australian Financial Review*, 19 February. Available from: www.afr.com/politics/federal/home-affairs-demanded-paladin-ceo-quit-then-paid-it-another-109m-20190219-h1bgkx.

Higgins, C. (2017). *Asylum by Boat: Origins of Australia's refugee policy*. Sydney: NewSouth Books.

Hirsch, A. (2017). Five quotes from the Turnbull–Trump call show the folly of Australia's refugee policy. *The Conversation*, 4 August. Available from: theconversation.com/five-quotes-from-the-turnbull-trump-call-show-the-folly-of-australias-refugee-policy-82072.

Hirsch, A., Hoang, K. & Vogl, A. (2019). Australia's refugee sponsorship program: Creating complementary pathways or privatising humanitarianism? *Refuge*, *35*(2): 109–22. doi.org/10.7202/1064823ar.

Joint Standing Committee on Migration. (1994). *Asylum, Border Control and Detention*. The Parliament of the Commonwealth of Australia. Canberra: AGPS. Available from: nla.gov.au/nla.obj-1665725393/view?partId=nla.obj-1669989612#page/n62/mode/1up.

Jupp, J. (1994). *Exile or Refuge? The settlement of refugees, humanitarian and displaced immigrants*. Canberra: AGPS.

Jupp, J. (2002). *From White Australia to Woomera*. Cambridge, UK: Cambridge University Press. doi.org/10.1017/CBO9781139195034.

Karp, P. (2019). Peter Dutton's department regains control of refugee settlement services. *The Guardian*, [Australia], 29 May. Available from: www.theguardian. com/australia-news/2019/may/29/peter-duttons-department-regains-control-of-refugee-settlement-services.

Kunz, E.F. (1988). *Displaced Persons: Calwell's new Australians*. Sydney: Australian National University Press.

Marr, D. & Wilkinson, M. (2004). *Dark Victory*. Sydney: Allen & Unwin.

Martin, J. (1965). *Refugee Settlers: A study of displaced persons in Australia*. Canberra: Australian National University Press.

Martin, L. (2017). Discretion, contracting, and commodification: Privatisation of US immigration detention as a technology of government. In D. Conlon & N. Hiemstra (eds), *Intimate Economies of Immigration Detention: Critical perspectives* (pp. 32–50). London: Routledge. doi.org/10.4324/97813157 07112.

Maylea, C. & Hirsch, A. (2018). Social workers as collaborators? The ethics of working within Australia's asylum system. *Ethics and Social Welfare*, *12*(2): 160–78. doi.org/10.1080/17496535.2017.1310918.

McKenzie, N. & Baker, R. (2021). Big profits in asylum-seeker contracts as workers say they felt 'cheated, exploited'. *Sydney Morning Herald*, 24 May. Available from: www.smh.com.au/national/big-profits-in-asylum-seeker-contracts-as-workers-say-they-felt-cheated-exploited-20210523-p57ucc.html.

McPhail, K., Okochi Nyamory, R. & Taylor, S. (2016). Escaping accountability: A case of Australia's asylum seeker policy. *Accounting, Auditing and Accountability Journal*, *29*(6): 947–84. doi.org/10.1108/AAAJ-03-2014-1639.

Mendes, P. (2017). *Australia's Welfare Wars: The players, the politics and the ideologies*. Sydney: UNSW Press. doi.org/10.11157/anzswj-vol29iss2id407.

Neumann, K. (2015). *Across the Seas*. Melbourne: Schwartz Publishing.

Nicholls, G. (1998). Unsettling admissions: Asylum seekers in Australia. *Journal of Refugee Studies*, *11*(1): 61–79. doi.org/10.1093/jrs/11.1.61.

Okhovat, S. (2018). *With Empty Hands: How the Australian government is forcing people seeking asylum to destitution*. Report, June. Sydney: Refugee Council of Australia. Available from: www.refugeecouncil.org.au/wp-content/uploads/2018/12/With-Empty-Hands_FINAL.pdf.

Palmer, M. (2005). *Inquiry into the Circumstances of the Immigration Detention of Cornelia Rau: Report*. Canberra: Commonwealth of Australia.

Paxton, G. (2020). *Refugee Policy and Timeline*. Melbourne: The Royal Children's Hospital Melbourne, Immigrant Health Service. Available from: www.rch.org.au/immigranthealth/clinical/refugee-policy-and-timeline/.

Pécoud, A. (2020). Introduction: The International Organization for Migration as the new 'UN migration agency'. In M. Geiger & A. Pécoud (eds), *The International Organization for Migration* (pp. 1–28). Houndmills, UK: Palgrave Macmillan. doi.org/10.1007/978-3-030-32976-1_1.

Price, C. (1981). Immigration policies and refugees in Australia. *International Migration Review*, 15(1–2): 99–108. doi.org/10.1177%2F0197918381015 001-213.

Refugee Council of Australia (RCOA). (2017). *Not Working: Experiences of refugees and migrants with Jobactive*. Report, March. Sydney: Refugee Council of Australia. Available from: www.refugeecouncil.org.au/jobactive-report/2/.

Refugee Council of Australia (RCOA). (2019). Review into settlement outcomes a 'well-considered examination of refugee settlement', Refugee Council of Australia says. Press release, 26 December, Sydney. Available from: www. refugeecouncil.org.au/review-into-settlement-outcomes-a-well-considered-examination-of-refugee-settlement-refugee-council-of-australia-says/.

Refugee Council of Australia (RCOA). (2020). Less than one third of refugees in Australia's humanitarian program are resettled from UNHCR. Press release, 9 May, Sydney. Available from: www.refugeecouncil.org.au/less-one-third-refugees-australias-humanitarian-program-resettled-unhcr/.

Refugee Council of Australia (RCOA). (2021). *Lifting of travel restrictions welcome news for refugee visa holders*. Sydney: Refugee Council of Australia. Available from: www.refugeecouncil.org.au/lifting_of_travel_restrictions_welcome_news/.

Refugee Council of Australia (RCOA). (2022). *Next steps to improve Australia's Settlement and Integration of Refugees*. Sydney: Refugee Council of Australia. Available from: www.refugeecouncil.org.au/wp-content/uploads/2022/07/Settlement-Services-Discussion-Paper-2022.pdf.

Review of Migrant and Multicultural Programs and Services (ROMAMPAS). (1978). *Migrant services and programs: Report of the review of post-arrival programs and services for migrants*. Parliamentary Paper No. 164/1978, May. Canberra: AGPS.

Richmond, D. (2011). *Review of Humanitarian Settlement Services Performance Measures and Contract Management*. Canberra: Commonwealth of Australia.

Roumeliotis, V. & Paschadilisi-Silas, E. (2013). Settlement and community development: Moving and shaping our civil society. In A. Jakubowicz and C. Ho (eds), *For Those Who've Come Across the Seas: Australian multicultural theory, policy and practice* (pp. 83–93). Melbourne: Australian Scholarly Publishing.

Save the Children & United Nations Children's Fund (UNICEF). (2016). *At What Cost? The human, economic and strategic cost of Australia's asylum seeker policies and the alternatives*. Melbourne & Sydney: Save the Children & UNICEF. Available from: www.unicef.org.au/Upload/UNICEF/Media/Documents/At-What-Cost-Report.pdf.

Senate Education and Employment References Committee. (2019*). Jobactive: Failing those it is intended to serve*. February. Canberra: Parliament of Australia. Available from: parlinfo.aph.gov.au/parlInfo/download/committees/reportsen/024217/toc_pdf/Jobactivefailingthoseitisintendedtoserve.pdf;fileType=application%2Fpdf.

Senate Select Committee for an Inquiry into a Certain Maritime Incident. (2002). *A Certain Maritime Incident*. Report, 23 October. Canberra: Parliament of Australia. Available from: www.aph.gov.au/Parliamentary_Business/Committees/Senate/Former_Committees/maritimeincident/index.

Shergold, P., Benson, K. & Piper, M. (2019). *Investing in Refugees, Investing in Australia: The findings of a review into integration, employment and settlement outcomes for refugees and humanitarian entrants in Australia*. February. Canberra: Department of the Prime Minister and Cabinet. Available from: www.homeaffairs.gov.au/reports-and-pubs/files/review-integration-employment-settlement-outcomes-refugees-humanitarian-entrants.pdf.

Shields, J., Drolet, J. & Valenzuela, K. (2016). *Immigrant settlement and integration services and the role of nonprofit providers: A cross-national perspective on trends, issues and evidence*. RCIS Working Paper No. 2016/1, February. Toronto: Ryerson Centre for Immigration and Settlement. Available from: digital.library.ryerson.ca/islandora/object/RULA%3A8408/datastream/OBJ/download/Immigrant_Settlement_and_Integration_Services_and_the_Role_of_Nonprofit_Service_Providers__A_Cross-national_Perspective_on_Trends__Issues_and_Evidence.pdf.

Snape, J. (2019). The new 'boat people'? How Labor's focus on air arrivals only hints at new immigration challenge. *ABC News*, 9 October. Available from: www.abc.net.au/news/2019-10-09/labor-concered-at-asylum-seeker-numbers-arriving-by-plane/11581494.

Spinks, H. (2009). *Australia's settlement services for migrants and refugees*. Parliamentary Library Research Paper No. 29 2008–09. Canberra: Parliament of Australia. Available from: www.aph.gov.au/About_Parliament/Parliamentary_Departments/Parliamentary_Library/pubs/rp/rp0809/09rp29.

Spinks, H., Barker, C. & Watt, D. (2013). *Australian Government spending on irregular maritime arrivals and counter–people smuggling activity.* Parliamentary Library Research Paper, Updated 4 September. Canberra: Parliament of Australia. Available from: www.aph.gov.au/About_Parliament/Parliamentary_Departments/Parliamentary_Library/pubs/rp/rp1314/PeopleSmuggling.

Taylor, S. (2005). The Pacific Solution or a Pacific nightmare? The difference between burden shifting and responsibility sharing. *Asia-Pacific Law and Policy Journal,* 6(1): 1–43.

United Nations High Commissioner for Refugees (UNHCR). (2020). *Figures at a Glance.* [Online]. Geneva: UNHCR. Available from: www.unhcr.org/figures-at-a-glance.html.

United Nations High Commissioner for Refugees (UNHCR). (2021). *Resettlement Data Finder.* [Online]. Geneva: UNHCR. Available from: rsq.unhcr.org/en/#3g1M.

Urbis Keys Young. (2003). *Evaluation of the Integrated Humanitarian Settlement Strategy (IHSS).* Canberra: Urbis Keys Young.

York, B. (2003). *Australia and Refugees, 1901–2002: An annotated chronology based on official sources.* Canberra: Parliamentary Library Social Policy Group. Available from: www.aph.gov.au/About_Parliament/Parliamentary_Departments/Parliamentary_Library/Publications_Archive/online/Refugees contents.

3

Out of sight, out of mind? Markets and employment services in remote Indigenous communities

Diana Perche

Introduction

The early waves of marketising reform in Australian government service delivery were relatively slow to impact on policies and programs targeting First Nations people. The portfolio of Indigenous Affairs is widely recognised as a highly complex area of policymaking, given the challenges of service delivery in remote areas, the language and cultural barriers and the long-term impacts of processes of colonisation, dispossession, exclusion and marginalisation. For many decades, the Commonwealth Government funded separate delivery of services and programs for First Nations people and supported a broad policy approach based on Indigenous self-determination. However, since the Howard era, marketisation in social services has been increasingly applied to Indigenous services and separate policy delivery has been replaced with 'mainstreaming' of services.

A notable feature of the market-based reform agenda has been that social policies have been piloted or trialled in Indigenous communities in far more draconian and punitive ways than among non-Indigenous populations. Examples include the implementation of income management for welfare recipients in remote communities in the Northern Territory and the banning of alcohol and pornography in specific communities as part of the Northern Territory Emergency Response (NTER), which was rolled out in 2007, and the introduction of the School Enrolment and Attendance Measure in remote communities, which applied penalties through the income-support system to families whose children did not attend school, between 2013 and 2017.

Employment service delivery in remote communities is another area of policy experimentation where the Commonwealth Government has applied a more punitive approach to Indigenous remote communities than in urban and regional centres where the non-Indigenous population is larger. This chapter concentrates on the application of market principles to employment service delivery in remote Indigenous communities and examines how providers have come to be seen as an extension of the government's power to punish and control individual behaviour.

This chapter begins with a summary of the development of policy around employment and welfare provision in remote Indigenous communities, from the adoption of the Community Development Employment Projects (CDEP) in 1977 through to the most recent implementation of the similarly named, but radically different, Community Development Program (CDP) in 2015. It shows the impact of institutional layering throughout this period, to the point where the original policy settings were seen as creating the very problems they were designed to mitigate. The chapter then examines the contractual arrangements with service providers under the CDP, observing the flawed design of the market and considering the implications in terms of the quality, efficacy and appropriateness of the services this market provides. Given the discernible risks of policy failure, the chapter concludes by reflecting on the factors motivating the adoption of market logic in this policy area, despite the lack of a viable labour market in remote parts of Indigenous Australia.

This chapter is written by a non-Indigenous scholar, observing the impact of government policy on First Nations people. It is well recognised that First Nations people are too often the subject of academic research that does not reflect their experiences, priorities and ways of knowing (Nakata 2007; Smith 2012). In this chapter, care has been taken to prioritise the voices of First Nations people in explaining the lived experience of the provision of employment services in remote areas, particularly as they have been recorded during parliamentary inquiries. It is important to acknowledge, however, that the author's interpretation of these records may not reflect the experience of all First Nations people who are affected by the government policy under examination here, and future policy development in this area should take this into account.

From community development to welfare dependence: Explaining the institutional history

This chapter will examine the institutional history of Commonwealth policy targeting employment for First Nations people in Australia, focusing particularly on labour market participation in remote communities. This is predominantly a story of incremental changes, particularly from the 1990s, which saw the well-established CDEP gradually undermined and transformed into a punitive work-for-the-dole scheme. Sanders (2016) observes the role of apparently small bureaucratic decisions that, over time, had a powerful, unforeseeable impact on the CDEP and contributed in different ways to its ultimate demise. Indeed: 'Such was the power of routine decisions within government that cumulatively they did most of the reframing of this once positively regarded program' (Sanders 2016: 32).

The incremental shift away from the original CDEP model of self-determination and separate treatment towards marketisation of employment services in remote Indigenous communities is usefully analysed using the five patterns of gradual institutional change identified by Streeck and Thelen (2005). These patterns are distinguished by the mechanisms used to bring about change and the extent to which opportunities are opened and exploited by actors inside or outside the institutional structures, at different times. The five modes are displacement, layering, drift, conversion and exhaustion, and the two most directly applicable in this case are layering and conversion. Layering is used to describe institutional change that does not attempt to terminate and replace an existing institution, protected as it is likely to be by vested interests, but rather to introduce amendments or revisions that appear to function alongside the existing arrangements. Once such apparently minor or peripheral amendments take hold, they can result in 'differential growth', where the new features attract support and new logic becomes acceptable. Because the amendments have been 'layered' over the existing arrangements, rather than displacing or attacking them directly, they do not produce a 'counter-mobilisation' in defence of the status quo (Streeck and Thelen 2005: 23–24). This reflects the risk of 'taken for grantedness' inherent in institutions, allowing for 'subversive' actors to take advantage of the ambiguities, 'gaps' and 'soft spots' within the rules (Mahoney and Thelen 2010: 10–11). The power dynamics will ultimately change, because 'while powerful veto players can protect the old institutions, they cannot necessarily prevent the addition of new elements' (Mahoney and Thelen 2010: 20).

The other applicable form of institutional change in Streeck and Thelen's typology is conversion, through which existing institutions are 'redirected to new goals, functions or purposes' (2005: 26). Conversion overturns the earlier institutional expectations and distribution of power to suit the interests of a different set of actors. According to Mahoney and Thelen (2010: 21): 'Conversion normally occurs when rules are ambiguous enough to permit different (often starkly contrasting) interpretations.' The process of conversion can be fraught: there is a potential for unintended consequences to emerge from the newly converted institution, along with political struggle between actors supporting or resisting change, taking advantage of ambiguities in the new rules and demanding compromises in their implementation (Streeck and Thelen 2005).

As will be examined in more detail in the next section, the design of the CDEP opened the possibility of seeing its participants as both paid employees and welfare-dependent. The Howard government exploited this ambiguity, using the crisis of the NTER to allow a substantial shift away from the Commonwealth's longstanding practice of treating remote labour markets differently and supporting Indigenous self-determination, to an adoption of markets in the delivery of employment services as part of a 'mainstream' welfare-based system. In this case, the institutional change consisted of the abandonment of the government's former commitment to community development in remote communities in favour of welfare combined with work obligations with no associated benefits for the community. After many years of incremental change through layering, there was little support left at the government level for retaining self-determination and community development. The conversion of the CDEP into a market-based system focusing on work for the dole has provoked considerable resistance from Aboriginal organisations and stakeholders, but little attention elsewhere.

The importance of the CDEP in Aboriginal communities over this period reflects the complex ways in which the policy as an institution shaped the lives and relationships of community members. Streeck and Thelen (2005: 9) offer a definition of institutions as 'collectively enforced expectations with respect to the behaviour of specific categories of actors', involving 'mutually related rights and obligations'. Institutions can also be understood as 'distributional instruments laden with power implications' (Mahoney and Thelen 2010: 9). Before the introduction of market logic, the design of the CDEP established institutional expectations about the treatment of Indigenous participation in the labour market as a separate policy problem, not subject to the same pressures and ideological expectations as people in the 'mainstream' labour market. This set of institutional expectations was originally based on the challenges of remoteness and lack of a viable labour market and infrastructure. The different treatment of Indigenous economic participation also considered the history of racism and discrimination in the labour market and the need to accommodate cultural differences with flexible work arrangements, along with aspects of historical and ongoing social exclusion affecting employability, including lack of access to education, adequate housing and health care. The CDEP thus saw the creation of local Aboriginal community-controlled organisations that received government funding and distributed it as wages for those working on community-led projects. The program provided a mechanism for substantial growth in the number and size of Aboriginal community-controlled organisations over time, shaping relationships and expectations at the local level as well as between communities and government. These organisations were understood to be a powerful reflection of Indigenous self-determination in action, with substantial resources and reach (Rowse 2002).

The Community Development Employment Projects

The CDEP initiative was introduced in 1977 by the Liberal–Country party Coalition government under Prime Minister Malcolm Fraser and was designed and administered by the Department of Aboriginal Affairs (DAA). The policy was a response to growing concern about the welfare of Aboriginal people in remote areas, many of whom had been forced to leave their low-paid work on outback stations because of the equal wages case and had little prospect of finding work in a very limited labour market (Jordan and Altman 2016; Fowkes and Li 2018). Indigenous Australians had been essentially excluded from the social security system until the 1960s, but as eligibility for welfare was expanded, concern grew about the risks of 'sit-down money' and the lack of formal employment opportunities in remote areas. The CDEP was a voluntary program that allowed Indigenous organisations or community councils in specific remote areas to employ participants for community development projects, paying them a basic wage out of a block grant that was notionally offset against the unemployment benefits they would otherwise have been eligible to receive, plus costs (Sanders 2001). Following early successes in pilot programs, the scheme was gradually expanded to include more remote communities under the Hawke Labor government (1983–91).

Key features of the CDEP distinguished it from other labour market programs targeting unemployed people. The scheme was voluntary, not compulsory, and communities could elect whether to participate. The flexibility associated with the block funding for the community-based organisations administering the projects ensured that community needs were met across a wide range of services and activities, ranging from road maintenance, housing construction and rubbish collection to child care and aged care, night patrols, postal services and running the community store and fuel outlet. The activities were often community services otherwise provided by municipal or state governments in less-remote parts of Australia (such as emergency services, meals on wheels, patient transport services and ranger programs), or were positions designed to support government-funded services such as Centrelink liaison officers, health workers and teaching assistants in schools (see, for example, Scott 2001: 207).

Block funding allowed the community organisations to design their own projects to meet the needs and priorities identified by their own residents, and to provide for flexibility in work arrangements to allow members of the community to continue their cultural obligations and practices. Critically, participants were considered employees, not welfare recipients. The pay system included a base rate for 15 hours a week at award wages, with the possibility of 'top ups' for those who elected to do more hours of work. Sanders emphasises the CDEP was not considered to be welfare or social security:

> Although the CDEP scheme grew out of the extension of social security entitlements to Indigenous Australians, it was not, in the late 1970s and the 1980s, in any way formally linked to the social security system. The scheme was not recognised by or referred to in the social security legislation and it was administered, at Commonwealth level, almost entirely by the Indigenous

affairs portfolio with little or no input from the social security portfolio. The link between the CDEP scheme and social security entitlement was simply an informal, notional financial offset. The CDEP scheme was outside the social security system, and participants in the scheme were essentially treated simply as low-income wage earners. (2001: 47)

This framing of the CDEP as a funding source, rather than a system of social security, would change considerably over time, as discussed in the next section.

To further underline this point, the work activities associated with the CDEP were not considered to be an early form of work for the dole or mutual obligation, as it would be understood today. Rather, the design of the CDEP enabled 'Indigenous self-management and community pride' (Fowkes 2018: 73). The Indigenous community-based organisations managing the CDEP exercised cultural authority in the local community and political authority in their relationship with the government (Rowse 2002). Work activities were based on traditional Aboriginal cultural values of reciprocity between the individual and his or her community or kinship groups—quite different from the more recent expectations of 'mutual obligation' between an individual and the government (Martin 2001: 32–33). As Rowse notes, participants in CDEP activities were active members of the community, contributing to projects that were the product of self-determination. Thus, CDEP workers were, 'in some respects, like shareholders in the CDEP' (Rowse 2001: 40).

Institutional layering: From the CDEP to the CDP

The early success of the CDEP prompted its expansion to cover a growing range of remote communities. The Hawke Labor government extended the program to non-remote areas, in recognition of the similar challenges faced there by Aboriginal people seeking employment (Blakeman 2016: 221). By 1990, the CDEP had reached urban communities in the southern states and eastern Queensland and was considered a national program. This section will examine the development of the CDEP as a process of institutional layering, from its expansion under the Hawke government through to its gradual dismantling by the Howard government and subsequent replacement by the Gillard government. The following section will outline the Abbott government's ultimate conversion of the program into the more punitive employment program, the CDP. These developments are summarised in Figure 3.1.

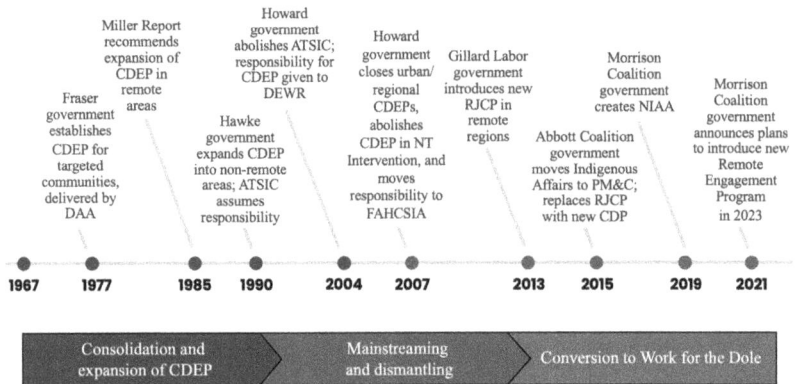

Figure 3.1 Timeline of key milestones in Indigenous employment policy
Source: Based on author's research.

In 1990, the Hawke government created the Aboriginal and Torres Strait Islander Commission (ATSIC) to replace the Department of Aboriginal Affairs. This new body was directed not by public servants, but by elected commissioners who represented Aboriginal and Torres Strait Islander people in a regional structure. The Hawke government intended ATSIC to serve as an important expression of Indigenous self-determination, with Indigenous leadership representing Indigenous interests to the government and making decisions about programs and funding that affected Indigenous people (Bradfield 2006). ATSIC was given administrative responsibility for the CDEP, which formed a substantial part of its budget and functions. At its peak, the CDEP included 272 projects, employed 33,000 participants nationwide and consumed one-third of the annual ATSIC budget (Jonas 2001: 13).

The following decade was characterised by a growing tension within different agencies of government, as the CDEP was increasingly understood as both a form of social security *and* paid employment (Sanders 2001). The first institutional layer had been applied by the Hawke government with a 1991 amendment to the *Social Security Act,* which excluded CDEP participants from unemployment benefits on the grounds they were already receiving a kind of income support from the government. In 1997, concern was expressed by the Human Rights and Equal Opportunity Commission about the range of social security supplementary payments that CDEP participants were unable to access (Blakeman 2016: 227). In 1997, in response to the Howard government's freeze on expansion of CDEP placements, ATSIC commissioned an independent review, known as the Spicer Review. This review observed that up to one-third of community members did little of the work expected of them under the CDEP, thus receiving little pay under the 'no work, no pay' rules, and it recommended these workers be transferred to unemployment benefits instead. Sanders (2001: 49) suggests ATSIC used this finding to make the distinction between the CDEP and social security clearer. In 1999, the Howard Liberal–National Coalition government's new Indigenous Employment Policy prevented further expansion of the CDEP and introduced incentive payments for CDEP participants who left the program for paid work, seeking to reframe the CDEP as a pathway to mainstream employment. The government also addressed the inequality of access to social security supplements for CDEP participants, and this new layer meant participants became Centrelink customers for the first time.

In 2004, the Howard government abolished ATSIC in line with its ideological rejection of Indigenous self-determination and separate representation and service delivery, having criticised the commission over many years for apparent conflicts of interest and mismanagement (Bradfield 2006). ATSIC's functions were moved into mainstream departments. The CDEP was moved to the Department of Employment and Workplace Relations (DEWR), which had responsibility for mainstream employment policy focused on welfare-to-work and labour market activation. This department was already well recognised for its extensive use of markets in providing employment services through the Job Network (Considine et al. 2011; Sanders 2001) and, within a short period, the same technique of competitive contracting was applied to organisations wishing to provide CDEP opportunities for their communities.

The demise of ATSIC would prove to be critical for the CDEP. Drawing on Mahoney and Thelen's (2010) observations about power shifts as a result of layering, it is clear ATSIC had been a powerful veto player, protecting the CDEP and its original values and objectives, based on Aboriginal self-determination and the appropriateness of separate policy treatment. Altman (2016: 208) argues that because the CDEP was ATSIC's largest program, it could be 'linked to ATSIC's perceived failure; redefined as an employment program, [CDEP] could be held responsible in part for the government's inability to close the employment gap'. Once ATSIC was removed, there were no other similarly powerful actors within the Commonwealth public service to defend the unique nature of the Indigenous remote labour market. It was difficult for the CDEP organisations themselves to mobilise resistance without a peak representative body. It was at this point that the institutional layering of the previous years turned to the possibility of conversion, and the Howard government's critique of self-determination combined powerfully with a critique of Indigenous-specific policy, which was dismissed as 'separatism' (Altman 2007: 309).

With the CDEP now administered by DEWR, the Howard government was quick to open the CDEP to marketisation, in the first sign of institutional conversion. In 2005, the Howard government applied a competitive purchasing process for CDEP contracts, along the lines of the mainstream Job Network scheme, and opened this to both non-Indigenous organisations and private providers. This caused some Indigenous organisations to lose contracts and forced others to merge or work across regional boundaries, outside their own communities, to remain competitive (Fowkes 2018: 78–79). Sanders (2007: 2) noted the earlier funding model for the CDEP organisations under the DAA and ATSIC were 'loyalty models, in which particular Indigenous organisations were funded and supported over extended period[s] of time because of their identification and links with the community being served'. The new scheme introduced in 2005 replaced this model with a 'new competitive contractualism' using short-term contracts and ending the security of funding (Sanders 2007; Altman 2016). As Fowkes (2018: 79) argues, 'the 2005 "reforms" broke the formal nexus between local Aboriginal control and program delivery, replacing it with a KPI/purchasing process and reframing CDEP as an instrument of government policy', rather than community-based development. The institutional expectations based on Indigenous self-determination and community control were substantially shifted. The Howard government also began to close CDEP programs in urban and regional areas from 2006 on the basis there were 'strong labour markets' in these areas, negating the need for separate treatment of Indigenous people.

In July 2007, the Howard government announced the Northern Territory Emergency Response—ostensibly to address child sexual abuse in remote communities. One of the prominent policy measures of the NTER was 'welfare quarantining', which aimed to prevent residents of the targeted remote communities using their social security payments to purchase alcohol or tobacco or to gamble. It soon became clear the CDEP would also be wound back in the affected communities to allow this income-management measure to be implemented. Jordan and Altman (2016: 8) record the Indigenous affairs minister Mal Brough's surprise that CDEP participants could not be covered by the income-management policy because they were technically employees not welfare recipients. This further demonstrates the extent to which the welfare frame for the CDEP had become widely accepted in government circles by this stage.

The Rudd Labor government was elected in late November 2007 and made the deliberate decision to continue the implementation of the five-year plan for the NTER. However, it paused the closure of CDEP activities in the Northern Territory while it considered its new Indigenous employment policy. The CDEP was moved to the Department of Families, Housing, Community Services and Indigenous Affairs. The plan to abolish the program in non-remote areas was implemented, with new participants moved on to social security payments and some participants in remote areas 'grandfathered' on CDEP wages for a fixed period. The Labor government took some time to develop its replacement for the CDEP and it was not until 2012 that the Gillard government announced the new Remote Jobs and Communities Program (RJCP). This new program replaced the CDEP and combined with the parallel services that were working in Indigenous communities by this stage, including mainstream Job Services Australia (JSA), the Disability Employment Service and the Indigenous Employment Policy. Participants would now receive social security payments rather than CDEP wages and would be subject to JSA-style obligations for participants to engage in work for the dole, as well as compulsory case management, including regular appointments and job plans (Fowkes 2019: 4). Some legacy of the abolished CDEP remained in initial allocations of funding for community development, though these were not retained after the change of government in 2013.

The RJCP was based on the market logic of contestability, with providers competing for tenders in a system that only allowed a single provider for each of the 60 identified remote regions. This was intended to make the system easier to navigate for local employers and participants (Fowkes 2018: 102). As in the earlier version of the Howard government's CDEP, contracts were open to local Indigenous organisations and regional councils, but also to for-profit and national non-government organisations— some working in partnership with Indigenous organisations. This was a period of 'rationalisation and amalgamations' (Hunter 2016: 80) as the market consolidated rapidly. The RJCP service contracts were issued for five years, in line with those used by the JSA. Providers were paid a basic service fee for holding monthly meetings with participants and developing individual 'participation plans' (Sanders 2016: 169). Providers in remote areas found they were forced to move away from organising work activities and community visits. Instead, they required new skills and new staff to manage the 'computer-based case management work', which did not fit the skills of the former CDEP staff (Sanders 2016: 170).

The implementation of the RJCP from 1 July 2013 marked the conversion of a labour creation program based on an understanding of Indigenous self-determination and community development to a marketised provision of employment services based on the mainstream JSA model. The earlier tension between the vision of the CDEP as a form of social security and as paid employment had been resolved definitively. The CDEP was replaced with a new program that adopted the mainstream welfare-to-work mechanisms of active jobseeking and work for the dole in return for social security payments. The gradual introduction of competitive contracting for the delivery of employment services had culminated in a contestable market, pitting Aboriginal community-controlled organisations against larger non-government and for-profit providers for a limited number of contracts for remote regions.

The new Community Development Program

In September 2013, just three months after the introduction of the RJCP, a new Coalition government under Prime Minister Tony Abbott was elected, bringing a radical new ideological approach to Indigenous affairs. Abbott centralised all aspects of the Indigenous affairs portfolio inside the Department of the Prime Minister and Cabinet (PM&C) and established five broad priority areas for the portfolio, one of which was employment. The government commissioned a wideranging review by businessman Andrew Forrest, which was published with the title *Creating Parity* (2014). The Forrest Review was deeply critical of 'welfare dependency' in Indigenous communities. Public servants from PM&C admitted the influence of the Forrest Review on Indigenous affairs policy, particularly with respect to the replacement of the RJCP, which the Abbott government pronounced 'a complete disaster' in its first months of implementation (SFPARC 2017d: 49–50). Within months, the government had introduced the new CDP in its place.

In line with the Forrest Review's critique of welfare dependence, the Abbott government introduced a new compulsory form of work-like activity and imposed it on all eligible CDP jobseekers (PM&C 2017).

The work-for-the-dole provisions of the CDP were noticeably more onerous than the equivalent expectations of participants in Jobactive—the mainstream employment placement program that had replaced the JSA—and were designed to address the perceived 'high level of idleness in communities' and to 'establish social norms' in remote Indigenous communities, as recommended by the Forrest Review (ANAO 2017: 27). The CDP applied to 60 regions, covering 75 per cent of the Australian landmass and incorporating approximately 1,000 isolated communities. While the program was not ostensibly targeted at Indigenous people, of the 33,000 participants in 2017, 85 per cent identified as Indigenous (SFPARC 2017d: 46).

Participants on income support living in the CDP-designated areas and aged between 18 and 49 years were initially required to undertake up to 25 hours of work-related activity over five days each week, for 46 weeks of the year, from the beginning of their enrolment in the program.[1] This was equivalent to working for $10.80 per hour—well below the minimum wage (of $19.84 per hour in 2020). In contrast, Jobactive participants between the ages of 30 and 59 at the same time were required to complete 15 hours per week, over 26 weeks of the year, after 12 months of unemployment, and these work-related activities were defined more broadly to include study, training and volunteer work (for a more detailed comparison, see Fowkes 2016a: 5). The government explained that the considerably higher expectation of work-related activity for CDP participants was due to the limited utility of them being required to complete 20 job searches per month, as required of Jobactive participants, thus acknowledging the extremely limited labour market in remote communities (PM&C 2017: 47).

The implementation of the CDP was notable for its lack of consultation and public debate. The program was implemented administratively, rapidly and out of public view, by amending contracts with providers and treating them as 'commercial in confidence'. The contract revisions were issued on 28 May 2015, with signatures required by 12 June, for rollout of the new program on 1 July. The government did present a Bill to Parliament to amend the *Social Security (Administration) Act 1999* in December 2015 (five months after the program's implementation).

---

1   From the start of 2019, this was reduced to 20 hours of work-related activity a week, as a measure introduced in the Commonwealth Government's 2018 budget (PM&C 2018) in response to widespread criticism.

The Bill was intended to support the new compliance system established under the CDP, though details were to be left to the minister to determine through legislative instruments. The Bill was reviewed by the Senate Finance and Public Administration Legislation Committee, which reported in March 2016. However, when the federal election was called in May 2016, the Bill lapsed and was not reintroduced. This meant there was very little in the way of parliamentary debate of the changes and similarly limited media attention. There was widespread criticism from peak bodies and advocacy organisations of the limited consultation process and rushed implementation, particularly for the apparent focus on provider perspectives only (for example, HRLC 2017: 5; Jobs Australia 2017).

Creating a market: Service provision in employment services

As observed earlier, contestability has been applied to employment services in remote communities since the Howard government, requiring providers to compete to win tenders to deliver publicly funded employment services. The Gillard government reduced the number of available contracts to one provider for each region, forcing considerable market consolidation. Consolidation was exacerbated with the Abbott government's introduction of the CDP in 2015. The first round of CDP contracts saw the 60 regions covered by providers in the following categories:

- 21 Indigenous corporations, covering 25 regions
- three regional councils (Northern Territory local government), covering five regions
- seven not-for-profit non-Indigenous corporations, covering 10 regions
- six for-profit non-Indigenous companies, covering 20 regions.[2]

This concentration of ownership was somewhat forced by the government. In a submission to the ANAO, Jobs Australia (2017) observed that the requirement for a single contract per region meant many existing providers

---

2   In response to widespread criticism of the lack of Indigenous organisations chosen as CDP providers, Minister for Indigenous Affairs Nigel Scullion announced all providers would be Indigenous organisations for the 2019 provider selection process (Scullion 2019). This has resulted in a number of joint ventures between local Aboriginal-controlled corporations and for-profit and not-for-profit employment service providers, and some reduction in the concentration of ownership (NIAA 2019).

who won contracts were required to deliver services to new cohorts, and some new providers had little to no experience in delivering employment services. Not all regions were subject to competition between potential providers—indeed, the government asked some organisations to partner with others after the closing date, to cover additional regions in the absence of viable alternatives, and they reported that they saw little choice because they thought they would lose other contracts. Some successful providers were given contracts with very little notice and had difficulty procuring the necessary computer equipment and training, and housing staff near the sites. This is clearly a very 'thin' market, with nonexistent competition in many areas, pointing to the inappropriate use of competitive tendering.

The consolidation of providers created further challenges, including a lack of local knowledge, a lack of experience working with Indigenous jobseekers and an absence of links to local communities and local employers. Many of these issues were identified in an inquiry held by the Senate Finance and Public Administration References Committee (SFPARC 2017a) into the 'Appropriateness and Effectiveness of the Objectives, Design, Implementation and Evaluation of the Community Development Program'. The inquiry received submissions and heard testimony from many providers and community organisations working in remote areas, including during hearings held in Kalgoorlie, Western Australia; Alice Springs in the Northern Territory; and Townsville and Palm Island, in Queensland.

The Senate inquiry noted the challenges raised by the significant distances between the providers' head offices and the remote communities they served. In several reported cases, the distances were too great to allow staff from the providers to visit work-for-the-dole sites to monitor attendance more than once a fortnight. Furthermore, the lack of cultural awareness among provider staff working with community members was exacerbated by the use of short-term staff with no local knowledge, including migrant workers on temporary visas.

CDP cost to government

The CDP proved to be a costly program to maintain. A performance audit conducted by the ANAO in 2017 noted the Abbott government redirected resources from other Indigenous programs into the CDP to fund the expensive 'work-like activities'. The CDP cost twice as much as the RJCP had per jobseeker ($10,494 per annum compared with $5,071 per annum) and the cost per jobseeker in the CDP in 2016–17 was five times the cost per jobseeker for Jobactive participants (ANAO 2017: 41).

The expenditure on the CDP was designed to be demand-driven, with payments to providers depending on the size of their caseload, the number of employment outcomes achieved and the delivery of activity fulfilment requirements. For example, providers were paid incentives for employment outcomes, where a CDP participant was placed in outside employment and retained the position for 13 and 26 weeks, resulting in payments to the provider of $2,250 and $5,250, respectively (Fowkes 2016b: 3). Payment for employment outcomes was a relatively small factor in the overall scheme, however, reflecting only $18.92 million (7 per cent) of the total $268.52 million expenditure for 2015–16 (PM&C 2017). The overall cost was dominated by the CDP Activity Outcome payment, which was paid to providers at a rate of $12,450 per annum per jobseeker for hours attended by participants in work-like activities (Fowkes 2016b: 3). This activity payment amounted to $204.2 million (76 per cent) of total spending on the program in 2015–16 (PM&C 2017). The incentives in this payment scheme were thus clearly skewed towards providing work-for-the-dole activities and monitoring attendance, rather than pursuing the (much riskier) employment outcomes requiring the participant to remain in a placement for 26 weeks (ANAO 2017).

Managing the providers

The market logic of activity-based payment was further reinforced in the performance management techniques applied by the government to contractors. The regulation of providers through close monitoring of KPIs is often presented as a mechanism to ensure efficient and effective delivery of services. It is clear, however, the performance measurements in this program did not measure service quality and the government had little recourse in the case of provider failure.

As public servants from PM&C explained in detail to the Senate inquiry (SFPARC 2017d: 50–53), the CDP providers were given three KPIs to meet.[3] The first related to the delivery of employment services and

---

3   Details of the contractual relationship between the government and the providers have been made publicly available since the NIAA took over responsibility for the administration of the CDP in 2019, and the operational guidelines and current sample head agreements can be found on the NIAA's website (NIAA 2020).

measured the number of jobseekers who had 'monthly contact' with providers documented in the government's information technology (IT) system and the number of jobseekers with an 'individualised job plan', and assessed a sample of 'tailored assistance and quality training to overcome barriers to employment' and 'quality post-placement support'. The second KPI related to the availability, attendance rates and appropriateness of work-like activities organised by the provider. The third measured the providers' performance against a regional employment target, using data from the Australian Bureau of Statistics and regional data on the labour market (SFPARC 2017d: 50).

Providers were assessed internally by PM&C every six months. For providers who fell below the expected standards, a Performance Improvement Plan could be developed, and providers would be 'dealt with directly' (SFPARC 2017d: 52). Assessments of performance were treated as commercial in confidence and not publicly available. The issue of provider performance is problematic, given the lack of feasible competition or choice in many regions and the secrecy surrounding the assessment process. The Senate inquiry heard that only two providers had been changed since the RJCP began in 2013, pointing to a problem of 'sunk costs' on the part of the government, given that even when PM&C did issue breach notices for poor performance, it had few options (Altman, in SFPARC 2017c: 18). The ANAO report also noted two cases of fraud in particular and observed that one provider had its funding agreement terminated after being found to be involved in fraud but was then subcontracted by the incoming provider to continue to deliver services (ANAO 2017: 35). According to a submission to the ANAO by the peak body Jobs Australia in 2017, 'most providers are judged to be underperforming' when measured against the unrealistic regional employment targets that do not adequately reflect historical performance or local labour market issues (Jobs Australia 2017: 12).

Clearly, the quantitative monitoring of provider performance missed many important aspects of service quality. PM&C admitted to the Senate that it did not monitor staff turnover or employee numbers in providers' offices (SFPARC 2017d: 56), even though other witnesses to the hearing suggested turnover was very high in many provider organisations. The ANAO reported on the wide variation in the ratio of jobseekers to staff across different providers, ranging from eight to 117 jobseekers to one CDP staffer, with an average of 28 jobseekers to one provider staff member (ANAO 2017: 42). PM&C paid no attention to the number of Indigenous staff in community-facing roles or the cultural competence of staff.

Other aspects of the providers' activities also demand closer examination. There was nothing in the KPIs designed to capture the quality of training provided to jobseekers or the actual cost of delivering quality work-like activities. The flat rate of payment for all jobseekers in work-for-the-dole activities created a risk for providers in expending extra funds on higher-quality activities if participants might not attend (Fowkes 2016b). The training arranged by providers was not necessarily designed to be useful to the needs of local employers (SFPARC 2017b: 9). Some witnesses deplored the 'training for the sake of training' offered in some regions, which allowed local contractors to make a profit while delivering training of poor quality with few participants (SFPARC 2017b: 28). Of even more concern was the lack of scrutiny of the compulsory job plans for every jobseeker, as there was no requirement to show the jobseeker understood the process or the obligations set out in the plan. As one Centrelink employee from Alice Springs suggested to the Senate inquiry:

> You could ask anyone that's been to one of the CDP providers what's in their job plan, and they will tell you that they don't know. That's purely because there is no access to interpreters when these people are negotiating their contract. (SFPARC 2017d: 18)

PM&C's simple checking for the existence of a plan in the IT system failed to capture the futility of the exercise for many participants. The focus on administrative compliance would not encourage providers to take risks in providing quality services—an issue observed in other similar markets for mainstream employment services (Considine et al. 2020).

Many witnesses and submissions to the Senate inquiry noted the lack of employment outcomes from the scheme and argued the CDP did not address the real reasons jobseekers in remote communities were unable to participate in the labour market. For example, witnesses pointed to issues of poor housing, homelessness and mobility as obstacles to finding employment (SFPARC 2017c: 8); the lack of recognition of carer obligations, which would prevent a participant from taking full-time work or working a long distance from home (SFPARC 2017b: 28, 34); and the impacts of intergenerational trauma and family violence, which make jobseeking very difficult (SFPARC 2017b: 33). Others pointed to structural factors including institutional racism and prejudice that mean 'Aboriginal people are seen as only being suitable for low-level jobs' (SFPARC 2017b: 34). One business leader from Kalgoorlie observed that local businesses could not afford to take on new staff due to insurance costs (SFPARC 2017b: 9). Another witness argued not enough support was offered through the CDP for those who were 'chronically unemployed' (SFPARC 2017b: 16).

During the Senate inquiry, providers also criticised the government's KPIs and the way they were monitored. Many pointed to the high administrative costs, which left little funding or time for the more purposeful activities including job training, mentoring and the development of appropriate activities. One provider observed: 'We feel that it's become an administrative program more than anything else. The outcomes that we can get back on the community are non-existent. We're chasing our tail, continually trying to administer the program as a whole' (Miller, in SFPARC 2017c: 2).

Another provider complained: 'We're having enough trouble just basically keeping our heads above water and … providing any real, solid training for people is just very difficult' (Coffey, in SFPARC 2017b: 40). Another estimated that between 30 and 40 per cent of the provider's funding went to the regular reporting of basic services and monitoring compliance, rather than providing mentoring, training or other services directly to the jobseekers (SFPARC 2017d: 15). The compliance system based on reporting multiple small activities (updating job plans, monthly appointments with jobseekers, daily reporting of attendance at work-related activities) was expensive, and the providers were not funded adequately to meet these requirements alongside delivering quality services (Bach-Mortensen and Barlow 2021).

The inadequacy of funding for the providers was further compounded by the costs of delivering services in remote areas. Many providers argued the government's funding agreements did not consider the issue of remoteness. For example, one provider in the West Australian Goldfields told the Senate committee:

> I'm based at Warburton and I can tell you that there is absolutely no recognition in the program about the isolation of the Warburton community, for example. It is a thousand miles from the nearest Centrelink office, it is a thousand miles from the nearest bank. The costs of providing these services out here are very different to what they are for a provider in Kalgoorlie or Alice Springs or another centre. (McLean, SFPARC 2017b: 35)

Another witness, a police superintendent in the Gascoyne region of Western Australia, explained the challenges of delivering quality work-like activities from a distance, considering the perverse incentives built into the PM&C payment structure, which left providers in a position of considerable uncertainty:

> If the CDP worker does not show up, which is quite often the case, the service provider doesn't get paid for it. Look at Burringurrah, which is about five or six hours out of Carnarvon. MAX Employment are based in Carnarvon, so they drive out to Burringurrah. There are 37 members that are registered for CDP at Burringurrah, but traditionally three people will show up, so it's not a good business proposition for them to go out all that way to get paid for three people who are going to show up. (Bolt, in SFPARC 2017b: 4)

The complexity of the government's IT system for reporting also created challenges for the providers and several moved the reporting function to central offices in larger urban areas, as local staff did not have the skills to use the system and the internet connections in remote areas were often inadequate. The lack of recognition of the complexity of service delivery in very remote areas was further compounded by a payment structure based on mutual obligation and enforcing jobseeker behaviours, which were out of the provider's control. The next section will look at the role of providers in reporting breaches, in the context of the incentive to avoid losing payments by reporting all 'no shows', without exception.

Managing the jobseekers

As observed earlier, the providers received the bulk of their payments for the CDP Activity Outcomes—paid only for eligible jobseekers attending work-like activities daily. Under the Job Seeker Compliance Framework, if a jobseeker did not attend an activity, they were reported as absent in the IT system and would be 'breached' for the nonattendance, unless they were deemed to have a 'valid excuse'. Jobseekers who were breached could lose one-tenth of their fortnightly income support for each day absent. If a penalty was applied but the jobseeker was 're-engaged' in work-like activities within two weeks, payments could be restored to the provider (but not to the jobseeker). Under the funding agreements, providers were penalised if they did not report a jobseeker's absence (Fowkes 2016b: 3). This system of penalising providers financially when they had not breached did not apply to providers in Jobactive.

This incentive built into the payment structure for CDP providers had a stark impact on the number of breaches reported by the providers. In several updated studies based on the quarterly data released by the Department of Jobs and Small Business, researcher Lisa Fowkes consistently showed the CDP breaches were disproportionate and excessive when compared with jobseeker breaches in the mainstream Jobactive program. For example, there were 23 times more Jobactive participants than CDP participants, yet from the time CDP was implemented, there have been consistently more penalties applied to CDP participants than to Jobactive participants. As Fowkes noted:

> In 2016, 111,086 *jobactive* participants took part in Work for the Dole, attracting 103,533 no show no pay penalties in that year— an average of about 0.9 penalties per participant. An estimated 30,000 CDP participants participated in Work for the Dole in that year, yet they received 161,507 no show no pay penalties—an average of more than 5 penalties per participant. (2019: 11–12)

The more consequential form of penalty that can be applied to CDP and Jobactive participants is for 'serious failure'. These penalties are imposed on jobseekers who are found to have refused suitable work, caused their unemployment by their own actions or engage in 'persistent noncompliance'—in particular, if they have had three no-show, no-pay breaches in a six-month period. The penalty is a suspension of income support for up to eight weeks at a time. As part of the Senate Estimates process in October 2017, PM&C reported in response to a question on notice that for the period from 1 July 2015 to 30 June 2017, across the CDP and Jobactive programs, 15,127 people received a serious failure penalty, of whom 92 per cent were Indigenous (Senate Finance and Public Administration Legislation Committee 2017). It is noteworthy that 3,493 of the Indigenous jobseekers penalised under this system had received five or more serious failure penalties over the two-year period—indicating the penalties are not the deterrent the government assumes and there are more likely to be systemic issues preventing Indigenous individuals from complying with program requirements.

One of the key issues identified in the Senate inquiry was the problematic role of Centrelink, as its services are very difficult to access from remote areas. Many communities affected by CDP have few functional telephone landlines and limited or no mobile phone coverage, few computers with internet connection and limited postal services. There are further challenges associated with accessing or providing information through the MyGov website, especially with the lack of interpreter services and low literacy and numeracy levels in many communities. Many witnesses observed the long waiting times on hold when calling Centrelink for jobseekers, who often used up limited mobile phone credit or were forced to use a telephone in a public area. With all these technological, communications and literacy challenges, contact with the government agency was widely experienced as 'cumbersome and ineffective' (Kral, in SFPARC 2017c: 20).

The effect of this system of no-show, no-pay and serious failure breaches on individual jobseekers and their families could be severe. As Victoria Baird from Save the Children in the East Kimberley of Western Australia noted during the Senate inquiry:

> The rules can be too strict, often not taking into consideration the fact that many don't have access to transport, often don't have credit on their mobile phone, and are frequently dealing with family violence and health concerns. Those who do find their payments have been stopped struggle to navigate the system to get their payments restarted ... [There are many] individuals who are not currently claiming payment because the thought of going through this process is too daunting. (Baird, in SFPARC 2017b: 13)

Another witness, Damien McLean, a community development advisor with the Ngaanyatjarra Council in Western Australia, observed that '[p]eople who are already very poor have become a good deal poorer' (SFPARC 2017b: 38). In some communities, the impact on household income has been extreme, as shown by this comment from the CEO of Ngaanyatjarra Council: '[B]etween 15 and 20 per cent of [our] jobseekers don't receive any money—that's just under 600 job seekers who aren't receiving any money' (Coffey, in SFPARC 2017b: 40). Community members also inevitably suffered from the consequences of these breaches. Witnesses to the Senate inquiry reported increased crime, families being separated, individuals accumulating debts and fines and risking incarceration, high levels of dependence on those family members with income and pressure exerted especially on older people receiving a pension. Community stores observed decreasing food sales, indicating high levels of poverty (for a more detailed discussion of this, see Staines and Smith 2021).

A further consequence of the high levels of punitive breaches associated with the CDP was the overall level of disengagement from the program, leaving individuals without any income at all, as they were neither in employment nor claiming income support. This is explained in part by the challenges of contacting Centrelink to negotiate a restoration of payments after a breach and the unwillingness, especially of younger people, to engage in a government program that appears illegitimate (Fowkes 2019: 18). Fowkes argues the diminishing caseload reported by PM&C indicates growing numbers of people who are leaving or failing to enrol in the CDP. She notes the 17 per cent drop in the CDP caseload, from 36,642 participants on 1 July 2015 to 30,380 on 30 June 2018, and observes that 59 per cent of the decline is among people under the age of 25 years. Altman gave similar evidence to the Senate inquiry, noting the median individual income dropped between 2011 and 2016 by approximately $200 per adult per week (SFPARC 2017c: 13).

The limited value of 'work-related experience'

The legitimacy and appropriateness of the work-for-the-dole activities offered by many CDP providers were questionable at best. In some cases, the 'make-work' nature of the activities was obvious. One witness to the Senate inquiry observed, for example, that '[w]ork-like activities are generally never specific to a location or across a region. They are activities for activities' sake' (Miller, SFPARC 2017c: 6). Another CDP case manager admitted: 'We need to get a balance between actively engaging people and boring them silly' (SFPARC 2017b: 60).

In other cases, the poor design of the program allowed providers to engage in exploitative behaviour, requiring participants to undertake work in 'actual jobs that need to be performed in the community' (such as working in the store or clinic), but only being paid unemployment benefits for doing so (SFPARC 2017b: 36–37)—effectively below the minimum wage. The National Campaign Coordinator from the Australian Council of Trade Unions also noted:

> Rather than creating employment opportunities, this program gives a pool of free labour where the program is in operation. One of the most pernicious things I have seen with this program is that the current government has opened it up to for-profit business … I personally have had a conversation with a CEO who told me he had some guys on sick leave and annual leave so he backfilled those positions with CDP workers. (Keys, in SFPARC 2017d: 21)

From a First Peoples' perspective, the lack of cultural appropriateness and dignity associated with the work-like activities is also a source of anger and frustration. Chansey Peach, member for Namatjira in the Northern Territory Legislative Assembly, spoke of his observations of 'demeaning' and 'insulting' activities, including Elders being obliged to 'pick up rubbish' and elderly women being taught 'art' or 'knitting'. He noted: '[T]hese are traditional women who would much rather go out on country and wild harvest bush tucker to meet wholesale and market demands' (Peach, in SFPARC 2017c: 34). Other witnesses noted the inappropriateness of requiring feuding families to attend CDP activities together at the same site (SFPARC 2017b: 15) or the 'alienating' experience of being forced to find work 'off country', away from community and culture (SFPARC 2017c: 44). This was very different to the more flexible arrangements under the old CDEP. The lack of respect for, and accommodation of, cultural and ceremonial obligations also prompted criticism. One witness from the Kalgoorlie–Boulder Chamber of Commerce and Industry observed:

> The feeling out there in the community is one of resentment, particularly when something comes up. We have cultural obligations we need to attend to and we have family obligations. All our obligations are different and they don't sit in the stereotypes of white people. So we have white people making these policies that don't take into consideration our obligations in the community. When they fulfil these obligations, they get penalised, and they get penalised for eight weeks. (Carmody, in SFPARC 2017b: 10)

For Aboriginal-controlled provider organisations, the desire to make sure their services were culturally appropriate had been discouraged by PM&C, as the chairperson of Western Australia's Aarnja Limited reported to the Senate inquiry:

> While we were trying down on our end to fit a cultural match to our organisation and ensure it had Aboriginal community control and that communities had a say, we saw these people come up from Canberra to tell us, 'This is how it is, we really don't care what you've done'. (Sibosado, in SFPARC 2017b: 56)

The contrast with the former CDEP—which had not only allowed for culturally appropriate flexibility, but also offered work that was meaningful and important to the community itself—was a theme raised by almost every Indigenous organisation represented at the Senate inquiry.

Conclusion: Market failure and ideology

The incremental shifts towards marketisation of remote employment services occurred over two decades and prompted relatively little counter-mobilisation or protest outside the First Nations organisations and communities most directly affected. For most of the Australian population and media, what happens in remote Indigenous communities is 'out of sight, out of mind', and successive governments have avoided sustained criticism. This incremental process of institutional change has profoundly disrupted the previously settled understanding of First Peoples' self-determination and the right to be treated separately, with policies and programs that are culturally appropriate and community led.

The marketisation of employment services in remote communities has revealed several major design flaws. The Productivity Commission identified several critical factors in evaluating the markets used in the delivery of human services in its 2016 report *Introducing Competition and Informed User Choice into Human Services: Identifying sectors for reform*, and stipulated several additional reasons for caution when considering service delivery in remote Indigenous communities. These included the considerably higher cost of service delivery in remote areas, along with the need to work effectively across cultural and language barriers and to cater to the needs of First Nations communities who were more likely to experience profound disadvantage across many interconnected areas including education, health, disability, housing, employment, cost of living and experience of the criminal justice system (PC 2016: Ch. 7). The Productivity Commission also noted the high levels of mobility among First Nations people, and the high likelihood of negative experiences of government service provision in the past. It observed that 'effective government stewardship is important' (PC 2016: 140), particularly in thin markets. On this basis, the commission recommended contestability be applied in social services with care, with provision made for an effective and accessible complaints process and the assurance that there is a 'provider of last resort' in the case of provider failure. The government failed to heed these warnings with the CDP.

Having examined the design of the employment services market in remote communities, it is clear the move to commissioning a single provider for each region resulted in the disappearance of many Aboriginal community-controlled organisations. The loss of these potentially viable alternatives meant there would be no 'credible threat of replacement' when a provider failed to deliver (PC 2016: 8). There was no apparent reward for providers who sought to improve the quality of their services or introduce innovations that were appropriate for the community they served. The design of the contestable market meant there was a complete disconnect between the government as purchaser and the users of employment services in affected communities. The government paid little attention to the user experience and gathered very little information about the challenges faced by providers at the front line. Instead, PM&C focused on monitoring narrow performance metrics and did not collect adequate information about the true cost and quality of the services provided. While the incentives driving the behaviour of the providers were aligned with the government's aims to reduce welfare dependency, the high disengagement rates among participants indicated the penalties were too high. Community resentment of the program and growing disengagement appear to have prevented the government from achieving its own objectives. In summary, the apparent advantages of a contestable market for service delivery were outweighed by the flawed design, which gave none of the usual market-based advantages of choice, control and empowerment for service users (Carey 2016: 36). Indeed, it seems reasonable to conclude—as the peak provider body Jobs Australia did in 2017—that 'CDP is doing more harm than good' (Jobs Australia 2017: 5).

In seeking to explain the decisions made over time to introduce market logic into Indigenous remote communities, it is noteworthy there is little for governments to gain in terms of electoral politics, given the relative invisibility of Indigenous policy in national politics. It seems more persuasive to assume the decisions have been motivated by a bipartisan ideological commitment to market forces, at the elite level, persisting in opening new areas of government service delivery to the for-profit and not-for-profit sectors (Meagher and Wilson 2015). Gingrich (2011: 6–7) argues that because there is considerable voter resistance to private businesses delivering services, the policy is more easily applied to services that are 'less salient or more marginal' than those that are more universal, and this certainly applies to the CDP in remote communities. The benefits appear to be relatively small for those providers who have entered the market, however, given the highly restrictive funding agreements that have been applied to the CDP providers. The compliance focus of the program appears to have been the more powerful driver for the government, as it attempted to modify the behaviour of apparently 'deviant' and 'dysfunctional' welfare recipients living in remote communities.

This evokes a deeper trend in Indigenous affairs, which reflects a path dependency stretching back to the early colonial era. The current treatment of unemployment in remote communities builds on earlier values associated with European settlers as colonisers that demand Aboriginal people assimilate, deny space for cultural difference and adopt a paternalistic and racist approach that justifies government-led interventions into Indigenous families and communities. Most striking is the abandonment of self-determination and the dismantling of the hundreds of Indigenous community-based organisations that had emerged during the CDEP era. These organisations had both cultural and political authority and were a source of Indigenous pride and purpose, but their economic power was built on government funding in the form of block grants received through the CDEP. The marketisation of employment services in remote communities is the next step in a path-dependent process designed to end self-determination, weaken the Aboriginal community-controlled sector and eliminate the Indigenous right to cultural difference.

Epilogue

As part of the 2021 budget, the Morrison Government announced its intention to substantially reform employment services for remote communities, indicating it would replace the CDP with a new 'remote engagement program' from 2023. In the interim, the government announced the mutual obligation requirement to engage in 'work-like activities' would be voluntary rather than compulsory from May 2021. This, combined with the decision in 2019 to only engage Indigenous organisations as CDP providers, suggests the Abbott government's risky conversion of the remote community development program to a mainstream work-for-the-dole program could potentially be undone.

This is a response to substantial efforts by First Nations peak bodies leading the Aboriginal community-controlled sector to encourage the government to adopt a partnership approach in determining policies that affect First Nations people. In particular, the peak bodies have worked closely with the government to 'refresh' the overarching 'Closing the Gap' targets that aim to reduce inequality between First Australians and non-

Indigenous Australians across a range of key indicators. The Coalition of Aboriginal and Torres Strait Islander Peak Organisations has co-designed the *National Agreement on Closing the Gap* with the Australian national, state and territory governments and, having participated in designing the targets, is now actively monitoring the implementation and sharing in the decision-making. This is a significant shift in the policy environment, reflecting a renewed commitment to self-determination through community-controlled organisations representing the interests and priorities of First Nations.

Details of the proposed reform for remote employment are not yet clear, however, the government is currently engaged in a two-year consultation process that, importantly, included 'roundtable' and 'town hall' consultation sessions in remote communities between September and November 2021. According to the National Indigenous Australians Agency (NIAA 2021), 'the program will be fit-for-purpose and better match the needs of Indigenous Australians and communities, reflecting the diversity of remote Australia'. Their discussion paper acknowledges the government's awareness of the need for locally formulated solutions, the lack of viable paid employment opportunities in some remote labour markets, the potential need for improved training better targeted to the needs of the participants and potential employers, the importance of addressing barriers to employment including culturally specific requirements and the need for mutual obligation programs to be 'fair and reasonable' (NIAA 2021). While these discussion points respond to many of the identified flaws in the CDP, the continuing role of market-based services is unclear. It will be critical to ensure new programs can deliver quality support and employment services to remote communities without punishing and discriminating against First Nations people. The involvement of First Nations community-controlled organisations in the design and delivery of these programs (as happened with the original CDEP) offers the chance to learn from past mistakes.

References

Altman, J. (2007). In the name of the market? In J. Altman & M. Hinkson (eds), *Coercive Reconciliation: Stabilise, normalise, exit Aboriginal Australia*. Melbourne: Arena Publications.

Altman, J. (2016). Bawinanga and CDEP: The vibrant life, and near death, of a major Aboriginal corporation in Arnhem Land. In K. Jordan (ed.), *Better than Welfare? Work and livelihoods for Indigenous Australians after CDEP*. CAEPR Monograph No. 36. Canberra: ANU Press. doi.org/10.22459/CAEPR36. 08.2016.

Altman, J. (2017). *Submission (No. 26) to the Senate Finance and Public Administration References Committee Inquiry into the Appropriateness and Effectiveness of the Objectives, Design, Implementation and Evaluation of the Community Development Program (CDP)*. Canberra: Parliament of Australia. Available from: www.aph.gov.au/Parliamentary_Business/Committees/Senate/ Finance_and_Public_Administration/CDP/Submissions.

Australian National Audit Office (ANAO). (2017). *Design and Implementation of the Community Development Programme*. The Auditor-General ANAO Report No. 14 2017–18, Performance Audit. Canberra: ANAO. Available from: www. anao.gov.au/sites/default/files/ANAO_Report_2017-2018_14a.pdf.

Bach-Mortensen, A.M. & Barlow, J. (2021). Outsourced austerity or improved services? A systematic review and thematic synthesis of the experiences of social care providers and commissioners in quasi-markets. *Social Science & Medicine*, *276*(May): 113844. doi.org/10.1016/j.socscimed.2021.113844.

Blakeman, B. (2016). Appendix 1: Annotated timeline of key developments. In K. Jordan (ed.), *Better than Welfare? Work and livelihoods for Indigenous Australians after CDEP*. CAEPR Monograph No. 36. Canberra: ANU Press. doi.org/10.22459/CAEPR36.08.2016.

Bradfield, S. (2006). Separatism or status-quo? Indigenous affairs from the birth of land rights to the death of ATSIC. *Australian Journal of Politics & History*, *52*(1): 80–97. doi.org/10.1111/j.1467-8497.2006.00409a.x.

Carey, G. (2016). Is the Productivity Commission still fit for purpose? In P. Smyth, E. Malbon & G. Carey (eds), *Social Service Futures and the Productivity Commission: A Power to Persuade dialogue*. [Online]. University of New South Wales & The Power to Persuade. Available from: www.powertopersuade.org. au/social-services-futures.

Considine, M., Lewis, J.M. & O'Sullivan, S. (2011). Quasi-markets and service delivery flexibility following a decade of employment assistance reform in Australia. *Journal of Social Policy*, *40*(4): 811–33. doi.org/10.1017/ S0047279411000213.

Considine, M., O'Sullivan, S., McGann, M. & Nguyen, P. (2020). Locked-in or locked-out: Can a public services market really change? *Journal of Social Policy*, *49*(4): 850–71. doi.org/10.1017/S0047279419000941.

Department of the Prime Minister and Cabinet (PM&C). (2017). *Submission (No. 36) to the Senate Finance and Public Administration References Committee Inquiry into the Appropriateness and Effectiveness of the Objectives, Design, Implementation and Evaluation of the Community Development Program (CDP)*. Canberra: Parliament of Australia. Available from: www.aph.gov. au/Parliamentary_Business/Committees/Senate/Finance_and_Public_ Administration/CDP/Submissions.

Department of the Prime Minister and Cabinet (PM&C). (2018). *2018–19 Budget: Community Development Programme reforms*. Budget factsheet. Canberra: PM&C. Available from: www.pmc.gov.au/sites/default/files/ publications/budget-fact-sheet-cdp-reforms_0.pdf.

Forrest, A. (2014). *Creating Parity*. Canberra: Commonwealth of Australia. Available from: www.niaa.gov.au/sites/default/files/publications/Forrest-Review.pdf.

Fowkes, L. (2016a). *Impact on social security penalties of increased remote work for the dole requirements*. CAEPR Working Paper No. 112/2016. Canberra: Centre for Aboriginal Economic Policy Research, The Australian National University. Available from: caepr.cass.anu.edu.au/research/publications/impact-social-security-penalties-increased-remote-work-dole-requirements.

Fowkes, L. (2016b). *Update on Impact of the Community Development Programme on Social Security Penalties*. Report for Jobs Australia, 9 September. Available from: web.archive.org/web/20210325184134/https://www.ja.com.au/sites/ default/files/cdp_penalties_-_september_update.pdf.

Fowkes, L. (2018). Settler-state ambitions and bureaucratic ritual at the frontiers of the labour market: Indigenous Australians and remote employment services 2011–2017. Unpublished PhD thesis, The Australian National University, Canberra.

Fowkes, L. (2019). *The application of income support obligations and penalties to remote Indigenous Australians, 2013–18*. CAEPR Working Paper No. 126/2019. Canberra: Centre for Aboriginal Economic Policy Research, The Australian National University. Available from: openresearch-repository.anu.edu.au/ bitstream/1885/156433/1/Working_Paper_126_2019.pdf.

Fowkes, L. & Li, J. (2018). Designing a remote employment program: Lessons from the past and a proposal for the future. *Journal of Australian Political Economy*, (82): 57–83.

Gingrich, J. (2011). *Making Markets in the Welfare State: The politics of varying market reforms*. Cambridge, UK: Cambridge University Press. doi.org/10.1017/ CBO9780511791529.

Human Rights Law Centre (HRLC). (2017). *Submission: A fair and community-led approach to remote community and economic development—Inquiry into the Community Development Programme (CDP) by the Senate Standing Committees on Finance and Public Administration.* 23 June. Melbourne: HRLC. Available from: www.hrlc.org.au/submissions/2017/6/28/submission.

Hunter, B. (2016). Some statistical content for analysis of CDEP. In K. Jordan (ed.), *Better than Welfare? Work and livelihoods for Indigenous Australians after CDEP.* CAEPR Monograph No. 36. Canberra: ANU Press. doi.org/10.22459/CAEPR36.08.2016.

Jobs Australia. (2017). *Submission in Response to the ANAO Audit: The design and implementation of the Community Development Programme.* April 2017. Armidale, NSW: Jobs Australia.

Jonas, W. (2001). CDEP, racial discrimination and social justice. In F. Morphy & W.G. Sanders (eds), *The Indigenous Welfare Economy and the CDEP Scheme* (pp. 11–18). CAEPR Research Monograph No. 20/2001. Canberra: ANU Press. doi.org/10.22459/CAEPR20.05.2004.

Jordan, K. & Altman, J. (2016). From welfare to work, or work to welfare? In K. Jordan (ed.), *Better than Welfare? Work and livelihoods for Indigenous Australians after CDEP.* CAEPR Monograph No. 36. Canberra: ANU Press. doi.org/10.22459/CAEPR36.08.2016.01.

Mahoney, J. & Thelen, K. (2010). *Explaining Institutional Change: Ambiguity, agency and power.* Cambridge, UK: Cambridge University Press. doi.org/10.1017/CBO9780511806414.

Martin, D. (2001). Community development in the context of welfare dependence. In F. Morphy & W.G. Sanders (eds), *The Indigenous Welfare Economy and the CDEP Scheme* (pp. 31–38). CAEPR Research Monograph No. 20/2001. Canberra: ANU Press. doi.org/10.22459/CAEPR20.05.2004.

Meagher, G. & Wilson, S. (2015). The politics of market encroachment: Policymaker rationales and voter responses. In G. Meagher & S. Goodwin (eds), *Markets, Rights and Power in Australian Social Policy* (pp. 29–96). Sydney: Sydney University Press. dx.doi.org/10.30722/sup.9781920899950.

Nakata, M.N. (2007). *Disciplining the Savages: Savaging the disciplines.* Canberra: Aboriginal Studies Press.

National Indigenous Australians Agency (NIAA). (2019). *Community Development Program Regions List and Map.* [Online]. Canberra: NIAA. Available from: www.niaa.gov.au/resource-centre/indigenous-affairs/community-development-programme-regions.

National Indigenous Australians Agency (NIAA). (2020). *Community Development Program (CDP) Head Agreement and Operational Guidance*. Canberra: NIAA. Available from: www.niaa.gov.au/resource-centre/indigenous-affairs/ cdp-agreement-operational-guidance.

National Indigenous Australians Agency (NIAA). (2021). *New remote engagement program: Public discussion paper*. August. Canberra: NIAA. Available from: www. niaa.gov.au/indigenous-affairs/employment/remote-engagement-program.

Productivity Commission (PC). (2016). *Introducing Competition and Informed User Choice into Human Services: Identifying sectors for reform*. Study Report, November. Canberra: Productivity Commission. Available from: www. pc.gov.au/inquiries/completed/human-services/identifying-reform/report.

Rowse, T. (2001). The political dimensions of community development. In F. Morphy & W.G. Sanders (eds), *The Indigenous Welfare Economy and the CDEP Scheme* (pp. 39–46). CAEPR Research Monograph No. 20/2001. Canberra: ANU Press. doi.org/10.22459/CAEPR20.05.2004.

Rowse, T. (2002). *Indigenous Futures: Choice and development for Aboriginal and Islander Australia*. Sydney: UNSW Press.

Sanders, W. (2001). Adjusting balances: Reshaping the CDEP scheme after 20 good years. In F. Morphy & W.G. Sanders (eds), *The Indigenous Welfare Economy and the CDEP Scheme* (pp. 47–50). CAEPR Research Monograph No. 20/2001. Canberra: ANU Press. doi.org/10.22459/CAEPR20.05.2004.

Sanders, W. (2007). *Changes to CDEP under DEWR: Policy substance and the new contractualism*. CAEPR Topical Issue No. 6. Canberra: Centre for Aboriginal Economic Policy Research, The Australian National University. Available from: caepr.cass.anu.edu.au/sites/default/files/docs/Sanders_CDEP_0.pdf.

Sanders, W. (2016). Reframed as welfare: CDEP's fall from favour. In K. Jordan (ed.), *Better than Welfare? Work and livelihoods for Indigenous Australians after CDEP*. CAEPR Monograph No. 36. Canberra: ANU Press. doi.org/ 10.22459/CAEPR36.08.2016.

Scott, H. (2001). Job creation and mutual obligation: Taparjatjaka Community Government Council, Northern Territory. In F. Morphy & W.G. Sanders (eds), *The Indigenous Welfare Economy and the CDEP Scheme* (pp. 207–8). CAEPR Research Monograph No. 20/2001. Canberra: ANU Press. doi.org/ 10.22459/CAEPR20.05.2004.

Scullion, N. (2019). Minister Scullion: 1,000 subsidised jobs and Indigenous service providers for the Community Development Program. Media release, Senator Nigel Scullion, Minister for Indigenous Affairs, 4 February, Canberra. Available from: www.indigenous.gov.au/news-and-media/announcements/ minister-scullion-1000-subsidised-jobs-and-indigenous-service-providers.

Senate Finance and Public Administration Legislation Committee. (2017). Question on Notice No. 215. Portfolio Question No. 90. *2017–18 Supplementary Budget Estimates.* Canberra: Parliament of Australia. Available from: www.aph.gov. au/api/qon/downloadestimatesquestions/EstimatesQuestion-CommitteeId1-EstimatesRoundId1-PortfolioId3-QuestionNumber215.

Senate Finance and Public Administration References Committee (SFPARC). (2017a). *Appropriateness and Effectiveness of the Objectives, Design, Implementation and Evaluation of the Community Development Program (CDP): Final report.* Canberra: Parliament of Australia. Available from: www.aph.gov.au/Parliamentary_Business/Committees/Senate/Finance_and_Public_Administration/CDP.

Senate Finance and Public Administration References Committee (SFPARC). (2017b). *Appropriateness and Effectiveness of the Objectives, Design, Implementation and Evaluation of the Community Development Program (CDP): Public Hearings, 23 August 2017, Kalgoorlie, WA.* Canberra: Parliament of Australia. Available from: parlinfo.aph.gov.au/parlInfo/search/display/display.w3p;query=Id:%22 committees/commsen/c8fe85ea-a3fd-4976-8c1c-e01ba9b406c6/0000%22.

Senate Finance and Public Administration References Committee (SFPARC). (2017c). *Appropriateness and Effectiveness of the Objectives, Design, Implementation and Evaluation of the Community Development Program (CDP): Public Hearings, 28 August 2017, Alice Springs, NT.* Canberra: Parliament of Australia. Available from: parlinfo.aph.gov.au/parlInfo/search/display/display.w3p;query=Id:%22 committees/commsen/ba158b80-9257-40fa-9c62-d546347ed7b2/0000%22.

Senate Finance and Public Administration References Committee (SFPARC). (2017d). *Appropriateness and Effectiveness of the Objectives, Design, Implementation and Evaluation of the Community Development Program (CDP): Public Hearings, 8 September, Canberra, ACT.* Canberra: Parliament of Australia. Available from: parlinfo.aph.gov.au/parlInfo/search/display/display.w3p;query=Id:%22 committees/commsen/c902f7cd-ff7c-4564-9eeb-d544f5aec5a2/0000%22.

Smith, L.T. (2012). *Decolonizing Methodologies: Research and indigenous peoples.* 2nd edn. London: Zed Books.

Staines, Z. & Smith, K. (2021). Workfare and food in remote Australia: 'I haven't eaten … I'm really at the end …'. *Critical Policy Studies, 16*(1): 36–59. doi.org/10.1080/19460171.2021.1893198.

Streeck, W. & Thelen, K.A. (2005). *Beyond Continuity: Institutional change in advanced political economies.* Oxford, UK: Oxford University Press.

4

A super market? Marketisation, financialisation and private superannuation

Adam Stebbing

Introduction

Many affluent Organisation for Economic Co-operation and Development (OECD) countries have recently adopted private retirement income policies to curb the pressures purportedly placed on national budgets by fiscal austerity and future population ageing. At the forefront of this international trend, Australia established a compulsory system of private occupational superannuation in the early 1990s that requires employers to make set contributions on behalf of their workers into individualised private super accounts. This has transformed the role of private superannuation from an exclusive occupational benefit for about one-third of the workforce in the 1970s to its current role as a retirement savings vehicle for more than 90 per cent of workers (Nielson and Harris 2009). The mandating of occupational superannuation has contributed to the rapid growth of the private super market, with total fund assets climbing from $41 billion in 1987 to a massive $2.6 trillion in 2018 (APRA 2018a).

The expansion of occupational super has coincided with—and contributed to—the increasing financialisation of the private superannuation market. This trend is perhaps most evident in the shift from defined-*benefit* schemes in public sector and corporate funds that guaranteed a private pension to a defined-*contribution* scheme that mandates contributions to be paid into individual savings accounts invested in financial markets. So, as private super has become a major source of lifetime savings, particularly for younger generations, the promise of a healthy and secure retirement for members of virtually every Australian household (of working age) has become increasingly entangled with financial markets over their life course, bringing new risks from volatility and market failure, and compounding existing inequalities.

Why does the transformation of private super matter? The financialisation of private superannuation matters because after decades of rapid expansion it now forms a second tier of retirement income policy, alongside the affluence-tested age pension that forms the first and primary tier (see Spies-Butcher and Stebbing 2011). Retirement income policy is a core social policy domain that addresses the greater risk of poverty or income insecurity households face during old age. It aims to ensure older households have incomes that support a dignified life in later stages of the life course.

This chapter explains how the shifting dynamics of the private superannuation market are reconfiguring the distribution of the financial risks of old age in Australia's retirement income system. The first section explains the conceptual framework that informs my analysis of how private superannuation has been transformed in recent decades. The second section charts how private super was transformed from an occupational benefit for an exclusive minority in the early 1970s into a market for private retirement savings and a second tier of retirement income policy in the 1990s. The third section explains how financialisation and recent reforms continue to restructure how the superannuation market manages financial risks. In concluding, I briefly reflect on the implications of this analysis of the superannuation market for retirement income policy. And finally, in the Epilogue, I reflect on how the early release of superannuation scheme during the Covid-19 pandemic and other recent reforms highlight some consequences of marketisation and financialisation.

Understanding the transformation of private superannuation

The private superannuation market was neither self-forming nor self-regulating, as anticipated by neoclassical economics. As recently as the 1970s, the private superannuation sector had few of the features associated with competitive market exchanges and a weak link with retirement savings. This section establishes the conceptual framework this chapter applies to analyse how private superannuation was transformed from an occupational benefit into a market for retirement savings.

The starting point for my analysis is to understand the private superannuation market as a social institution. This accords with a growing body of research in political economy and economic sociology that theorises markets, such as that for superannuation, as social arenas of exchange that use competitive mechanisms to allocate goods, services and information (Fligstein and Dauter 2007: 107; Gingrich 2011: 8). As social institutions, markets are governed by legislation, regulation, practices and norms that constrain and enable the various actors engaged in exchanging goods and services (Vogel 2007: 26). This understanding refocuses analysis on the complex interactions between the market and the state in particular contexts, rather than assuming with neoclassical economics that state intervention simply reduces market competition (Swedberg 2006: 233). In fact, even if it is not always successful, state action has been shown as necessary to 'craft' the conditions for markets to operate and thrive (Vogel 2018: 4–5; also see Polanyi 1944).

The transformation of private superannuation into a market is often linked to broader claims about how neoliberalism has restructured the welfare states of affluent countries such as Australia over the past four decades.[1] According to Hall and Thelen (2009: 22–24), neoliberalism has become an umbrella concept that is too encompassing to usefully explain the institutional character of recent changes in a specific policy context.

---

1   Neoliberalism is the subject of a burgeoning literature that employs at least four distinct meanings: as the hegemonic ideology of our times, as the political project that reorders state institutions to market logic, as a form of rationality encroaching on everyday life and as the latest phase of contemporary capitalism (Brown 2015; Fox Piven 2015; Harvey 2005; Mirowski 2013; Wacquant 2012). This concept has been deployed widely to explain diverse political and economic developments in myriad contexts (Thelen 2012: 145).

Recent changes widely associated with neoliberalism have been captured with greater analytical clarity by the related concepts of marketisation and financialisation.

Marketisation refers to action by the state that reconfigures the policy architecture of the state and/or builds new institutions that imbue market logic. Market logics have two central attributes: the use of competitive mechanisms to allocate services and products, and the use of incentives to influence the behaviour of consumers and producers (Gingrich 2011: 7). Marketisation takes many forms, including state actions that support and/or constitute market actors, define the products to be exchanged, construct social arenas and the rules for market exchange, promote for-profit provision and encourage consumer choice and competition (Vogel 2018: 15).[2] The project of marketisation is neither a purely technical nor a purely (right-wing) political endeavour. Rather, it has been pursued by governments of the centre-left and centre-right to meet distinct policy goals and benefit core constituencies (Gingrich 2011).

Financialisation captures a broader shift in the political economy that integrates financial ways of thinking and acting into how state and private (for-profit and not-for-profit) institutions—and, by implication, households—operate (Bryan and Rafferty 2018: 9; van der Zwan 2014). Financial ways of thinking apply complex calculations to quantify the potential risks and returns for the available options in each situation (Bryan and Rafferty 2018: 22). These calculations convert each option into 'transactions on balance sheets of assets and liabilities, and as business-like profit and loss accounts' (Bryan and Rafferty 2018: 10). Financial ways of acting involve choosing the option that is calculated (estimated) to maximise return without unwarranted exposure to risk. In practice, financialisation includes using financial criteria such as returns and risks to assess organisational performance, managing organisations to maximise shareholder value and introducing regulatory reforms that facilitate profit-seeking (Cutler and Waine 2001: 99–100). By counterposing neoliberalism with the concepts of marketisation and financialisation, my analysis of private superannuation differentiates the impact of recent market-oriented social policy reforms and broader changes to economic activity (although there is some overlap between the two as financial markets are a form of market).

---

2   In the case of superannuation, marketisation is akin to what Vogel (2018) terms 'marketcraft'.

As marketisation and financialisation involve complex institutional changes, the impact of both processes on private superannuation is explained drawing on insights from historical institutionalism. Historical institutionalism comprises a loose camp of interdisciplinary approaches that claim that institutional developments over the longer term tend to be more consequential than specific policy choices at a point in time because institutions can become 'embedded' and impact subsequent developments through intended or unintended 'feedback effects' (Pierson 2004: 15). Imposing constraints or conferring resources that impede or promote certain actions, feedback effects may stem from multiple sources in different historical and political contexts—including state and market institutions, political interests and other policy actors and/or political ideas (Hacker 2004: 244). My analysis focuses on the sequence of policy developments and related feedback effects from the 1970s to the present, since this is the period over which superannuation has been transformed from an occupational benefit into a market for private retirement savings.

Policy models differ in how responsibility for managing the financial risks of poverty and income insecurity in old age is distributed between households, the state, employers and/or private (financial) markets. These responsibilities are often actively constructed by political actors in policy discourse using frames that strategically represent policy issues by linking shared norms, cultural values and/or ideological claims to a particular construction of a problem and its solution (Campbell 2004: 94; Rein and Schon 1993: 153). Retirement income policy may spell out de jure responsibilities explicitly framed in legislation, regulations and/or policy discourse that mandate households, the state, employers and/or private markets to take certain actions. Retirement income policy may also imply de facto roles for households, employers and/or private markets that either alter incentive structures or imply voluntary actions in the absence of state intervention. In the ensuing analysis, I consider to what extent, if at all, the transformation of private super in recent decades has reconfigured the distribution of de jure and de facto responsibilities for the financial risks of Australian retirement income policy.

From occupational benefit to private market? The transformation of superannuation

This section establishes the contours of the private superannuation sector in the 1970s and reflects on its role in what I call the 'traditional' model of retirement income policy. It then draws on the concepts set out above to identify the following three phases in the development of this market (see Figure 4.1):

1. localised industrial campaigns for occupational super and the development of early union super funds (mid-1970s to early 1980s)
2. national industrial campaigns for occupational super in Accords and establishment of industry super funds, as operational standards developed (early to late 1980s)
3. foundations of superannuation market established via legislation for occupational super and operational standards (early to mid-1990s).

By the end of this three-phase process, superannuation had become the second tier of the two-tier model of retirement income policy that has been gradually reshaping the de jure and de facto responsibilities for the financial risks of old age.

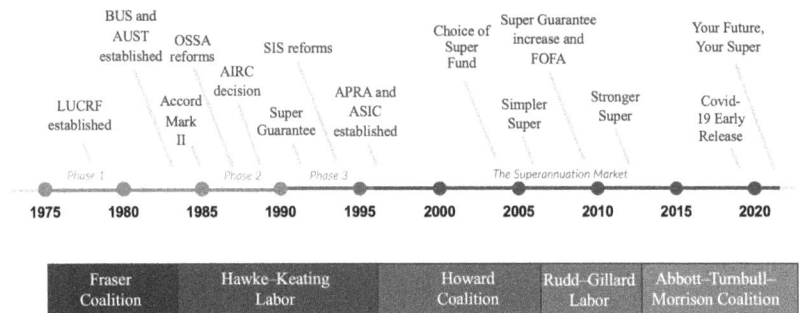

Figure 4.1 The superannuation market: A timeline of key developments
Source: Based on author's research.

Before the super market: Superannuation and traditional retirement income policy

Private superannuation did not function as a market in the early 1970s. The private and public sectors did not supply a retirement savings product that was routinely preserved until old age or portable between different employers and super funds. Employers limited membership of superannuation funds and schemes as an occupational benefit through invitation to workers after extended service (St Anne 2012: 27). Superannuation benefits were reserved for workers who remained with the employer until the scheme matured and pensions were calculated relative to an individual's salary and years of service (St Anne 2012: 27). Without a retirement product to exchange, tight controls on fund membership and benefits decoupled from fund performance, superannuation funds did not compete with one another or seek to maximise investment returns (or market share). Rather, employers used superannuation to reward loyal employees in the competitive postwar labour market and, with no investment controls, many smaller funds supplied cheap lines of credit to be reinvested in the employer's business (Dixon and Foster 1982: 9).

Private superannuation functioned as an occupational benefit rather than a retirement product for about one-third of workers in the early 1970s. Most members received super as lump-sum benefits with severance pay when changing jobs before retirement. In the early 1980s, about 80 per cent of super payments were received as lump sums by workers aged under 55 years when leaving an employer (Aaron 1984: 356–57). Often, lump-sum benefits were equivalent to contributions made without interest or investment returns (Knox 1983: 6). The remaining 20 per cent of super payments paid as retirement benefits accounted for more than 80 per cent of total payments (Aaron 1984: 357). It follows that, at most, 9 per cent of the national workforce had defined-benefit schemes that paid private annuities in the early 1980s.[3] Evidence indicates superannuation benefits—lump sum or defined—were concentrated among older men with high incomes in managerial and professional salaried positions who had been employed by large organisations for extended periods (NSCI 1976: 8).

---

3   As noted below, about 44 per cent of workers had superannuation in 1982; 20 per cent of this amount is about 9 per cent of the workforce.

The weak link between superannuation and retirement income reflected the organisation of the sector into employer-level schemes, which had diverse benefit structures and no mechanism to transfer balances between funds when employees moved. The superannuation sector was bifurcated by persistent differences between public and private sector schemes. Public sector super schemes were self-administered on a not-for-profit basis and largely funded from general revenue when account-holders became eligible for benefits (Knox 1986: 43). Covering about 58 per cent of government employees, public schemes provided a defined benefit or a lump sum calculated as equivalent to super contributions that would have been funded at stipulated rates (Knox 1983: 6; NSCI 1976: 5).

Private sector super funds ranged from large corporate funds for (mostly) white-collar employees that paid defined benefits and retail funds established by life insurance offices to small employer schemes for employees of a particular business (Bateman 2003: 119; Knox 1983: 6). Evidence suggests the small employer funds with fewer than 10 members were most prevalent and made up more than 80 per cent of private sector funds in the early 1970s (NSCI 1976: 9). Most super contributions were funded and, except for a small portion of retail funds, private sector schemes operated on a not-for-profit basis. Private sector schemes covered about 21 per cent of private sector employees and mostly paid lump-sum benefits (NSCI 1976: 5, 11).

Financial institutions had limited roles in a superannuation sector dominated by not-for-profit funds. Both public and private sector super funds were instituted as trusts and managed by trustees appointed by those constituting them. Trust deeds outlined the rights and obligations of trustees (who controlled super funds), employers (where relevant) and members (Castillo 2012: 23). Government departments and agencies appointed trustees for public sector funds. Private sector employers often acted as trustees for their own super funds, generally appointing directors and senior managers (Dixon and Foster 1982). Other small super funds were often established by individual trustees to minimise tax liabilities (Castillo 2012: 23). This limited the role of financial institutions to providing financial services to private non-profit super funds; mutual life insurance offices had the largest direct role in administering—in part or in full—most private sector super funds (Knox 1986: 43).

The state also had a minimal role in the superannuation sector (apart from in public sector schemes) during the 1970s. It subsidised private super via tax concessions that applied to certain super contributions, fund investment earnings and lump-sum benefits (Nielson and Harris 2009). To access the concession for investment earnings, private super funds had to adhere to the 30/20 rule to invest 30 per cent of their assets in government bonds, of which 20 per cent had to be held in Commonwealth bonds (Holt 1961: 1155). Otherwise, superannuation was only lightly regulated and not subject to specialised legislation. The state did not impose investment controls, nor did it require funds to preserve benefits until retirement or routinely vest account holdings (that is, inform members of the estimated value of contributions and investment earnings).

Given its weak link to retirement savings, superannuation unsurprisingly had a minimal role in the traditional model of retirement income policy, in which the 'first tier', the age pension, was more or less universal. Accordingly, the traditional model largely distributed responsibility for the financial risks of old age between the state and households. The state had de jure responsibility in this model, collectively pooling the financial risks of old age by funding the affluence-tested age pension from general tax revenue.[4] Although technically funded by taxes collected today, the age pension can be understood to have an income-smoothing function in that taxes are collected at high-income stages of an individual's working life and the pension provides them with a modest income stream at retirement. In other words, taxes collected over an individual's working life can be conceived of as at least partially covering the cost of the age pension they receive in retirement. Because of the pension's modesty, the traditional model has relied on retirees having low housing costs to achieve low poverty rates (Castles 1997; Yates and Bradbury 2010). Households had a de facto role in securing low housing costs through homeownership in this model, which is often conceived as a fourth pillar of social insurance (Yates and Bradbury 2010).[5] The state encourages homeownership directly by excluding the family residence from the pension's asset test and indirectly by only providing highly residual social housing (Yates 2010).[6]

---

4   Low health costs to individuals from the universal health insurance scheme Medicare, established in 1985, have also become important.
5   Although predicated on high homeownership rates, the traditional model of retirement income policy relies primarily on the reduced living costs for owner-occupiers rather than the potential for retirees to access equity from housing assets through sale or financial instruments.
6   Social housing peaked at 6 per cent of housing stock (Yates 2010).

The traditional model of retirement income policy conferred few responsibilities for the financial risks of old age on to employers and financial markets. However, several large corporate and public sector employers did assume de facto responsibility for managing the financial risks of old age by paying annuities or lump-sum benefits for an exclusive minority of workers when defined-benefit schemes matured at retirement. Profit-seeking financial market institutions had even fewer responsibilities than employers in the traditional model, with most super funds operating as not-for-profit trusts, typically controlled by employers and administered by mutual life insurance offices.

Phase 1: Early pioneers of the super market — Market-savvy unionists and occupational super

Although they had a modest short-term impact, union campaigns for occupational super in the mid-1970s paved the way for later transformations of occupational superannuation by forging super into a product that had the potential to be transferred between certain funds and linking benefits to the financial performance of the fund. These campaigns started to expand coverage of the second tier of retirement income policy, making it less of an exclusive benefit for higher-income–earners. In these campaigns, market-savvy unionists established a new 'union' model of super fund that provided a precursor for later industry funds, combining a not-for-profit organisational structure with accumulation member accounts. Before a market had been established, these new super funds established a financialised model to the extent that their growth spread accumulation accounts managed by financial institutions and invested assets to maximise returns for account-holders (Stebbing 2015: 130–31). Seeking to capitalise on the growth in coverage, large life insurance offices—including National Mutual and the Australian Mutual Provident Society (AMP)—and investment banks also spread the accumulation account model by actively expanding their retail superannuation business (Morris 2018: 59–60).

Union campaigns for occupational super in the mid-1970s established the foundations of the second tier of retirement income policy as a fallback position following a failed campaign for a national public superannuation scheme. Political campaigns for national superannuation—a single state-administered super scheme for workers—gathered momentum in the early 1970s following growing concerns about the adequacy of the age pension (Olsberg 1997: 76). Having promoted employer-funded super benefits since the 1950s, the union movement was a key proponent of national super (Morris 2018: 59). This campaign peaked with bipartisan support for national super at the 1972 election and the establishment of the National Superannuation Committee of Inquiry (NSCI, or Hancock Inquiry) in the same year by the incoming Whitlam Labor government to develop policy proposals. Bipartisan support for national super, however, was short-lived and the campaign stalled after the Fraser Coalition government took office in late 1975. Industrial campaigns for wage increases were also constrained in the mid-1970s—initially, by unions' commitment to wage restraint in return for national wage indexation from the Whitlam government and then by the anti-inflationary monetary policies of the Fraser government (Olsberg 1997: 75–76).

Against this backdrop, unions developed the 'deferred wages of workers' frame in their campaigns to justify pursuing occupational super through industrial bargaining in the arbitration system to improve worker remuneration. This frame primarily constructed occupational superannuation as an industrial issue, establishing employer super contributions as equivalent to a 'wage increase' (rather than a gift from employers). Unions also used the 'deferred wages' frame to argue that, as benefits were delayed until retirement (or when workers left their job), occupational super would not fuel short-term inflation. As well as providing the rationale for union campaigns in the mid-1970s, this frame has had an enduring influence on how unions and other key proponents have conceived of private superannuation in subsequent campaigns.

Just as significant to influencing the later composition of the industry was the establishment by market-savvy unions of a new financialised model of super fund in these campaigns. Early union funds, including the Stevedoring Employees Retirement Fund established by the Waterside Workers' Federation of Australia in 1967, expanded the scope of occupational super funds to cover employees across a sector of the economy (Morris 2018: 59). Developed by the Federated Storemen and Packers' Union of Australia (FSPU) in 1978, the Labour Union Cooperative Retirement Fund (LUCRF) established a fund model with a distinctive organisational structure, investment strategy and account structure (St Anne 2012: 72). This model had a not-for-profit organisational structure managed by a board of trustees with union and employer representatives who were responsible for maximising investment returns for fund members (St Anne 2012: 13). Financed mainly by employer contributions, superannuation was held in accumulation accounts that operated like other individual savings accounts managed according to financial criteria (Olsberg 1997: 286).

Union funds initiated the financialisation of superannuation by expanding the role of the financial sector in the 1970s. The financial sector remained highly segmented during the 1970s, with state regulations placing controls on the operations of banks and other financial institutions, which limited particular types of institutions to offering a specified range of products (Lewis and Wallace 1993: 4).[7] The financial institutions most involved in private superannuation were life insurance offices and finance companies involved in managed funds (Covick and Lewis 1993: 183). Like most employer funds, early union funds—notably excluding LUCRF—were administered by life insurance offices (Olsberg 1997: 286). Private super (including employer and union funds) became increasingly important to life insurance offices, with the latter holding about 43 per cent of their assets in super by 1981 (Lewis and Wallace 1993: 10). Early union funds also employed financial sector intermediaries to manage assets, including subsidiaries owned partly by state-owned savings banks. Although the outsourcing of asset management and administration functions opened a pathway for private for-profit firms to enter, the short-term impact of this trend was minimised by the limited scale of union funds and the not-for-profit structure of most super funds, life insurance offices and financial entities (some of which were state-owned) involved in the sector.

Union campaigns for occupational super stalled by 1980 but succeeded in extending coverage to 44 per cent of workers by 1982 (ABS 1982: 8). Union super funds did not supplant the prevalence of defined-benefit schemes nor the dominance of public sector, corporate and employer super funds (Covick and Lewis 1993: 177). These funds also did not alter the practice of individuals receiving super benefits as lump-sum payments before retirement. Rather, union campaigns were significant for establishing a political strategy and new institutions that later served as 'proofs of concept' for financialised superannuation products invested to maximise returns in funds co-managed by unions and employers.

---

7   These regulations included restricting entry to the banking sector to domestic institutions that met specified criteria, strictly demarcating the permissible activities of banks and other types of financial organisations, limiting cross-ownership of different types of financial institutions, setting official interest rates and requests on lending, and enacting statutory minimum deposits (Daugaard and Valentine 1993: 40; Lewis and Wallace 1993: 7).

Phase 2: An 'industrial revolution' — Establishing the preconditions for the super market

Building on the platform provided by earlier campaigns for occupational super, Labor governments in partnership with the Australian Council of Trade Unions (ACTU), the union movement's peak body, established the preconditions for a national superannuation market in the 1980s. This policy coalition marketised private superannuation during this phase by enlarging the potential market by extending coverage to workers, establishing and facilitating the expansion of industry super funds that were to become key market actors, transforming private super into a retirement savings product and promoting consumer choice and fund competition. As these preconditions for a market were established, private super was financialised by the spread of the accumulation account model and broader liberalisation of the financial sector.

During these years, Australian Labor Party (ALP) governments relied on eight Accords (1983–95), which were neocorporatist wage-fixing agreements between the ALP and the ACTU under which unions agreed to moderate wage demands in return for an expanded 'social wage'. Although the Accords identified national superannuation as a priority, these agreements became the vehicle through which the Hawke Labor government and the ACTU pursued further expansion of occupational super in the 1980s (Morris 2018: 73). Occupational super was not on the immediate agenda after Labor took office, though it had a critical role in securing the first Accord. The Accord—the government's signature economic policy—was put in jeopardy after the Australian Industrial Relations Commission (AIRC) in 1984 rejected the building unions' proposal to have benefits owed to workers disbursed as over-award payments (St Anne 2012: 70). Falling back on the industrial strategy developed in the 1970s, the building unions mobilised the 'deferred wages' frame when negotiating to have these over-award payments disbursed as occupational super into the first industry super fund, the Builders Unions Superannuation Fund (BUS).

Established in 1984, BUS and the Allied Unions Superannuation Trust (AUST) were the first industry super funds developed to manage the super holdings of workers paid under a particular award or set of awards.[8] Industry super funds were an Australian innovation modelled on ACTU principles that were, in turn, informed by the experience of early union super funds in the 1970s and the industrial partnerships established between unions and businesses in the Nordic countries (St Anne 2012: 72–74). Industry funds shared with early union super funds fully vested and portable investments held in accumulation accounts (St Anne 2012: 75). As former FSPU officials Bill Kelty and Simon Crean were among the senior ACTU officials tasked with formulating union superannuation policy, LUCRF heavily informed the industry fund model (St Anne 2012: 72). Like LUCRF, early industry super funds had a not-for-profit organisational structure managed by a board of trustees with equal representation from unions and employers tasked with maximising investment returns for members. In contrast to LUCRF, early industry super funds did not outsource investment management to private financial service providers (Sword 1986: 105).

BUS and AUST provided important proofs of concept that unions were able to responsibly establish and jointly manage with employers centralised super funds for employees from thousands of businesses (St Anne 2012: 72). The design of BUS—including the composition of its board, investment strategy and use of inhouse investment managers— was intended to 'sustain legitimacy in the eyes of the employers, the government and the public' (Olsberg 1997, in Morris 2018). This design was controversial among some sectors of the union movement which recognised that accumulation accounts offered less security than defined-benefit schemes (St Anne 2012: 76). But the design also reflected practical difficulties in securing financial sector sponsors to guarantee defined benefits, considering the low level of contributions from multiple employers for a large pool of workers (Kingston et al. 1992: 141). The Hawke government and the ACTU actively promoted BUS as a union prototype, emphasising its industry-level coverage, funding through employer contributions and 'vested' investments.

Earlier industrial campaigns for occupational super and industry super funds paved the way for Labor and the ACTU to incorporate employer-financed super contributions at the national level in the Prices and Incomes Accord Mark II of 1986. In 1985, the government came to agree with business that wages should not be indexed (as previously negotiated

---

8   For instance, BUS administered the super of builders and AUST managed the super of workers covered by awards in the construction industry.

in the Accord) as fiscal conditions worsened due to high inflation and interest rates, a growing current account deficit and a declining currency (Stilwell 1986: 17–18). Both the ACTU and the government adopted the 'deferred wages' frame as the rationale for including 'award super'— as these employer-financed super contributions were called—set at 3 per cent of wages as part of the social wage in the Accord Mark II (Treasury 2001: 78). Award super also appealed to unions as a means of expanding industry funds, which were set as the default funds, and enabled the expansion of superannuation without requiring employers without super funds to establish them (Sharp 1992: 35). The Accord negotiation was reinforced by both close institutional ties between Labor and the ACTU and personal ties between Treasurer Paul Keating and lead union negotiator Bill Kelty (Kelly 2008: 262).[9]

Award super was established at the national level through the arbitration system, effectively building on the distinctive wage-earner institutions developed in the early twentieth century (Castles 1994: 135). In the 1986 National Wage Case, the AIRC approved award super set at 3 per cent of wages being paid into various industry super funds (Treasury 2001: 79). While the Accord Mark II proposed award super for the labour force, the AIRC decided on award-by-award negotiations due to concerns about the management of super funds and required the government to ensure operational standards were met (Treasury 2001: 79). The award super provisions had some success in increasing super coverage, which rose to 51 per cent of workers by 1988 (Australian Government 1988: 1). Award super also increased the scale of industry super funds, which held accounts for most workers in 18 sectoral awards and many workers in a further 11 awards by the late 1980s (St Anne 2012: 92).[10]

---

9   Award super also divided business interests. On one hand, employer interests opposed award super as it increased their expenses and decreased the role of employer super funds. On the other hand, life insurance offices and the financial services sector supported award super as it provided a major source of equity for the financial sector and decreased the role of employer super funds that competed against them as a source of cheap business loans (Sharp 2009: 200, 202).

10   Despite the transformation award super represented, the bifurcated structure of private superannuation became more pronounced in the short term, with 71 per cent of *public* super funds offering defined-benefit schemes and 86 per cent of *private* super funds managing accumulation accounts in 1991 (ISC 1994: v). Small, typically employer super funds remained the most common; more than 90 per cent of super funds held assets of less than $500,000 (ISC 1993: v). With most accumulation accounts having low balances, defined-benefit funds held 56 per cent of all assets (ISC 1994: v).

In response to the AIRC's concerns, the Hawke government introduced operating standards for superannuation products and funds in the *Occupational Superannuation Standards Act 1987* (*OSSA*). This legislative package marketised superannuation by fashioning it into a retirement product and introducing measures aimed at increasing choice and competition. It established a preservation age of 55 years, which forged the link between superannuation and retirement (Bateman 2003).[11] This legislation aimed to increase consumer choice and fund competition through vesting that decreased information asymmetries by requiring funds to provide annual valuations of super balances in preservation stage, and increasing portability to give members the choice of transferring accounts between funds.[12]

The *OSSA* also introduced measures that financialised superannuation by requiring super funds established after 1985 to embody 'financial ways of acting' that curbed potential conflicts of interest and risky behaviour. This package prevented trustees from carrying out inhouse lending to trustees or members, lending more than 10 per cent of fund assets to employers or contributors to the fund, or borrowing funds (Castillo 2012: 20). It also favoured the industry fund model by requiring larger super funds with more than 200 members to appoint account-holders or representatives to half of trustee positions (Treasury 2001: 79). To oversee these operating standards, the Hawke government established the Insurance and Superannuation Commission (ISC) (Bateman 2003: 122). But, as the commission lacked direct constitutional power to legislate for superannuation, super funds failing to meet these standards were denied access to the tax concession for super investments rather than facing legal sanctions or other penalties (Covick and Lewis 1997: 273).[13]

These operating standards contributed to the financialisation of private superannuation in the 1980s, along with the rise of industry super and the liberalisation of the financial sector. Despite their not-for-profit structure, industry super funds spread the accumulation account model, elevating

---

11   To hold super paid before retirement age, Approved Deposit Funds were established until account-holders reached 65 years of age (ISC 1990: 3).
12   This also effectively prevented super funds from paying benefits equal to total contributions without investment earnings.
13   The 30/20 rule the Hawke government abolished in 1983 operated in a similar way. This rule required super funds to invest 30 per cent of their assets in government bonds and 20 per cent of these in Commonwealth bonds to receive the tax concession for super investments. Funds that did not meet this requirement did not receive the tax concession.

the aim of maximising investment returns for individual members over the collective pooling of resources (Stebbing 2015). This shift to accumulation accounts reflected a broader international trend towards financialisation in other private pension markets, as nonstate pension funds aimed to maximise returns and reduce liabilities, particularly from potential shortfalls from defined-benefit schemes due to increased longevity (Stebbing 2015: 131). The rise of industry funds also created the potential for later competition by increasing the economies of scale in the private super sector from employer to award-level funds. So, as private superannuation became a less-exclusive occupational reward, it increasingly became a household asset to manage and invest to maximise returns.

The financial sector was liberalised through a suite of reforms enacted by the Hawke government, accelerating the pace of financialisation in the Australian economy and in the superannuation system. The reforms included regulations that enabled foreign and new domestic organisations to enter the sector, institutions to select the range of financial services and products offered, cross-ownership of financial institutions that offered different services and the limited privatisation of state-owned financial entities (Wallace and Lewis 1993: 4). Liberalisation acted as the catalyst for rapid consolidation across the financial sector, with for-profit banking groups—the four major banks and their subsidiaries—accounting for more than 60 per cent of total financial assets by 1990 (Wallace and Lewis 1993: 9). As for-profit banking groups have come to dominate a consolidated financial sector, financial institutions have placed greater emphasis on maximising shareholder value, including those in the retail super subsector and other superannuation activities.

By the end of the 1980s, the perceived success of 'award super' gave Labor and the ACTU a political stake in private super (Stebbing 2015: 123). This was a major factor behind the Hawke government's policy shift in the 'Better Incomes' policy statement of 1989 to replace national super with occupational super as the second arm of retirement income policy (alongside the pension) (Howe 1989: 4). Labor strategically used major government reports to justify this policy shift. Notably, both the Cass Social Security Review and the Senate Standing Committee on Community Affairs framed national super as involving excessive startup costs and recommended occupational super to replace it as the supplementary retirement income policy (Foster 1988: 190; SSCCA 1988: xliv). Occupational super was also better attuned with prevailing policy ideas about limiting the role of the state and the long tradition of the state mandating occupational welfare (Castles 1997). After the government postponed wage rises in 1989, Labor and the ACTU included a provision to increase award super to 6 per cent of wages in the Accord Mark VI; however, the AIRC refused to ratify the Accord in 1991, pointing to employer noncompliance with award super provisions and restating concerns about super funds' operational standards (AIRC 1991: 61). This institutional obstacle ended the industrial campaign for award super. In the next phase, the ALP government pursued a legislative strategy to extend occupational superannuation.

Phase 3: Financialising wages — Establishing the institutional foundations of the super market

Circumventing the obstacle presented by the AIRC's decision, the Hawke–Keating Labor government changed strategy to pursue legislation—notably, for the Superannuation Guarantee Scheme and the Superannuation Industry Supervision (SIS) regulations—to advance the earlier campaigns for 'award super'. These reforms established the institutional foundations of the superannuation market during this phase by extending an occupational scheme to near universal coverage of the workforce, increasing mandated employer contributions from 3 to 9 per cent of wages over the following decade, limiting employer contributions to only those super funds that complied with the existing operating standards that fashioned super into a retirement product and reinforcing these operating standards to shore up financially responsible behaviour among trustees. As well as establishing these market foundations, the Superannuation Guarantee reinforced the financialisation of private super by shoring up the accumulation account model and the growth of both industry and retail super funds.

The Superannuation Guarantee Scheme represented a seismic shift in retirement income policy that established a national occupational super scheme that expanded the consumer base of the superannuation market to almost the entire workforce.[14] Announced in the 1991–92 budget,

---

14 The scheme did not require employers to make super contributions for workers earning less than $450 per month, working part-time and/or not aged between 18 and 65 years (Treasury 2001: 84). Initially, organisations with payrolls exceeding $500,000 per year would be required to pay the higher 5 per cent contribution rate, but mandatory super contributions were to increase gradually to (at least) 9 per cent of wages by 2002 (Borowski 2005: 52).

the Super Guarantee mandated employers to make super contributions, initially set at either 3 per cent or 5 per cent of their workers' wages, into a complying industry, employer or retail super fund stipulated in industrial agreements (Borowski 2005: 52; Kerin 1991: 4; Olsberg 1994: 287).[15] This scheme amounted to the mandatory financialisation of wages, with workers forced to relinquish a portion of their wages to private superannuation, which would incrementally increase to a contribution of 9 per cent of wages by 2002, and manage this financial investment until preservation age (Bryan and Rafferty 2018: 86). Employers were required to either make contributions into a complying super fund nominated in enterprise agreements or pay the Superannuation Guarantee Levy to finance equivalent government contributions into a fund (Kerin 1991: 4). Superannuation funds were obliged to comply with the *OSSA* to receive employer contributions for workers but did not have to guarantee a particular level of investment return or final benefit to those workers.

The Superannuation Guarantee was the subject of partisan politics. Predictably, Labor and the ACTU were the chief proponents of the scheme and were able to coordinate their campaigns, buoyed once again by close institutional and personal ties (Mann 1993: 41).[16] The Liberal and National (Coalition) parties were the chief parliamentary opponents of the Super Guarantee, framing its compulsion as stifling the choices of consumers (workers), while prompting concerns about its potential to put further pressure on unemployment (which was at 10 per cent) and inflation during the recession (Hewson 1991). The scheme split business interests in line with their self-interest, with the financial industry in support and employer organisations opposing. However, the Australian Council of Social Services, as well as organisations representing women and pensioners, also opposed the Superannuation Guarantee as it would reinforce market inequalities, providing little benefit to low-income–earners (Mann 1993).

Despite its support from powerful interests, the Superannuation Guarantee initially failed to secure support in the Senate. Without a Senate majority, Labor's main obstacle to enacting the guarantee came in securing the support of Australian Democrats senators, who held the balance of power. The Democrats supported the Super Guarantee in principle but expressed

---

15 The higher contribution rate was to apply to organisations with payrolls of more than $500,000.
16 Keating's elevation to the prime ministership in December 1991 arguably bolstered Labor's commitment, given his reliance on ACTU support, his previous support for occupational super and ties to pro-reform ACTU officials (Mann 1993: 49).

concerns about the inequity of the superannuation tax concessions, the regulatory integrity of super funds, the lack of Treasury modelling and the capacity of small employers to finance employee super contributions (Cleary 1992; Maley 1992). Labor secured the Democrats' support by agreeing to increase the preservation age for superannuation to 60 years and reduce the impact on employers by lowering the higher contribution rate to 4 per cent (Mann 1993: 30).[17] Notwithstanding their initial concerns, the Democrats' support increased the durability of the Super Guarantee after its enactment (particularly when compared with the AIRC decisions that ratified the Accords), as the minor party held the balance of power in the Senate until 2002.

Responding to concerns raised by the AIRC and the Democrats, the Keating government enacted the SIS legislation of 1993 and 1994 to tighten the regulatory framework for private super.[18] The SIS legislation secured the regulatory foundations of the superannuation market by requiring funds to adhere to the preservation age, portability of balances and vesting requirements established by the *OSSA* (Bateman 2003: 122). But, in contrast to the *OSSA*, under the SIS legislation, super funds were required to comply because it was enacted using the corporations, pensions and taxation powers of the Australian Constitution (Covick and Lewis 1997: 274). The SIS legislation also codified the responsibilities of trustees and financial service providers, as well as increasing the ISC's oversight of private super (Bateman 2003: 122). The SIS legislation also established incentives for trustees to be financially responsible, obliging them to establish funds for the sole purpose of retirement provision and giving the ISC responsibility for enforcing new civil and criminal penalties for breaching fiduciary duties (Bateman 2003: 122; Castillo 2012: 82). This legislation also further limited inhouse investments to 5 per cent of total fund assets and prohibited borrowing.[19]

These reforms establishing the foundations of the contemporary superannuation market contributed to the increasing financialisation of the sector. Although it did not preclude defined-benefit schemes, the

---

17 The threshold at which the higher rate was also increased in negotiations to employers with payrolls of $1 million or more (Mann 1993: 30).

18 The SIS reforms were legislated in the *Superannuation Industry (Supervision) Act 1993* and the *Superannuation Industry (Supervision) Regulations Act 1994* (Covick and Lewis 1997: 273).

19 The Keating government announced 'L-A-W tax cuts' in the leadup to the 1993 election, but afterwards said these would be directed into increasing the Superannuation Guarantee to 12 per cent of wages in the 2000s. However, this never eventuated, because the Howard Coalition government did not support increases to compulsory super contributions over 9 per cent.

Superannuation Guarantee accelerated the shift to defined-contribution accounts that operated to financial criteria and reinforced the market distribution of income.[20] Whereas 80 per cent of super accounts had a defined-benefit structure as recently as 1980, 85 per cent were accumulation accounts by 2000.[21] The Super Guarantee underpinned the shift to accumulation accounts because it specified only the portion of wages that must be contributed to super and these contributions were not set at a level (especially initially) sufficient to fund an annuity (see Stebbing 2015). Albeit for different purposes, both industry and retail super funds that were typically nominated in enterprise agreements sought to maximise investment returns and provided members' accumulation accounts, particularly when compared with the operation of public sector and corporate super funds that had offered defined benefits.[22] The SIS legislation also reduced the appeal of corporate and small employer funds by increasing fund administration and preventing new entrants from reinvesting employee contributions inhouse.[23] Still, important differences from the free-market model that animates neoclassical economic theory persisted; not-for-profit super funds dominated the sector, consumers could not opt out and typically did not choose their fund, and competition between funds remained limited.

By the end of this phase, superannuation was established as the second tier of the two-tier model of retirement income policy that is reconfiguring how the financial risks of old age are managed and distributed. In this model, the state largely retains de jure responsibility for the affluence-tested age pension, but it formally transfers de jure responsibility to households for financing additional retirement income to supplement (or substitute for) the pension by mandating superannuation contributions over a working life. This also extends the time horizon over which households are required to manage the financial risks of old age from across working life into retirement, which holds out the promise of higher retirement incomes but carries with it prolonged exposure to new risks from volatility and market failure. Employers' expanded role in financing

---

20   This trend is partly attributable to the low level of contributions specified by the Superannuation Guarantee, which were unlikely to mature into substantial private annuities for most workers (even at 9 per cent of wages in 2002), and to uncertainty about the long-term contributions level.

21   This figure should be read with some caution, given the high incidence of lump-sum super benefits paid as severance pay before retirement age in the 1980s.

22   Only three of 100 industry super funds offered defined-benefit schemes in 1992 (Kingston et al. 1992: 141).

23   These reforms were 'grandfathered', so did not require existing corporate funds or small funds operated by employers to change their investment portfolios (Covick and Lewis 1997).

contributions for employees does not expose them to financial risk because 'compulsory' amounts to 'compulsory saving out of wage income' (Bryan and Rafferty 2018: 86). Private super funds and financial service providers benefit from second-tier policies, receiving de facto support through the Superannuation Guarantee and super tax concessions, but have only the de jure responsibility to maximise returns and act in their members' best interests. In sum, the rise of superannuation as the second tier of retirement income policy shifted responsibility for the financial risks of old age, at least partially, onto households.

Financialisation in the super market since the early 1990s

The financialisation of the superannuation market has continued unabated since the early 1990s as private super has become increasingly important to both retirement income policy, as coverage of the workforce has become nearly universal, and the financial sector, as the total value of super assets has rapidly expanded. Financialisation has coincided with the consolidation of institutional private super funds, with their number declining from 4,734 in 1996 to 202 in 2018 (see Figure 4.2). The focus here is on 'institutional' super funds that hold the superannuation of most workers and, by extension, a large majority of Australian households. Notably, this excludes self-managed super funds (SMSFs), which are typically favoured by a well-off majority and have become increasingly popular. Between 1996 and 2018, the number of SMSFs increased from 100,000 to 596,000 and their assets multiplied from $28 billion to $750 billion. The increasing importance of SMSFs to private superannuation and the financial sector is a parallel process of financialisation to that discussed here and requires a separate treatment that is beyond the scope of this chapter. As private super funds have consolidated their operations, superannuation has been financialised by expanding the scale and scope of profit-seeking financial entities, refocusing not-for-profit super funds on maximising short-term investment returns for individual members and replacing defined-benefit schemes that collectively pooled risks with individualised accumulation accounts. Successive governments have embraced and advanced financialisation by introducing a new regulatory framework that supports consolidation and reforms that aim to make fund trustees, financial advisors and consumers behave more like rational financial actors.

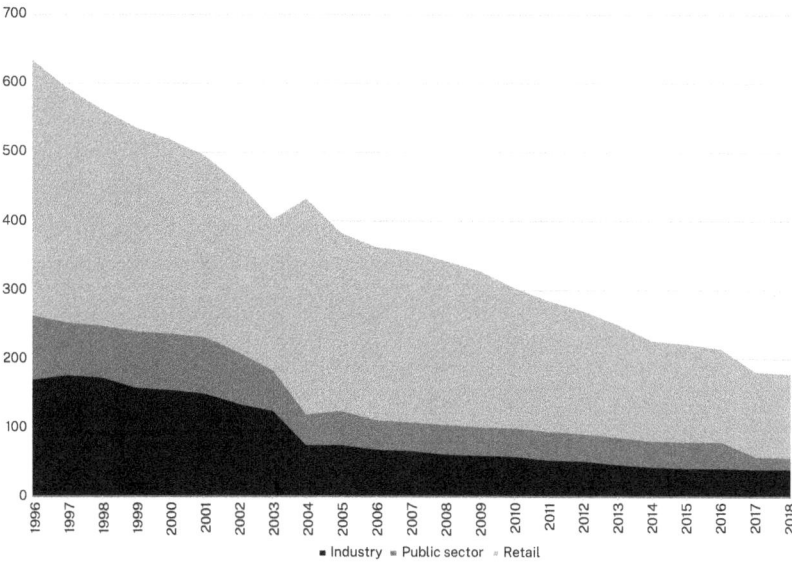

■ Industry ■ Public sector ▪ Retail

Figure 4.2a Consolidation of industry, retail and public sector super funds, 1996–2018

Sources: The data source for 1996–2003 is APRA (2007); for 2004–16, APRA (2016); and for 2017 and 2018, APRA (2018a).

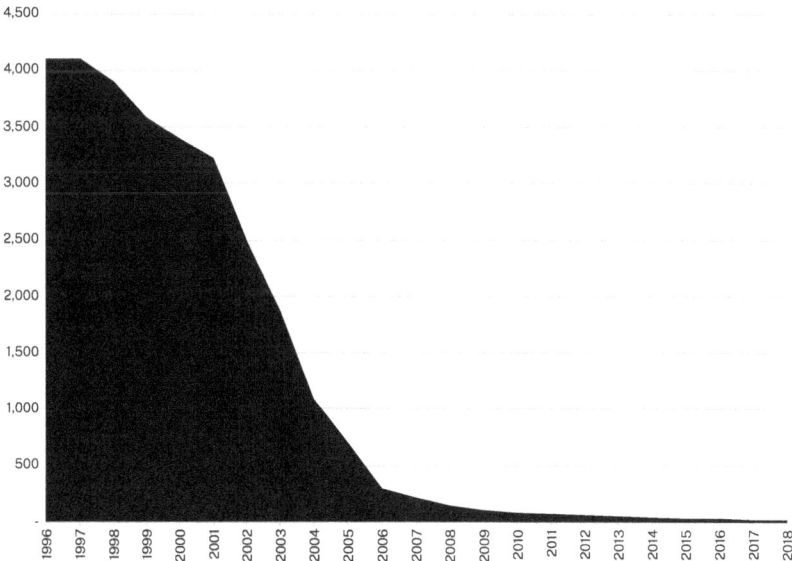

Figure 4.2b The collapse of the corporate not-for-profit super sector, 1996–2018

Sources: The data source for 1996–2003 is APRA (2007); for 2004–16, APRA (2016); and for 2017 and 2018, APRA (2018a).

Profit-seeking retail super funds and financial services have expanded and consolidated their operations since the mid-1990s. Retail super funds expanded their assets tenfold, from $60 billion in 1996 to $622 billion in 2018 (see Figure 4.3). Retail funds increased their market share from 24 to 36 per cent of assets between 1996 and 2004, before declining to 23 per cent of assets in 2018.[24] This expansion is the result of retail super funds and financial service providers actively increasing their stakes in the superannuation market as well as the twin processes of privatisation and demutualisation. Retail super funds have consolidated their operations, decreasing from 372 to 121 in number between 1996 and 2018. This consolidation reflects broader structural change in the financial sector, which has increasingly been dominated by large domestic and international profit-seeking conglomerates since the mid-1990s. Financial institutions, including those demutualised or privatised around this time, became part of larger banking groups or large financial conglomerates through mergers, acquisitions or purchases of other private enterprises (Keneley 2001: 164). Most retail super funds are owned by the four major banking groups: NAB, ANZ, Westpac and the Commonwealth Bank (Taylor et al. 2017: 261).

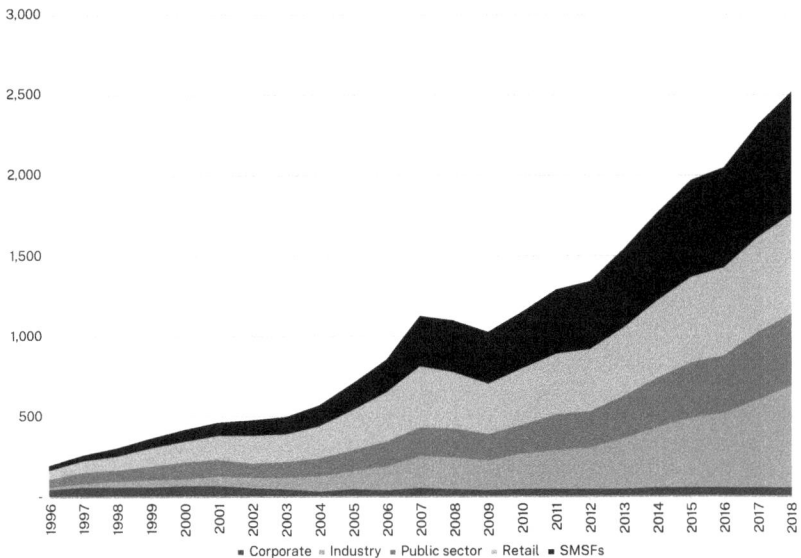

■ Corporate ■ Industry ■ Public sector ■ Retail ■ SMSFs

Figure 4.3 Total assets held by super fund type, 1996–2018

Note: The data for the period 1996–2003 include SMSFs, small APRA-regulated funds and approved-deposit funds.

Sources: Data source for 1996–2003, APRA (2007); for 2004–16, APRA (2016); and for 2017–18, APRA (2018a).

---

24   The decline in the market share of retail funds is largely attributable to the growth of SMSFs.

Privatisation and demutualisation were different sides of the same coin. Privatisation converted state-owned institutions into profit-maximising entities during the 1990s, including the Commonwealth Bank, four state banks and many other financial service providers. While the Commonwealth Bank was privatised via a public float, most of the state banks and other financial service providers were purchased by private enterprises (RBA 1997: 14–16). Demutualisation has transformed the not-for-profit super funds and financial service providers that dominated the pre-market private super sector into profit-maximising entities (Stebbing 2015: 127). Initiated by senior managers, demutualisation was typically framed as necessary to access capital, expand business and compete with industry super funds (Keneley 2001: 162; Morris 2018: 83). Large not-for-profit life insurance offices—including major players in retail super as well as financial services providers for corporate and industry super funds such as AMP and National Mutual—demutualised between 1991 and 1998 (Morris 2018: 83; Stebbing 2015: 127). As a result, the share of total financial assets held by not-for-profit life insurance offices shrank from 58 per cent to 1 per cent between 1985 and 1998 (Morris 2018: 83).

Industry super funds have, to some extent, emulated the for-profit sector by consolidating their operations as their role in the superannuation market has rapidly expanded since the mid-1990s. Industry super funds have expanded their assets to become larger than retail funds, increasing their assets more than thirtyfold, from $20 billion in 1996 to $631 billion in 2018 (see Figure 4.3). This has increased their market share from 8 per cent to 23 per cent of total super assets over the same period (APRA 2018a). Although retaining their not-for-profit structure, industry funds represent a financialised form of not-for-profit organisation as they aim to maximise investment returns for individual members rather than collectively pool risk (Stebbing 2015: 127). Industry funds consolidated their operations through mergers and collaborative ventures (Clare and Cranston 2017: 17). The number of industry super funds declined from 169 in 1996 to 39 in 2018 (APRA 2007: 20; 2018a). Spearheaded by the ACTU, industry super funds collaborated—often with what were mutual funds at the time—in ventures by pooling resources to lower costs and increase control over investments (Brown and Davis 2009: 11). Consolidation among industry funds has served a similar purpose to that of for-profit funds in seeking to maximise short-term returns, but for the benefit of members rather than shareholders.

The collaborative ventures of industry funds were instituted to pool the costs of diversifying their investment portfolios without attracting the high fees charged by profit-seeking financial service providers.[25] These ventures have included the Development Australia Fund with AMP in 1990 to invest in public infrastructure projects, Industry Fund Services (IFS) with Colonial Mutual to offer financial services for super funds and members in 1994 and the Super Members Home Loan Program by National Mutual with support from the ACTU in 1994 (Brown and Davis 2009: 13). The last was expanded into Members Equity Bank, which obtained its banking licence in 2002 and is a venture half-owned by IFS and AXA (which purchased National Mutual) that increases the capacity of industry funds to manage large investments (Morris 2018: 86). Industry super funds became the sole owners of Members Equity Bank by purchasing AXA's stake in 2006 (Brown and Davis 2009: 13). And, in 2007, Industry Super Holdings was established, with IFS, Industry Funds Management, Members Equity Bank and Members Equity Portfolio Management as subsidiaries (Brown and Davis 2009: 10). Although these collaborative ventures have continued to expand, industry funds still source various services from profit-seeking financial service providers.

Consolidation among larger super funds is a major factor behind the increasing dominance of the accumulation account model in the superannuation market. Of those held with larger super funds, 95 per cent were accumulation accounts by 2018 (APRA 2018b: 18). On the one hand, this trend is explained by the rising market shares of retail and industry super funds that favoured the accumulation account model. Between 1996 and 2018, the market share of industry and retail super funds climbed from 37 to 64 per cent of the total assets held by larger super funds (APRA 2007, 2018a). On the other hand, this also reflects the decline of defined-benefit schemes among single-employer super funds. The market share of public sector schemes declined slightly, from 20 to 17 per cent of total fund assets between 1996 and 2018, as superannuation rapidly expanded. But public sector funds limited their future liabilities by closing defined-benefit schemes to new entrants and replacing these with accumulation accounts in the early 2000s. During the same period, the corporate super subsector collapsed, declining from 4,100 to 24 funds, and from holding 19 to 2 per cent of total assets, between 1996 and 2018

25 These collaborative ventures were at least partly instituted as separate financial entities because super funds were unable to carry out non-retirement savings operations due to the sole-purpose test established by the SIS legislation in the early 1990s.

(see Figures 4.2 and 4.3). These funds were closed, outsourced to retail funds or, in the case of smaller businesses, converted into SMSFs (Castillo 2012: 22; Morris 2018: 71).

Intentionally or otherwise, regulatory changes enacted by governments of both major political parties have advanced the financialisation of the superannuation market. Shortly after taking office in 1996, the Howard Coalition government established the Wallis Inquiry into the regulatory structure of the financial system. The government used the Wallis Inquiry to legitimise restructuring the regulatory framework of the financial system, including private super, along lines favoured by the Treasury, from an institutional base that treats the same kind of financial institutions similarly to a function-based approach that treats services with identical functions the same (Bakir 2003: 527, 531). The function-based approach has advanced financialisation by streamlining the regulations for large conglomerates that have come to dominate the financial sector and blurring former institution-based boundaries. This underpinned the government's replacement of the ISC with the two regulatory agencies currently responsible for institutional superannuation: the Australian Prudential Regulation Authority (APRA) and the Australian Securities and Investments Commission (ASIC), which is responsible for consumer and investor protections (Bateman 2003: 122). These new regulators supported consolidation in the superannuation market by streamlining the rules and procedures for financial conglomerates (Gizycki and Lowe 2000: 203).

The Howard government also used the Wallis Inquiry and other reports, such as that by the National Commission of Audit, to reframe and realign policy debates on superannuation with its economic policy and provide the rationale for further reform (Spies-Butcher and Stebbing 2019: 1419).[26] Notably, the Wallis Inquiry framed private super as principally about reducing the future fiscal pressure that population ageing will place on the state from increasing age pension costs (Wallis 1997: 127). The inquiry recast the role of superannuation in retirement income policy as a substitute for the age pension, rather than a supplement to it, as Labor and the union movement had argued in the 1980s. Consistent with the Treasury's submission, the inquiry framed the lack of competition between super funds as a policy problem and constructed greater consumer choice,

---

26 As Bakir (2003: 531) notes, the shift towards the government's agenda is unsurprising as the inquiry 'was independent neither of government nor [of] business'.

particularly in regards to employees' choice of fund for compulsory employer contributions, as the solution (Treasury 1997: 4; Wallis 1997). The Howard government and retail super funds subsequently mobilised the 'competition and choice' and 'pension substitute' frames to build the rationale for reform both groups supported. These frames highlight how the politics of marketisation and financialisation overlap. Consumer choice and provider competition are staples of market organisation, and the choice and competition frame has been repeatedly deployed to argue for the greater access of profit-seeking financial entities to compulsory occupational super.

The Howard government mobilised the Wallis Inquiry to frame a series of proposals as increasing consumer choice. In 1996, the government announced the Choice of Super Fund Reforms that aimed to expand the choice individuals had in selecting a super fund for compulsory contributions to be paid into (Morris 2018: 70). The major banking groups and retail super funds advocated for the reforms, which they perceived as an opportunity to increase their share of compulsory employer contributions (Davis 1998). The Labor Party, industry and corporate super funds opposed the government's legislation, which was viewed as increasing complexity and targeted at weakening industry super because it was a powerbase for unions and, by extension, Labor (Davis 1998). The reforms were contentious in the Senate, where the government lacked a majority, and did not pass Parliament until the support of the Democrats was secured in the third attempt in 2004 (Morris 2018: 70). In 1998, the government expanded choice to non-superannuation products by introducing bank-operated retirement savings accounts that attracted the same concessional tax treatment as super funds (Morris 2018: 70). But, with lower returns than super funds, these accounts proved unpopular (St Anne 2012: 205–6).

For the remainder of its term, the Howard government framed its reforms as encouraging financially responsible behaviour among trustees and consumers. In 2004, the government framed Registrable Superannuation Entity (RSE) licences for trustees as encouraging financially responsible behaviour (Morris 2018: 70). RSE licences conferred on trustees additional obligations around disclosure and financial advice as well as the duty 'to act in the best interests of superannuation fund members' (APRA 2018b: 1).[27] By making trusteeship more onerous, RSE licences

---

27   Trustees were required to substantiate these obligations with supporting evidence to APRA or ASIC when requested (Clare and Cranston 2017: 9).

were a disincentive (in addition to those identified earlier) for employers to administer their own super fund and were a factor in their rapid decline in the early 2000s (see Figure 4.2b). In 2006, the government framed its 'Simplified Super' reforms as encouraging self-provision in retirement by removing tax on super benefits in the retirement phase and providing tax incentives for consumers to make extra super contributions. These reforms also conferred the political advantage of benefiting the core Coalition constituency of high-income earners in the leadup to the 2007 federal election.

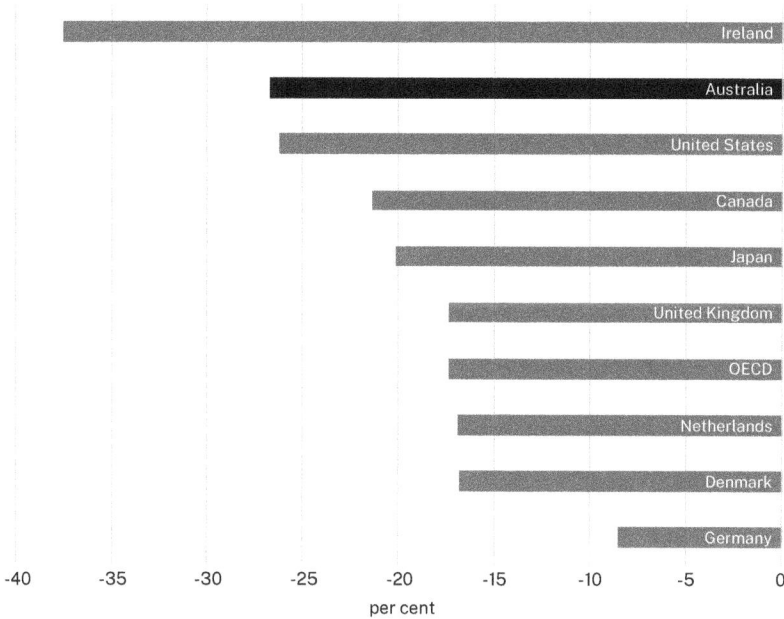

Figure 4.4 Private pension funds' real investment returns in 2008
Source: OECD (2009).

Shortly after the Rudd Labor government took office, the superannuation market was hit hard by the Global Financial Crisis (GFC). The OECD estimated superannuation funds had experienced real investment losses of 27 per cent in Australia at the height of the crisis in 2008 (Figure 4.4; OECD 2009: 1). Considerably higher than the OECD average of 17 per cent, Australia had the second-largest investment losses for private pensions among the organisation's 30 member countries (OECD 2009: 1). Notwithstanding these high losses, private super funds avoided financial collapse during the GFC and its immediate aftermath as the investment risks (and losses) were borne mostly by the holders of accumulation

DESIGNING SOCIAL SERVICE MARKETS

accounts. The Rudd–Gillard Labor governments (2007–13) used three reviews—the Rippoll Inquiry (2009), the Henry Tax Review (2010) and the Cooper Super System Review (2010)—to prosecute the case for further regulatory reforms consistent with the 'competition and choice' frame constructed by the Coalition parties and retail super funds, but focused more on protecting consumers than on enriching shareholders.

The Rudd–Gillard governments used the Rippoll Inquiry (in 2009) into corporate collapses during the GFC to build the case for the 'Future of Financial Advice' (FOFA) reforms that targeted the behaviour of financial advisors. The Rippoll Inquiry found that existing product disclosure protocols were insufficient and financial advisors faced many potential conflicts of interest, particularly from fee structures and rolling commissions (Morris 2018: 166). The Gillard government responded with the FOFA reforms to establish a 'best interest duty' that compelled financial advisors to act in the best interests of their clients, a ban on 'conflicted remuneration structures' such as commissions and a requirement that consumers opt in to ongoing financial advice at least every two years (ASIC 2018). Industry super funds welcomed these reforms, for which they had advocated in their submission to the inquiry and subsequent media campaigns (Whiteley 2010). Despite Labor justifying the reforms as stimulating 'choice and competition' by requiring consumers to make active choices, the Coalition parties and financial planning industry opposed the reforms, arguing the package limited consumer choice (Kahler et al. 2010).[28] Although not focused on super, these reforms were aimed at reducing risks for households and reducing predatory market behaviour by financial market operatives.

The Rudd government used both the Henry Tax Review and the Cooper Super System Review to justify policies directed at aligning the behaviour of super account-holders with the calculative rationality expected of active consumers in neoclassical economics. The Henry Tax Review (Henry 2010) purported to be the most extensive root-and-branch review of the taxation system since 1975. In its reply to the Henry Review, the Rudd government announced further financialisation by gradually increasing the Superannuation Guarantee to 12 per cent of wages (see Stebbing 2015). Despite bipartisan support for this increase, the Gillard and Abbott governments froze the Superannuation Guarantee at 9.5 per cent of wages until fiscal conditions improved, and it remains frozen.

---

28   A later Coalition government wound back some of these protections.

The Cooper Super System Review (Cooper 2010) reframed the policy problem of private super as the failure of consumers to actively select super products based on their performance and thus stimulate competition between private super funds. The Cooper Review claimed many account-holders were disengaged, lacking interest in what was perceived as a compulsory investment and/or perceiving themselves to have insufficient financial literacy to assess and compare super fund performance (Cooper 2010: 6). The review's solution to this rendering of the policy problem was to recommend new regulations to simulate market conditions and curb predatory behaviours, including a default super option and streamlined super fund administrative systems (Cooper 2010). Although sharing with the Coalition's 'competition and choice' frame an understanding of the policy problem as a lack of competition between super funds, the 'consumer protection' frame was employed to justify regulations that simulate rational consumer behaviour among disengaged account-holders and limit the discretion of private super funds.

The Gillard government used the Cooper Review to justify the 'StrongerSuper' package, including the 'MySuper' and 'SuperStream' proposals, between 2011 and 2015. Designed to be cost-effective and easy to compare, MySuper products became the default super option from July 2013, with a standardised fee structure and one diversified investment strategy aimed at achieving identified levels of return and risk (Australian Government 2011: 5). Private super funds were limited to providing one MySuper option and, although not compulsory, had to offer such a product to be nominated in an industrial award (Australian Government 2011: 3). Private super funds also had to transfer existing default members to this new product by July 2017 (Australian Government 2011: 3). The SuperStream reforms aimed to increase efficiency by introducing standardised protocols for managing larger super funds and automating fund administration (Australian Government 2011: 9). These reforms represented attempts to address the 'deficient consumer' frame; while MySuper products sought to direct disengaged fund members to act as rational consumers and shield households from predatory market behaviour, SuperStream was aimed at increasing efficiency to make funds act more competitively.

The segmented super market and the two-tier model of retirement income policy

The financialisation of the superannuation market has coincided with the growing importance of the two-tier model of retirement income policy. But the impact of private superannuation on retirement income policy is tempered by two factors. First, the retention of the age pension moderates the extent to which superannuation alters the distribution of financial risk. Second, compulsory superannuation is not set to mature until the mid-twenty-first century, at which time it is anticipated individuals will retire after having made super contributions set to at least 9 per cent of their wages over their entire working lives. Until then, the impact of second-tier super policies on the distribution of risk, and in particular, those risks managed by the state, will be limited—but gradually increase—as successive generational cohorts enter retirement after having made compulsory super contributions for larger fractions of their working life.

The superannuation market has expanded the role of employers without increasing—and, in some cases, by diminishing—their exposure to financial risk. Public sector employers retain some de facto responsibility for the financial risks their employees face in old age by managing inhouse super funds, but this is limited by the replacement of defined-benefit schemes with accumulation accounts for employees commencing after 2005. In contrast, most private sector employers have withdrawn from taking de facto responsibility for their employees' financial risks by closing those corporate and small funds that had offered defined-benefit schemes (even if few of these matured). Further, not all employers meet their legal obligations to make super contributions and, as compulsory super is a component of wage income, thereby commit a form of wage theft (Bryan and Rafferty 2018: 86–87). Wage theft is a pervasive risk to retirement income borne by a significant minority of households, reducing their super contributions and investment earnings in the longer term. Evidence suggests employers failed to pay $5.6 billion of compulsory super contributions, with 2.7 million employees losing $2,000 on average in 2013–14 alone (Senate Economics References Committee 2017: ix).

The main beneficiaries of the two-tier model of retirement incomes are private super funds and financial service providers. Private super funds benefit from the state's de facto role in reducing their exposure to financial risk through second-tier policies subsidising their operations; while compulsory employer contributions directed $66 billion into private super funds, the tax subsidies for super amounted to about $38 billion of revenue forgone in 2016–17 (PC 2018: 320; Treasury 2018: 19).[29] Private super funds charged account-holders a further $9 billion in fees in 2017 (APRA 2018b). According to Taylor (2011: 267), compulsory super is a financial windfall for the superannuation market and the financial sector more generally that guarantees their growth and insulates them from the consequences of poor performance.

A further aspect of the favourable legislative and regulatory conditions that superannuation market actors enjoy is that their de jure responsibilities are limited to a duty to maximise returns for members and act in their best interests. Alarmingly, state regulators appear to have little capacity to enforce this duty, with Morris (2018: 47) arguing the current regulatory framework of the financial services sector is too complex and not focused on super fund fees or investment performance. There is also no obligation for super funds either to achieve a minimal rate of investment return or to deliver a minimum benefit for retirees. Taylor et al. (2017: 258) argue the limits to the regulatory system stem from regulatory capture, with governments under pressure from the intense lobbying of the banking and financial services sector to protect the interests of private financial institutions over those of super fund members.

Instead, the financial risks of superannuation largely fall on households, although they are borne unevenly. The MySuper reforms have had only mixed success at reducing investment risk for inactive members because the performance of these default options has varied widely and individuals can change super funds but have no non-financialised alternative (PC 2018: 91; Taylor 2011: 267). When super funds incur investment losses, both active and inactive account-holders still pay fees. This was highlighted by the experience of the GFC, particularly among the losses incurred by super account-holders who belonged to age cohorts at or close to retirement age. It remains up to the discretion of individuals to select less-risky investment portfolios to reduce their exposure to market volatility in the leadup to retirement.

---

29   These figures include estimates for larger super funds and SMSFs. Most tax benefits for superannuation are paid out to individuals when they withdraw super benefits.

As the second tier of retirement income policy, superannuation is gradually extending patterns of income and wealth inequality from working life into retirement. This is partly because compulsory super contributions are determined by the level of labour market income and partly because investment returns tend to relate to the value of super assets held. Households with higher incomes and savings rates over their working life are best placed to supplement compulsory super with voluntary contributions and maximise the tax advantages. In contrast, households with lower incomes over their working life are least likely to receive large super benefits and could satisfy more immediate needs with that portion of income quarantined into superannuation such as saving for a home deposit or paying off other debt (Bryan and Rafferty 2018: 87). This is exacerbating broader social inequalities—including those pertaining to family and working life—since low-income households (of working age) are more likely to have members who are single parents, full-time informal carers, live alone, have a disability, privately rent housing, rely on income support, work part-time, receive a lower income due to the gender pay gap and/or are unemployed or underemployed (ACOSS 2018).[30]

Conclusions

Private superannuation has been transformed since the mid-1970s from a bifurcated occupational benefit for exclusive minorities in the public and private sectors into a tradable retirement product in a segmented market with almost universal workforce coverage. In the mid-1970s, superannuation was typically offered by employers in inhouse super funds. Despite the prevalence of defined-benefit schemes, super had a weak link with retirement because it was paid out when employees changed employer and there was no preservation age or portability. Superannuation was fashioned into a marketable retirement product through two decades of campaigns and reform, resulting in the current dominance of the accumulation model and regulations for portability,

---

30 While the top fifth of households receiving the highest incomes hold more than 45 per cent of super assets, the bottom 40 per cent of households earning the lowest incomes hold only 15 per cent (ACOSS 2018: 56). Households of retirement age were least likely to be receiving the highest incomes (ACOSS 2018: 39). While accounting for 15 per cent of households overall, only 6 per cent of households in the fifth income quintile (the 20 per cent of households with the highest incomes) had at least one member aged 65 years and over (ACOSS 2018: 39). In contrast, 29 per cent of households in the first income quintile and 19 per cent of those in the second income quintile were aged 65 years and over (ACOSS 2018: 3).

preservation and vesting that have transformed it into a retirement savings vehicle. Since the mid-1990s, financialisation has been restructuring superannuation into a segmented market, with one segment comprising larger institutional super funds and another segment consisting of SMSFs.

The superannuation market was established by a policy coalition of the union movement and Labor governments through three phases of mobilisation from the mid-1970s to the 1990s. In the first phase, the union movement developed the 'deferred wages' frame and instituted early prototypical union funds that combined a not-for-profit organisational structure with accumulation accounts for members. The union movement used these as political resources in the second phase; the 'deferred wages' framed was employed to prosecute the case for award super in the Accords and industry super funds were modelled on the prototypical union funds of the 1970s. Committed to the Accords as a signature policy, Labor governments pressed the case for award super to the AIRC and, after the latter's concerns constrained the ambitions of award super, enacted super fund operating standards. When the AIRC halted the industrial campaign for award super in 1990, Labor (with union support) circumvented this institutional hurdle in the third phase by legislating compulsory employer super contributions and regulatory operating standards in the early 1990s. According to Taylor et al. (2017: 267), the resulting superannuation market is 'extremely complex, publicly mandated, but privately controlled'.

After the institutional foundations were established, the superannuation market has been increasingly financialised by state and market restructuring since the mid-1990s. Larger super funds have consolidated their operations, following broader trends in the financial sector after the liberalisation of the 1980s and 1990s, increasing the scale of super assets held by profit-seeking financial conglomerates and industry super funds. As the experience of the GFC highlights, however, individuals ultimately bear the financial risks for private super held in accumulation accounts and the risks borne by financial actors are moderated by the future investments guaranteed from compulsory employer super contributions and fees for services routinely rendered. Subsequent reforms of both Labor and Coalition governments have sought not to change this, but to realign the behaviour of super funds, financial advisors and account-holders with that anticipated in competitive markets.

The apparent bipartisanship over compulsory private superannuation since the mid-1990s conceals the ongoing importance of partisan ideas and interests. On one hand, when in government, the Coalition and the retail super funds (with support from banking groups) developed the 'competition and choice' frame to construct insufficient competition between super funds as the policy problem and increasing consumer choice as the solution. This policy coalition used this frame to pursue reforms aimed at granting profit-seeking actors greater access to compulsory employer contributions, introducing new financial vehicles such as SMSFs that increased the role of financial service providers, and opposed Labor's legislation that sought to protect consumers (the FOFA reforms). On the other hand, Labor governments and industry super funds (with union support) have constructed a 'consumer protection' frame to justify reforms aimed at curtailing excessive rent-seeking among financial service providers (FOFA) and encouraging account-holders to act as consumers. These partisan differences demonstrate both the interest-based politics of superannuation policy and the risks, as Taylor et al. (2017) note, of regulatory capture.

The financialisation of private superannuation has coincided with its rapid expansion to become the secondary tier of retirement income policy. It follows that the expansion of superannuation has financialised retirement income policy, requiring members of virtually every Australian household (of working age) to invest in financial assets managed by private super accounts over their working life to shore up security in old age. The financialisation of retirement income policy is, nevertheless, partial because the age pension still collectively pools protection from the financial risks of old age and acts as the risk manager of last resort if superannuation investments fail. Still, the rising importance of superannuation to retirement income policy has transferred the risks to households without increasing those borne by employers or the financial sector. This transfer accentuates intragenerational inequalities, as households must stretch labour market incomes to cover both the purchase of the family home, which is increasingly unaffordable (especially in major cities), and the accumulation of private retirement income in the context of rising financial market volatility.

Epilogue: Self-funded stimulus during a global pandemic (and more)

Further consequences of both financialisation and marketisation for retirement policy have become evident since this chapter was written, particularly from the scheme for temporary early release of superannuation and reforms to superannuation in 2020. Among its early fiscal stimulus measures in response to the economic consequences of the Covid-19 pandemic, the Morrison Coalition government temporarily loosened the restrictions on the early release of superannuation. This allowed eligible individuals under retirement age experiencing financial hardship early in the pandemic to access up to $20,000 of super savings, from April to December 2020 (Treasury 2020). Super benefits accessed via this temporary scheme were exempt from tax. This scheme had a high take-up rate, with 4.8 million individuals (98 per cent of applicants) withdrawing $36.4 billion by January 2021 (APRA 2021). Evidence suggests most individuals accessing superannuation through this scheme spent it on rent, mortgage repayments or other household bills (ABS 2021).

Although surpassed in dollar terms by other stimulus measures, the temporary early release of super scheme is noteworthy in highlighting how financialised social policy can compound the role that households have in managing risks over the life course. The early release of super scheme amounted to a privatised stimulus measure that gave eligible households access to their private savings otherwise preserved for their retirement invested with private funds. This scheme amounted to individualised income-smoothing that did not require public spending (except for tax expenditures on super benefits), in which participating households had to self-manage the relative risks of withdrawing super early during the pandemic or preserving their investments until retirement for their financial security over the life course. Most applicants to the early release of super scheme belonged to groups who could afford it least and were unlikely to benefit from the tax concessions, being aged less than 40 years and having incomes of less than $90,000 (ATO 2021). For at least some of these households, the early release of super scheme was the main additional option available to respond to the financial insecurity presented by the pandemic as it pre-dated both JobKeeper and JobSeeker—the government's payments to employers and unemployed people, respectively, which were its eventual fiscal responses to the pandemic during 2020 and early 2021 (Elmas 2021). In granting access to private assets and individualising risk, the early access to superannuation scheme contrasts markedly with the collective risk-pooling typical of government stimulus measures funded by public debt or that of European social insurance schemes. It is also difficult to imagine European governments raiding social insurance schemes to pay for fiscal stimulus during an economic crisis.

Beyond the early release of superannuation scheme, the Morrison government introduced the 'Your Future, Your Super' reform package in late 2020. The government argued this package would reduce consumer fees and increase consumer choice. The reforms aimed to reduce fees by 'stapling' employees to their existing super accounts when they changed jobs, introducing caps on the fees for low-balance super accounts and banning exit fees (Frydenberg 2020). The government also claimed the package would increase choice by improving the transparency and accountability of super funds, with measures that require funds to invest to maximise financial returns, establish a new online comparison tool and introduce new reporting requirements to inform account-holders of underperformance. At first glance, these reforms may seem consistent with the 'consumer protection' frame outlined above in aiming to reduce rent-seeking and enable consumers (Karp 2021). But, the Your Future, Your Super reforms signalled the continuation of interest-based politics rather than heralding a new bipartisanship. Both Labor and the industry super funds opposed the government's reforms, arguing that 'stapling' would primarily benefit underperforming retail funds and the new investment rules sought to curb the activities of industry super funds (Karp 2021). Partisan contestation over superannuation policy should not be overstated, however, given the Coalition government recently increased the Superannuation Guarantee to 10 per cent of wages with Labor's support.

So, where to from here for retirement policy? With both major parties and powerful financial interests mostly supporting the status quo of the age pension and mandatory occupational super, incremental reforms to retirement policy seem much more likely than radical revisions over the next few years. Incremental reforms can, nevertheless, have far-reaching impacts in a $2.6 trillion super market. In closing, I briefly mention three potential reforms that could help to address (but clearly not solve) unresolved issues highlighted earlier in this chapter. First, as the financial impact of investment losses is far greater for those approaching (or at) retirement age, the government could require individuals to select 'safer' investment options once they reach a certain age to mitigate the risk.

Second, as recent reforms intended to encourage consumer choice and fund competition have had limited success, the government could set limits on annual fund fees. And third, as reduced super balances from extended absences from paid employment can reinforce intragenerational inequities, the Superannuation Guarantee should apply to paid parental leave and government benefits for working-aged individuals.

References

Aaron, H.J. (1984). Social welfare in Australia. In R.E. Caves & L.B. Krause (eds), *The Australian Economy: A view from the north* (pp. 349–90). Sydney: Allen & Unwin.

Australian Bureau of Statistics (ABS). (1982). *Superannuation Australia*. Canberra: ABS.

Australian Bureau of Statistics (ABS). (2021). Early access to superannuation used to pay household bills. Media release, 21 April, Canberra. Available from: www.abs.gov.au/media-centre/media-releases/early-access-superannuation-used-pay-household-bills.

Australian Council of Social Service (ACOSS). (2018). *Inequality in Australia 2018*. Sydney: ACOSS & University of New South Wales.

Australian Government. (1988). *Reform to the Taxation of Superannuation*. Canberra: Australian Government.

Australian Government. (2011). *Stronger Super*. Canberra: Australian Government.

Australian Industrial Relations Commission (AIRC). (1991). *National Wage Case October 1991: Reasons for decision*. Canberra: Australian Government.

Australian Prudential Regulation Authority (APRA). (2007). A recent history of superannuation in Australia. *APRA Insight*, 2: 3–10.

Australian Prudential Regulation Authority (APRA). (2016). *Annual Superannuation Bulletin*. Canberra: APRA.

Australian Prudential Regulation Authority (APRA). (2017). *Annual Superannuation Bulletin*. Canberra: APRA.

Australian Prudential Regulation Authority (APRA). (2018a). *Annual Superannuation Bulletin*. Canberra: APRA.

Australian Prudential Regulation Authority (APRA). (2018b). *Quarterly Superannuation Performance*. Canberra: APRA.

Australian Prudential Regulation Authority (APRA). (2021). *COVID-19 Early Release Scheme—Issue 36*. 8 February. Canberra: APRA. Available from: www.apra.gov.au/covid-19-early-release-scheme-issue-36.

Australian Securities and Investments Commission (ASIC). (2018). *Future of Financial Advice (FOFA) Reforms*. Canberra: ASIC. Available from: asic.gov.au/regulatory-resources/financial-services/regulatory-reforms/future-of-financial-advice-fofa-reforms/.

Australian Taxation Office (ATO). (2021). *COVID-19 Early Release of Super Report (20 April – December 2020)*. Canberra: ATO. Available from: www.ato.gov.au/super/sup/covid-19-early-release-of-super-report-(20-april---31-december-2020)/.

Bakir, C. (2003). Who needs a review of the financial system in Australia? The case of the Wallis inquiry. *Australian Journal of Political Science, 38*(3): 511–34. doi.org/10.1080/1036114032000134029.

Bateman, H. (2003). Regulation of Australian superannuation. *Australian Economic Review, 36*(1): 118–27. doi.org/10.1111/1467-8462.00272.

Borowski, A. (2005). The revolution that faltered: Two decades of reform of Australia's retirement income system. *International Social Security Review, 58*(4): 45–65. doi.org/10.1111/j.1468-246X.2005.00225.x.

Brown, C. & Davis, K. (2009). Is pension fund collaboration possible and sustainable? Insights from the Australian experience. Unpublished paper, Melbourne.

Brown, W. (2015). *Undoing the Demos: Neoliberalism's stealth revolution*. New York, NY: Zone Books.

Bryan, D. & Rafferty, M. (2018). *Risking Together: How finance is dominating everyday life in Australia*. Sydney: Sydney University Press.

Campbell, J.L. (2004). *Institutional Change and Globalization*. Princeton, NJ: Princeton University Press.

Castillo, J. (2012). Entrusting the trustees: The regulation of self-managed superannuation funds in Australia. Unpublished PhD thesis, University of Tasmania, Hobart. Available from: eprints.utas.edu.au/16743/2/whole-castillo-thesis-2013.pdf.

Castles, F.G. (1994). The wage earner's welfare state revisited: Refurbishing the established model of Australian social protection 1983–93. *Australian Journal of Social Issues*, *29*(2): 120–45. doi.org/10.1002/j.1839-4655.1994. tb00939.x.

Castles, F.G. (1997). The institutional design of the Australian welfare state. *International Social Security Review*, *50*(2): 25–34. doi.org/10.1111/j.1468-246X.1997.tb01065.x.

Clare, R. & Cranston, A. (2017). *The Australian Superannuation Industry.* Sydney: Association of Superannuation Funds of Australia.

Cleary, P. (1992). Democrats asked to formalise wish list. *Sydney Morning Herald*, 5 June.

Cooper, J. (2010). *Super System Review: Final report.* Canberra: Australian Government.

Covick, O. & Lewis, M.K. (1993). Insurance, superannuation and collective investments. In M.K. Lewis & R.H. Wallace (eds), *The Australian Financial System* (pp. 136–213). Melbourne: Longman Cheshire.

Covick, O. & Lewis, M.K. (1997). Insurance, superannuation and managed funds. In M.K. Lewis & R.H. Wallace (eds), *The Australian Financial System: Evolution, policy and practice* (pp. 221–93). Melbourne: Addison Wesley Longman.

Cutler, T. & Waine, B. (2001). Social insecurity and the retreat from social democracy: Occupational welfare in the long boom and financialization. *Review of International Political Economy*, *8*(1): 96–118. doi.org/10.1080/09692290010010308.

Daugaard, D. & Valentine, T.J. (1993). The banks. In M.K. Lewis & R.H. Wallace (eds), *The Australian Financial System* (pp. 39–82). Melbourne: Longman Cheshire.

Davis, I. (1998). The super divide. *Australian Financial Review*, 15 December.

Dixon, D. & Foster, C. (1982). *Alternative Strategies to Meet the Income Needs of the Aged.* Canberra: Social Welfare Policy Secretariat.

Elmas, M. (2021). Superannuation raids cost Australians thousands of dollars: Fund bosses. *The New Daily*, [Melbourne], 8 July. Available from: thenewdaily. com.au/finance/superannuation/2021/07/08/superannuation-early-release/.

Fligstein, N. & Dauter, L. (2007). The sociology of markets. *Annual Review of Sociology*, *33*(1): 105–28. doi.org/10.1146/annurev.soc.33.040406.131736.

Foster, C. (1988). *Towards a national retirement incomes policy: An overview*. Social Security Review Issues Paper No. 6. Canberra: Department of Social Security.

Fox Piven, F. (2015). Neoliberalism and the welfare state. *Journal of International and Comparative Social Policy*, *31*(1): 2–9. doi.org/10.1080/21699763.2014. 1001665.

Frydenberg, J. (2020). Supporting Australian workers and business. Joint media release, The Hon. Josh Frydenberg MP, Treasurer of the Commonwealth of Australia, with The Hon. Scott Morrison MP, Prime Minister, 22 March, Canberra. Available from: ministers.treasury.gov.au/ministers/josh-frydenberg-2018/media-releases/supporting-australian-workers-and-business.

Gingrich, J. (2011). *Making Markets in the Welfare State: The politics of varying market reforms*. Cambridge, UK: Cambridge University Press. doi.org/10.1017/ CBO9780511791529.

Gizycki, M. & Lowe, P. (2000). The Australian financial system in the 1990s. In D. Gruen & S. Shrestha (eds), *The Australian Economy in the 1990s* (pp. 180–215). Sydney: Reserve Bank of Australia. Available from: www.rba. gov.au/publications/confs/2000/pdf/conf-vol-2000.pdf.

Hacker, J. (2004). Privatizing risk without privatizing the welfare state: The hidden politics of social policy retrenchment in the United States. *American Political Science Review*, *98*(2): 243–60. doi.org/10.1017/S0003055404001121.

Hall, P. & Thelen, K. (2009). Institutional change in varieties of capitalism. *Socio-Economic Review*, *7*(1): 7–34. doi.org/10.1093/ser/mwn020.

Harvey, D. (2005). *A Brief History of Neoliberalism*. Oxford, UK: Oxford University Press. doi.org/10.1093/oso/9780199283262.001.0001.

Henry, K. (2010). *Australia's Future Tax System: Final report*. Canberra: Treasury.

Hewson, J. (1991). *Budget Reply Speech 1991–92*. Canberra: Parliament of Australia.

Holt, H. (1961). *House of Representatives Debates*, 26 April (pp. 1151–55). Canberra: Parliament of Australia.

Howe, B. (1989). *Better Incomes: Retirement incomes policy into the next century*. Canberra: Australian Government.

Insurance and Superannuation Commission (ISC). (1990). *Private Sector Superannuation Funds and Approved Deposit Funds 1987–88 and 1988–89*. Canberra: AGPS.

Insurance and Superannuation Commission (ISC). (1993). *Superannuation Bulletin 1991–92*. Canberra: AGPS.

Insurance and Superannuation Commission (ISC). (1994). *Superannuation Bulletin 1993–94.* Canberra: AGPS.

Kahler, A., Fielding, Z., Priest, M. & Mather, J. (2010). Shake-up for financial planners. *Australian Financial Review,* 27 April.

Karp, P. (2021). Australian superannuation changes: What do they mean for you? *The Guardian,* [Australia], 18 June. Available from: www.theguardian.com/australia-news/2021/jun/18/australian-superannuation-changes-what-do-they-mean-for-you.

Kelly, P. (2008). *The End of Certainty: Power, politics and business in Australia.* 2nd edn. Sydney: Allen & Unwin.

Keneley, M. (2001). The evolution of the Australian life insurance industry. *Accounting, Business & Financial History, 11*(2): 145–70. doi.org/10.1080/09585200122306.

Kerin, J. (1991). *Budget Speech 1991–92.* Canberra: Parliament of Australia.

Kingston, G., Piggott, J. & Bateman H. (1992). Customised investment strategies for accumulations superannuation. In K. Davis & I. Harper (eds), *Superannuation and the Australian Financial System* (pp. 139–56). Sydney: Allen & Unwin.

Knox, D. (1983). Employer-sponsored superannuation in Australia. *Current Affairs Bulletin,* February: 4–13.

Knox, D. (1986). Occupational superannuation in Australia: Present and future. In R. Mendelsohn (ed.), *The Finance of Old Age* (pp. 35–50). Canberra: Centre for Research on Federal Financial Relations.

Lewis, M.K. & Wallace, R.H. (1993). *The Australian Financial System.* Melbourne: Longman Cheshire.

Maley, K. (1992). Super law to be torpedoed. *Sydney Morning Herald,* 13 June.

Mann, K. (1993). Supermen, women and pensioners: The politics of superannuation reform. *International Journal of Sociology and Social Policy, 13*(7): 29–62. doi.org/10.1108/eb013179.

Meagher, G. & Goodwin, S. (2015). Introduction: Capturing marketisation in Australian social policy. In G. Meagher & S. Goodwin (eds), *Markets, Rights and Power in Australian Social Policy* (pp. 1–28). Sydney: Sydney University Press. doi.org/10.30722/sup.9781920899950.

Mirowski, P. (2013). *Never Let a Serious Crisis Go to Waste: How neoliberalism survived the financial meltdown.* New York, NY: Verso.

Morris, N. (2018). *Management and Regulation of Pension Schemes: Australia— A cautionary tale.* London: Routledge. doi.org/10.4324/9781315268132.

National Superannuation Committee of Inquiry (NSCI). (1976). *Occupational Superannuation in Australia: Final report of the Superannuation Committee of Inquiry.* Canberra: Australian Government.

Nielson, L. & Harris, B. (2009). *Chronology of Superannuation and Retirement Income in Australia.* Canberra: Department of Parliamentary Services.

Olsberg, D. (1994). Australia's retirement income revolution: A new model for retirement savings and investment politics. *Economic and Industrial Democracy, 15*(2): 283–91. doi.org/10.1177/0143831X94152008.

Olsberg, D. (1997). *Ageing and Money: Australia's retirement revolution.* Sydney: Allen & Unwin.

Organisation for Economic Co-operation and Development (OECD). (2009). *Pensions at a Glance: Retirement incomes systems in OECD countries.* Paris: OECD Publishing.

Patten, S. (2012). Banks seek financial advice concessions. *Australian Financial Review*, 16 October.

Pierson, P. (2004). *Politics in Time: History, institutions and social analysis.* Princeton, NJ: Princeton University Press.

Polanyi, K. (1944). *The Great Transformation: The political and economic origins of our time.* 2nd edn. New York, NY: Beacon Press.

Productivity Commission (PC). (2018). *Superannuation: Assessing efficiency and competitiveness.* Draft report. Canberra: Productivity Commission.

Rein, M. & Schon, D. (1993). Reframing policy discourse. In F. Fischer & J. Forrester (eds), *The Argumentative Turn in Policy Analysis and Planning* (pp. 145–66). Durham, NC: Duke University Press.

Reserve Bank of Australia (RBA). (1997). Privatisation in Australia. *Reserve Bank of Australia Bulletin*, December: 7–16.

Senate Economics References Committee. (2017). *Superbad: Wage theft and non-compliance of the Superannuation Guarantee.* May. Canberra: Parliament of Australia. Available from: www.aph.gov.au/Parliamentary_Business/Committees/Senate/Economics/SuperannuationGuarantee/Report.

Senate Standing Committee on Community Affairs (SSCCA). (1988). *Income Support for the Retired and the Aged: An agenda for reform.* Canberra: Parliament of Australia.

Sharp, R. (1992). The rise and rise of occupational superannuation under Labor. *Journal of Australian Political Economy*, *30*: 24–41.

Sharp, R. (2009). The super revolution. In G. Bloustein, B. Comber & A. Mackinnon (eds), *The Hawke Legacy* (pp. 198–211). Adelaide: Wakefield Press.

Spies-Butcher, B. & Stebbing, A. (2011). Population ageing and tax reform in a dual welfare state. *Economic and Labour Relations Review*, *22*(3): 45–64. doi.org/10.1177/103530461102200304.

Spies-Butcher, B. & Stebbing, A. (2019). Mobilising alternative futures: Generational accounting and the fiscal politics of ageing in Australia. *Ageing & Society*, *39*(7): 1409–35. doi.org/10.1017/S0144686X18000028.

St Anne, C. (2012). *A Super History: How Australia's $1 trillion+ superannuation industry was made*. Sydney: Major Street.

Stebbing, A. (2015). The devil's in the detail: The shift to private retirement incomes. In G. Meagher & S. Goodwin (eds), *Markets, Rights and Power in Australian Social Policy* (pp. 115–52). Sydney: Sydney University Press. doi.org/10.30722/sup.9781920899950.

Stilwell, F. (1986). *The Accord and Beyond: The political economy of the Labor government*. Sydney: Pluto Press.

Swedberg, R. (2006). Markets in society. In N.J. Smelser & R. Swedberg (eds), *The Handbook of Economic Sociology* (pp. 233–53). 2nd edn. Princeton, NJ: Princeton University Press.

Sword, G. (1986). The Storemen and Packers' Union superannuation scheme. In R. Mendelsohn (ed.), *The Finance of Old Age* (pp. 95–106). Canberra: Centre for Research on Federal Financial Relations.

Taylor, S. (2011). Captured legislators and their twenty billion dollar annual superannuation cost legacy. *Australian Accounting Review*, *21*(3): 266–81. doi.org/10.1111/j.1835-2561.2011.00142.x.

Taylor, S., Asher, A. & Tarr, J.A. (2017). Accountability in regulatory reform: Australia's superannuation paradox. *Federal Law Review*, *45*(2): 257–89. doi.org/10.1177/0067205X1704500205.

Thelen, K. (2012). *Varieties of Liberalization and the New Politics of Social Solidarity*. Cambridge, UK: Cambridge University Press. doi.org/10.1017/CBO9781107282001.

The Treasury. (1997). *Submission to the Financial System Inquiry*. Canberra: Australian Government.

The Treasury. (2001). Toward higher retirement incomes for Australians: A history of the Australian retirement incomes system since Federation. *Economic Roundup*, Centenary Edition: 65–92.

The Treasury. (2018). *Tax Expenditure Statement*. Canberra: Australian Government.

The Treasury. (2020). Early access to superannuation. *Fact Sheet: Economic response to the coronavirus*. Last updated 17 April. Canberra: Australian Government. Available from: treasury.gov.au/sites/default/files/2020-04/Fact_sheet-Early_Access_to_Super.pdf.

van der Zwan, N. (2014). Making sense of financialization. *Socio-Economic Review*, *12*(1): 99–129. doi.org/10.1093/ser/mwt020.

Vogel, S. (2007). Why freer markets need more rules. In M.K. Landy, M.A. Levin & M. Shapiro (eds), *Creating Competitive Markets: The politics of regulatory reform* (pp. 25–42). Washington, DC: Brookings Institution Press.

Vogel, S. (2018). *Marketcraft: How governments make markets work*. Oxford, UK: Oxford University Press. doi.org/10.1093/oso/9780190699857.001.0001.

Wacquant, L. (2012). Three steps to a historical anthropology of actually existing neoliberalism. *Social Anthropology*, *20*(1): 66–79. doi.org/10.1111/j.1469-8676.2011.00189.x.

Wallace, R.H. & Lewis, M.K. (1993). Introduction. In M.K. Lewis & R.H. Wallace (eds), *The Australian Financial System* (pp. 1–10). Melbourne: Longman Cheshire.

Wallis, S. (1997). *Financial System Inquiry: Final report*. Canberra: Australian Government.

Whiteley, D. (2010). Both parties need to back these changes into law. *The Australian*, 24 April.

Yates, J. (2010). Housing and tax: The triumph of politics over economics. Paper prepared for the Conference on Australia's Future Tax System: A post-Henry review, Sydney, 21–23 June.

Yates, J. & Bradbury, B. (2010). Home ownership as a (crumbling) fourth pillar of social insurance in Australia. *Journal of Housing and the Built Environment*, *25*(2): 193–211. Doi.org/10.1007/s10901-010-9187-4.

5
Marketisation in disability services: A history of the NDIS

Georgia van Toorn

Introduction

The National Disability Insurance Scheme (NDIS) has instituted a hyper-marketised model of disability service provision in Australia since its introduction in 2013. While disability services have long been provided by a mix of public, not-for-profit and for-profit providers, the NDIS aims to use the mechanism of individualised funding to establish a national competitive market. Individualised funding cashes out government funding as individual budgets that recipients can use to purchase services from providers or have services purchased on their behalf by third-party brokers. Whereas the previous system was governed at the state and territory level using contracts and competitive tendering between state governments and providers, the NDIS is the first federally regulated scheme to provide monetary payments in lieu of services provided or funded directly by government. While state governments are withdrawing from direct service provision, the federal government is committed to 'as minimal interference as possible in the market' (NDIA 2016c: 20). Consequently, the NDIS represents an important shift in the political economy of disability service provision, prioritising the role of markets in addressing social needs.

The NDIS is one of the largest, most costly and most rapidly implemented social policy reforms in Australia's history. Despite this, little has been written about its origins.[1] Scholars and commentators who are otherwise critical of market-based social service models initially suspended criticism of the NDIS, given its progressive reputation and links with the disability movement. More recently, however, issues of privatisation, unequal access, poor regulation, bureaucratic gatekeeping and workforce are receiving critical attention in both popular media and scholarship (Cortese et al. 2021; Cortis and van Toorn 2022; Malbon et al. 2019; Murphy 2020; Schultz 2020; Wilson et al. 2021).[2] Questions are being raised about how and why a scheme intended to empower disabled Australians has unintended consequences that, prima facie, seem to have the opposite effect. Such questions prompt critical reflection on the NDIS and the politics that have shaped its evolution.

Much of the existing literature on the NDIS emphasises its endogenous roots, playing down how the Australian experience accords with global trends in individualised, market-based disability provision. The policy's origins have been located in the Third Way social investment paradigm embraced by the Australian Labor Party (Needham and Dickinson 2018), the 'pro-market, pro-privatisation pedigree' of Australia's top policy advisors (Miller and Hayward 2017: 133) and in the human rights framework through which the Australian disability movement pressed its demands (Thill 2015).

While these accounts provide valuable insights, my aim in this chapter is to broaden the analysis beyond the nation-state by exploring some of the exogenous sources of policy learning and resource mobilisation that led to the adoption of individualised disability funding in Australia. I do so by tracing the transnational linkages and pathways through which individualised funding has travelled from the United Kingdom, paying particular attention to the role of disability and civil society advocacy groups in sourcing and translating ideas from abroad. I identify a variety of civil society groups whose advocacy work was central to Australia's adoption of individualised funding. I explore these transnational networks and examine what effects they had on domestic disability politics and policy

---

1   There has been relatively greater academic interest in the history of public health care in Australia, which is financed via an equivalent mechanism (that is, a designated tax levy) but delivered through a different funding model.
2   These issues are discussed further in the Epilogue to this chapter.

formation. To understand how such networks become implicated in the wider marketisation reform process, however, it is essential to look beyond the network itself. I therefore also consider the conditioning contexts that influence advocacy and the political arenas where ideas are remoulded, re-signified and repurposed in the service of other agendas. In so doing, we can appreciate how political and economic factors external to the network also shaped and constrained the way individualised funding was sold to, and implemented by, Australian social reformers. That is, we can begin to see how policy cooption occurs because of advocates acting in and on their immediate political environment.

The chapter is based on original empirical material collected through interviews as well as secondary sources. A key policy figure featured in this chapter, Jane Sinclair, was a founding member of advocacy group In Control Australia.[3] Her account details the behind-the-scenes advocacy that shaped government thinking in the years leading up to and during the scheme's development. To supplement her account, I also draw on In Control publications and promotional materials as textual artefacts of its advocacy and lobbying efforts. Another set of key actors is disabled people engaged in policy advocacy and activism as members or representatives of disabled people's organisations (DPOs). DPOs are distinguished from non-user-led collectives, such as In Control, by the fact they are run by and for disabled people, according to principles of self-advocacy and self-determination (Barnes et al. 1999). The advocates and activists featured in this chapter include Therese Sands, who, at the time of interview, was the director of Australia's peak body of DPOs, Disabled People's Organisations Australia, and writer and activist El Gibbs. The final set of actors with firsthand insight into how global trends in individualised funding have manifested in Australia are the policymakers and bureaucrats who witnessed the construction of the NDIS as inside observers. Their accounts offered valuable insights into the internal processes and priorities shaping the design of the scheme. Also important for the purposes of this chapter is the way the scheme has been made *operational* through ongoing processes of institutional restructuring. As the case of the NDIS shows, marketisation is made possible through the relatively radical reordering of the state and its institutions. Once we begin to think about policy as a means of transforming the form and function of state institutions, a much wider range of actors comes into play, aside from those who 'make' policy.

---

3   'Jane' is a pseudonym to protect her identity.

For instance, even though the design of the NDIS is formally a federal government responsibility, the states have been implicated in the scheme's implementation, having agreed to dismantle various state government agencies and privatise their service functions—ostensibly to 'support the successful implementation of the NDIS' (NSW Government n.d.).[4] State officials therefore have a role in the scheme's operationalisation. Their decisions to withdraw as the 'provider of last resort' have been hugely important in facilitating privatisation under the scheme. One such official is featured in this chapter to shed light on the motivations behind these privatisations and to underscore some of the more contradictory and contested elements of the scheme's operation.

The chapter's structure reflects this dual concern with the micro and macro aspects of policy formation. Following a brief overview of the conceptual and institutional design of the NDIS, I consider several key policy players, processes and events that shaped the development of the scheme. This is followed by an analysis of the intermediary role of In Control Australia and other advocacy groups who mobilised around individualised funding. I pay particular attention to the In Control network because their transnational advocacy, among other things, facilitated the spread of individualised funding from the United Kingdom to Australia. The final section situates these processes in the changing political economy of disability service provision. These macro-structural dynamics are, I argue, key to understanding the specific and highly marketised form individualised funding has taken in Australia.

The anatomy of the NDIS

The NDIS has been described as a 'hybrid' scheme, combining several different and potentially conflicting principles and design features (Miller and Hayward 2017; Needham and Dickinson 2018). Framed broadly as a social insurance program, the scheme is available to all Australians regardless of income, wealth and work status, provided they meet a set of criteria related to disability. Access to NDIS funding is determined through the rules governing eligibility, under which prospective participants must have 'substantially reduced functional capacity' due to impairment/s that

---

4   In the case of New South Wales, for example, the agreement to 'support the transition of existing NSW services to the non-government organisation sector' was set out in a bilateral agreement between the Commonwealth and the State of New South Wales (COAG 2015: 4).

are permanent, affect their capacity for social or economic participation and necessitate life-long support under the NDIS (NDIA 2019). To be approved as part of a person's individual package, supports must be judged 'reasonable and necessary' by the statutory authority overseeing the scheme, the National Disability Insurance Agency (NDIA), and included in the participant's individual plan (which outlines individuals' goals and aspirations and how funded supports will contribute to fulfilling these) (Laragy and Fisher 2020). All NDIS participants have a plan developed with the NDIA and the option of self-managing their funds or using an NDIA planner or external brokerage service. It was estimated that by 2019–20, 475,000 Australians—those (and only those) classified as having a permanent and severe disability—would be in receipt of an individualised budget, and the time of writing that number had reached 535,000 (NDIA 2020; NDIA 2022).

The insurance aspect is related to how support is costed and how the scheme itself is financed. Rather than governments funding services through block grants, funding is allocated based on individual needs, which are calculated annually but expected to continue through an individual's life course. Theoretically, this creates an incentive for the insurer—in this case, the state—to intervene early and fund the necessary supports to enhance independence later in life, in the hope of reducing future dependence on the system (Steketee 2013). Under the new scheme, funding for disability services is a federal government responsibility, with state and territory governments now returning a portion of their revenue to fund the NDIS alongside federal revenue streams—namely, the 0.5 per cent increase to the Medicare Levy[5] introduced in 2014 (PC 2017).

Another key feature of the scheme is the invocation of human rights norms as a basis for entitlement to individualised, self-directed support from the state. Passed in 2013 by a Labor government, with support from the conservative Coalition, the *National Disability Insurance Scheme Act 2013* (*NDIS Act*) was the first in Australia's history to place a statutory duty on the state to provide for needs arising from disability (Soldatic et al. 2014). It is strongly framed around Australia's obligations under the United Nations Convention on the Rights of Persons with Disabilities to grant disabled citizens equal rights to 'determine their own best interests,

---

5   The Medicare Levy is charged on taxable income, collected by the Australian Taxation Office and paid into consolidated revenue, to assist with the costs of Australia's national public health insurance system, Medicare.

including the right to exercise choice and control … in decisions that will affect their lives' (*NDIS Act* [Cth], s. 4.8). The Act gives expression to these rights by enabling participants to access public funding for the supports included in their individual plan.

The NDIS has, prima facie, the appearance of a 'big-government' social insurance program. Notions of shared risk, collective responsibility and social investment characterise the scheme as 'analogous to the postwar Beveridge reforms of the welfare state' (Needham and Dickinson 2018: 732). The scheme is projected to cost more than $30 billion a year by 2024–25, by which time the level of public spending on the NDIS will have surpassed the spending on Medicare (Australian Government 2021). As part of this institutional reordering of the state and its functions, the government has taken on new roles in regulating, legislating and supporting the development of a competitive market for disability services (Carey et al. 2018). As a stimulatory measure, this unprecedented injection of disability funding is expected to create 'clear incentives for [market] growth, expansion and entrance by new organisations' (NDIA 2016c: 7). So, while the scheme may have the appearance of a Keynesian-era social welfare program, what is in fact emerging is a new institutional apparatus and regulatory regime dedicated to the optimal functioning of a 'radically new disability marketplace', based on principles of competition, economic efficiency and cost containment (NDIA 2016c: 3).

As Bode (2009: 167) reminds us, 'welfare delivery, including its marketized forms, take[s] shape *through organisational action*, hence the need to consider the very agencies which make welfare markets work'. The agency tasked with making the NDIS market 'work' is the NDIA. The logic of marketisation is captured in the NDIA's governing ethos. One of its main aims is to facilitate the growth of 'a vibrant, multifaceted, open and competitive marketplace'—a role it terms 'market stewardship' (NDIA 2016c: 3). This role involves almost no direct service provision and very minimal commissioning. It does, however, entail some intervention in the supply side of the market, by ensuring a business-friendly environment for service providers and, importantly, by fostering in them an entrepreneurial mindset (NDIA 2016c). The NDIA (2016c: 11) maintains that '[e]xisting providers need to adapt their business models to a contestable marketplace … They will need to operate efficiently without direct government procurement, and in a way that is attractive to consumers'. 'Market readiness' is the term often used in reference to what the agency is seeking to achieve in its work with these organisations (NDIA 2016a: 26; 2016b: 30). Rather than intervening in the market—through, for example, monitoring the supply of services and supplementing the market where supply is not meeting demand—its more circumscribed role seems to entail simply setting 'the rules of the game (e.g. prices)', overseeing the provider registration process and establishing a nationally consistent set of quality and safeguarding mechanisms on the basis of which providers are expected to self-regulate (Carey et al. 2018: 18; Cortis and van Toorn 2022).

The NDIS is premised, then, on two parallel and contradictory framings—one based on social insurance principles, the other on a market logic of demand-driven service provision. It is the melding of these two conflicting design principles that makes the NDIS unique in Australia. Whereas social insurance implies a collective, state-centric and universal means of social protection, individualised funding delivers social supports on an individual basis via the mechanism of the market. To the extent these two frames coexist alongside and in conflict with one another, it is no accident. Each frame is a historical artefact of the way the NDIS was conceptualised by the various actors and groups involved in its design. Both the insurance and the market-oriented aspects of the scheme can be traced back to several key policy processes, players and events.

The making of the NDIS

The first key event in the making of the NDIS was a national leaders' summit hosted in 2008 by the then Labor prime minister, Kevin Rudd (see Figure 5.1). The Australia 2020 Summit, as it was called, brought together more than 1,000 of Australia's leading thinkers 'to tackle the long-term challenges confronting Australia' (Davis 2008: 1). It was here the idea of a national disability insurance scheme was first publicly floated. Its broad outlines had been sketched by Bruce Bonyhady, a prominent economist and policy advisor, a father of two sons with disability and a former chair of Yooralla, one of Australia's largest and most generously funded non-government disability service providers. He went on to play a leading role in the design of the scheme and later became inaugural chair of the NDIA (Manne 2011). Bonyhady did not attend the summit, but had his proposal championed by delegates (Crabb 2016). His idea, in essence, was to incorporate insurance principles within a publicly funded, national individualised funding scheme. The scheme he envisaged would guarantee all Australians the right to individualised support should they be born with or acquire a disability before the age of 65, provided they met the eligibility criteria. As mentioned above, the scheme would take an individual and lifetime approach to disability funding, in contrast to the previous system, which was funded cyclically and hence prone to cost-cutting and capping (Bonyhady 2016). Framing it as insurance, rather than 'welfare', Bonyhady hoped, would also help instigate a shift from a charitable to a rights-based approach to disability service provision (Bonyhady 2016). The scheme was considered one of the most promising and innovative ideas to come out of the summit (Davis 2008; Soldatic and Pini 2012).

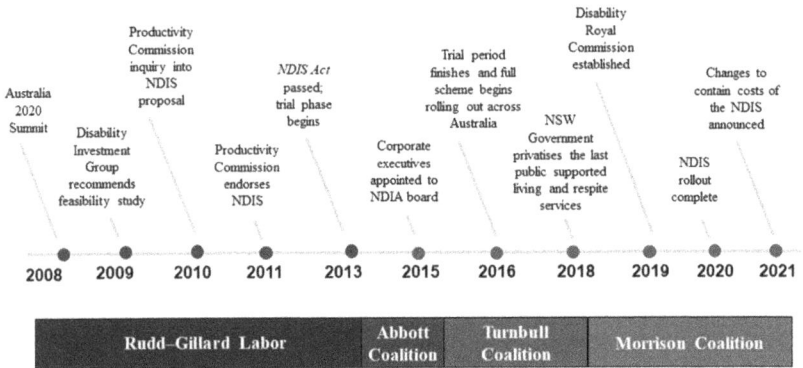

Figure 5.1 Timeline of NDIS policy developments
Source: Based on author's research.

Following the summit, the issue of disability care became the focus of unprecedented political discussion. Labor's Parliamentary Secretary for Disability Services Bill Shorten promptly appointed a group of experts, including Bonyhady and John Walsh, an actuary at business services firm PricewaterhouseCoopers, to 'explore innovative funding ideas from the private sector that will help people with disability and their families access greater support and plan for the future' (PwC 2009: 1). The Disability Investment Group, as it was called, published a report calling for 'structural reform' to the disability service system, using an individualised 'social insurance type approach' (PwC 2009: v). This echoed the findings of an important report, called *Shut Out: the experience of people with disabilities and their families in Australia*, in which a cross-sector alliance of disability advocacy bodies, carers' groups and service providers described the system as 'irretrievably broken and broke, chronically under-funded[,] under-resourced, [and] crisis driven' (National People with Disabilities and

Carer Council 2009). The Disability Investment Group recommended the government commission a feasibility study into a national disability insurance scheme, to which the government responded by referring the matter to the Australian Productivity Commission.

The second significant event in the making of the NDIS was the ensuing public inquiry conducted by the Productivity Commission in 2010–11. The inquiry comprised an extensive public consultation with disability, industry and policy stakeholders. During the inquiry, the NDIS was reframed in ways that more closely resembled the Productivity Commission's own ideological predispositions and practical mission. The commission's raison d'être is to promote competition and the use of market mechanisms to solve all manner of policy problems. Its bias towards market solutions was evident in the issues paper it released to inform consultations. In it, stakeholders were invited to comment on the proposed approach, whereby:

> under individualised funding, people with disabilities or their families would have a greater capacity to choose the services that best met their needs. Service provision would then be consumer-focused (as in most markets), and block funding of service providers by governments would largely disappear. (PC 2010a: 25)

This was the beginning of a shift in the way individualised funding was conceptualised and promoted by elite policy communities. Bonyhady's 'social insurance–type approach' still provided an overarching policy framework but with a strong added emphasis on competition and consumer choice. During the inquiry, the commission received more than 1,000 public submissions. Through these, it received widespread endorsement, or at least qualified support, from civil society and other stakeholders for the market-based model it was proposing. Stakeholders across the political spectrum viewed the scheme as consistent with the maximisation of consumer choice and control (see, for example, In Control Australia 2010; NDS 2010; NSW Government 2010). Through the consultation process, a modified vision of the NDIS emerged, which was then more fully elaborated in the commission's report to the government (PC 2011b).

The commission's vision for the NDIS was for a market-based system of disability provisioning in which consumer demand, as an expression of individual needs and preferences, would drive the quality and supply of services. Its report placed a heavy emphasis on 'consumer choice', stressing that currently, the government was 'the main constraint on competition and responsiveness to people with disability and carers' (PC 2011b: 407). Individualised funding would also serve a market-disciplinary function. While consumers would enjoy greater choice and control over their support, service providers would be compelled to compete to 'satisfy the needs of consumers, given that they would otherwise lose their business' (PC 2011b: 357).

Such statements reveal the values animating advocates of market-based models of welfare in general and the NDIS in particular. On the one hand, these include the assumption that government, by definition, is unresponsive to the needs and preferences of service users. In this view, government represents a kind of bureaucratic sludge through which users must labour, and which ultimately restricts the efficient allocation of social services. On the other hand, government is assumed to constrain competition and therefore undermine the quality of services that a functioning market would otherwise guarantee. On both points, it is an article of faith that the market rather than government holds the key to cheaper and better outcomes.

Behind the scenes, both before and after the Australia 2020 Summit and the Productivity Commission's inquiry, disability advocacy groups were also working among the nation's top federal Labor politicians and members of the public service to cultivate support for a Commonwealth-funded individualised scheme. This advocacy work was crucial in so far as it helped build consensus and support for the scheme among politically polarised groups, including disability and carer organisations as well as powerful industry stakeholders. In what follows, I explore the role of advocates in more depth—in particular, the role of transnational advocacy networks in facilitating the spread of market-based models of state restructuring.

Framing disability: Transnational advocacy in the age of marketisation

From a neo-institutional perspective, the evolution of policy is viewed as a path-dependent process. This means the way a policy develops owes much to decisions already taken and patterns of decision-making that, over time, become institutionally entrenched (Brenner and Theodore 2002). If historical memory is to some degree encoded into formal decision-making processes, the domain of civil society advocacy must have its own policy-shaping path dependencies, too. Following the cultural turn in social movement theory, these path dependencies have tended to be viewed in normative-symbolic terms, as frameworks that guide collective action and advocacy on a given issue (Benford and Snow 2000). Tarrow, for example, argues that certain trends or cultures of advocacy begin to crystalise when 'a given collective action frame becomes part of the political culture—which is to say, part of the reservoir of symbols from which future movement entrepreneurs can choose' (quoted in Keck and Sikkink 1999: 95). In other words, the way in which issues have been framed in the past will continue to shape future framings.

The Australian disability movement is unique in having long framed disability as a consumer rights issue, as opposed to a human rights or social justice issue (Newell 1996). Newell (1996) argues this consumer orientation has its roots in the dominance of non-disabled professionals, bureaucrats and service providers in disability advocacy. He suggests organisations *of* disabled people have not had the same social, human and financial capital as the welfare and service provider lobbies. Consequently, disabled people have lacked an effective political voice. By contrast, organisations *for* disabled people, such as the Australian Council for Rehabilitation of the Disabled (ACROD), were considered well organised and highly effective at representing the interests of service providers (Newell 1996). ACROD, now called National Disability Services (NDS), as the peak body for private and charitable disability providers, is still one of the leading lobby groups and was one of the driving forces behind the $5 million campaign for the NDIS (NDS 2013).[6] Professional advocacy bodies like NDS tend to operate within the fairly circumscribed parameters of state-sanctioned consumer advocacy and political discourse. While they may be prepared to lend their support to consumer causes in the belief that 'increased consumer choice will help to assure quality [service provision]', they are less inclined to weigh into debates about the desirability or otherwise of market-led reform strategies (NDS 2015: 2). Hence, it has been left to user-led groups to defend their interests against the 'many things [that] have been done in the name of the "rights" of people with disabilities', including the extension of market forces into disability services (Newell 1996: 430).

---

6   For further discussion of the 'Every Australian Counts' campaign, see Thill (2015), NDS (2013) and Steketee (2013).

Yet disabled people and their organisations, Newell (1996) argues, have also contributed to the framing of disability issues in ways that resonate with policy agendas of marketisation and privatisation. Newell noted in the mid-1990s that:

> [i]n Australia the last 10 years has featured organisations of people with disabilities defining themselves as 'consumers', attaching themselves to the politically stronger discourse of consumerism. Via this discourse political ends have been achieved, including representation in government and non-government arenas ... Hence, predominantly in Australia many do not identify as 'the disability rights movement' but as 'consumers with disability'. (1996: 429)

Disability advocacy groups are no longer in the business of consumer advocacy—at least not to the extent Newell described in 1996—and most now firmly identify with the disability rights orientation to which Newell refers. As the case of the NDIS shows, however, such groups still at times selectively appropriate consumer discourse to help give their proposals more widespread political appeal.

To appreciate how consumer discourse came to feature in advocacy around individualised funding and the NDIS, we can distinguish two distinct phases in this advocacy, separated by the Productivity Commission inquiry. The first phase saw disability advocates and other supporters of individualised funding look to other countries as exemplars of individualised approaches. Here, the advocacy group In Control played an important, behind-the-scenes role. In Control Australia was established in 2008 and was formally affiliated with, and partly modelled on, the original In Control non-government organisation (NGO) based in England and founded by Simon Duffy, an influential disability advocate and the architect of the United Kingdom's 'personalised budgeting' system (Epstein-Frisch 2009). The Australian network described itself as a 'collaboration involving a number of individuals and agencies around Australia', who 'share a determination to see self-directed funding [or] Individualised Funding ... available as a standard option for people living with disability' (In Control Australia 2010: 3). Its mission was to promote the idea, support the small number of individualised funding programs already operating across Australia and bring international evidence and experience to bear on developments in Australia (In Control Australia 2010). The network saw its role as providing 'an avenue for information exchange, critical inquiry, dialogue, collaboration, leadership and influence', with the 'common use of the name [signalling] a common interest in discovering and sharing best practice, on an "open source" basis' (In Control Australia 2010: 3). While not the most prominent or influential voice in the chorus of disability reform/advocacy groups, In Control Australia managed to carve out a role for itself as an organisation of individualised funding policy specialists.

As interest in, and support for, an Australian individualised funding scheme began to mount after the Australia 2020 Summit, In Control found there was a growing audience for its ideas. The network played an intermediary role in bringing these ideas to the attention of key politicians and bureaucrats. Its approach was to marshal the 'wealth of evidence and experience of how [individualised funding] has been successfully implemented in international jurisdictions', including the United Kingdom, and present this to government as a working model of how it could operate in Australia (In Control Australia 2010: 6). At the time, the UK arm of In Control was overseeing an open-source repository of individualised funding–related information, research, practice guidelines and success stories (In Control 2011). Members of In Control Australia disseminated these materials in high-level discussions with governments in the years leading up to the 2010–11 Productivity Commission inquiry. As one of its founding members explained to me in an interview:

> [In Control] was a tool for informing the sector here in Australia and for lobbying government ... There was new information from In Control UK that one just gets by email and keeping in touch with certain people. And we caught a momentum. [In Control Australia] was very effective because there was lots of new stuff coming out of the UK and I would just read it and pass on materials to the senior people in [the NSW Department of Ageing, Disability and Home Care] ... In Control Australia became a place of ... 'authoritative information'—up-to-date perspectives, and what have you. And we could just flood decision-makers ... In Control UK was terrific ... [Using the In Control name] gave it authority. (Jane, individualised funding advocate)

The effectiveness of this strategy is evident in the fact that all the major individualised funding program evaluations conducted by In Control in the United Kingdom were subsequently cited in the Productivity Commission's report (PC 2011c). The Productivity Commission found these studies provided 'compelling evidence', 'generally revealing highly positive views about the impacts of self-directed funding' on both individuals and the economy (PC 2011a: 1–2).

As the idea of a national disability insurance scheme gained momentum after the 2008 leaders' summit, and the national Disability Investment Group was investigating issues of feasibility, there was interest among Labor ministers, federal public servants and the group itself in how individualised funding operated elsewhere, and how it could work in Australia (PwC 2009). Identifying the opportunity to contribute ideas and expertise, In Control Australia began staging events to bring members of the extended network into contact with Australian decision-makers (Epstein-Frisch 2009). Reflecting on the group's intermediary role, an In Control Australia founding member recounted that during this time:

> [W]e were able to use UK people to host … quite a number [of] events … We had some In Control folk come out to Australia and what was exciting in those days was that we knew more than government. And so we would bring out people and they would clamour, senior [ministers] … you know, I had a seminar with someone talking about [the UK resource allocation system] and I had the minister and his policy staff and they wanted their own event. (Jane, individualised funding advocate)

The informant goes on to explain how at the time:

> everyone was kind of struggling with questions around resource allocation, etc., and … I hosted a roundtable … [with] people from [the departments of the] Prime Minister [and Cabinet], Premier and Cabinet, and Treasury … the central agencies, not just [state] agencies … we were the resource that could put them in touch with experts from overseas about how these mechanisms worked. (Jane, individualised funding advocate)

In the second phase, there was a marked shift in emphasis and in the language of advocacy, starting around the time the Productivity Commission began its inquiry in 2010. Whereas advocacy for individualised funding had previously emphasised social inclusion, citizen agency and self-empowerment, In Control and large sections of the disability rights lobby increasingly adopted the commission's own framing of the NDIS as a pro-market enterprise promising greater consumer 'choice'. That is not to say that advocates themselves were adherents of marketisation per se, but that their vision of how individualised funding would work was framed in ways that were compatible with that agenda. For example, in its submission to the Productivity Commission's inquiry, In Control Australia argued:

> [Individualised funding] calls on services providers to operate under the commercial conditions that are taken for granted in other sectors. It creates a competitive marketplace in which service organisations grow or fail according to their ability to respond to the demands of their customers. This in turn means that the range of services will be shaped by the demand[s] of people with disabilities, largely removing the need for state-driven service commissioning. (2010: 85)

In a similar vein, the peak body, NDS, argued that in the interests of fairness, equality and self-empowerment, disabled 'consumers should have choice about the services they receive' (NDS 2010: 16). A content analysis of the transcripts of 23 public hearings conducted by the Productivity Commission during the inquiry shows the words 'consumer' and 'choice' were used 597 times by the participants and commissioners. While there was some dissenting opinion, the emphasis on consumer choice was overwhelmingly positive, with many agreeing that '[e]nabling people with disabilities to exercise choice and control … would provide a significant incentive for service providers to offer a greater variety of better quality services' (PC 2010b: 95).

By appealing to the logic and language of consumer choice, the disability lobby achieved what Snow and Benford (1988) call 'frame resonance': alignment 'between an organization's interpretive work and its ability to influence broader public understandings' (Keck and Sikkink 1999: 95). It was able to project an image of its preferred policy that resonated with the prevailing logic of marketisation and that 'hooked' its solution—individualised funding—to the problem of disabled people's disenfranchisement. Arguments in favour of consumer choice were a powerful endorsement for the market model proposed in the Productivity Commission's report. They lent weight to the notion that the rights of disabled Australians were not just compatible with, but also in fact demanded, the creation of a national competitive market for disability services. They also provided a persuasive rationale for the privatisation, or 'transfer', of government-owned and operated services to the non-government sector. The inquiry's transcripts suggest many of the people and organisations consulted displayed a somewhat passive acceptance of marketisation and privatisation as inevitable parts of the trend towards person-centred service provision. When a representative of In Control was asked at a public hearing for her opinion on whether states should remain in the business of service delivery, she answered:

> I think [the] state government is ... outsourcing service provision wherever it can to the non-government sector. I think that there will continue to be a non-government sector. I imagine under a national disability insurance scheme we'd also see a strengthening of the private for-profit sector. (PC 2010b: 698)

As this statement implies, processes of marketisation and privatisation were already in motion by the time disability advocates began mobilising to support the NDIS. These structural changes in the political economy of disability services had a momentum of their own that was not reducible to individual advocates and their chosen strategies, although their buy-in was crucial in terms of building public support for the scheme. Their deployment of consumerist language and logic also had the effect of disarming, or at least 'complicating', arguments against the marketisation of disability services (Miller 2017: 104). However, their role in the reform process should be understood in light of the prevailing policy trend towards greater marketisation. Their advocacy was effective because it was consistent with the direction in which disability policy was already headed. Advocacy discourses centred on consumer choice found a receptive audience not only among social progressives, but also among leading neoliberal reformers intent on increasing the role of markets in such provisioning. The scheme that eventuated was an imperfect expression, but an expression nonetheless of advocates' demands for greater choice. There is always a discrepancy between the programs and practices that advocates might advance and the institutions that subsequently form, which are agglomerations of new ideas and existing institutional realities.

The discussion so far has centred on domestic and transnational civil society advocacy and the strategies used to instigate one of the largest social reforms in Australia's history. This line of analysis is useful in so far as it helps explain the specific form individualised funding has taken in Australia. Yet it is unable to account for the dramatic structural changes to the political economy of disability service provision, which constitute the conditions of constraint and enablement in which transnational advocacy networks and actors pursue their specific agendas. I now turn to these political-economic conditions.

The changing political economy of Australia's 'disability marketplace'

The NDIS has been rolled out at a time of significant change in the political economy of disability service provision in Australia. It is no coincidence that its national implementation has seen the dismantling of public service infrastructures and policy agencies at the state level. In fact, a logic of privatisation was built into the scheme via a series of intergovernmental agreements that specified how the scheme was to be implemented in each state and territory. New South Wales, in particular, has been the focal point of one of the largest public service privatisation programs in recent history (Sansom 2014). The launch of the NDIS in the Hunter region of New South Wales in 2016 was underpinned by an agreement between the Liberal (conservative) NSW and federal Coalition governments to transfer all government-owned and operated specialist disability services, including specialist disability housing stock, to the non-government sector (COAG 2015). Under the new system, NDIS participants could access funding for specialist disability housing via their individual budget, but neither the state government nor the NDIA would provide these services directly, nor retain ownership of housing assets (NDIA 2015). The withdrawal of state governments from disability services, under the guise of giving people greater choice of providers, would eliminate entirely the state's role in the direct provision of services under the NDIS. As part of the transition to a fully privatised system, the NSW Government would no longer function as the 'provider of last resort' for people with no other means of support, as it had in the past. The last tranche of supported living and respite services was transferred out of public hands in June 2018 (NSW Government 2018).

Before these changes, about 40 per cent of services—including accommodation support, personal assistance, speech pathology, occupational therapy and respite services—were provided directly by the NSW Government (Browne 2016). Ageing, Disability and Home Care (ADHC), part of the NSW Department of Family and Community Services, was by far the largest provider of in-home support and personal care, delivering 70 per cent of services of this kind to disabled people and the elderly (Belardi 2015). In 2013, the government passed legislation enabling public assets to be transferred to the non-government sector, and later sold, as part of the transition to the new market-based system

(Lewis 2017). Two years later, the Home Care Service of NSW[7] was sold for $114 million to a private health insurer (Belardi 2015). By May 2018, 9,500 public sector jobs had been transferred to the non-government sector (Kirkwood 2018) and ADHC had been disbanded (ADHC 2017). At the time, these moves were justified as the logical 'next steps' in preparing for the rollout of an individualised, consumer-oriented scheme with choice and control at its core (ADHC 2017).

The rationale given by a senior NSW state bureaucrat for the government's withdrawal from disability services illustrates how notions of choice and empowerment feature in elite accounts of privatisation. In his view, markets were attuned to the needs of consumers and personalised service provision was impossible to achieve so long as public providers remained part of the service mix:

> So, we are exiting all service delivery ... All of our services are being transferred into the NGO sector [because] it happens to be the right thing in terms of flexibility, responsiveness and so on. When you've got people with disability able to be that potent, as consumers, governments are just too slow and frankly too inefficient ... the state [currently] provides 40 per cent of the market, so to say that we should be staying there, that is antithetical to increasing the variety in the market. [Government withdrawing] will in fact maximise the range of choice that people with disability have. (John, state government bureaucrat)

While there is nothing new about the use of 'empowerment' in defence of privatisation, in this case, the government had in the disability advocacy lobby an additional, external source of legitimacy for its consumer choice agenda. It could make the claim that by letting the market and the non-government sector play a larger role in the delivery of services, it was merely responding to demands from the disability sector for more individual choice and agency. As the NSW Government official said:

> [F]or the first time, you have a system which is genuinely and fully empowering of those individuals. They are not dependent on organisations or on government, per se. And that empowerment, not only is it the right thing to do, but it will actually drive a whole

---

7   The Home Care Service was the NSW Government's provider of home-based care to support older people, people with disability and their carers to live independently in their own homes. Its funding predominantly comprised Commonwealth funds for the Home and Community Care program and the NSW Community Care Supports Program.

host of market responses ... This aligns perfectly—perfectly—to the interests of the person with disability, which is why it is so empowering. (John, state government bureaucrat)

While the disability lobby was broadly supportive of increased choice and competition in the disability sector, there was some ambivalence about the government's divestment program. Disability groups vehemently defended the closure of large, state-run residential centres, which for them represented the worst aspects of the old model of institutionalised care (O'Reilly 2014). However, there has been concern among these groups that a system with no public provider of last resort could fail to cater to individuals with particularly acute and complex needs—individuals with whom NGOs might refuse to work or who may not gain access to NDIS funding in the first place. According to disability advocate Therese Sands:

> [T]here's not a great deal of confidence in the private sector in terms of being able to meet the needs of particular groups of people with disability, particularly, say, those people in the criminal justice system, those who perhaps have more complex needs, those that are labelled with challenging behaviours, people ... that have traditionally received supports from the mental health service sector. There are just real concerns about what happens to people who aren't eligible for the NDIS. Where will you get your disability support? (Therese Sands, DSO representative)

Reflecting on what privatisation will mean for people who are ineligible for support under the NDIS, disability activist and commentator El Gibbs likewise noted:

> [T]he privatisation of ADHC, I think it's a disaster, in lots of respects. Because it means that if you don't qualify for the NDIS, you will get nothing. There are now no services in NSW for anyone who doesn't qualify for the NDIS.

The pitfalls of a system that relies exclusively on market mechanisms and private providers for the provision of social needs are exemplified in the case of a Victorian man, Francis, aged 20, who has autism and an intellectual disability. Amid the transition to the NDIS, the Victorian State Government is also withdrawing from direct provision of disability services (Milligan 2017). Following an assault, Francis was put in jail on remand. He received no sentence for the offence but remained in jail for three months. This was because, despite having an NDIS individual budget worth an annual $1.5 million allocated to him, no private or voluntary agency would provide him with the support required. Legal Aid workers reported that providers were refusing clients like Francis on the grounds they presented a 'business risk' to their organisation (Milligan 2017). Victorian Legal Aid lawyers told a federal government committee reviewing the scheme's performance they had four other clients in Francis's position and were aware of others in New South Wales. Neither the NDIA nor the government would accept responsibility for supporting these individuals. According to the lawyers, 'the clients' families were being told by the [NDIA] it was simply an "insurer or a bank", and by the Victorian Department of Health and Human Services that it was simply a "landlord"' (Milligan 2017). Cases like these are often described in terms of 'market failure', the implication being that the market mechanism—in this case, individualised funding—has failed to work in the way one might expect. In fact, the opposite is true. The market's response to Francis's case was in fact optimal, with market players acting according to financial incentives, to protect themselves against perceived risks and threats to profitability. The response to Francis was logical and perhaps predictable in a system that transforms services into commodities and in which market actors expect to, and are in fact required to, generate a surplus from their provision. At a microlevel, the logic of this system dictates that when a person's need comes into conflict with a provider's perceived 'business risk', the need for support will be subordinated to the financial imperatives of profit-making. At the macrolevel, the absence of an overarching coordinating mechanism or provider of last resort means there is no responsibility by any provider to meet any individual's needs, and equally, no means to ensure all needs are met. This demonstrates the importance of a public provider operating outside the market to help mitigate problems of inequity and unmet need in social service markets (see Chapter 9 for a detailed discussion of the rationale for and role of public providers).

Conclusion

I began this chapter by noting the recent shift in Australian disability policy towards more individualised, market-based models of disability provisioning. This was the starting point for a deeper exploration of the mechanisms that facilitated the transnational movement of individualised funding as a concept and as a working model of disability reform. Disability advocates organised through transnational advocacy networks including In Control, along with other local groups and alliances, were shown to have played a major role in the transmission and favourable reception of these concepts. Their advocacy efforts not only convinced the government of the merits of individualised funding, they also helped marshal public support for the NDIS and—perhaps inadvertently— diffused opposition by claiming for themselves the trope of 'consumer choice' and tying this to a defence of disabled people's rights as citizens.

In a climate of broader neoliberal restructuring, advocates of individualised funding faced a unique set of political opportunities and constraints. Elements within the disability movement found that hitching their demands to a broader project of market-oriented state restructuring was an effective political strategy. By appealing to an agenda that celebrates consumer choice and control, and links it to rights, disability advocates seized the opportunity to affect change in line with their vision of a just society. But in so doing they also re-signified and reinvigorated that agenda, vesting it with the moral force of an emancipatory project and bestowing on it the imprimatur of leftist social progressivism. Moves to outsource and privatise services gained a Left cover, as no sooner was the NDIS introduced than these privatising moves were touted as ways to liberate and empower disabled people. Disability advocates for their part seemed loath to question these developments, lest funding for the scheme be cut and its political support jeopardised.

It would be wrong, therefore, to attribute the highly marketised nature of the NDIS to the political sensibilities and strategies of the Australian disability lobby alone. In making their case for the scheme, key advocates deployed the language and logic of the market to great effect. This helped build consensus and support for the scheme among politically disparate parties and interest groups. Yet the sensibilities and strategies of these advocates were, like the scheme itself, a function of the political and economic climate in which they were operating. Policy ideas and discourses borrowed from elsewhere are always filtered through local political cultures, institutional configurations and path dependencies, which in Australia's case were heavily weighted in favour of marketisation. Individualised funding was layered into this existing institutional landscape in such a way that the resulting scheme was infused with neoliberal market rationales and notions of consumer citizenship. Individualised funding in its institutionally embodied form owes much to the unique constellation of neoliberal political and institutional paths that characterise the contemporary Australian welfare state.

Epilogue: Recent developments and future challenges for the NDIS

Since this chapter was written, the Covid-19 pandemic, the Royal Commission into Violence, Abuse, Neglect and Exploitation of People with Disability, and changes to the NDIS made by the conservative Coalition government have further highlighted the contradictions and tensions inherent in the scheme. In the first half of 2020, when Covid-19 cases were on the rise in Australia, frontline disability support workers and people with disability more generally were overlooked in the pandemic response, including in the national distribution of personal protective equipment. The health risks to workers delivering NDIS services and NDIS participants themselves were amplified by problems of poor management, under-resourcing, low pay, poor job security, multiple job-holding and unpaid work (Cortis and van Toorn 2020). While Covid-19 shone a spotlight on these problems, they pre-dated the health crisis and were closely bound up with the long-running marketisation of the sector. To protect the safety of NDIS workers and participants in (post-)Covid-19 conditions, more planning and investment are needed in critical overheads and infrastructure (for example, for staff training, supervision, safety and reporting), and government regulators including the NDIA must ensure the NDIS pricing schedule can adequately cover at least minimum entitlements for workers.

The need for regulatory reform of the disability sector was further highlighted by the Disability Royal Commission. Established in April 2019, the commission found that 'inappropriate funding structures' combined with a lack of regulatory oversight had enabled provider organisations to prioritise financial imperatives over client safety and wellbeing (Australian Government 2020: 20). The safety implications of marketisation were underscored by testimony from NDIS participants who felt that 'some providers of disability services saw people with disability as a "commodity"' (Australian Government 2020: 181). Better regulation of providers will go some way towards remedying these issues. However, NDIS participants will continue to face risks to their safety and wellbeing if providers are incentivised to prioritise profits over the quality of services.

In 2021, the NDIA drastically increased its projections for the number of people anticipated to be in the scheme by 2030, from 582,860 to 870,761 (Disability Intermediaries Australia 2021). While the assumptions and information on which these projections are based have not been made public, the Coalition government has made clear its intentions to try to contain the cost of the scheme, which is now expected to reach an estimated $60.3 billion by 2030 (NDIA 2021: 15). Notwithstanding the accuracy or otherwise of these figures, they are currently dominating debate over the future of the NDIS. They have been used to justify a range of measures, including government plans to take control of the assessment process through which a person's eligibility for NDIS funding is determined and cede it to government-contracted health professionals and computer algorithms (van Toorn, forthcoming). These plans were recently abandoned in the face of strong opposition by disability, legal and medical groups, who argued the new assessment process would undermine the scheme's core principles of choice and control. Against the backdrop of these various developments, the Coalition government allocated an extra $13.2 billion to the NDIS over four years in the 2021–22 budget. However, it remains to be seen whether this additional funding will achieve its intended purpose or simply further enable profiteering by large commercial care providers.

References

Ageing, Disability and Home Care (ADHC). (2017). *About ADHC*. Sydney: NSW Department of Family and Community Services. Available from: web.archive.org/web/20171215141902/www.adhc.nsw.gov.au/about_us.

Australian Government. (2020). *The Royal Commission into Violence, Abuse, Neglect and Exploitation of People with Disability: Interim report*. 30 October. Canberra: Commonwealth of Australia. Available from: disability.royalcommission.gov.au/system/files/2020-10/Interim%20Report.pdf.

Australian Government. (2021). *Budget 2021–22: Securing Australia's recovery—Guaranteeing the essential services*. Canberra: Australian Government. Available from: budget.gov.au/2021-22/content/download/glossy_ges.pdf.

Barnes, C., Mercer, G. & Shakespeare, T. (1999). *Exploring Disability: A sociological introduction*. Cambridge, UK: Polity.

Belardi, L. (2015). NSW govt strikes deal with Australian Unity for sale of home care service. *Australian Ageing Agenda*, 28 August. Available from: www. australianageingagenda.com.au/2015/08/28/nsw-govt-strikes-deal-with-australian-unity-for-sale-of-home-care-service/.

Benford, R. & Snow, D. (2000). Framing processes and social movements: An overview and assessment. *Annual Review of Sociology*, *26*(1): 611–39. doi.org/10.1146/annurev.soc.26.1.611.

Bode, I. (2009). On the road to welfare markets: Institutional, organizational, and cultural dynamics of a new European welfare state settlement. In J. Hendricks & J. Powell (eds), *The Welfare State in Post-Industrial Society: A global perspective* (pp. 161–77). New York, NY: Springer. doi.org/10.1007/978-1-4419-0066-1_9.

Bonyhady, B. (2016). Reducing the inequality of luck: Keynote address at the 2015 Australasian Society for Intellectual Disability National Conference. *Research and Practice in Intellectual and Developmental Disabilities*, *3*(2): 115–23. doi.org/10.1080/23297018.2016.1172021.

Brenner, N. & Theodore, N. (2002). Cities and geographies of 'actually existing neoliberalism'. *Antipode*, *34*(3): 349–79. doi.org/10.1111/1467-8330.00246.

Browne, R. (2016). Fears for future as NSW government sheds disability services. *Sydney Morning Herald*, 29 April. Available from: www.smh.com.au/nsw/fears-for-future-as-nsw-government-sheds-disability-services-20160428-goh33l.html.

Carey, G., Dickinson, H., Malbon, E. & Reeders, D. (2018). The vexed question of market stewardship in the public sector: Examining equity and the social contract through the Australian National Disability Insurance Scheme. *Social Policy & Administration*, *52*(1): 387–407. doi.org/10.1111/spol.12321.

Cortese, C., Truscott, F., Nikidehaghani, M. & Chapple, S. (2021). Hard-to-reach: The NDIS, disability, and socio-economic disadvantage. *Disability & Society*, *36*(6): 883–903. doi.org/10.1080/09687599.2020.1782173.

Cortis, N. & van Toorn, G. (2020). *The Disability Workforce and COVID-19: Initial experiences of the outbreak*. Sydney: Social Policy Research Centre, University of New South Wales. doi.org/10.26190/5eb0e680cbb04.

Cortis, N. & van Toorn, G. (2022). Safeguarding in Australia's new disability markets: Frontline workers' perspectives. *Critical Social Policy*, *42*(2): 197–219. doi.org/10.1177/02610183211020693.

Council of Australian Governments (COAG). (2015). *Bilateral Agreement between the Commonwealth and New South Wales: Transition to a National Disability Insurance Scheme.* 16 September. Canberra: COAG. Available from: content. webarchive.nla.gov.au/gov/wayback/20151020011806/www.coag.gov.au/ sites/default/files/NSW_Bilateral_Agreement_Transition_%28Turnbull%29 _signed.pdf.

Crabb, A. (2016). Disillusioned with politics? Then take heart in July 1. *The Drum*, [ABC TV], 28 June. Available from: www.abc.net.au/news/2016-06-28/crabb-disillusioned-with-politics-then-take-heart-in-july-1/7549008.

Davis, G. (2008). *Australia 2020 Summit: Final report.* Canberra: Department of the Prime Minister and Cabinet. Available from: apo.org.au/node/15061.

Disability Intermediaries Australia. (2021). *Deep Dive into NDIS Sustainability.* Melbourne: Disability Intermediaries Australia. Available from: www. intermediaries.org.au/news/deep-dive-into-ndis-sustainability/.

Epstein-Frisch, B. (2009). *PWD E-Bulletin.* Issue 56, August. Sydney: People with Disability Australia. Available from: web.archive.org/web/20090911232544/ pwd.org.au/e-bulletin/PWD_E-Bulletin_56.html.

In Control. (2011). *Resources.* [Online]. Wythall, UK: In Control. Available from: web.archive.org/web/20120115174751/www.in-control.org.uk/resources.aspx.

In Control Australia. (2010). *Submission to the Productivity Inquiry into Disability Care and Support: In Control Australia.* August. Brisbane: In Control Australia. Available from: www.pc.gov.au/inquiries/completed/disability-support/submissions/sub0570.pdf.

Keck, M. & Sikkink, K. (1999). Transnational advocacy networks in international and regional politics. *International Social Science Journal, 51*(159): 89–101. doi.org/10.1111/1468-2451.00179.

Kirkwood, I. (2018). NDIS and disability privatisation to be examined by NSW parliamentary committee. *Newcastle Herald,* 23 June. Available from: www. newcastleherald.com.au/story/5484292/inquiry-into-disability-privatisation/.

Laragy, C. & Fisher, K. (2020). Choice, control and individual funding: The Australian National Disability Insurance Scheme. In R.J. Stancliffe, M.L. Wehmeyer, K.A. Shogren & B.H. Abery (eds), *Choice, Preference, and Disability: Promoting self-determination across the lifespan* (pp. 133–54). Cham, Switzerland: Springer. doi.org/10.1007/978-3-030-35683-5_7.

Lewis, D. (2017). NDIS: Mother of daughter with severe disability fears privatisation of NSW group homes. *Background Briefing*, [ABC Radio National], 28 July. Available from: www.abc.net.au/news/2017-07-28/mother-daughter-disability-fears-group-home-privatisation-ndis/8748414.

Malbon, E., Carey, G. & Meltzer, A. (2019). Personalisation schemes in social care: Are they growing social and health inequalities? *BMC Public Health*, *19*(805). doi.org/10.1186/s12889-019-7168-4.

Manne, A. (2011). Two nations: The case for a National Disability Insurance Scheme. *The Monthly*, August. Available from: www.themonthly.com.au/issue/2011/august/1314794058/anne-manne/two-nations.

Miller, P. (2017). 'The age of entitlement has ended': Designing a disability insurance scheme in turbulent times. *Journal of International and Comparative Social Policy*, *33*(2): 95–113. doi.org/10.1080/21699763.2017.1302893.

Miller, P. & Hayward, D. (2017). Social policy 'generosity' at a time of fiscal austerity: The strange case of Australia's National Disability Insurance Scheme. *Critical Social Policy*, *37*(1): 128–47. doi.org/10.1177%2F026101831666 4463.

Milligan, L. (2017). Emergency intervention to remove disabled man left in prison after NDIS providers refused to care for him. *7.30*, [ABC TV], 9 November. Available from: www.abc.net.au/news/2017-11-09/emergency-intervention-to-remove-disabled-man-stuck-in-prison/9133634.

Murphy, K. (2020). Coalition plan on NDIS assessments has echoes of 'aged care debacle', Liberal MP says. *The Guardian*, [Australia], 8 December. Available from: www.theguardian.com/australia-news/2020/dec/08/coalition-plan-on-ndis-assessments-has-echoes-of-aged-care-debacle-liberal-mp-says.

National Disability Insurance Agency (NDIA). (2015). *Operational Plan Commitment between the National Disability Insurance Agency (NDIA), New South Wales Government and Commonwealth Government for Transition to Full Implementation of the NDIS*. Geelong, Vic.: NDIA. Available from: www.ndis. gov.au/media/540/download?attachment.

National Disability Insurance Agency (NDIA). (2016a). *Market Position Statement: Tasmania*. July. Geelong, Vic.: NDIA. Available from: vtphna.org.au/wp-content/uploads/2019/05/PB-market-position-statement-TAS-PDF.pdf.

National Disability Insurance Agency (NDIA). (2016b). *NDIA Annual Report 2015–16*. Geelong, Vic.: NDIA. Available from: www.ndis.gov.au/about-us/publications/annual-report/annual-report-2015-16.

National Disability Insurance Agency (NDIA). (2016c). *NDIS Market Approach: Statement of opportunity and intent.* November. Geelong, Vic.: NDIA. Available from: www.ndis.gov.au/media/448/download?attachment.

National Disability Insurance Agency (NDIA). (2019). *Access to the NDIS: The disability requirements.* Geelong, Vic.: NDIA. Available from: www.ndis.gov.au/about-us/operational-guidelines/access-ndis-operational-guideline/access-ndis-disability-requirements.

National Disability Insurance Agency (NDIA). (2020). *Q3 2019–2020: COAG Disability Reform Council quarterly report.* 31 March. Geelong, Vic.: NDIA. Available from: www.ndis.gov.au/media/2351/download.

National Disability Insurance Agency (NDIA). (2021). *Annual Financial Sustainability Report Summary: Interim update.* Geelong, Vic.: NDIA. Available from: www.ndis.gov.au/news/6590-ndis-financial-sustainability-report-release.

National Disability Insurance Agency (NDIA). (2022). *Report to disability ministers for Q4 of Y9 Full report.* Geelong, Vic.: NDIA. Available from: www.ndis.gov.au/media/4615/download?attachment.

National Disability Insurance Scheme Act 2013 [NDIS Act] (Cth) No. 20, 2013. Available from: www.legislation.gov.au/Details/C2013A00020.

National Disability Services (NDS). (2010). *Productivity Commission Inquiry into Disability Care and Support: NDS submission.* Canberra: National Disability Services. Available from: www.pc.gov.au/inquiries/completed/disability-support/submissions/sub0454.pdf.

National Disability Services (NDS). (2013). *Annual Report 2012–2013.* Canberra: National Disability Services. Available from: www.nds.org.au/images/files/NDS_AnnualReport_2013.pdf.

National Disability Services (NDS). (2015). *National Disability Insurance Scheme (NDIS) Quality & Safeguarding System Submission: National Disability Services (NDS) May 2015.* Canberra: National Disability Services. Available from: www.nds.org.au/pdf-file/IMPORTED-5AE2-45F0-8034-2C3F7C5C1536.

National People with Disabilities & Carer Council. (2009). *Shut Out: The experience of people with disabilities and their families in Australia.* National Disability Strategy Consultation Report. Canberra: Commonwealth of Australia. Available from: www.dss.gov.au/sites/default/files/documents/05_2012/nds_report.pdf.

Needham, C. & Dickinson, H. (2018). 'Any one of us could be among that number': Comparing the policy narratives for individualized disability funding in Australia and England. *Social Policy & Administration, 52*(3): 731–49. doi.org/10.1111/spol.12320.

Newell, C. (1996). The disability rights movement in Australia: A note from the trenches. *Disability & Society*, *11*(3): 429–32. doi.org/10.1080/09687599627705.

NSW Government. (n.d.). Transfer of New South Wales disability services. *About the NDIS in New South Wales*. Sydney: NSW Government. Available from: web.archive.org/web/20170308015514/ndis.nsw.gov.au/about-ndis-nsw/transfer-of-nsw-disability-services/.

NSW Government. (2010). *The Productivity Commission Inquiry into a National Disability Long-Term Care and Support Scheme: Draft NSW Government submission*. August. Sydney: NSW Government. Available from: www.pc.gov.au/inquiries/completed/disability-support/submissions/sub0536.pdf.

NSW Government. (2018). When services are transferring. *About the NDIS in New South Wales*. Sydney: NSW Government. Available from: web.archive.org/web/20180922214150/ndis.nsw.gov.au/about-ndis-nsw/transfer-of-nsw-disability-services/when-services-are-transferring/.

O'Reilly, S. (2014). Why closing Stockton Centre divides disability advocates: Opinion. *Newcastle Herald*, 7 April. Available from: www.newcastleherald.com.au/story/2203275/why-closing-stockton-centre-divides-disability-advocates-opinion/.

PricewaterhouseCoopers (PwC). (2009). *Disability Investment Group: National Disability Insurance Scheme final report*. October. Canberra: Commonwealth of Australia. Available from: www.dss.gov.au/sites/default/files/documents/05_2012/pwc_ndis_report_2009.pdf.

Productivity Commission (PC). (2010a). *Disability care and support*. Productivity Commission Issues Paper, May. Canberra: Productivity Commission. Available from: content.webarchive.nla.gov.au/gov/wayback/20110601220630/www.pc.gov.au/__data/assets/pdf_file/0007/98026/issues.pdf.

Productivity Commission (PC). (2010b). *Productivity Commission Inquiry into Disability Care and Support: Transcript of proceedings at Melbourne on Tuesday, 8 June 2010, at 9.11am*. Canberra: Productivity Commission. Available from: www.pc.gov.au/inquiries/completed/disability-support/public-hearings/20100608-melbourne.pdf.

Productivity Commission (PC). (2011a). Appendix E: Impacts of self-directed funding. In *Disability Care and Support: Productivity Commission Inquiry report*. No. 54, 31 July. Canberra: Productivity Commission. Available from: www.pc.gov.au/inquiries/completed/disability-support/report/29-disability-support-appendixe.pdf.

Productivity Commission (PC). (2011b). *Disability Care and Support: Productivity Commission Inquiry report. Volume 1.* No. 54, 31 July. Canberra: Productivity Commission. Available from: www.pc.gov.au/inquiries/completed/disability-support/report/disability-support-volume1.pdf.

Productivity Commission. (2011c). *Disability Care and Support: Productivity Commission Inquiry report. Volume 2.* No. 54, 31 July. Canberra: Productivity Commission. Available from: www.pc.gov.au/inquiries/completed/disability-support/report/disability-support-volume2.pdf.

Productivity Commission (PC). (2017). *National Disability Insurance Scheme (NDIS) Costs: Productivity Commission study report—Overview.* October. Canberra: Productivity Commission. Available from: www.pc.gov.au/inquiries/completed/ndis-costs/report/ndis-costs-overview.pdf.

Sansom, M. (2014). Tensions over 14.5k NSW jobs shift in NDIS. *Government News*, [Sydney], 7 August. Available from: www.governmentnews.com.au/2014/08/tensions-14-5k-nsw-jobs-shift-ndis/.

Schultz, A. (2020). How do we hold dodgy disability services to account? *Crikey*, 14 August. Available from: www.crikey.com.au/2020/08/14/ndis-disability-complaint-accountability/.

Snow, D.A. & Benford, R.D. (1988). Ideology, frame resonance, and participant mobilization. In B. Klandermans, H. Kriesi & S. Tarrow (eds), *International Social Movement Research: From structure to action* (pp. 197–218). Greenwich, CT: JAI Press.

Soldatic, K. & Pini, B. (2012). Continuity or change? Disability policy and the Rudd government. *Social Policy & Society*, *11*(2): 183–96. doi.org/10.1017/S1474746411000510.

Soldatic, K., van Toorn, G., Dowse, L. & Muir, K. (2014). Intellectual disability and complex intersections: Marginalisation under the National Disability Insurance Scheme. *Research and Practice in Intellectual and Developmental Disabilities*, *1*(1): 6–16. doi.org/10.1080/23297018.2014.906050.

Steketee, M. (2013). How a forty-year-old proposal became a movement for change. *Inside Story*, 22 October. Available from: insidestory.org.au/how-a-forty-year-old-proposal-became-a-movement-for-change.

Thill, C. (2015). Listening for policy change: How the voices of disabled people shaped Australia's National Disability Insurance Scheme. *Disability and Society*, *30*(1): 15–28. doi.org/10.1080/09687599.2014.987220.

van Toorn, G., (forthcoming) Automating the welfare state: the case of disability benefits and services. In R. Chang, R. Loeppky & D. Primrose (eds.) *Routledge Handbook of the Political Economy of Health and Healthcare*. London: Routledge.

Wilson, E., Campain, R., Pollock, S., Brophy, L. & Stratford, A. (2021). Exploring the personal, programmatic and market barriers to choice in the NDIS for people with psychosocial disability. *Australian Journal of Social Issues*, *57*(1): 164–84. doi.org/10.1002/ajs4.154.

6

Making a profitable social service market: The evolution of the private nursing home sector

Gabrielle Meagher and Richard Baldwin

Introduction

Nearly one-quarter of a million older Australians received residential aged care (RAC) services, including housing, support with activities of daily living and health care, during 2019–20 (ACFA 2021: 56). RAC facilities—often called nursing homes—are largely publicly funded. They are a major budget item for the Australian Government, which spent $13.4 billion on this social service in the 2019–20 financial year. Older people themselves contributed a further $4.9 billion (ACFA 2021: 10). Although mostly publicly funded, most nursing homes are privately owned, and provision is organised in a marketised system in which tendering, competition and consumer choice are the main instruments on which governments rely to drive quality, innovation and diversity.

Nursing homes have been much in the news in recent years and the marketisation of the system has been questioned. Well before the Covid-19 pandemic exposed the vulnerability of older people living in nursing homes, evidence of poor-quality care in some services prompted the establishment of the Royal Commission into Aged Care Quality and Safety in late 2018. The commission's interim report, called simply

Neglect, 'found that the aged care system fails to meet the needs of our older citizens in the delivery of safe and quality care' (Royal Commission into Aged Care Quality and Safety 2019a). The commission has argued that the direction of reform has put 'too much faith in market forces and consumer choice as the primary driver of improvement in the aged care system' (Royal Commission into Aged Care Quality and Safety 2019b: 3), and it flagged its intention to explore alternatives to market organisation for the sector in its final report (Royal Commission into Aged Care Quality and Safety 2019c: 80).

Two aspects of the marketisation of nursing homes over recent decades have been the increasing market share and growing size of for-profit businesses among providers, which are the focus of this chapter. In 2020, the share of RAC places operated for profit was 41 per cent (ACFA 2021: 58)—up from 27 per cent in 2000 (DHAC 2000: 5). Across this period, the number of places increased from about 140,000 to more than 217,000, and for-profit facilities accounted for more than two-thirds of this growth. What can we learn about the relationship between market design and market structure from this trend? Specifically, have—and, if so, how have—Commonwealth Government policies[1] shaped the ownership structure of the sector?

The question is important for two reasons. First, while there is an impressive body of research exploring the policy-driven development of the RAC sector over several decades (Cullen 2003; Fine 1999; Gibson 1998; Howe 1990, 2000; Le Guen 1993; Parker 1987), there has been no study of how changing market design has affected the ownership structure within the RAC market in the past half-century.[2] Second, and more importantly, the weight of evidence in international research is that quality is, on average, lower in for-profit nursing homes than in non-profit and public facilities. For example, a recent systematic review of 50 studies of the relationship between nursing home ownership and performance in the United States found:

> For-profit nursing homes tend to have better financial performance, but worse results with regard to employee well-being and client well-being, compared to not-for-profit sector homes …

---

1   It is not possible within this chapter to discuss the complex role of state and local government policy on the development of the RAC market—or 'markets'—since differences between the states remain today, long after the establishment of encompassing Commonwealth funding and regulation.
2   R.A. Parker's marvellous book is an exception; it covers the period up to the mid-1980s only (Parker 1987).

> [T]he better financial performance of for-profit nursing homes
> seems to be associated with worse employee and client well-being.
> (Bos et al. 2017: 352)

The limited available Australian research confirms this pattern (Baldwin et al. 2015). Further, emerging evidence from the Covid-19 pandemic suggests for-profit homes and homes with characteristics associated with for-profit status (including larger size and less-skilled staff) are linked to worse outcomes (Bach-Mortensen et al. 2021).[3] By examining the relationship between market design and ownership of RAC provision over time, our analysis could help identify risks with the current direction of residential aged care policy (see also Baldwin et al. 2015), to inform policies that steer the sector away from these risks.

Market design and ownership structure

Our analysis is framed broadly around Gingrich's (2011) typology of 'welfare markets'. Gingrich distinguishes between two dimensions of service provision: allocation (how services are funded and distributed) and production (how services are delivered). When allocation is organised through market mechanisms such as user payments, the amount and/ or quality of services people receive are more affected by how much they can afford. When allocation is organised more collectively, through public financing of a regulated system, access to good-quality services is less affected by the capacity to pay (Gingrich 2011: 10). In social service markets, production can be organised according to different structures of competition, which vary by how much control they give to the state, individual service users or private providers. Members of these groups have divergent primary aims: in Gingrich's account, governments seek efficiency, service users seek quality and producers seek profits and rents,[4] and different rules of the market give more or less power to one or another group to pursue its aims (Gingrich 2011: 10–12).

---

3   In Australia, while most deaths from Covid-19 in 2020 were of older people living in residential care, the relatively small size of the pandemic and the few facilities involved meant these associations have not been found (Ibrahim et al. 2021).

4   At this most abstract level, Gingrich's theory is framed starkly and differences between types of producers (for-profit, non-profit, professionals) are not accounted for. Accordingly, whether non-profit providers have the pursuit of profit and rent as their primary aim is an open question. Theories of institutional logic start from the position that different producer types have different primary aims (Thornton et al. 2012).

By exploring the different ways responsibility for allocation of services and control over their production can be distributed, Gingrich generates six ideal types of market design. In each, governments' chosen design settings present a specific set of incentives to providers and consumers and shape the extent to which the aims of each group are likely to be realised (Gingrich 2011: 12–19). In state-driven 'managed markets', governments retain more power over providers' cost structures with 'clear standards and tight control' on the production dimension, while on the allocation dimension, users are protected by guaranteed access. In state-driven 'austerity markets', the state retains power over public funding to providers on the production dimension, but limits access on the allocation dimension by, for example, targeting and increasing user charges. In consumer-driven 'consumer-controlled markets', users' choices drive producer behaviour on the production dimension, supported by strong regulation of access and collective financing on the allocation dimension. In consumer-driven 'two-tier markets', producers also respond to users' choices on the production dimension, but on the allocation dimension, more costs fall to users and governments do less to compensate for differences of, for example, income among users. In producer-driven 'pork-barrel' markets, the combination of generous public financing on the allocation dimension and lax regulation of private providers on the production dimension leaves providers relatively free to increase profits through rent-seeking from the state. In producer-driven 'private-power' markets, providers respond to tighter fiscal constraints in a weakly regulated environment by charging users more or reducing service quality.

In addition to theorising how market designs vary in their allocation and production dimensions, Gingrich emphasises the importance of partisan preferences in governments' policy choices. She argues that right and left parties use markets differently, 'as tools to empower groups who support their particular long-term partisan goals' (Gingrich 2011: 4–5). Partisan preferences are relevant to our analysis because some major marketising policies have been introduced by Labor as well as by Coalition governments (as might be expected) in Australia.

One aspect of market design theory that Gingrich does not develop fully is how policy choices affect the ownership profile of private provision, because she assumes that both non-profit and for-profit providers respond to the incentives that market designs establish and pursue rents or profits over the interests of governments or consumers when the opportunity arises. However, she does recognise that non-profit and for-profit providers may have different motivations, and 'incentives to seek profits by overcharging users and/or cutting costs … are amplified when providers are privately owned and responsive to shareholders' (Gingrich 2011: 11). This is an important concession that implies that market instruments that put few constraints on producers are those most likely to draw in for-profits, even if non-profit providers might also seek rents and profits when the opportunity presents. These instruments include, on the allocation dimension, generous subsidies and/or weakly regulated consumer co-payments and weak regulation of access to the subsidised market for both consumers (no, few or weak eligibility criteria) and providers (by enabling them to select clients). On the production dimension, instruments that may draw in for-profits include weakly regulated entry (few or only basic conditions of market access; removal of any proscription on for-profit provision), allowing providers to choose where they operate and weak regulation of quality.[5] It is also important to recognise that specific profit and rent opportunities arise in RAC because it offers accommodation, which entails real property, as well as care. Thus, for example, if governments liberalise policies on sources of capital for developing properties or control fees for care but not accommodation, new opportunities to make money from property investment in residential facilities emerge. Gingrich's concession also points to a related aspect of diversity among providers: the amplification of profit-orientation in those with shareholders. In other words, not all for-profit providers are the same; corporate operators that typically manage multiple facilities are likely to be more profit-oriented, while for operators with a single facility, 'the profit motive might [be] secondary to some professional motive to provide good quality care' (Morris 1999: 141).

The changing market for residential aged care in Australia

It was not until the 1950s that what we understand today as residential aged care became an object of Commonwealth Government policy, and not until the 1960s that market logic was introduced and the sector came to approximate its current form. Nevertheless, a variety of institutions had fulfilled the analogous social function since Governor Lachlan Macquarie, military ruler of the colony of New South Wales, first funded the charitable Benevolent Society to provide care to Sydney's 'poor and

---

5   Thanks to Bob Davidson for encouraging me to include a list of these instruments and for providing a handy distillation of them.

indigent' in 1821 (Cummins & NSW Department of Health 1971). In so doing, Macquarie used an approach that would persist to the present: providing public financial aid to an external organisation for services that he recognised would not be otherwise provided by voluntary (or market) means, judging that '[t]his would be cheaper and attract less opprobrium than direct government control' (Dickey 1987: 17). Between Macquarie's time and the entry of the Commonwealth Government, a mix of public and private institutions continued to offer accommodation and care for a subset of older people, albeit often poorly (Cullen 2003: 5–6), with a mix of public (state and local government) and private funding.

Within the general approach of public subsidies for largely private provision that has persisted across two centuries, the institutional organisation of RAC has changed considerably. This is because public funding of private provision does not always create or shape a 'market' for the service in question. Macquarie's intervention did not create a market for residential care for older people, for example. Rather, it supported private provision organised within the charitable logic of voluntary assistance of the time,[6] as did the Commonwealth Government's first intervention in the sector in the 1950s, which is discussed in more detail below. And as Gingrich's framework highlights, social service markets are not all the same. While market logic first began to shape the sector in the 1960s, governments' market design interventions since then have changed how both the allocation and the production of RAC are organised. In what follows, we divide the past nearly seven decades into six phases, drawing out how changing market designs have shaped—intentionally or otherwise—the ownership structure of the sector.[7]

Phase 1: 1954–63 — Supporting the development of 'homes for the aged'

The first phase of Commonwealth Government involvement in residential aged care began in 1954, with the *Aged Persons Home Act 1954*, legislated by the ruling Liberal–Country party Coalition as part of its policy response to the postwar housing shortage. The shortage was partly driven by strong population growth after the war, but older people also emerged as a target

---

6   See Thornton et al. (2012). The framework discussed there does not include a 'charitable logic', which was more dominant in the early nineteenth century than organised mutual aid within the working class, which is better characterised as being organised by what Thornton et al. would call an associational logic. We have taken the liberty of adapting their general argument to include charity.

7   Others have created periodisations; see Footnote 8.

group because of another demographic change: the prewar decline of the three-generation household, which left more old people living—poorer— in their own households (Snooks 1994: 91).

The *Aged Persons Home Act* legislated for matching grants to be made to 'religious and charitable organizations towards the capital costs of building homes for the aged' (HRSCE 1982: 10). The minister for social services of the time praised 'the devotion and unselfishness' of these volunteer organisations, which the government assumed were assisting the 'needy aged' (HRSCE 1982: 10). Note that neither public nor for-profit providers were eligible for these capital grants; public provision of general housing for low-income people was financed separately under the Commonwealth–State Housing Agreement established by Labor in the early postwar years, while the failure of the private market to provide affordable housing for poor older Australians was the problem the 1954 Act was seeking to remedy.

The Act did not support the building of what we would understand today as 'residential aged care facilities'; no parallel legislated support was made until the 1960s for the provision of 'care services' to older people. In general, this phase might be best understood as the last in the prehistory of the policy-shaped market for RAC. Government intervention sought to address a (housing) market failure, but it did so by reference to the associational logic of the voluntary sector, which stepped in when the foundational institution of the family was absent (HRSCE 1982: 10–11). When family care was unavailable, there existed scattered small business providers of something resembling RAC alongside some charitable and state long-term care institutions, but competition and the pursuit of profit were not organising dynamics of the sector during this time. Nevertheless, this phase did enable the development of valuable real property assets in the non-profit sector in the form of hostel accommodation, to which later policies would attach new incentives and opportunities that were, in turn, extended to for-profit providers.

Phase 2: 1963–72 — Creating a producer-driven market promoting for-profit provision

The Commonwealth Government's next intervention targeted what we would now understand as residential aged care (Wheelwright 1992: 112) and was decisive in the consolidation and growth of a large, private nursing home industry.[8] This intervention was directed at managing a problem in the health system.[9] While the states had responsibility for social service provision, and long provided and regulated the quality of care for older people, the Commonwealth Government co-funded hospital care. Having declined to introduce a national insurance system in the early postwar years, the Commonwealth paid a hospital benefit for patients in both public and approved private hospitals. By the early 1960s, many old people needing long-term care lived in institutions licensed as hospitals, but hospital financing (via a mix of the Commonwealth benefit and private insurance) did not cover them adequately (Parker 1987: 11). To deal with this group, in 1962, the government amended the *National Health Act 1953* to create two new categories of beneficiary: 'nursing home patients' and 'approved nursing homes'. The latter included some institutions already licensed as hospitals but was also extended to include others that had not been recognised as hospitals (Sax 1984: 63–64). Significantly, both for-profit and non-profit operators could be approved as nursing homes, which became eligible to receive a benefit of $2 per patient per day, with no means test and no regulation of patient admission. In 1963, when this subsidy became available, the states administered around half of all nursing home beds (SSCPHNH 1985: 16). Between 1963 and 1968, the number of nursing home beds increased 48 per cent and 95 per cent of new beds were run by private organisations—non-profit and for-profit. By as early as 1965, half the non-public sector was run for profit (SSCPHNH 1985: 16).

The *Aged Persons Homes Act 1954* did not subsidise the building of nursing home beds, because its aim was to drive the building of more independent forms of housing. However, as residents in subsidised independent housing aged, their needs increased and the measures implemented under the Act also changed—without amendment to the Act itself (HRSCE 1982: 12–14). These changes led to further growth in nursing home accommodation, specifically in the non-profit sector. First, in 1966, capital grants were extended to subsidise non-profit providers to build up to one-third of any new properties as nursing home accommodation. Further changes in 1969 enabled these non-profit, subsidised providers to

8   There are several excellent histories and analyses of this period—notably, Parker (1987), Howe (1990) and Wheelwright (1992). Others have called it the 'laissez faire' period (Howe 1990) or the period of 'commodification and entitlement' (Fine 1999: 12).
9   Parker (1987: 7–13) gives a detailed account of this period.

consolidate their nursing home beds into larger facilities and to take over the nursing home entitlements of organisations that did not wish to use them (HRSCE 1982: 14).

In 1969, matching capital grants were also made available to state governments to provide nursing home accommodation to older people of 'limited means' under the States Grants (Nursing Homes) Bill (Cullen 2003: 32). However, few funds were allocated to this scheme and state co-contributions were required—suggesting weak Commonwealth Government commitment to public provision.[10] Indeed, a member of the Labor opposition argued 'the Government's whole policy has been to provide minimal assistance in this field, and to allow private enterprise to come in on the basis of profit motive'.[11] Labor's assessment was evidently well founded. In the end, only half the allocated money was drawn on by the states (Cullen 2003: 32), so this measure had a negligible impact on both the ownership structure of the sector and the provision of beds.

Subsidies for care were also changed in 1969, affecting both non-profit providers of hostel accommodation and all nursing home providers, of which a majority were for-profit. Together, these changes filled in the continuum between independent accommodation at one end and hospital health care at the other, laying the foundation for the broader policy category of 'residential aged care' that would later encompass both hostels and nursing homes. Towards the independent end, a subsidy for personal care in *hostels* was introduced as a measure under the *Aged Persons Homes Act 1954*, to enable frailer residents to remain longer in this more independent form of accommodation, rather than moving to a nursing home (HRSCE 1982: 14). Towards the healthcare end, a supplementary benefit for nursing home residents who needed intensive nursing care was introduced under the *National Health Act 1953* (Cullen 2003: 50–51). The government saw this benefit 'as much as a means of maintaining the increasingly key private sector as of helping poorer patients pay their way'; the Labor opposition agreed with the first of these assessments, expressing concern that 'the extra benefit would "serve to subsidise private

---

10   Opposition leader Gough Whitlam pursued this issue on more than one occasion, asking about it in 1969 (*House of Representatives Hansard*, Wednesday, 28 May 1969, p. 2430, available from: parlinfo. aph.gov.au/parlInfo/search/display/display.w3p;query=Id%3A%22hansard80%2Fhansardr80% 2F1969-05-28%2F0150%22) and again in 1970 (*House of Representatives Hansard*, Thursday, 16 April 1970, p. 1311, available from: historichansard.net/hofreps/1970/19700416_reps_27_hor66/).
11   *House of Representatives Hansard*, Thursday, 27 August 1970, available from: parlinfo.aph.gov.au/ parlInfo/search/display/display.w3p;query=Id%3A%22hansard80%2Fhansardr80%2F1970-08-27 %2F0064%22.

enterprise even further"' (Parker 1987: 23). A senior bureaucrat from the administering Department of Social Security offered an explanation: 'The financial stimulus provided by the intensive care benefit apparently helped promote amongst investors a widespread belief that nursing homes were low risk, high profit financial ventures' (Wilson 1973–74: 22). At any rate, rapid growth in private, for-profit nursing home beds continued.

As noted above, the opposition Labor Party criticised the growth of the for-profit sector. Members used parliamentary debates on these measures to argue that housing and care for older people should not be opportunities for 'ruthless investors ... looking for profits'.[12] They also lamented the poor quality of services in some private facilities, often citing media reports.[13] For example, Leader of the Opposition Gough Whitlam argued in May 1969 that abuses were 'excessively prevalent among that class of private nursing home which caters for persons who can pay little more than their age pension and the Commonwealth nursing home benefit'.[14] Labor members also criticised some subsidised (and so non-profit) providers of independent housing for demanding 'donations' that were effectively 'key money', and which meant providers favoured older people with more resources.[15]

By the end of the second phase of Commonwealth involvement in RAC, what Gingrich (2011: 17–19) would call a producer-driven 'private-power market' was firmly established—the result of conservative governments' efforts to foster the growth of private provision, both non-profit and for-profit, with very few controls. On the allocation dimension, collective financing was available, in the form of various direct care subsidies to all providers (non-profit, for-profit and public) along with capital grants to non-profit and, later (and minimally), to state providers. However,

---

12   Albert James, member for Hunter, Thursday, 13 April 1967, during the debate on the second reading speech on the Aged Persons Homes Bill 1967 (available from: parlinfo.aph.gov.au/parlInfo/search/display/display.w3p;query=Id%3A%22hansard80%2Fhansardr80%2F1967-04-13%2 F0073%22).
13   See, for example, this speech by Labor Member Hector McIvor, also during the debate on the Aged Persons Homes Bill 1967 (available from: parlinfo.aph.gov.au/parlInfo/search/display/display. w3p;query=Id%3A%22hansard80%2Fhansardr80%2F1967-04-13%2F0085%22).
14   During the debate on the reading of the States Grants (Home Care) Bill 1969 (*House of Representatives Hansard*, Wednesday, 28 May 1969, p. 2388, available from: parlinfo.aph.gov.au/parl Info/search/display/display.w3p;query=Id%3A%22hansard80%2Fhansardr80%2F1969-05-28%2 F0150%22).
15   These were the entry contributions for hostel accommodation that eventually became accommodation bonds. See, for example, the speech by Fred Collard, member for Kalgoorlie, available from: parlinfo.aph.gov.au/parlInfo/search/display/display.w3p;query=Id%3A%22hansard8 0%2Fhansardr80%2F1967-04-13%2F0083%22.

collective financing was extended without admission controls and user fees were unregulated, with 'operators … free to charge residents whatever fee they desired' (Cullen 2003: 49). On the production dimension, providers controlled the size and structure of the market in their own interest, since the government did not regulate entry into the sector, nor the size and placement of facilities. Further, the government's 'hands-off approach' gave for-profit operators many opportunities to push costs on to consumers through fees and/or to cut costs, including by carefully selecting residents and skimping on the quality of food, accommodation and care (Cullen 2003: 49–50).

By the late 1960s, rising costs to governments and to consumers became recognised policy problems. One policy response was to begin to direct resources at developing community-based supports for old people to remain at home.[16] But addressing problems in the nursing home sector— rising costs, uncontrolled growth and the unnecessary admission of old people—would also become policy goals for the Liberal–Country party Coalition (Parker 1987: 30). As Parker (1987: 30) puts it: 'Ten years of an uncoordinated and unregulated free-for-all financed by guaranteed public subsidies was to be brought to a halt.' Yet various aspects of the market established during the second phase—not least a large role for the private sector and the establishment of organised private interests (Howe 1990: 155)—had a long legacy.

Phase 3: 1972–86 — State attempts to manage the market

Over the next decade and a half, care for older people was the subject of much policy activity. Several inquiries and legislative and regulatory changes occurred, as successive governments of both colours grappled with the legacy of the 'free-for-all' enabled during the earlier period. While the balance of provision between residential and home-based care was one object of policy, residential aged care was often subject to particular attention as the largest budget item by an order of magnitude. Both ownership and profits were explicitly discussed and policies made to address issues thereby identified.

---

16   Accordingly, subsidies to the states to arrange home care were legislated in the *States Grants (Home Care) Act 1969* and the *States Grants (Paramedical Services) Act 1969*. The Commonwealth Government sought to share the cost of these services with the states and to promote, 'stimulate and coordinate' voluntary organisations as well as state and local governments to provide them (HRSCE 1982: 15).

Regulatory efforts to increase public control over costs both to the Treasury and to residents, as well as the entry of both producers and consumers into the residential care system, began in 1972, with amendments to the *National Health Act 1953* by a Coalition government. As Le Guen (1993: 5) outlines, admission to a nursing home now required approval by a medical practitioner. Responding to concern about conflicts of interest among doctors who could approve entry for old people into homes they themselves owned, approvals became subject to oversight by a Commonwealth Medical Officer. The fees charged by private nursing homes also became regulated, such that, after 1 January 1973, approved homes could not charge more than the maximum determined by the Department of Social Services (DSS).

Further efforts to rebalance aged care away from nursing homes and towards home care and less-intensive residential care were made by the Coalition government in 1972 (Le Guen 1993: 6–7). The new Domiciliary Nursing Care Benefit would subsidise family care as an alternative to institutional care, in line with conservative social thinking,[17] while the *Aged Persons Hostels Act 1972* provided further significant capital subsidies to non-profit providers of housing for older people, specifically to build hostel accommodation.[18]

In late 1972, Labor came to power for the first time in more than two decades. There were some significant continuities in approach to RAC policy between the outgoing and incoming governments, including the desire to shift the balance towards community rather than institutional care, and to gain and maintain some control over the size, growth and cost of institutional care. Indeed, Labor took over implementation of the reforms that were designed to gain some control over the growth and shape of the sector outlined above. Nevertheless, partisan differences are evident—notably, in the attitude to ownership of residential care facilities. While Labor's Minister for Social Security Bill Hayden felt the need to allay for-profit providers' anxiety that the new government might nationalise

---

17   See, for example, the statement in Parliament on 29 August 1972 by Dr Jim Forbes, acting minister for health, in which he argues for the need to go beyond (mere) admiration of those 'who feel deeply a sense of family totality and who make considerable sacrifices to keep elderly relatives within the home even when they may require constant nursing' (available from: parlinfo.aph.gov.au/parlInfo/search/display/display.w3p;query=Id%3A%22hansard80%2Fhansardr80%2F1972-08-29%2F0081%22).

18   Hostel building was already subsidised under the *Aged Persons Homes Act 1954* but was less well developed than independent housing (which was more lucrative for providers) on one hand, and nursing homes (which were more expensive for government), on the other (Cullen 2003: 33).

for-profit nursing homes, 'he did make plain that he was much concerned about standards and profits' (Parker 1987: 36–37). Some measures were addressed directly to this end—for example, by building on Coalition price-control policies. For-profit providers were funded under the new Participating Nursing Home Scheme, under which Commonwealth nursing home benefits were supplemented with controlled user fees for the minority of residents who paid them (Cullen 2003: 53).

However, in line with its social thinking, Labor also sought to encourage alternatives to for-profit provision of residential care. On the accommodation front, in 1973, capital matching grants to non-profit providers were extended to allow the building of nursing home places freed from the previous requirement that the provider also offer hostel places, and to allow the purchase of for-profit nursing homes that were for sale (Cullen 2003: 34–35; Le Guen 1997: 9; Parker 1987: 40). On the care front, the government recognised that operating costs were already stretching the resources of many non-profit providers, who would likely find it difficult to develop new property stocks without increased operational revenue flows (Parker 1987: 40). Accordingly, under the *Nursing Homes Assistance Act 1974*, an alternative to nursing home benefits was offered to non-profits, in the form of the Deficit Financing Scheme, which, as its name suggests, funded deficits incurred in running nursing homes.

Parker (1987: 40–41) documents Coalition criticisms of the new arrangements as a deliberate attempt to squeeze the private sector and a threat to the autonomy of religious organisations (assistance to which it was difficult for them to condemn). Parliamentary debates and policy differences reflected divergent partisan ideologies about the role of the non-profit sector: for Labor, it was a higher-quality alternative to for-profit provision; for the Coalition, it was to be protected from state incursions as an expression of religious freedom. The deficit financing scheme enabled non-profit nursing home providers to develop or acquire further properties, but the care subsidy remained too low in hostels for capital grants to significantly boost hostel development. Therefore, further assistance was given to non-profits through the Personal Care Subsidy for hostel residents, the value of which was tripled between 1972 and 73, and 1975 and 76 (Cullen 2003: 61).

The Labor government was dismissed in 1975 amid a constitutional crisis (Madden 2020). The incoming, small government–minded Fraser administration sought to gain yet more financial and planning control of the sector (Parker 1987: 59). One response was a four-year experiment with shifting some of the costs of nursing home care off the public accounts, by obliging private health insurers to replace the Commonwealth subsidy for nursing home residents insured with them. Problems in the design of this measure and poor compliance of nursing home proprietors saw funding revert to the Commonwealth in 1981, with little evidence of savings (Le Guen 1993: 10–11; Parker 1987: Ch. 7).

The failure of the fee-control regime introduced in 1972 to contain costs was a significant, ongoing problem recognised by two major inquiries during the early 1980s, led by Labor's Leo McLeay and Patricia Giles.[19] The fees private nursing home proprietors could charge to supplement the Commonwealth nursing home benefit were set in relation to that benefit, which was reviewed annually, and between annual reviews, proprietors could apply to the Department of Health for approval to increase their fees (Dreyfus 1984: 91; Parker 1987: 34, 61). Guidance for departmental determinations under the *National Health Act 1953* was vague, so several decisions were challenged by nursing home proprietors in court (Dreyfus 1984; Wheelwright 1992).[20] At their root, these cases concerned the profitability of nursing home enterprises. During this time, the department responded to court decisions by elaborating more explicit guidelines for decision-making,[21] which themselves were challenged in court and struck down as outside the authority granted by the Act.

---

19   At the beginning of the 1980s, two inquiries dealing with RAC policy were established. In 1980, the House of Representatives Standing Committee on Expenditure decided to inquire into accommodation and home care for the aged, resulting in the 1982 report *In a Home or at Home* (HRSCE 1982). The committee, chaired by Labor's Leo McLeay, aimed 'to identify the reasons for the continued dominance of expenditure on institutional care and establish a framework which allows governments to make cost effective decisions on provision of both Accommodation and Home Care for the Aged' (HRSCE 1982: vii). In late 1981, the Australian Democrats called for a Senate inquiry into private hospitals and nursing homes and the Fraser Coalition government did not have the numbers in the Senate to prevent it. The background to the inquiry, chaired by Patricia Giles, were 'a number of areas of concern with respect to the nursing home industry', including the poor standard of care (which had been receiving negative press attention), that proprietors were making too much profit or too little and were facing bankruptcy, that there was an oversupply of beds and that admission procedures were inadequate (SSCPH&NH 1985: xiv).

20   See Dreyfus (1984) and Wheelwright (1992) for detailed analyses of the legal problems and cases. The remainder of this paragraph is drawn from these two sources.

21   An 'Efficiency Audit of Commonwealth Administration of Nursing Home Programs' by the Commonwealth Auditor-General in 1981 criticised the department's inconsistent administration and weak control of the nursing home benefits, and guidelines were further changed in response.

When Labor regained government in 1983, the relevant provisions of the *National Health Act* were amended to allow the minister to formulate more detailed principles for determining fees and approving new nursing homes (Parker 1987: 71). In his second reading speech, Minister for Health Neal Blewett argued this was necessary 'to permit [the minister's] delegates to take account of the lack of normal market constraints on the nursing home industry' (cited in Dreyfus 1984: 105). Principles for fee determination were introduced in 1984 but did not solve the ongoing problem; the same year, the Giles Committee's report called the system 'an administrative disaster' (SSCPHNH 1985: 67).

The core problem in setting fees arose from the nature of the nursing home market itself: half of all beds were in for-profit facilities that relied on public funding for the bulk of their revenue. Policymakers—legislative, judicial and administrative—were aware of the dilemmas this situation posed and, over the years, variously favoured either proprietors' profits or consumers and the public purse (Wheelwright 1992; Parker 1987: 61–65). The fee-setting regime put ministers and their delegates in the invidious position of determining the 'reasonable return' the Giles Committee argued was due to 'an honest proprietor'. On one hand, containing costs to the Treasury and ensuring the affordability and accessibility of services to consumers with low incomes pulled in the direction of lower subsidies and fees, respectively. On the other hand, keeping for-profit providers satisfied enough to remain in the sector and allowing them enough of a margin to provide services of an adequate, even improving, level pulled in the direction of higher subsidies and fees. Indeed, as late as 1985, a Labor government convened a Working Party on Nursing Home Profitability and took up its recommendation that providers could charge higher fees when 'the profit component [was] below a certain level' (Cullen 2003: 63).

The fear of 'unreasonable profits' made at public expense led governments to take available opportunities to restrict and control providers (Parker 1987: 63). Nevertheless, as Parker notes, the rarity of bankruptcies and the large sums paid for goodwill by purchasers of homes suggested the sector remained sufficiently lucrative for investors throughout these years. The strong overall growth in beds and particularly in public spending on nursing home benefits in the late 1970s and the first half of the 1980s reinforces Parker's assessment of the positive expectations of nursing home business owners (Cullen 2003: 55).

Meanwhile, the number of non-profit nursing home beds and the costs of their deficit financing also grew steeply between 1975 and 1987 (Cullen 2003: 58). As noted above, Labor's aim was to increase the share of non-profits because they were seen as offering better-quality care. However, policy-shaped market conditions also presented non-profit organisations with incentives that pulled against successive governments' attempts to manage growth in the number and cost of nursing home beds. The 'blank cheque' design of deficit financing made cost control difficult (Parker 1987: 66), while the integration of many non-profit nursing homes into campuses on which independent living and hostel accommodation were also found 'encouraged an internal progression from one level to the next', thereby maintaining demand for nursing home beds—whether or not that was the best option for older people (Parker 1987: 69).

During the third phase of Commonwealth involvement in RAC, governments attempted to gain some control over the producer-driven private-power market that the policies of the first two phases had engendered. However, they had limited overall success, measured by control over spending, access to the industry for providers, placement in and affordability of a nursing home for consumers and the quality of care (Parker 1987: Ch. 9). On the allocation dimension, collective financing continued to be available, while on the production dimension, provider decisions continued largely to determine the size and structure of the market, and the location of facilities. Quality requirements were inconsistent because they were largely under state jurisdiction, and systems of monitoring remained underdeveloped. Little headway was made on diverting resources from residential to home-based care, although important groundwork was laid with the Labor government's legislation of the Home and Community Care program in 1985 (Cullen 2003: 82–85).

Between 1972 and 1984, the number of nursing home beds increased by 45 per cent—largely in line with the share of older people in the population (see Figure 6.1). There was absolute growth in all ownership types, but the pace of growth differed among them. The number of beds in government homes increased by 17 per cent, in for-profit homes by 20 per cent and in non-profit homes by 163 per cent. Accordingly, the share of nursing homes in public ownership fell from 25 to 20 per cent, the share in for-profit ownership fell from 56 to 46 per cent and the share in non-profit ownership nearly doubled—from 18 to 33 per cent. Further, the geographical distribution of homes was uneven, since providers primarily decided where to locate, leaving some areas underserved and others with a surfeit of places.

Partisan differences were once again evident and the ownership structure of the market changed, if not its rising costs and otherwise relatively undirected growth. A Coalition government in 1972 put in place the first controls on fees and entry into a nursing home and sought to promote both family care and hostel accommodation as alternatives to nursing home care. The Labor government of 1972–75 continued these, but also sought to and succeeded in increasing the share of nursing homes run by non-profits (see Figure 6.1). The Coalition government of 1976–83 faced a tension between its desire to restrict government spending and intervention and its desire to foster the growth of the private sector, which seemed to demand liberal subsidies. Its experiment with private financing via private health insurance failed, and the attempt to restrict collective financing through tougher cost controls met resistance from 'subsidised private sector interests [that sought] to entrench those interests through the mechanism of judicial review' (Wheelwright 1992: 148).[22]

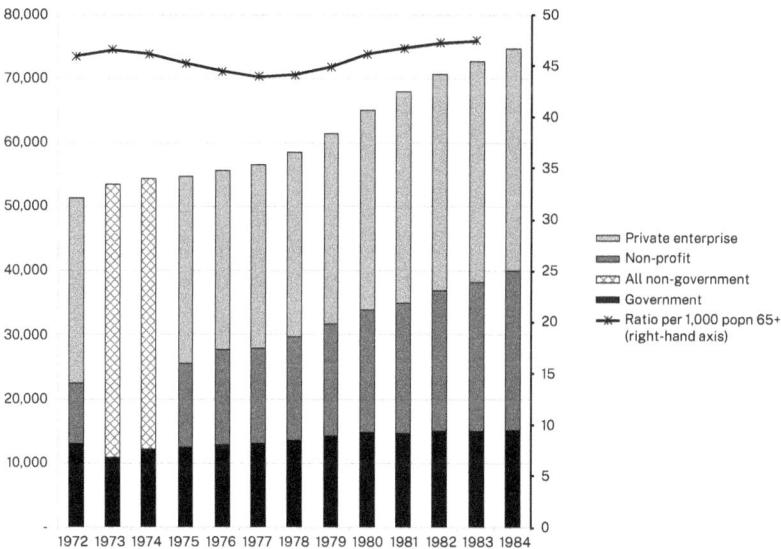

Figure 6.1 Ownership of nursing home beds and ratio of beds per 1,000 population aged 65 years and over, Australia, 1972–84

Note: This includes nursing homes only, not hostel facilities.

Source: SSCPHNH (1985: Table 1.8, p. 17; Table 1.5, p. 12).

---

22   The incoming Labor government faced a significant increase in litigation by for-profit providers challenging the fees determined for their nursing homes (Department of Health 1985: 120) and, in 1984, Minister Blewett announced 'the Government had agreed in principle to introduce a new system of calculating nursing home profitability which would greatly assist the private nursing home sector' (Blewett 1984).

Increasing community and hostel care was an important plank in the election platform of the Labor government elected in 1983. The new government quickly amended the *National Health Act* and the *Nursing Homes Assistance Act*, changing the process of approving new nursing homes to control their growth (Department of Health 1985: 116) and instituting an 18-month freeze on new approvals in March 1983 (DCS 1986: 21). In 1984, the new Hostel Care Subsidy, which contributed to funding for meals, laundry, cleaning and emergency on-call services, inter alia, was introduced alongside the existing Personal Care Subsidy (Cullen 2003: 62). New research was instigated to inform quality management, funding and staffing in residential care, and to chart new directions for community care (Department of Health 1985: 118–19). Yet, problems with the private-power market still needed to be managed and, in 1986, a programmatic 'Statement on the care of aged people' was made by the minister for the new portfolio of Community Services, Senator Don Grimes. Although some key reforms had already begun to be implemented, the statement clearly marked a new phase in aged care policy.

Phase 4: 1986–97 — Further towards a managed market

Senator Grimes's statement set out further dimensions of what had come to be known as Labor's Aged Care Reform Strategy (Gibson 1996)— effectively the first attempt by an Australian government to develop an integrated *system* for the provision of appropriate support to older people. Framed within the government's broader Social Justice Strategy (Howe 1997: 302), Senator Grimes's statement emphasised consultation, planning, innovation, coordination and improving both quality and access for people who were disadvantaged or had special needs. In addition to these egalitarian and technocratic considerations, implementation of the Aged Care Strategy would also be strongly shaped by the 'economic rationalist'[23] policy framework that informed how Labor governments understood policy problems and their solutions during these years (Head 1988; Cahill and Toner 2018). This framework emphasised efficiency

---

23   Or 'neoliberal', as it would now be called. Public administration and public policy researchers also use the concept of New Public Management (Hood 1991).

and accountability—often to be achieved by the market mechanism of competition and through management models derived from private business.[24]

A key aim of the strategy was to address two decades of 'huge and largely uncontrolled growth in expenditure on nursing homes' (Grimes 1986) by further tightening government control over supply and demand for residential care and rebalancing provision away from nursing homes towards care in hostels or at home. As the previous section showed, successive governments of both major parties had pursued these goals for more than a decade with limited success. This time, the government's efforts were more concerted and achieved some success. Legislative changes sought to address system-level problems identified in several reports, including those of the McLeay and Giles committees, and a review of nursing homes and hostels the government commissioned in 1985 (Howe 1990).

During this phase, among reforms to aged care too many to analyse here, three key sets of measures are most relevant to our concern with the policy drivers of the ownership structure of residential care and the distribution of power in the sector:[25] stronger controls on the number, type and location of residential care beds; a new funding formula for nursing home subsidies; and a freeze on Commonwealth benefits to state government–owned nursing homes.

Under the first set of measures, stronger controls on the number, type and location of residential care beds were introduced in 1987, building on the government's already revised nursing home approval process. In the new system, needs-based planning replaced the earlier process, which assessed submissions from prospective providers. Planning benchmarks set ambitious targets to drive the growth of hostel places and to effectively reverse the ratio of nursing home to hostel beds, from where it stood at 67:33 in 1984 to 40:60 within three years. In addition to driving growth in hostel places, the government sought to use the available and new policy levers to increase equity of access to and the quality of hostel care, while also containing costs. Amendments to the *Aged or Disabled Persons Homes*

---

24   As a policy framework, economic rationalism under Labor had a complex relationship with more traditional Labor values of equality. In social policy, attempts to target support to the neediest in aged care coexisted with more universal approaches, such as the introduction of the national health insurance scheme, Medicare.

25   See Gibson (1996), Howe (1997) and Cullen (2003) for more comprehensive and detailed accounts of the Aged Care Reform Strategy.

Act 1954 in 1987 sought to use the design of capital grants to non-profit providers to target new hostel places to frailer and disadvantaged older people. In the parliamentary debate, the Coalition opposition pushed for access to the hostel sector for for-profit providers. They argued that private sector investment was necessary to meet the growing demand for hostel care and the government should welcome it, especially since it was willing to consider privatising publicly owned airlines.[26] Minister Blewett countered with the claim: 'This Government does not believe that we can treat issues such as aged care and child care in the same way as we treat commercial organisations.'[27]

Further changes to hostel funding were implemented in 1989. Despite Minister Blewett's rhetoric, these changes effectively repositioned hostel providers and older people as more like businesses and their consumer rights–bearing customers (Staples 1988a). 'Entry contributions'—a form of private financing of aged care—had been chargeable to residents between 1954 and 1969, when they were disallowed because they gave hostel providers an incentive to offer accommodation to people who could afford contributions rather than to those who needed it (Cullen 2003: 39–40). The government reinstated these contributions, along with enhanced protections for hostel residents and their assets and incomes (Staples 1988a: 2–3). In 1990, the relatively new Hostel Care Subsidy was removed for residents who were not 'financially disadvantaged', creating the first means test for a subsidy in residential aged care (Gibson 1996: 167).[28] In an even more profound break with the past, for-profit providers of hostel care became eligible for recurrent (although not capital) hostel subsidies. While this decision was not justified at length, it was apparently related to the new nursing home funding model (discussed below), which treated for-profit and non-profit providers the same way.[29]

---

26 See, for example, debate on the Community Services and Health Legislation Amendment Bill 1987 (*House of Representatives Hansard*, Monday, 23 November 1987, p. 2508, available from: parlinfo. aph.gov.au/parlInfo/search/display/display.w3p;query=Id%3A%22chamber%2Fhansardr%2F1987-11-23%2F0069%22).

27 Ibid., continuing the 23 November 1987 debate.

28 Alarmed by the loss of revenue removing the subsidy would cause, providers protested this measure, with support from the Coalition and Democrats; in response, the government further amended the legislation to make application prospective only (Le Guen 1993: 26).

29 Minister for Finance Ralph Willis's brief explanation noted that 'private enterprise has been a major provider in the nursing home industry over many years' and pointed to their historical exclusion from eligibility for the hostel subsidy program. To receive the subsidy, 'private enterprise organisations will be required to comply with *the same requirements* as religious and charitable organisations', and would be subject to all the same regulation, including the planning and approvals system. Notably, the general conditions of the Act were to be amended to allow for-profit providers to make a profit (Willis 1990; emphasis added).

The second set of measures was the new funding formula for calculating recurrent subsidies for nursing homes, announced with the 1986–87 budget and phased in over the following years.[30] Under the *Nursing Homes and Hostels Legislation Amendment Act 1987*, all homes—both non-profit and for-profit—were to be funded in the same way, removing, in the interests of efficiency and equity, the very wide variation by state and by ownership status identified in various reports (Gibson 1996: 165). Legislated at the same time, fee controls restricted resident charges to a maximum of 87.5 per cent of the age pension (and rent assistance, where applicable), on the reasoning that nursing care was free in public hospitals under the universal health insurance scheme, Medicare, which the ALP government had recently introduced (Howe 2000: 61). Up to 6 per cent of beds in each state would be approved to charge a higher rate to wealthier older people 'who wish[ed] to pay for care and accommodation outside these funding arrangements' (Staples 1988b).

The new formula separated funding into three modules, each with specific built-in incentives (for details, see Cullen 2003: 68–70; Le Guen 1993: 16–17). The Standard Aggregated Module was a uniform subsidy per resident per day to meet infrastructure and hotel costs. Unspent funds from this module, which was designed to promote efficiency, could be retained as profit. The Care Aggregated Module funded a certain number of nursing and personal care hours per week per resident in a home, based on individual need (dependency), as assessed under a new five-point Resident Classification Instrument. Providers' spending of funds from this module, which was designed to improve quality, drive efficiency and increase the supply of care, was audited under a 'validation program'. The third module, Other Cost Reimbursed Expenditure, reimbursed providers for non-wage costs of staffing, such as superannuation and payroll tax.

The third measure that directly impacted the distribution of ownership and power in RAC was a decision, in 1985, to freeze Commonwealth benefits to state government nursing homes in some states and territories— again, to address wide variation in subsidy levels. The freeze appears to have contributed to the ongoing decline in the share of public providers

---

30   Both the McLeay and the Giles reports (HRSCE 1982; SSCPHNH 1985) had recommended that a new standardised system of program grants replace the differential arrangements for non-profit and for-profit homes (via the Deficit Financing and Participating Nursing Homes schemes, respectively). Reviews by the Department of Community Services of nursing homes and hostels and hostel care subsidy arrangements in 1985 and 1986 made similar recommendations. The new system was based on these recommendations.

(AIHW 1993: 228). The freeze was lifted in the 1992–93 budget and state homes were moved on to the funding system that applied to all private providers (Le Guen 1993: 12).

During the fourth phase of Commonwealth involvement in RAC, consecutive Labor governments had more success than governments in the third phase in gaining control over the private-power market that had evolved over three decades. By 1996, the sector had moved towards what Gingrich (2011) calls a 'managed market'. On the allocation dimension, collective financing continued to be available and older people's access to residential care was determined based on need under the new, publicly provided Aged Care Assessment Program. A new funding model largely removed providers' opportunities to negotiate (or litigate) higher operational subsidies and reduced incentives to avoid admitting more frail residents. Meanwhile, resident fee controls increased accessibility and strictly limited providers' capacity to shift costs on to consumers. On the production dimension, the government gained substantial control over the supply and distribution of RAC places through the new planning and approval processes. New mechanisms for quality oversight and for empowering residents had been introduced, in the form of national outcome standards for nursing homes and hostels (implemented in 1987 and 1991, respectively). Two of the three streams of funding (the Care Aggregated Module and Other Cost Reimbursed Expenditure) could be spent on staff expenses only, and unspent funds could not be retained. These requirements were enforced through the validation program, thereby retaining in the government's hands a critical lever over care quality. 'User rights advocacy services' were introduced in 1989, followed by the 'Charter of residents' rights and responsibilities in nursing homes and hostels' in 1990. Taken together, these policies put a brake on providers' capacity to profit from cream-skimming and cost-cutting.

By the end of the period, the government had advanced its goals of reducing the ratio of nursing home to hostel places, and reducing overall provision of institutional care.[31] The average level of funding for more dependent residents was higher, while the share of the least frail in nursing

---

31   The number of residential care places increased by nearly 30 per cent between 1985 and 1996 and almost all this increase (89 per cent) was in hostel places. The share of nursing home places fell from 67 per cent to 54 per cent and, while the number of residential care places increased, places per 1,000 people aged 70 and over fell from 99 to 91 (AIHW 1995: Table 5.17; 1997: Table 8.16).

homes fell, and savings from residential care were carried into community care, including the new, more intensive home care 'packages' introduced in 1992, which would become increasingly important in the next phase.

Despite increased controls, for-profit providers remained interested in RAC and nursing homes became more profitable: return on investment increased from $4.89 to $9.89 per resident per day between 1984 and 1985, and 1991 and 1992 (Cullen 2003: 70). Indeed, the for-profit share of nursing homes increased slightly from 46 per cent in 1984 to 48 per cent at the end of 1996 and their share of subsidised hostel care also began to grow— from zero to 7 per cent across the same period (PC 1998: Table 9A.28). The growth in for-profit hostels almost compensated for the policy-driven constraint on growth in nursing home beds. Taking nursing homes and hostels together, the share of for-profit provision fell from 31 to 29 per cent between 1985 and 1996. Meanwhile, public provision of nursing homes fell from 20 per cent in 1984 to 14 per cent at the end of 1996.

The Labor Party governed for the entire period, but partisan differences are clearly observable in parliamentary debates along predictable battlelines. The Labor government sought to gain financial and management control over the mostly private sector and to ensure that benefits did not go too disproportionately to better-off older people, at public expense, albeit using some market discourse alongside the social justice and human rights ideas that informed various aspects of its reforms. To achieve what favouring the non-profit sector had done in the past, the government appears to have been relying on measures aimed at increasing equity of access, service quality and older people's rights within the system.

The Coalition opposition recognised the importance of high-quality RAC to older people's wellbeing and professed to agree in general with the direction of government policy.[32] However, on providers' behalf, the opposition rejected the government's characterisation of private providers as 'profit hungry entrepreneurs'[33] and vociferously resisted increased state control. In Parliament, opposition members, citing providers, complained

---

32   See, for example, the contribution from Opposition's Spokesman on Community Services Charles Blunt to the debate on the Second Reading Speech on the Community Services and Health Legislation Amendment Bill 1987 (*House of Representatives Hansard*, Monday, 23 November 1987, p. 2508, available from: parlinfo.aph.gov.au/parlInfo/search/display/display.w3p;query=Id%3A%22 chamber%2Fhansardr%2F1987-11-23%2F0069%22).

33   Charles Blunt, this time in a debate on aged care as a Discussion of a Matter of Public Importance (*House of Representatives Hansard*, Wednesday, 13 April 1988, p. 1463, available from: parlinfo.aph. gov.au/parlInfo/search/display/display.w3p;query=Id%3A%22chamber%2Fhansardr%2F1988-04-13%2F0040%22).

that the processes for determining the Standard Aggregated Module and Care Aggregated Module were shrouded in 'secrecy' and the administering department was 'using Gestapo-type tactics to harass and intimidate proprietors' in a 'denial of natural justice'.[34] The role of assessors as 'gatekeepers' in the new system to determine the eligibility of older people for nursing home entry was strongly resisted, as was the 'unfair', 'intrusive' and 'insurmountable' validation of expenditure.[35] Opposition members rejected fee controls and the restriction on places catering to those who wanted to pay more to get better accommodation and care as 'the politics of envy' and 'socialism gone mad'.[36]

In general, despite their overwhelming reliance on public funding, providers resisted what they framed as a violation of their rights as proprietors. While the opportunity existed, they continued the time-honoured strategy of seeking administrative review of their fees.[37] Across a decade, through their advocates among opposition parliamentarians, but also in submissions to inquiries, advertisements in newspapers and other means, private providers contested the tightening controls, which significantly disrupted business as usual, despite their staged introduction. In submissions to the review of 'the structure of nursing home funding arrangements' conducted by economist Bob Gregory, for example, a major provider industry association proposed major reversals, including fee deregulation and market competition (Gregory 1994: 31).

Labor's policies were contentious, intensively reviewed and amended in various ways. However, they remained largely in place when, in March 1996, Labor lost power to a new Coalition government under John Howard, which introduced new policies that industry preferred.

---

34   Charles Blunt; see speech cited at note 32.
35   Cited in a speech by Shadow Minister for Social Security David Connolly (*House of Representatives Hansard*, Thursday, 12 November 1992, p. 3297, available from: parlinfo.aph.gov.au/parlInfo/search/display/display.w3p;query=Id%3A%22chamber%2Fhansardr%2F1992-11-12%2F0113%22).
36   Bob Woods (Liberal) in the debate on the Community Services and Health Legislation Amendment Bill 1988 (*House of Representatives Hansard*, Thursday, 28 April 1988, p. 2358, available from: parlinfo.aph.gov.au/parlInfo/search/display/display.w3p;query=Id%3A%22chamber%2Fhansardr%2F1988-04-28%2F0150%22); between two periods in Parliament, Woods also worked as a lobbyist for Doug Moran, owner of the largest chain of nursing homes at the time (Bagwell 1997).
37   In 1989, Minister Staples defended the introduction of a charge on providers seeking such reviews, following an increase in requests from an average of 20 annually to about 600 in 1987–88, which he argued was the result of 'an orchestrated form of protest' by the industry against the nursing home reforms; see *House of Representatives Hansard* (Thursday, 10 November 1988, p. 2844, available from: parlinfo.aph.gov.au/parlInfo/search/display/display.w3p;query=Id%3A%22chamber%2Fhansardr%2F1988-11-10%2F0112%22).

Phase 5: 1997–2013 — A new *Aged Care Act* increases private power

In a now well-established tradition of incoming Coalition governments (Weight 2014), on its election, the Howard government (1996–2007) established a National Commission of Audit (NCOA) to review the role of government and recommend how its efficiency could be improved. Like others since, the NCOA's report expressed a market logic. The NCOA (1996) found aged care insufficiently market-like and predicted exponential rises in outlays unless the government made changes, including introducing means-tested user charges and entry contributions for all residential facilities, not just hostels. Within a few months of receiving the NCOA's report, and picking up its proposals, the government announced plans for 'structural reform of residential aged care' in its first budget, 'to address major flaws in the existing system … and save $479 million over 4 years' (Costello 1996).

Accordingly, the Howard government legislated the *Aged Care Reform Act* in 1997, and various provisions came into force over the following years (see Howe 2000). The Act made sweeping, interrelated changes to the structure, funding and regulation of residential aged care, affecting both the real estate and the service aspects of its business model. The new policies opened the system to renewed growth of for-profit provision, including the proliferation and expansion of large corporate providers. They also shifted some power away from government and older people back to providers and increased the costs, both financial and administrative, for older people. Many proposed measures were controversial and the government faced opposition in the Senate, where it was in minority, and from religious and community groups.

Structural reform under the Act removed the distinction between nursing homes and hostels, unifying them into a single RAC program, as it is known today. The change was justified partly by reference to the concept of 'ageing in place', such that an older person in a hostel (or what became a 'low-care' place) would not need to move to a new facility when their needs increased to the level offered in a nursing home (what became a 'high-care' place). This policy aimed to address problems arising from the different funding models for nursing homes and hostels, which increasingly had resident populations with overlapping need profiles

(Cullen 2003: 73–75).[38] One important effect of this integration of the system and the associated funding changes was to align the policy treatments of for-profit and non-profit providers.

The Act changed policies for funding capital costs and accommodation and the recurrent costs of care and hostel services. The review of (Labor's) nursing home funding arrangements (Gregory 1993, 1994) had concluded that funding and incentives for capital investment were insufficient and the quality of accommodation was often poor, especially in for-profit homes. While Labor responded by rewarding providers that offered better-quality accommodation with higher public subsidies (Cullen 2003: 38), the Howard government's approach to remedying these problems aligned with its market-oriented policy goals and sought to shift costs to older people deemed to have the capacity to pay. Accordingly, the first Howard–Costello budget abolished general capital assistance programs for residential care, retaining only a small residual capital funding program to support some providers, such as those catering to special needs groups. The new *Aged Care Act* restructured recurrent funding by separating care and accommodation costs and requiring older people to make means-tested contributions to both. To drive providers to increase the quality of accommodation, building certification requirements were introduced and providers who failed to meet them risked losing their subsidies.

To cover the costs of accommodation and property maintenance and development, the government proposed to extend to high-care places (that is, to nursing homes) the user contributions to capital costs that had long existed in what were now called low-care places (hostels). Under the policy, the amount and payment of an 'accommodation bond', as they were called, were to be mostly a private matter between provider and client. Providers could not charge an older person so much that they would be left with assets below a specified (low) threshold;[39] there was no upper limit. The extension of bonds to high-care places was a very controversial proposal. On one hand, bonds were eyed with great interest by the owners of for-profit nursing home as a source of interest-free capital. The peak

---

38 As Cullen (2003: 73–75) explains, two people with similar needs profiles could attract different levels of subsidy if one lived in a nursing home and the other in a hostel. Whether the integrated system functioned as intended is another matter; see Howe (2000).

39 The threshold was set at the equivalent of 2.5 times the annual rate of the single age pension (which was a bit more than $9,000 in early 1998). The family home was exempt from the assets test under certain conditions, such as if a partner or dependent child of the resident continued to live in it (Gray 2001: 65–66).

body for this group urged the government to 'stand firm and resist calls for more concessions' (Dodson 1997). Non-profit providers mostly preferred ongoing public capital funding to user-paid bonds. They were concerned about the lack of prudential regulation, which left older people exposed to significant losses, and about the equity impacts of unregulated upper limits on bonds, which had the potential to promote selection of clients on the basis of their capacity to pay a (larger) bond and to promote 'a two-tiered system of care' with 'rich, plush nursing homes' in wealthier areas and 'poor, badly maintained homes' elsewhere (Hatfield and Jamal 1997). More politically decisive was the anxiety older people felt at the prospect of selling their family home to access a high-care place. Thus, towards the end of 1997, the government backed down, restricting bonds to low-care (hostel) places only (Howard 1997).

The policy quickly succeeded in drawing in more resources from older people: in the three years after the implementation of these changes, the proportion of people paying bonds and the average amount of bonds both grew (Gray 2001: 65–69). Under an amendment to the *Aged Care Act* in 1998, people occupying high-care places were obliged to pay a means-tested, capped accommodation charge instead of a bond. The charge initially had an annual cap and payment was limited to five years (Howe 2000: 63), but the five-year limit was later removed for residents entering care from July 2004 (Department of Health and Ageing 2005: 49). Residents whose resources fell below the (low) means-test threshold were not required to pay for their accommodation; instead, the government paid providers a daily accommodation supplement.

Subsidies for care and other recurrent costs (such as meals, cleaning and recreation) were determined across the now-unified sector using an eight-category 'resident classification scale', which linked funding per resident to need as determined by the scale. All residents were expected to (continue to) pay a 'standard resident contribution', which was set at 85 per cent of the single aged pension for the majority of residents.[40] However, additional, income-tested fees now applied across nursing homes as well as hostels. User fees were primarily an instrument of public cost control; provider subsidies were reduced by the amount charged to residents.

---

40   This payment was the only user contribution to nursing home care required under Labor's policy before the introduction of the *Aged Care Act 1997*. The *Two-Year Review of Aged Care Reforms* reports that among new residents entering facilities after the reforms (from 1998 to 2000), 93–94 per cent paid the (lowest) pensioner rate of the standard resident contribution (Gray 2001: 62–63).

While providers decided the level of care fees, consumers received some protection as providers could not charge them more than the applicable subsidy. Within two years, these policies tripled the proportion of older people who paid fees, from 11 per cent (who had paid fees in hostels before the reform) to 33 per cent in 2000 (Gray 2001: 64).[41] In 2003, five years after the policy came into force, 40 per cent of residents paid care fees (Department of Health and Ageing 2003: 26).

While the new care funding model protected consumers from fee-gouging by providers, it did not protect them from cost-cutting that could critically compromise the quality of care. Under the Coalition's pro-market, deregulatory approach, quality and accreditation requirements were 'light touch'. Accordingly, the new system for subsidising care removed the obligations on providers to allocate specific proportions of the funding they received to care staff and to acquit public funding against expenditure on staffing, both of which had been required under the previous Labor governments' funding model. Further, while nursing staff ratios were specified in the original Act (as passed in 1997), they were soon removed in amendments, following 'consultation with providers and aged care professionals' (Gray 2001: 19). Instead, responsibility was delegated to providers 'to maintain an adequate number of appropriately skilled staff to ensure that the care needs of care recipients are met'.[42] These policies had a profound effect on the business opportunity related to recurrent costs in residential aged care and providers took this opportunity over the ensuing decades by replacing more expensive professional staff with cheaper workers with lower skill levels. The Labor opposition predicted this outcome in parliamentary debates on the Bill in 1997; one member described it as a 'reckless act by a government that has been captured by the private nursing home-owners lobby'.[43] At any rate, anticipatory

---

41 'High-care' users subject to fees paid more, having paid nothing beyond the basic resident contribution under Labor, while low-care users potentially paid less, since hostel user fees had not hitherto been regulated (Gray 2001: 64).

42 See *Aged Care Act 1997* (Cth), s. 54-1 (1)(b) (available from: www.legislation.gov.au/Details/C2004C01675).

43 The latter part of this remark may have some basis in reality; hospital and nursing home magnate Doug Moran is widely reported as the source of key reform proposals (Bagwell 1997; Dodson, 1996). See also speech by Brenda Gibbs (Labor) (*Senate Hansard*, Tuesday, 24 June 1997, p. 5042, available from: parlinfo.aph.gov.au/parlInfo/search/display/display.w3p;query=Id%3A%22chamber%2Fhansards%2F1997-06-24%2F0120%22).

excitement about the business opportunities in RAC was high in 1997. Property developers, investment banks and private equity companies entered the market over the coming years.[44]

Despite this optimistic behaviour by new market entrants, the Howard government's structural reforms fell prey to the stubbornly persistent problem of RAC policymakers in Australia. The government's expressed ambitions to solve existing problems and put the system to rights once and for all notwithstanding, conflict with providers over funding design and levels endured and intermittent scandals about care quality emerged. Accordingly, policy shifts and restructuring of the administrative architecture—often following reviews and scandals—continued to roil the sector over the decade 1997–2007, during which there were no fewer than seven responsible ministers.[45]

The 2002–03 budget papers included the first *Intergenerational Report*, which aimed to provide 'a basis for considering the Commonwealth's fiscal outlook over the long term, and identifying emerging issues associated with an ageing population' (Treasury 2003: iii). The report projected the Commonwealth's aged care costs as a share of gross domestic product would increase by nearly 150 per cent over the coming 40 years (Treasury 2003: 39). The report and its projections contributed to the framing of ageing as a fiscal problem and underpinned ongoing emphasis on the need to increase the share of costs paid by service users.[46]

---

44   To give a sense of the evolving business interest in residential aged care, House (1999) reports the entry of listed investor Development Capital of Australia (DCA) into the sector, noting it 'spent $7.5 million on two nursing homes to seed its newly formed aged-care group', and planned to spend a further $50–60 million on acquisitions over the coming year. DCA Agedcare was part of the share market–listed DCA Group acquired in 2006 by private equity firm CVC Asia Pacific for $2.7 billion. In October 2007, CVC sold DCA Agedcare to Bupa for $1.2 billion. At the time, Bupa (primarily a health insurance company based in the United Kingdom) owned 300 facilities in the United Kingdom and 43 in Spain (Reuters 2007), while DCA's Amity chain of RAC facilities in Australia and its Guardian chain in New Zealand owned 96 facilities across the two countries (CVC Capital Partners 2007). The bidding process before the sale drew interest from several large private equity companies, investment banks and healthcare corporations, including AMP Capital, Babcock & Brown Communities Group, Macquarie Bank, FKP Property Group and Ramsay Health Care (Clegg and Wilmot 2007).
45   These were Judi Moylan, Warwick Smith, Bronwyn Bishop, Kevin Andrews, Julie Bishop, Santo Santoro and Christopher Pyne. Whether this turnover was a symptom or a cause of ongoing problems with aged care policy is a question for another day.
46   For a critique of generational accounting and its implications for framing policy problems, see Spies-Butcher and Stebbing (2019).

In the 2002–03 budget, the government also announced it would commission a wide-ranging Review of Pricing Arrangements in Residential Aged Care. Led by academic economist Professor Warren Hogan, the review was published in 2004. Hogan made short, medium and long-term recommendations, many of which reflected his discipline's confidence in market mechanisms. One major short-term recommendation was that the resident classification scale, which determined funding per resident, be revised to reduce the 'administrative burden' on providers. Others included an expanded list of resident needs that would attract a funding supplement, better prudential regulation of accommodation bonds, improved information about service quality, including a star-rating system for consumers, and stricter reporting requirements about corporate owners and key personnel when places were transferred, to protect residents from providers who might evade the departmental process for approving providers[47] (Hogan 2004).

The government responded to the review's recommendations over the following years. The new Aged Care Funding Instrument (ACFI) was used to classify all residents entering care from mid-March 2008. The government also proposed to establish a provider-financed guarantee fund for accommodation bonds, instead of the stronger prudential oversight of providers Hogan had recommended. What eventuated, following consultations, Senate committee review and consultant reports, was a government-funded guarantee (ACFA 2017: 36–38). Hogan

---

47   In a change that would have far-reaching implications for service quality and oversight, the *Aged Care Act* had redefined the relationship between the government (as public funder), residential care facilities, their owners and the provision of services to older people. Under the *National Health Act 1953*, specific premises defined as nursing homes were subsidised to provide care in a specified number of approved beds (Herd et al. 1998). As Herd et al. explain, the *Aged Care Act* detached 'places' for which a subsidy could be paid from certain premises and allocated places instead to 'approved providers', who were corporate (or government) entities that met specified conditions. To become an approved provider, the applicant must satisfy the secretary of the relevant department that they are a corporation and that none of their key personnel (executive managers, anyone responsible for nursing services or day-to-day operations) is a 'disqualified person'—that is, a convicted criminal, bankrupt or of unsound mind (Hogan 2004: 165). Applicants were also required under the Act and associated 'Aged Care Principles' to meet accreditation standards (related to service quality and governance), have systems in place to ensure they could do so and certification standards (related to building quality) (Hogan 2004: 21). Places were (and are) traded in a secondary market, and approved providers were also required to notify the department within 28 days of any changes in their 'key personnel' (Hogan 2004: 290). However, as Hogan (2004: 290) pointed out, departmental oversight could be 'circumvented by the … practice of selling the entity owning places rather than the places themselves'. This practice, which became more common over time as the sector consolidated, may have concealed the entry of some very dubious characters (Houston 2021).

also recommended bonds be used as an alternative to accommodation payments in high care; however, the government was not yet prepared to take this political risk.

In the election of 2007, the Coalition lost to the ALP led by Kevin Rudd and reviews of, and policy tinkering with, the aged care system continued.[48] The new government introduced the *Aged Care Amendment (2008 Measures No. 2) Act 2008*, which included measures to improve protections for older people and to clarify lines of regulatory oversight, along lines recommended by the Hogan Review (see Elliot 2008). Interestingly for our purposes, the documents and debate relating to the Act referred to the growing role of corporate providers and indicated the bipartisan political consensus on this development. The existing:

> regulatory framework reflected the 'cottage' nature of the sector as it then was. In recent years a different model of aged care has emerged, one in which the owner and operator of a facility have distinct roles and responsibilities and may function quite separately. The last decade has also seen a significant increase in the level of investment in the sector from large corporate entities. The regulatory framework has not kept pace with this shift in business practice. (Elliot 2008: 1)

Labor member James Bidgood argued in favour of the Bill: 'It is obviously extremely important in terms of consumer confidence and *to maintain and increase the level of corporate investment* in the sector that the regulatory framework that governs these financial arrangements is as robust and current as possible.'[49] The opposition supported the Bill.

As part of Prime Minister Rudd's ambitious plans for sweeping reform of the healthcare system, in 2010, the Council of Australian Governments (COAG) agreed to a federal takeover of aged care, which saw state government co-funding of home and community care and coregulation of residential care removed over the ensuing years. That same year, the (now) Gillard Labor government asked the Productivity Commission 'to examine all aspects of Australia's aged care system, and to develop detailed

---

48 For details on legislative changes made each year, see the appendices to the annual *Reports on the Operation of the* Aged Care Act (available from: www.gen-agedcaredata.gov.au/Resources/Reports-and-publications/2020/September/Report-on-the-operation-of-the-Aged-Care-Act).
49 Emphasis added. James Bidgood (*House of Representatives Hansard*, Monday, 24 November 2008, p. 11177, available from: parlinfo.aph.gov.au/parlInfo/search/display/display.w3p;query=Id%3A%22chamber%2Fhansardr%2F2008-11-24%2F0171%22).

options to ensure it can meet the challenges facing it in coming decades' (Butler 2010). The commission's report, *Caring for Older Australians* (PC 2011), proposed further marketisation of aged care and emphasised expansion of home-based care and increasing consumer choice. Informed by the Productivity Commission's report, the ALP government released its Living Longer, Living Better (LLLB) policy in 2012. With bipartisan support, a suite of five Acts gave effect to the policy in June 2013, for implementation from July 2014, as discussed in the following section (see DSS 2013: 128–29).

Meanwhile, how and by how much the sector was funded were questions of ongoing contention with providers and of government efforts to control public expenditure and meet (remaining) partisan goals. As noted above, the *Aged Care Act 1997* had removed the requirement that providers spend a specified proportion of their funding on staff. Further, the Aged Care Funding Instrument, introduced in 2008, left providers to assess incoming residents' needs for the purposes of determining the level of funding for their care; whether higher amounts of care were delivered was not monitored. As the cost of ACFI funding grew, these policy settings meant governments looked to adjust the assessment criteria and to audit assessments to exercise some control over the amount and use of public spending. Accordingly, in the 2012–13 budget, the government proposed cutting spending by $1.6 billion over five years, through 'improving' the ACFI by 'tightening the assessment criteria' and enhancing the compliance powers of the Department of Health and Ageing. The rationale was to 'better align the funding claimed by aged care providers with the level of care being offered' (Swan and Wong 2012: 184). However, in the same budget, Labor committed $1.2 billion over five years to a 'workforce compact', with funding tied to measures that would improve pay, conditions, career structures and training (Swan and Wong 2012: 180). This funding had the potential to contribute to improved care quality by requiring providers to devote it to staffing costs of various kinds.

During this phase, there were both Coalition (1997–2007) and Labor (2007–13) governments, yet the general direction of reform was largely consistent. The *Aged Care Act 1997* was a decisive turning point towards re-empowering providers, which Labor resisted at the time. However, when in government, Labor acted within what appears to be a bipartisan consensus on marketisation and the appropriateness of for-profit provision, although it increased some protections for residents and workers, as might be expected. After a shaky start in an uncertain policy environment, the share of for-profit RAC provision increased from 26 to 33 per cent during the Howard years and from 33 to 35 per cent during the years of the ALP government (see Figure 6.2). Another important development was the increasing role of large corporations operating chains of facilities.

At the end of this fifth phase, residential aged care seemed to have the features of austerity and private-power markets. On the allocation dimension, access to services was controlled by government-managed needs assessment (which had a collective logic). Collective financing remained in place for most residents but, over time, the government sought to squeeze public contributions and means-tested user charges with relatively low thresholds were levied on care and accommodation. Older people were, as before, expected to find and choose facilities themselves (on a consumer logic) and to make decisions based on increasingly complex, poor-quality information.

On the production dimension, the number and regional placement of facilities continued to be controlled through the planning and approval system (state power). But the changed funding system (the ACFI) increased producers' opportunities for rent-seeking by delegating the assessment of residents' needs to them, and therefore the level of funding received. The ACFI also presented opportunities for provider profiteering, since it increased their control over service quality, by removing dedicated funding for, and regulation of, staffing. More providers also gained access to cash and interest-free capital through user fees and accommodation bonds in low care. Quality was regulated, but ongoing changes to complaints and oversight arrangements and scandals about care quality persisted.

Phase 6: 2013–22 — More austerity and the consolidation of private power

In September 2013, the ALP lost government to the Coalition under Tony Abbott. A National Commission of Audit followed in short order, reporting in 2014. In general, the commission supported the (marketising) direction of change, although proposed taking it further.[50] Policymaking has since been a mix of attempts to restrain public expenditure and

---

50 Emphasising the need to ensure the system is 'sustainable', the NCOA's recommendations called for a deepening of user-pays principles, for both consumers (through including the family home in asset tests) and providers (through private insurance to cover the risk of bond default), in line with the Productivity Commission's earlier proposals that no government had yet taken up.

loosen restrictions on providers that might be expected from Coalition governments, along with the need to respond to consequent problems by enacting some consumer protections. Some changes were developed in a 'red tape reduction plan' (Department of Health 2019) put together by the government and the Aged Care Sector Committee—one of a long line of tripartite sectoral consultative bodies.[51] With an ideological flourish, following the work of a 'red tape committee', the government legislated the *Omnibus Repeal Day (Autumn 2014) Act 2014*. The Act, the first of a series, removed building certification requirements for RAC providers.

However, critical changes also occurred when Labor's LLLB policy came into force on 1 July 2014. The Productivity Commission had recommended including the full value of the family home in aged care means testing but, like many before it, both Labor and Coalition, in framing the LLLB reforms, the then Labor government baulked at doing so. And, in line with Labor's weaker commitment to user-pays principles for more universal services, the LLLB introduced annual and lifetime caps on means-tested care fees for both home and residential care. However, the reforms also allowed for optional additional fees for 'additional services',[52] such as 'enhanced entertainment or lifestyle choices' (Department of Health 2012: 11). Significantly, the LLLB completed a transformation attempted by the Howard government more than a decade before and which would be decisive for the future structure of the sector. With accommodation payments now well established for low-care places, the LLLB also introduced lump-sum accommodation bonds—now to be called 'refundable accommodation deposits'—for all places (along with abolishing the distinction between high and low care in assessments). As Rick Morton (2017) put it: '[T]he immediate effect was to create

---

51   The use, and outcomes, of industry consultative bodies in aged care policymaking has not been systematically studied. The Aged Care Sector Committee (ACSC) replaced the Aged Care Reform Implementation Council that was established by Labor to support the rolling out of the LLLB reforms. Some key personnel remained unchanged across the transition—not least the chair, Professor Peter Shergold, who left the ACSC in November 2014 to chair the board of Opal Aged Care, a private equity–owned chain of residential care facilities and Australia's largest for-profit provider (Richardson 2021). He was replaced on the ACSC with David Tune.

52   There had long been provision for a small number of facilities or beds offering a higher standard of accommodation and hotel services under special arrangements, including the 'exempt homes' outside the public subsidy system during the 1980s and 'extra service' places under the *Aged Care Act 1997*, which were subject to specific regulations. Neither of these schemes is discussed here for reasons of space. 'Additional services' could be offered in all RAC facilities and are only very lightly regulated, as discussed below.

a modern-day gold rush … opening up vast pools of capital in relation to residents classified as high care … and laying the foundation for the corporatisation of care.'

Further changes by the Coalition government worked in the same direction. With the *Aged Care Amendment (Red Tape Reduction in Places Management) Act 2016*, the requirement that providers apply to the Department of Health for approval to transfer places to another provider was removed; previously, the requirement to seek approval gave the department a routine opportunity for oversight of to whom ownership of places was transferred, for the protection of older people (see Hogan 2004: 290; Footnote 50, this chapter). And while many of the LLLB reforms continued the marketisation of RAC under bipartisan agreement, one area of partisan difference was Labor's support for workforce development. Funding for the 'workforce compact' was 'reprioritised' in the Coalition's budget of 2014–15 and redirected into an (temporary, as we shall see) untied increase in funding to providers (Hockey and Cormann 2014: 208).

In 2015, the government also set in train yet another policy review process to inform future changes to the system. This time, the Aged Care Sector Committee—now chaired by David Tune (former secretary of the Department of Finance)—was commissioned to provide a 'roadmap' for the future of aged care. The resulting document pressed familiar themes, proposing further deregulation and marketisation (ACSC 2016). In 2017, the Legislated Review of Aged Care promised under the LLLB legislation, also undertaken by David Tune, recommended the removal of annual and lifetime caps on user fees to reduce costs to governments, and the removal of planning ratios in aged care, to allow the market to determine supply (Tune 2017).

However, despite the deregulatory direction of Coalition policy and the recommendations of reviews, provider discretion did not escape scrutiny when the risks fell on the public purse. After 2014, when the 'goldrush' took off, the government became concerned about 'continued higher than expected growth in ACFI expenditure' (Morrison and Cormann 2016: 101). As Morton (2017) also noted at the time: 'Politicians want deregulation—as well as control.' Thus, in the 2016–17 budget, the instrument's 'scoring matrix' was changed with the goal of saving $1.2 billion over the coming four years (Morrison and Cormann 2016: 101). The minister, Sussan Ley, emphasised the inconsistency in claims, the high rates of downgrading on audit and the need for a more independent and transparent approach to assessment (Cranston 2016). The sector resisted, as market analysts downgraded profit predictions for newly listed corporate chains (Cranston 2016), and representatives of for-profit providers called for fee deregulation and changes to means testing to bring in more funds from users if government funding was going to be cut (White et al. 2016). A government-commissioned review documented accelerating growth in ACFI claims after 2014, and noted as drivers the entry of new companies, the growing share of for-profit providers and the use of consultants to maximise funding (Applied Aged Care Solutions 2017: 36). In 2017, (yet another) Minister for Aged Care Ken Wyatt commissioned the 'resource utilisation and classification study' that would result in (yet another) system for determining need and linking it to funding in RAC. The Australian National Aged Care Classification will be used from 1 October 2022 (Department of Health 2021b).

Since 2013, more of the constraints on provider power and profitability introduced by ALP governments in the 1980s have been dismantled or proposed for dismantling. These include government controls over fees and over the number and location of RAC places through the planning ratios and annual tendering processes that are providers' main opportunity to gain access to the market (Aged Care Approval Rounds).[53] Proponents of marketisation have railed against the Aged Care Approval Rounds for several years, including the Productivity Commission (2011), the Aged Care Sector Committee (2016) and the Legislated Review of Aged Care (Tune 2017). In the budget of 2018–19, the government announced a plan to phase out the Aged Care Approval Rounds process (Department of Health 2018). Effectively deregulating the supply side of the market, and justified as 'increasing choice' for consumers, all residential care places will be allocated directly to older people assessed as eligible from 1 July 2024, rather than to approved providers (see Department of Health 2022). In 2019, the government also announced that the independent and publicly funded and provided aged care assessment process would be put out to tender in 2020. This proposal was withdrawn early in 2020 following strong resistance from state governments, which currently provide these services (O'Keefe 2020). However, it resurfaced in 2021 in the former Coalition government's response to the royal commission.

---

53 Acquiring existing places is the alternative.

The royal commission's reports have shown that regulation of the quality of residential care has often been ineffective. While the accreditation process is part of the problem, rent-seeking by providers in the context of weak regulation of care 'production' is at least as important. There is clear evidence, for example, that providers took the opportunity to reduce their own costs by substituting less-skilled for more-skilled labour after staffing ratios were removed under the *Aged Care Act 1997*. Data on the skill mix have been available only since 2003; they show that between 2003 and 2020, the share of (more expensive) registered nurses fell from 21 per cent of the equivalent full-time staff to 15 per cent, the share of enrolled nurses fell from 14 to 8 per cent and the share of allied health workers fell from 8 to 4 per cent. These highly skilled workers were replaced with personal care workers, for whom there is currently no mandated minimum qualification and whose share of the full-time-equivalent workforce grew from 57 to 72 per cent across the period (Mavromaras et al. 2017: Table 3.3; Department of Health 2021c: Table 2.2).

Further, the costs to consumers in residential aged care are driven by user-pays principles, enacted through weakly regulated provider-determined accommodation charges and fees for 'additional services', in addition to means-tested, publicly imposed care fees. Along with weak regulation of quality, user-pays policies have presented significant opportunities for rent-seeking by for-profit providers (Allard 2016). For-profit providers are consistently and significantly overrepresented in the highest quartile of average annual revenue per resident, driven primarily by higher accommodation charges (ACFA 2015, 2021). The Royal Commission into Aged Care Quality and Safety (2021b: 199) heard evidence from a member of the board of Opal Aged Care, the largest for-profit chain, that 'accommodation is currently the only component on which aged care providers are able to earn a return, the aged care sector has effectively become a property industry rather than a care industry'.

Additional service charges cover 'amenities' such as food choices and entertainment, not care. Consultants Ansell Strategic euphemistically described these charges as a way providers could 'maximise sustainability' in the context of constrained public funding (Cox and Koumoukelis 2016). Charges are regulated in a minimal way in line with the logic of consumer protection[54] and providers can levy them as a condition of entry into a facility. There are few official data collected about them (ACFA 2021: 64), but available evidence suggests they are a small but rapidly growing source of provider income (ACFA 2021: Table 6.10), that for-profit providers are much more likely to use the model of bundled services for a regular fee rather than fees for ad hoc services and that many providers now charge for services they previously provided 'free' as part of their usual offering (Pride Living Group 2019). As might have been foreseen by the government, large for-profit providers found multiple creative ways to raise additional revenue from residents. Regulation of additional service charges has had to evolve, following interventions against providers by the Department of Health and the Australian Competition and Consumer Commission (Gadens 2018; Groshinski et al. 2020). The two largest for-profit chains, Bupa and Regis, ended up in the Federal Court, which found that various of their additional charges on residents were illegal.

During this sixth phase, there have been three Coalition governments, the first of which implemented the LLLB policies legislated under the ALP. Since 2013, the share of for-profit providers increased from 36 to 41 per cent (see Figure 6.2). Another important development, starting in the early 2000s and advancing rapidly since 2014, is the proliferation and consolidation of large corporations—some owned by families, some by private equity and some listed on the stock exchange. These providers tend to develop large facilities in which quality tends to be lower than in smaller ones (Royal Commission into Aged Care Quality and Safety 2021b: 168).

Changes during this phase further increased provider power. On the allocation dimension, access to services remained controlled by government-managed needs assessment (which has a collective logic). Collective financing, including the lifetime cap on care charges, continued. However, governments held down public subsidies and significantly expanded user charges, giving all providers potential access to interest-free capital and capacity to charge 'market rates' for accommodation and for 'additional services'. In future, though, if funded and overseen appropriately, the new Australian National Aged Care Classification model has strong potential to ensure needs-based funding for the care component of RAC.

---

54 According to the Aged Care Financing Authority: 'An additional service fee can only be charged for services that have been agreed to by the resident, that are over and above those paid for by the Commonwealth under the Schedule of Specified Care and Services, and from which aged care residents receive a direct and tangible benefit' (2021: 64).

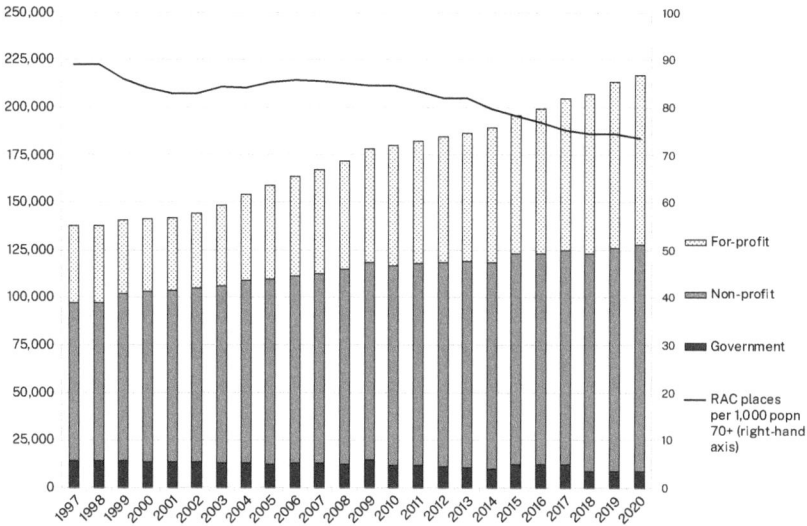

Figure 6.2 Ownership of residential aged care places, and places per 1,000 population aged 70 years and over, Australia, 1997–2020

Sources: Data provided in appendix tables of chapters on aged care in PC (various years).

As the vignettes in the introduction to this collection show, older people's challenges in navigating the aged care market continue. If not of very low means, they face high administrative burdens in negotiating their accommodation costs and other charges. Producers have incentives for cream-skimming (selecting less needy and/or more resource-rich clients), and there is strong sorting between providers by capacity to pay, especially for better accommodation.

On the production dimension, government controls on the number and regional placement of facilities persist but are scheduled for removal, which will increase private power. New opportunities to profit from both the service and real property dimensions of RAC accelerated corporate interest in the sector. Producer control over service quality remained high. Regulation of quality standards was in place, but its effectiveness continued to be limited.

The private power of providers has been scrutinised and criticised, for example, in a Senate Economic References Committee (2018) inquiry into the financial and tax practices of for-profit aged care providers, which recommended greater transparency. The Royal Commission into Aged Care Quality and Safety has also provided a forum for questioning the role of profit in aged care, and one of its commissioned reports has pointed to the complex business structures in aged care corporations that obscure how they use their revenues and derive profits. In 2020, in the absence of any government response to the Senate Economic References Committee report, independent Senator Stirling Griff proposed the Aged Care Legislation Amendment (Financial Transparency) Bill 2020. The Coalition government voted it down. The royal commission's final report did not explicitly question the role of the market as it had identified in its interim report.

Pressed by regulatory failures and media scandals into calling the royal commission, the Coalition government was obliged to respond to at least some of its recommendations (Department of Health 2021a). In the crucial area of staffing, the Morrison government committed to implementing the recommended minimum care time standard–in October 2024–of 200 minutes of care per day, including a specified proportion by a registered nurse. This is the most significant regulatory fetter on private power in the RAC market in decades.

Conclusion

The early and most recent phases of marketisation have empowered providers, while maintaining significant public funding. Profit-making and private power within the market have not been systematically problematised by policymakers as concepts of 'competitive neutrality' (between for-profit and non-profit providers) and arguments about the necessity of drawing in private capital to fund growth of the sector now have strong currency. The argument that private investment is needed to fund future property development is difficult to understand, given repayments on private borrowings are largely funded from the public purse. On its own terms, the market has failed: economists have found no evidence of increasing quality or falling prices and point to growth in the number of 'large and dominant providers that has further reduced competition and choice' (Yang et al. 2021). Meanwhile, in the face of market failure, successive revisions of systems of quality oversight do not appear to have maintained or improved service quality across the sector.

Some of the policies discussed above have been decisive in driving the development of for-profit provision in the first instance, followed by increased use of market practices in residential aged care (see Figure 6.3).

Weakly regulated subsidies offered to providers in the 1960s underpinned the growth of a large for-profit sector that, once established, sought mostly successfully to defend its position. Governments have attempted to contain the 'institutional power' (Busemeyer and Thelen 2020) they had seeded and ceded to the private sector with measures designed to contain costs or (perhaps less successfully) protect the interests of older people. Often these efforts have had partisan inflections. However, in recent years, confidence in market organisation of aged care and an unproblematised role for private businesses have become largely bipartisan. This does not mean governments no longer regulate residential aged care, but rather they do so in the context of the path-dependency and feedback effects of the early growth of for-profit provision.

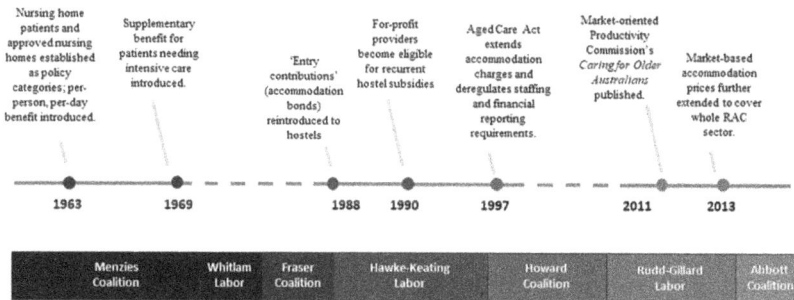

Figure 6.3 Timeline of decisive reforms for for-profit growth and marketisation of RAC

Source: Based on authors' research.

That most older Australians would prefer to remain in their own homes is a foundational assumption of aged care policymakers today. On this basis, home care programs have been expanded significantly in recent years and have themselves been marketised. Yet residential care will always have an important role to play in assisting some older people. They will need skilled, compassionate care and support to live as well as they can; Australia is a rich country and our collective resources are up to the task of ensuring they get it.

Epilogue

Market 'solutions' retain broad bipartisan support. However, the Covid-19 pandemic has put the government under considerable pressure to improve the quality of aged care and, along with the royal commission, has increased the political salience of this important social service. The royal commission's recommendations call for a new *Aged Care Act* to underpin 'a system of aged care based on a universal right to high quality, safe and timely support and care' (Royal Commission into Aged Care Quality and Safety 2021a: 205). Enshrining a universal right to care would be a good start.

Part of the problem with the current system, the royal commission found, was that 'mission-based, social purpose and government aged care services have lost out to the expansion of the private sector' (Royal Commission into Aged Care Quality and Safety 2021a: 50). Accordingly, the structure of the sector (facility size and ownership) needs to become an object of policy again. The history presented above shows it is possible to drive differential growth by selectively offering support to preferred provider types. Careful design would be needed today to avoid running up against competition policy constraints. The establishment of networks of small, public facilities in regional health districts would be one good option,[55] rooting homes in local communities, responding to the call for more 'home-like' facilities and better enabling connections with health services.

Regulation of quality is another lever the government can pull to drive providers' behaviour. The incoming Labor government has at least partly recognised this. One of its first acts was to introduce legislation that, among other things, brings forward the implementation of the mandated minimum 200 care minutes per resident per day to October 2023, and increases daily care minutes to 215 in October 2024.

Further, the institutional power of business to resist regulatory oversight by threat of exit is not infinite. As the ABC Learning case in child care showed the exit of a large provider can be managed in an orderly fashion, especially with government support (Sumsion 2012). As with many problems in social service systems today, including weak regulatory oversight of providers external to the public sector, the loss of capacity in public organisations is one important driver (Ansell et al. 2021). Well-funded institutions of oversight with highly skilled and committed staff are more likely to be able to build genuine partnerships with providers and thereby re-establish trust within the system (Braithwaite et al. 2007). In a system where high trust is well founded, the risk of rent-seeking and

---

55   See Davidson (Chapter 9, this volume) for the case for public providers in human service markets. See also Eagar (2020).

misuse of funds is diminished. Accordingly, regulatory procedures can be less burdensome, and tight oversight of providers' activities and taxpayers' and service users' funds is less likely to be necessary. In another promising action, the Labor government announced in July 2022 a 'capability review' of the ACQSC to consider whether it has the resources, knowledge and skills required to fulfil its responsibilities (Wells 2022). This is a step in the right direction.

Finally, many have pointed out how the pandemic has revealed who the real essential workers are: healthcare workers, supermarket, transport and other workers who help us all meet our daily needs, and those who look after children, people with disabilities and old people who need assistance. Yet (much like childcare and disability workers) aged care workers receive very low wages, their working conditions are typically poor, there are no mandated minimum training requirements for non-professional employees and career paths are weakly developed. In yet another promising action, the incoming Labor government has also supported aged care workers' application for a substantial pay increase that recognises the value of their work (Commonwealth of Australia 2022). Governments and employers can act to remedy these problems and thereby improve the lives of care workers themselves and the quality of care of older people.

References

Aged Care Financing Authority (ACFA). (2015). *Factors Influencing the Financial Performance of Residential Aged Care Providers.* May. Canberra: Department of Social Services. Available from: www.dss.gov.au/sites/default/files/documents/06_2015/acfa_report_-_standard_-_final.pdf.

Aged Care Financing Authority (ACFA). (2017). *The Protection of Residential Aged Care Lump Sum Accommodation Payments.* Study report. Canberra: Department of Health. Available from: webarchive.nla.gov.au/awa/2019 1107015817/agedcare.health.gov.au/reform/the-protection-of-residential-aged-care-accommodation-lump-sum-accommodation-payments.

Aged Care Financing Authority (ACFA). (2021). *Ninth Report on the Funding and Financing of the Aged Care Sector.* Canberra: Department of Health.

Aged Care Sector Committee (ACSC). (2016). *Aged Care Roadmap.* Canberra: Department of Health. Available from: www.health.gov.au/sites/default/files/aged-care-roadmap_0.pdf.

Allard, T. (2016). Rise in nursing home profits not matching the quality of care. *Sydney Morning Herald*, 2 January.

Ansell, C.K., Comfort, L., Keller, A., LaPorte, T. & Schulman, P. (2021). The loss of capacity in public organizations: A public administration challenge. *Perspectives on Public Management and Governance*, 4(1): 24–29.

Applied Aged Care Solutions. (2017). *Review of the Aged Care Funding Instrument. Report part 2: Main report.* June. Melbourne: Applied Aged Care Solutions Pty Ltd. Available from: www.health.gov.au/sites/default/files/documents/2019/11/review-of-the-aged-care-funding-instrument-acfi-review-of-the-aged-care-funding-instrument-acfi-part-2-main-report_0.pdf.

Australian Government. (2007). *Australian Government's Final Response to the Review of Pricing Arrangements in Residential Aged Care.* 8 May. Canberra: Commonwealth of Australia. Available from: web.archive.org.au/awa/2014 0802155607mp_/www.health.gov.au/internet/main/publishing.nsf/Content/633DD703F8CAEEC7CA257BF0001CFE77/$File/Final%20Response%20 Table.pdf.

Australian Institute of Health and Welfare (AIHW). (1993). *Australia's Welfare 1993.* Canberra: AIHW.

Australian Institute of Health and Welfare (AIHW). (1995). *Australia's Welfare 1995.* Canberra: AIHW.

Australian Institute of Health and Welfare (AIHW). (1997). *Australia's Welfare 1997.* Canberra: AIHW.

Bach-Mortensen, A., Verboom, B., Movsisyan, A. & Degli Esposti, M. (2021). A systematic review of the associations between care home ownership and COVID-19 outbreaks, infections and mortality. *Nature Aging*, 1(10): 948–61. doi.org/10.1038/s43587-021-00106-7.

Bagwell, S. (1997). How Doug Moran looks after himself. *Australian Financial Review*, 18 October.

Baldwin, R., Chenoweth, L. & dela Rama, M. (2015). Residential aged care policy in Australia: Are we learning from evidence? *Australian Journal of Public Administration*, 74(2): 128–41. doi.org/10.1111/1467-8500.12131.

Baldwin, R., Chenoweth, L., dela Rama, M. & Liu, Z. (2015). Quality failures in residential aged care in Australia: The relationship between structural factors and regulation imposed sanctions. *Australasian Journal on Ageing*, 34(4): E7–E12. doi.org/10.1111/ajag.12165.

Blewett, N. (1984). Increase in nursing home profitability. Media release, Minister for Health, The Hon. Neal Blewett, 23 October, Parliament House, Canberra. Available from: parlinfo.aph.gov.au/parlInfo/search/display/display.w3p;query= Id%3A%22media%2Fpressrel%2FHPR03001864%22.

Blewett, N. (1987). Community Services and Health Legislation Amendment Bill 1987. Second Reading, Wednesday, 4 November. *House of Representatives Hansard.* Available from: parlinfo.aph.gov.au/parlInfo/search/display/display. w3p;query=Id%3A%22chamber%2Fhansardr%2F1987-11-04%2F0071 %22.

Bos, A., Boselie, P. & Trappenburg, M. (2017). Financial performance, employee well-being, and client well-being in for-profit and not-for-profit nursing homes: A systematic review. *Health Care Management Review, 42*(4): 352–68. doi.org/10.1097/HMR.0000000000000121.

Braithwaite, J., Makkai, T. & Braithwaite, V.A. (2007). *Regulating Aged Care: Ritualism and the new pyramid.* Cheltenham, UK: Edward Elgar Publishing. doi.org/10.4337/9781847206855.

Busemeyer, M.R. & Thelen, K. (2020). Institutional sources of business power. *World Politics, 72*(3): 448–80. doi.org/10.1017/S004388712000009X.

Butler, M. (2010). Foreword. *Report on the Operation of the Aged Care Act 1997 – 1 July 2009 to 30 June 2010.* Canberra: Commonwealth of Australia.

Cahill, D. & Toner, P. (2018). Introduction: Situating privatisation and economic reform. In D. Cahill & P. Toner (eds), *Wrong Way: How privatisation and economic reform backfired.* Melbourne: La Trobe University Press.

Clegg, B. & Wilmot, B. (2007). CVC offers aged homes for $1bn. *Australian Financial Review,* 2 July.

Commonwealth of Australia. (2022). *Work Value Case – Aged care industry.* Submissions of the Commonwealth to the Full Bench of the Fair Work Commission, 8 August. Available from: www.fwc.gov.au/documents/sites/work-value-aged-care/submissions/am202099-63-65-sub-aust-govt-080822.pdf.

Costello, P. (1996). *Budget Speech 1996–97, delivered on 20 August 1996 on the Second Reading of the Appropriation Bill (No. 1) 1996–97 by the Honourable Peter Costello, MP Treasurer of the Commonwealth of Australia.* Canberra: Parliament of Australia. Available from: archive.budget.gov.au/1996-97/ speech/speech.pdf.

Cox, D. & Koumoukelis, A. (2016). Utilising additional services to maximise sustainability. *News,* November. Perth: Ansell Strategic. Available www.ansell strategic.com.au/utilising-additional-services-maximise-sustainability-2/.

Cranston. M. (2016). Frailty of aged care. *Australian Financial Review*, 11 June.

Cullen, D. (2003). *Historical perspectives: The evolution of the Australian Government's involvement in supporting the needs of older people.* Background Paper (Review of Pricing Arrangements in Residential Aged Care) No. 4. Canberra: Department of Health and Ageing.

Cummins, C.J. & NSW Department of Health. (1971). *The Development of the Benevolent (Sydney) Asylum, 1788–1855.* Sydney: NSW Government.

CVC Capital Partners. (2007). CVC agrees to sell DCA Agedcare Group to BUPA for A$1.225 billion. Media release, 3 October, CVC Capital Partners, Sydney. Available from: www.cvc.com/media/press-releases/2007/10-03-2007-123721599.

Department of Community Services (DCS). (1986). *Nursing Homes and Hostels Review.* Canberra: AGPS.

Department of Health. (1985). *Annual Report of the Director-General of Health 1983–84.* Canberra: AGPS.

Department of Health. (2012). *Living Longer. Living Better: Aged care reform package.* April 2012. Canberra: Commonwealth of Australia. Available from: www.health.gov.au/sites/default/files/documents/2019/10/foi-request-1295-extra-service-fees-living-longer-living-better-aged-care-reform-package-april-2012_0.pdf.

Department of Health. (2018). *Better Access to Care: Impact analysis of allocating residential aged care places to consumers instead of providers. Health Budget 2018–2019.* Canberra: Commonwealth of Australia. Available from: webarchive.nla.gov.au/wayback/20190509110120/www.health.gov.au/internet/budget/publishing.nsf/Content/budget2018-factsheet78.htm.

Department of Health. (2019). *Red Tape Reduction Action Plan: Aged care.* Canberra: Commonwealth of Australia. Available from: www.health.gov.au/sites/default/files/documents/2019/12/red-tape-reduction-action-plan-aged-care.docx.

Department of Health. (2021a). *Australian Government Response to the Final Report of the Royal Commission into Aged Care Quality and Safety.* May. Canberra: Commonwealth of Australia. Available from: www.health.gov.au/sites/default/files/documents/2021/05/australian-government-response-to-the-final-report-of-the-royal-commission-into-aged-care-quality-and-safety.pdf.

Department of Health. (2021b). *Residential Aged Care Funding Reform.* Canberra: Commonwealth of Australia. Available from: www.health.gov.au/ health-topics/aged-care/aged-care-reforms-and-reviews/residential-aged-care-funding-reform.

Department of Health. (2021c). *2020 Aged Care Workforce Census Report.* Canberra: Commonwealth of Australia. Available from: www.health.gov.au/sites/default/ files/documents/2021/10/2020-aged-care-workforce-census.pdf.

Department of Health. (2022). Competition in residential aged care. *Initiatives and Programs.* Canberra: Commonwealth of Australia. Available from: www.health. gov.au/initiatives-and-programs/improving-choice-in-residential-aged-care.

Department of Health and Aged Care (DHAC). (2000). *Report on the Operations of the* Aged Care Act 1997: *1 July 1999 to 30 June 2000.* Canberra: Commonwealth of Australia.

Department of Health and Aged Care (DHAC). (2001). *Report on the Operation of the* Aged Care Act 1997: *1 July 2000 to 30 June 2001.* Canberra: Commonwealth of Australia.

Department of Health and Ageing. (2003). *Report on the Operation of the* Aged Care Act 1997: *1 July 2002 to 30 June 2003.* Canberra: Commonwealth of Australia.

Department of Health and Ageing. (2005). *Report on the Operation of the* Aged Care Act 1997: *1 July 2003 to 30 June 2004.* Canberra: Commonwealth of Australia.

Department of Social Services (DSS). (2013). *2012–2013 Report on the Operation of the* Aged Care Act 1997. Canberra: Commonwealth of Australia.

Dickey, B. (1987). *No Charity There: A short history of social welfare in Australia.* 2nd edn. Sydney: Allen & Unwin.

Dodson, L. (1996). Look who was helping John Howard. *Australian Financial Review*, 30 August.

Dodson, L. (1997). Govt stands by nursing home bonds. *Australian Financial Review*, 29 October.

Dreyfus, M. (1984). Nursing home fee determinations: Judicial supervision of departmental procedure. *Federal Law Review*, *15*(2): 89–108. doi.org/10.117 7%2F0067205X8401500201.

Eagar, K. (2020). *Aged Care System Governance*. Submission to Royal Commission into Aged Care Quality and Safety. August. Wollongong, NSW: Australian Health Services Research Institute, University of Wollongong. Available from: agedcare.royalcommission.gov.au/system/files/2020-10/AWF.670.00037. 0001.pdf.

Elliot, J. (2008). Aged Care Amendment (2008 Measures No. 2) Bill 2008— Explanatory Memorandum. Accessed from: parlinfo.aph.gov.au/parlInfo/ search/display/display.w3p;query=Id%3A%22legislation%2Fems%2Fr3095 _ems_67d540e9-9406-4f20-9de2-47976aa8c4a0%22 [page discontinued].

Fine, M. (1999). *The responsibility for child and aged care*. SPRC Discussion Paper No. 105. Sydney: Social Policy Research Centre, University of New South Wales.

Gadens. (2018). Federal Court determines that asset replacement charges and capital refurbishment fees are prohibited under the *Aged Care Act 1997*. Media release, 16 March, Gadens, Sydney. Available from: www.gadens.com/ legal-insights/federal-court-determines-asset-replacement-charges-capital-refurbishment-fees-prohibited-aged-care-act-1997/.

Gibson, D. (1996). Reforming aged care in Australia: Change and consequence. *Journal of Social Policy*, 25(2): 157–79. doi.org/10.1017/S00472794000 00295.

Gibson, D. (1998). *Aged Care: Old policies, new problems*. Melbourne: Cambridge University Press.

Gingrich, J. (2011). *Making Markets in the Welfare State*. Cambridge, UK: Cambridge University Press. doi.org/10.1017/CBO9780511791529.

Gray, L. (2001). *Two-Year Review of Aged Care Reforms*. Canberra: Department of Health and Aged Care.

Gregory, R.G. (1993). *Review of the Structure of Nursing Home Funding Arrangements, Stage 1*. Canberra: AGPS.

Gregory, R.G. (1994). *Review of the Structure of Nursing Home Funding Arrangements, Stage 2*. Canberra: AGPS.

Grimes, D. (1986). Statement on the care of aged people by Senator Don Grimes, Minister for Community Services, August, Parliament of Australia, Canberra. Available from: parlinfo.aph.gov.au/parlInfo/download/media/pressrel/HPR 09021663/upload_binary/HPR09021663.pdf;fileType=application%2F pdf#search=%22media/pressrel/HPR09021663%22.

Groshinski, K., Eden, P., Gordon, T., Shannon, S. & Thomas, M. (2020). Aged care extra services under ACCC spotlight: Insights into the Bupa case. *Health in Focus*, 13 May. Sydney: Minter Ellison. Available from: www.minterellison.com/articles/aged-care-extra-services-under-accc-spotlight.

Hatfield, L. & Jamal, N. (1997). Nursing a grievance. *Sydney Morning Herald*, 17 February.

Head, B. (1988). The Labor government and 'economic rationalism'. *The Australian Quarterly*, (Summer): 466–77. doi.org/10.2307/20635508.

Herd, B., Sutherland, D. & O'Connor, A. (1998). Aged care comes out of retirement: And spawns a legislative boom. *The Proctor, 18*(7): 20–23.

Hockey, J. & Cormann, M. (2014). *Budget 2014–15: Budget measures*. Budget Paper No. 2, 2014–15, 13 May. Canberra: Commonwealth of Australia. Available from: archive.budget.gov.au/2014-15/bp2/BP2_consolidated.pdf.

Hogan, W.P. (2004). *Review of Pricing Arrangements in Residential Aged Care: Final report*. Canberra: Department of Health and Ageing.

Hood, C. (1991). A public management for all seasons? *Public Administration, 69*(1): 3–19. doi.org/10.1111/j.1467-9299.1991.tb00779.x.

House, K. (1999). Development Capital buys into aged care. *Australian Financial Review*, 16 March.

House of Representatives Standing Committee on Expenditure (HRSCE). (1982). *In a Home or at Home: Accommodation and home care for the aged*. Parliament of the Commonwealth of Australia. Canberra: AGPS.

Houston, C. (2021). Chicken killing brothers fail to refund bonds from aged care homes. *The Age*, [Melbourne], 12 July.

Howard, J. (1997). Television interview with Ray Martin. *A Current Affair*, [Channel 9], 5 November. Transcript. Available from: pmtranscripts.pmc.gov.au/release/transcript-10580.

Howe, A. (1990). Nursing home care policy: From laissez faire to restructuring. In H.L. Kendig & J. McCallum (eds), *Grey Policy: Australian policies for an ageing society* (pp. 150–69). Sydney: Allen & Unwin.

Howe, A. (1997). The Aged Care Reform Strategy: A decade of changing momentum and margins for reform. In A. Borowski, S. Encel & E. Ozanne (eds), *Ageing and Social Policy in Australia* (pp. 301–26). Melbourne: Cambridge University Press.

Howe, A. (2000). Rearranging the compartments: The financing and delivery of care for Australia's elderly. *Health Affairs*, (May–June): 57–71. doi.org/10.1377/hlthaff.19.3.57.

Ibrahim, J.E., Li, Y., McKee, G., Eren, H., Brown, C., Aitken, G. & Pham, T. (2021). Characteristics of nursing homes associated with COVID-19 outbreaks and mortality among residents in Victoria, Australia. *Australasian Journal on Ageing, 40*(3): 283–92. doi.org/10.1111/ajag.12982.

Le Guen, R. (1993). *Residential care for the aged: An overview of government policy from 1962 to 1993*. Background Paper No. 32 1993. Canberra: Parliamentary Research Service.

Madden, C. (2020). The dismissal: 45th anniversary. *FlagPost*, [Blog], 11 November. Canberra: Parliamentary Library. Available from: www.aph.gov.au/About_Parliament/Parliamentary_Departments/Parliamentary_Library/FlagPost/2020/November/The_dismissal.

Mavromaras, K., Knight, G., Isherwood, L., Crettenden, A., Flavel, J., Karmel, T., Moskos, M., Smith, L., Walton, H. & Zhang, W. (2017). *The 2016 National Aged Care Census and Survey: The aged care workforce, 2016*. Canberra: Department of Health.

Morris, J.R. (1999). Market constraints on child care quality. *Annals of the American Academy of Political and Social Science, 563*(1): 130–45.

Morrison, S. & Cormann, M. (2016). *Budget 2016–17: Budget measures*. Budget Paper No. 2, 2016–17, 3 May. Canberra: Commonwealth of Australia. Available from: archive.budget.gov.au/2016-17/bp2/BP2_consolidated.pdf.

Morton, R. (2017). Adrift in the uncertain market for aged care. *The Australian*, 29 April.

National Commission of Audit (NCOA). (1996). *Report to the Commonwealth Government, June 1996*. Canberra: AGPS. Available from: web.archive.org/web/20170122051236/www.finance.gov.au/archive/archive-of-publications/ncoa/coaintro.htm.

National Commission of Audit (NCOA). (2014). *Towards Responsible Government: The report of the National Commission of Audit—Phase one*. Canberra: AGPS. Available from: web.archive.org/web/20140705110858/www.ncoa.gov.au/report/phase-one/index.html.

O'Keefe, C. (2020). 'Unlikely to proceed': Hunt backs away from privatisation of aged care teams. *Sydney Morning Herald*, 28 February.

Parker, R.A. (1987). *The Elderly and Residential Care: Australian lessons for Britain.* Aldershot, UK: Gower.

Pride Living Group. (2019). *Additional Services Industry Insights Report.* December. Sydney: Pride Living Group. Available from: prideliving.com.au/download/1693/.

Productivity Commission (PC). (Various years). *Report on Government Services.* Canberra: Productivity Commission.

Productivity Commission (PC). (1998). *Report on Government Services 1998.* Canberra: Productivity Commission.

Productivity Commission (PC). (2011). *Caring for Older Australians: Final inquiry report.* Report No. 53. Canberra: Productivity Commission.

Reuters. (2007). BUPA's billion dollar buy-out. *Australian Ageing Agenda,* 8 October. Available from: www.australianageingagenda.com.au/executive/bupas-billion-dollar-buy-out/.

Richardson, A. (2021). *Australia Industry (ANZSIC) Report Q8601: Aged care residential services in Australia.* Melbourne: IbisWorld.

Royal Commission into Aged Care Quality and Safety. (2019a). About the interim report. Media release, 31 October, Canberra.

Royal Commission into Aged Care Quality and Safety. (2019b). *Aged care program redesign: Services for the future.* Consultation Paper 1, December. Canberra: Commonwealth of Australia.

Royal Commission into Aged Care Quality and Safety. (2019c). *Interim Report: Neglect.* Canberra: Commonwealth of Australia.

Royal Commission into Aged Care Quality and Safety. (2021a). *Final Report: Care, dignity and respect. Volume 1: Summary and recommendations.* Canberra: Commonwealth of Australia.

Royal Commission into Aged Care Quality and Safety. (2021b). *Final Report: Care, dignity and respect. Volume 2: The current system.* Canberra: Commonwealth of Australia.

Sax, S. (1984). *A Strife of Interests: Politics and policies in Australian health services.* Sydney: George Allen & Unwin.

Senate Economic References Committee. (2018). *Financial and Tax Practices of For-Profit Aged Care Providers.* Canberra: Parliament of Australia. Available from: www.aph.gov.au/Parliamentary_Business/Committees/Senate/Economics/Taxpractices-agedcare.

Senate Select Committee on Private Hospitals and Nursing Homes (SSCPHNH). (1985). *Private Nursing Homes in Australia: Their conduct, administration and ownership*. Canberra: AGPS.

Snooks, G.D. (1994). *Portrait of the Family within the Total Economy: A study in longrun dynamics, Australia 1788–1990*. Melbourne: Cambridge University Press.

Spies-Butcher, B. & Stebbing, A. (2019). Mobilising alternative futures: Generational accounting and the fiscal politics of ageing in Australia. *Ageing & Society, 39*(7): 1409–35. doi.org/10.1017/S0144686X18000028.

Staples, P. (1988a). Massive boost for aged people's accommodation. Media release, The Hon. Peter Staples MP, Minister for Housing and Aged Care, 23 December, Parliament House, Canberra. Available from: parlinfo.aph.gov. au/parlInfo/download/media/pressrel/HPR08017449/upload_binary/HPR 08017449.pdf;fileType=application/pdf#search=%221980s%20hostels%20 fees%20January%20entry%20contributions%22.

Staples, P. (1988b). Community Services and Health Legislation Amendment Bill, Second Reading, Thursday 21 April. *House of Representatives Hansard*. Available from: parlinfo.aph.gov.au/parlInfo/search/display/display.w3p;quer y=Id%3A%22chamber%2Fhansardr%2F1988-04-21%2F0099%22.

Sumsion, J. (2012). ABC Learning and Australian early education and care: A retrospective ethical audit of a radical experiment. In E. Lloyd & H. Penn (eds), *Childcare Markets Local and Global: Can they deliver an equitable service?* (pp. 209–25). Bristol, UK: Policy Press.

Swan, W. & Wong, P. (2012). *Budget: Budget measures*. Budget Paper No. 2, 2012–13, 8 May. Canberra: Commonwealth of Australia. Available from: archive.budget.gov.au/2012-13/bp2/bp2.pdf.

The Treasury. (2003). *Intergenerational Report 2002–03*. Canberra: Commonwealth of Australia.

Thornton, P.H., Ocasio, W. & Lounsbury, M. (2012). *The Institutional Logics Perspective: A new approach to culture, structure, and process*. Oxford, UK: Oxford University Press. doi.org/10.1093/acprof:oso/9780199601936.001.0001.

Tune, D. (2017). *Legislated Review of Aged Care 2017*. Canberra: Department of Health. Available from: www.health.gov.au/sites/default/files/legislated-review-of-aged-care-2017-report.pdf.

Weight, D. (2014). *Budget reviews and commissions of audit in Australia.* Parliamentary Library Research Paper 2013–14, 9 April. Canberra: Parliament of Australia. Available from: www.aph.gov.au/About_Parliament/Parliamentary _Departments/Parliamentary_Library/pubs/rp/rp1314/CommOfAudit.

Wells, A. (2022). Capability review of the Aged Care Quality and Safety Commission. Media release, 28 July. Available from: www.health.gov.au/ ministers/the-hon-anika-wells-mp/media/capability-review-of-the-aged-care-quality-and-safety-commission.

Wheelwright, K. (1992). Nursing homes: Policy, profit and litigation. *Griffith Law Review, 1*(2): 103–51.

White, A., Loussikian, K. & Tasker, S. (2016). Aged care and fast money make for unhealthy mix. *The Australian*, 11 June.

Willis, R. (1990). Community Services and Health Legislation Amendment Bill (No. 2) 1990. Second Reading, Thursday, 8 November. *House of Representatives Hansard*. Available from: parlinfo.aph.gov.au/parlInfo/search/display/display. w3p;query=Id%3A%22chamber%2Fhansardr%2F1990-11-08%2F0100 %22.

Wilson, D. (1973–74). Nursing Home Benefits: The first ten years and the new arrangements. *Social Security Quarterly, 3*: 21–25.

Yang, O., Yong, J., Zhang, Y. & Scott, A. (2021). Competition isn't improving the aged care sector. *Pursuit*, [University of Melbourne], 21 April. Available from: pursuit.unimelb.edu.au/articles/competition-isn-t-improving-the-aged-care-sector.

7

The marketisation of social housing in New South Wales

Laura Wynne, Kristian Ruming, Pranita Shrestha
and Dallas Rogers

Introduction

In 2016, the state government of New South Wales, Australia's most populous state, released the *Future Directions for Social Housing in NSW* policy document—the strategic policy framework for funding and managing social housing. The policy announced the social housing sector would be transformed from 'one which is dominated by public sector ownership, control and financing' to one that includes 'greater involvement of private and non-government partners in financing, owning and managing' social and affordable housing assets (FACS 2016: 5). While framed as addressing decades of underfunding in social housing in New South Wales and as a means to increase housing supply through partnership with the private and not-for-profit sector, the policy has been criticised as an extension of a neoliberal policy framework that continues the state's long-term retreat from direct social housing provision (Morris 2017b). For Morris (2017a: 461), social housing is identified by government 'as a public asset and ongoing expense that should be privatised if at all possible or alternatively handed over to community housing'.

This chapter explores the processes of marketisation and financialisation that underpin 'Future Directions' as the latest iteration of a policy shift transforming social housing in New South Wales. Marketisation and financialisation are drivers of what has been described as the 'hyper-commodification' of housing—a concept that captures the ways in which housing is becoming 'ever less an infrastructure for living and ever more an instrument for financial accumulation' (Madden and Marcuse 2016: 26). While much research has focused on how individual owners and corporatised landlords mobilise housing assets to generate financial return, we argue, following Jacobs and Manzi (2019), that marketisation and financialisation are equally observed in the public sector, as the state seeks to outsource funding and management of housing, realise financial value by leveraging public assets and reduce ongoing expenditure.

We use New South Wales as a case study throughout this chapter. Though the precise nature of changes in each Australian state differs slightly, there is a broad trend away from state provision of housing towards privatised, financialised systems of low-income housing provision. Across the country, the social housing stock has declined, while the community housing stock has more than doubled (AIHW 2019).[1] While this growth in community housing has led to an increase in the absolute numbers of social housing stock, proportionally, there has been a decline in the national social housing stock, from 5.1 per cent in 2007–08 to 4.6 per cent in 2018–19 (AIHW 2019). About 22 per cent of social housing is being managed by community housing providers. In recent decades, there has also been a decline in the number of households living in social housing in New South Wales, from 5.6 to 5.1 per cent between 1996 and 2001 and from 5.1 to 4.6 per cent between 2001 and 2016 (ABS 2016).

We provide an overview of several of the key mechanisms in the transformation of the social housing sector, describing how social housing estate redevelopments, the sale of social housing, the transfer of assets to community housing providers and the increasing use of financial mechanisms increasingly leverage housing assets to access finance via the private market (Wynne and Rogers 2020). In addition to providing a historical view of policy and funding changes at both the

---

1   It is not clear from the available data what proportion of this shift is accounted for by transfers of public housing to community sector ownership.

state and the national levels, we investigate the intentions outlined in the NSW Government's Future Directions policy, as well as key programs implemented across the state.

The following section provides an overview of research exploring the marketisation and financialisation of housing. Following this, we map the historical trajectory of public and social housing in Australia, noting the transition from well-supported public infrastructure to an underfunded, residualised and stigmatised form of housing. The third section traces more contemporary practices of marketisation and financialisation, focusing on the growing reliance on public housing estate redevelopment projects funded via public–private partnerships (PPPs), the sale of social housing assets, the growth of community housing providers and the growing prevalence of market mechanisms in the management of social housing assets.

Understanding recent policy shifts: Neoliberalisation, marketisation and financialisation

It is important to clarify several terms and concepts—marketisation, neoliberalisation, financialisation, public housing and social housing— before we move into the analysis. Public housing refers to a housing system in which the state is the landlord. Social housing, by comparison, refers to a housing system in which a not-for-profit or 'community' housing manager is the landlord. Under these definitions, a move from public housing to social housing is predicated on a move from the government giving up its landlord responsibilities and handing these over to a community housing manager. As we discuss later, the shift from describing subsidised housing as 'public housing' to 'social housing' in Australia is recent and significant, and illustrative of a shift from a government-dominated sector to one with high levels of involvement by non-government and for-profit actors. We have followed Gilmour and Milligan's (2012) definition of the term 'social housing' to encompass housing that is built, owned and/or managed by the state or community housing providers.

The term 'marketisation' is also a slippery one in housing studies. David Harvey, in his seminal book, *The Limits to Capital* (2018), argued that, over time, the use value of land has been 'profoundly degraded' (Christophers

2017: 64), while its exchange value has been afforded greater weight. Housing or other infrastructure that sits on the land is increasingly viewed as an asset, to be bought and sold not according to its use value *as a home* for its inhabitants but 'according to the rent it yields' (Harvey 2018: 347). Housing has long been considered a commodity of sorts, although, as Madden and Marcuse (2016: 26) note, its 'commodity character' has always 'ebbed and flowed'. The increasing emphasis on exchange value described by Harvey is reflected in the processes of land and housing commodification we see in Australia, with 'all the material and legal structures of housing—buildings, land, labour, property rights'—being turned into commodities (Madden and Marcuse 2016: 26).

Following neoliberalisation scholars like Harvey, housing scholars prefer to use the concept of neoliberalisation rather than marketisation. We will use the term marketisation in this chapter to maintain consistency with other chapters in this book, but what we mean when we say the marketisation of housing is really three key features of the neoliberalisation of housing—namely, privatisation, deregulation and financialisation. Thus, we are interested in the marketisation of housing running along three vectors. The first is the privatisation of public housing and the public land on which this housing sits. The second is the deregulation of the welfare state in general and public housing policy specifically. The third is financialisation, which refers to the penetration of finance and financial instruments into the shift from public to social housing, the redevelopment of public housing and the management of social housing.

While the ideas of privatisation and deregulation are now well established, financialisation is still something of a buzzword (Christophers 2015). It usefully points to the increasing 'prominence of actors and firms that engage in profit accumulation through the servicing and exchanging of money and financial instruments' (Madden and Marcuse 2016: 31). It is a process whereby financial logic and processes are incorporated into individual, corporate and government planning and decision-making (Bryan and Rafferty 2018). Everything comes to be viewed as either an asset or a liability/risk on a financial balance sheet (Bryan and Rafferty 2018). In their review of the financialisation of housing in the United Kingdom, Jacobs and Manzi (2019) outline three scales at which the process has occurred: financialised governance, where financialisation is an extension of neoliberal policymaking that pursues the commodification of housing, the privileging of homeownership and the dismantling of the housing welfare system; the financialised firm, where a new set of housing organisations, such as community housing providers, is established and takes on a role in funding, developing and managing housing assets; and the financialised subject, where individuals—primarily, homeowners—mobilise their housing assets to accumulate wealth.

Financialisation involves the extension of calculative practices into the domains of everyday life, such as housing, and these practices can be used by investors (Murphy 2015). In terms of property, financialisation has seen the increased involvement of actors who do not build, live in or even see the properties being bought and sold, but who buy, sell, finance and speculate on the housing market. The social function of housing is detached from its status as a capital investment asset (Farha and Porter 2017). Global financial integration throughout the 1980s to the 2000s, coupled with deregulation, led to transformations in the mortgage market that have paved the way for housing to be increasingly treated as a liquid asset (Fields and Uffer 2014). Property emerges as an asset for profit extraction by equity firms, investment funds, developers and lenders.

At another scale, homeowners have experienced easier access to finance, often through relaxed mortgage lending practices and the ability to access equity capital, allowing them to emerge as entrepreneurial investors, using their homes as a commodified asset that can be leveraged to invest and achieve (hopefully) long-term financial security (Smith 2008); homeowners are repositioned as investor subjects (Christophers 2015). However, these practices of financialisation occur within the context of a retreating welfare state that requires individuals to engage in risky investment strategies to fund their later life (Jacobs and Manzi 2018).

In research on financialisation, there is a growing emphasis on the reconfiguration of social housing systems globally (Aalbers et al. 2017; Jacobs and Manzi 2019). Financialisation involves breaking assets into smaller parts and services that can be leveraged—bought, sold, contracted out—such that each aspect of the housing chain becomes a candidate for financialisation; a key example is the securitisation of mortgages (Adkins et al. 2020). While most clearly apparent in the private sector, a multitude of processes have been enacted to achieve the financialisation and marketisation of social and public housing. These are subject to significant local variations but have largely comprised the retrenchment of government agencies as landlords and their replacement with either third-sector (not-for-profit) or private (for-profit) organisations (Christophers 2017; Fields 2017; Madden and Marcuse 2016).

A history of social housing policy and funding in Australia

Since World War II in Australia, state governments have undertaken the construction and management of public housing, while the Commonwealth has supplied funding through a series of periodically negotiated arrangements, such as the Commonwealth–State Housing Agreement (CSHA) and, more recently, the National Affordable Housing Agreement (NAHA) and the National Housing and Homelessness Agreement (NHHA). However, despite a long history of providing public housing, Australian governments have historically tended to be 'reluctant landlords' (Hayward 1996). The shift from 'public housing' to 'social housing' in Australia is recent and significant and is illustrative of a shift from a government-dominated sector to a sector with increasingly high involvement of not-for-profit and for-profit actors. Figure 7.1 presents a timeline of key public housing policies in Australia until 1990.

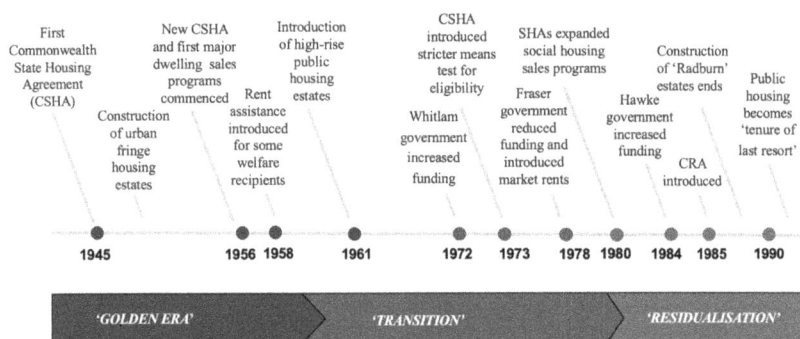

Figure 7.1 From 'golden era' to 'residualisation': Timeline of public housing policies, 1940s to 1990s

Note: CSHA – Commonwealth State Housing Agreement; CRA – Commonwealth Rent Assistance; SHA – State Housing Authority.

Source: Based on authors' research.

The first CSHA, finalised in 1945, emerged as a product of wider welfare state ideologies that informed the Labor government of the time, for whom the provision of housing for low-income households was a central policy concern after the Depression and World War II. The initial CSHA did not impose a means test for people seeking public housing, though it did specify that public housing should be allocated to those 'in need of proper housing' and set aside 50 per cent of dwellings for ex-servicemen.

This agreement was intended to 'complement and offset the vagaries of the private land and housing market' (Groenhart and Gurran 2015: 231). It made it difficult for states to sell public housing, by making the full value of loans repayable on the sale of dwellings (Hayward 1996: 15). The so-called golden era of public housing in Australia ran from 1945 to 1956, following this first CSHA (Hayward 1996: 29). Public housing is estimated to have peaked at about 5 per cent of total housing stock, which is much lower than in other countries.

The first CSHA saw rapid growth in the number of public housing dwellings constructed across Australia (Hayward 1996). Geographically, construction of new public housing estates tended to be in greenfield locations on the outer fringes of cities or—in the case of Sydney and Melbourne, where funds for public housing coincided with calls for the improvement of inner-city workers' housing (Allport 1988)—a few inner-city highrise towers (Troy 2009). Importantly, especially for fringe estates, dwellings tended to be built using low-cost materials that would lead to quality and maintenance issues in future decades.

The 1956 CSHA, negotiated under a right-leaning Coalition government, reoriented the focus to prioritising and encouraging homeownership among low-income households. One of the key changes eased conditions restricting sales of public housing, which resulted in some public housing properties being sold to existing tenants. In New South Wales, between 1947 and 1948, and 1968 and 1969, 37 per cent of CSHA-funded dwellings were sold to the private market (Hayward 1996: 17). Moreover, most homes sold by state housing authorities (SHAs) tended to be the best dwellings in the best locations, while those that remained included both the hastily constructed and maintenance-intensive dwellings built between the late 1930s and the late 1950s and the very unpopular highrise estates built thereafter (Hayward 1996: 22).

Between 1972 and 1984, a series of CSHAs was renegotiated between the Commonwealth and state governments. Across this period, support and funding for public housing provision tended to align with the underlying political ideology of the party in government at the time. For example, CSHAs negotiated under the Whitlam (in 1972) and Hawke (in 1984) Labor governments increased funding for public housing, while the CSHA negotiated by the Fraser Coalition government in 1978 reduced funding. Nevertheless, across this period, the level of funding allocated to public housing provision declined in real terms (Hayward 1996). The

1980s saw SHAs sell significant sections of their portfolios to existing tenants (Hayward 1996). The reduced level of Commonwealth funding flowing to public housing provision (under the CSHA) resulted in low construction rates, and the sale of existing social housing stock resulted in the decline in the level of stock increasingly targeted towards low-income households (Jones et al. 2007).

Reduced funding was accompanied by growing support for private market provision through more restrictive public housing eligibility criteria, a rapid increase in Commonwealth Rent Assistance (CRA) payments (a subsidy for low-income households in the private rental market) and a series of funding and taxation regimes that supported home purchase (Groenhart and Gurran 2015). As a result, private rental (and the related growth of private investment properties)—via regulatory reforms, taxation settings (negative gearing) and demand-side interventions (CRA)—emerged as the primary form of housing for a growing number of low-income households seeking affordable housing options.

The above was paralleled with a rapid increase in demand for public housing, as a growing number of low-income households were unable to secure affordable housing in the private market. There was an estimated shortfall of about 5 per cent in private rental properties at the lower end of the market, concentrated in Sydney (Yates and Wulff 2005: 7). Together, these processes worked to restrict access to public housing to the most disadvantaged households; by the 1990s, public housing in Australia had 'genuinely become welfare housing' for the first time (Hayward 1996: 27). Public housing was thus 'residualised', emerging as a tenure of last resort, providing accommodation to the most disadvantaged people who were unable to secure housing in the private sector (Atkinson and Jacobs 2008).

The 2003 CSHA, negotiated during the Coalition government of John Howard, broadened the definition of social housing to include a range of community, not-for-profit and private sector alternatives to state-owned and managed public housing (Berry et al. 2006: 308). The funding for public housing, which was historically the domain of the government, was dwindling. This was an important shift in policy rhetoric at the Commonwealth level, which called for private and non-profit providers to move in to provide social housing, as the government began to withdraw. Australia has, due to this broadened definition, since seen a discursive shift from 'public' housing, through 'community' housing (Darcy 1999), to 'social' housing.

In 2009, the Rudd Labor government replaced the CSHA with the NAHA. Like the CSHA before it, the NAHA outlined the roles and responsibilities of the Commonwealth and states and set funding arrangements. However, the emphasis on 'affordable housing' represented a further discursive shift in housing policy, which worked to downplay the focus on public housing and open policy and funding opportunities to a wider set of funding, development and management forms. Increasingly, affordable housing (be it home purchase, private rental or social rental) could be provided via the private market.

Redevelopment of public housing estates in New South Wales

The residualisation of public housing as a tenure, combined with the physical design legacies of the 1960s and 1970s, meant public housing became highly stigmatised (Arthurson 2004). Consequently, by the 1980s, SHAs across Australia began to undertake 'renewal' projects of public housing estates to reduce concentrations of social deprivation (Ruming 2018). Early area-based renewal schemes, which typically involved private interests and market mechanisms, sought to address issues related to the concentration of poverty by improving degraded housing stock and the physical environment (Pawson and Pinnegar 2018; Randolph and Judd 2000). From the 1990s, these efforts adopted broader 'community renewal' objectives, including programs to address socioeconomic disadvantage among residents. By the 2000s, there was an observable shift in the form of renewal taking place in public housing estates across Australia, and in New South Wales in particular. Figure 7.2 puts the redevelopment of public housing estates in New South Wales in the context of the broader neoliberalisation of housing in Australia.

In 2000, the NSW Government described redevelopment as 'a process where old Department of Housing dwellings are demolished and replaced with modern accommodation' (SGS Urban Economics & Planning 2000). Characterising these programs as involving demolition and replacement does not, however, quite capture the breadth of transformation associated with most estate redevelopments, which involved privatisation, transfer of stock and the creation of 'socially mixed communities' (Ruming 2018). Arthurson describes redevelopment in the 1990s as serving dual purposes. First, it offered a solution to help housing authorities seeking to 'overcome the existing physical limitations of the stock', which by the

1990s included 'ageing', 'poor design' and failing to meet the needs of tenants whose household structures varied significantly from those housed decades earlier. Second, it worked to increase public housing's 'potential for private sale' (Arthurson 1998: 35).

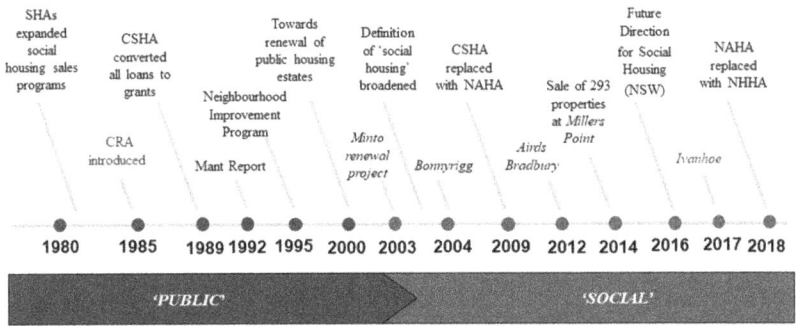

Figure 7.2 From 'public' to 'social' housing: A timeline of neoliberalisation of public housing policies in Australia, 1980s onwards

Note: CSHA – Commonwealth State Housing Agreement; CRA – Commonwealth Rent Assistance; SHA – State Housing Authority; NAHA – National Affordable Housing Agreement; NHHA – National Housing and Homelessness Agreement.

Source: Based on authors' research.

Renewal schemes increasingly involved the demolition of public housing estates and the redevelopment of mixed neighbourhoods, often at higher densities (Arthurson 2012). The appeal of mixed-tenure redevelopments was twofold. First, they were viewed as a mechanism for households living in private housing to act as role models for social housing tenants (who are positioned by the state as deviant citizens who fail to adhere to the neoliberal ideal of the individualistic, self-supporting citizen). This is despite the numerous studies from both Australia and overseas that have illustrated that public and private residents of these neighbourhoods rarely interact (Arthurson 2010; Fraser et al. 2012; Ziersch et al. 2018). Second, state governments viewed this urban renewal as new opportunities to leverage private market funding, delivery and management of public housing assets (Groenhart and Gurran 2015; Pawson and Pinnegar 2018), which were justified through the need to repair dilapidated stock and increase the social housing portfolio. Table 7.1 outlines key renewal projects in New South Wales, identifying the government programs with which they were associated and the redevelopment model used.

A key component of the marketisation of housing in general is the privatisation of public housing (Madden and Marcuse 2016). Since the 1990s, this has been achieved using several key strategies within the overall redevelopment of public housing estates (Pawson and Pinnegar 2018). The following subsections outline some of these key strategies: the sale of social housing assets and the creation of a social mix, and the transfer of social housing assets into non-government management.

Selling housing assets and social mix

In March 2014, the NSW Government announced that '293 properties in Millers Point, Gloucester Street and the Sirius building in The Rocks will be sold, due to the high cost of maintenance, significant investment required to improve properties to an acceptable standard, and high potential sale values' (FACS 2014). As Darcy and Rogers explain:

> In early colonial days the steady winds on the high peninsula made it a suitable place for windmills, leading to the name Millers Point. But for most of the last two centuries its proximity to major wharves and maritime industries saw the place develop as a largely low-income, working class neighbourhood which, in the early 1970s, was saved from modernist redevelopment by 'Green Bans' imposed by building unions. (2016: 47)

The sale of properties in Millers Point is perhaps one of the clearest examples of what David Harvey (2008) calls 'accumulation by dispossession', in which the city's poor are evicted to make way for capital investment. These events reflect a paradigm in which the land housing occupies is rationalised as an asset—to be capitalised on—rather than as a home.

Darcy and Rogers (2016) also note the justification for the sale of housing at Millers Point varied from that given to explain the redevelopment of other public housing. In earlier renewal projects, such as those at Minto and Bonnyrigg in Sydney's south-west, the degraded physical conditions of the estate were the primary justification drawn on by the government, which saw redevelopment as an opportunity to inject private capital into declining areas through the privatisation of public land (Darcy and Rogers 2016). However, the NSW Government claimed the sale of housing at Millers Point was aimed at freeing up capital to allow the government to build public housing elsewhere (Darcy and Rogers 2016). In contrast with the government's prevailing concern with the social mix in other areas, the effect of the Millers Point redevelopment has been to 'unmix' the neighbourhood by displacing tenants to parts of the city where 'land values more closely reflect their socio-economic status' (Darcy and Rogers 2016).

Table 7.1 Major renewal projects in New South Wales

Key public housing estates in NSW	Year of redevelopment/ sale	Government programs	Redevelopment model
Minto	2002	Living Communities Project	Estate type: Radburn* Model: State-led Social mix: 70% private housing, 30% public housing
Bonnyrigg	2004	Living Communities Project	Estate type: Radburn Model: PPP Social mix: 70% private housing, 30% public housing
Airds Bradbury	2012	Communities Plus	Estate type: Suburban Model: Led by Landcom (state agency) Social mix: 70% private housing, 30% public housing
Millers Point	2014		Estate type: Inner-city medium-density dwellings Model: Sale of all social housing assets Social mix: 100% private housing
Ivanhoe	2017	Communities Plus Future Directions for Social Housing in NSW	Estate type: Suburban Model: PPP Social mix: 70% private and affordable housing, 30% social housing
Redfern/ Waterloo	Announced in 2015, planning under way	Communities Plus Future Directions for Social Housing in NSW	Estate type: Inner-city highrise towers and medium-density dwellings Model: PPP Social mix: 70% private and affordable housing, 30% social housing

PPP = public–private partnership

* Radburn is an urban design in which the backyards of the houses face the street and the houses face one another, overlooking a common open space.

Source: Authors' research.

Crucial to increasing the attractiveness of public housing estates to the private market is the dismantling of estates that concentrate the location of social housing. Redevelopment has been in large part justified through its role in creating 'mixed communities'—a new policy paradigm that has gained traction as justification for the redevelopment of public housing across Europe and the United States (Galster 2007; Joseph 2006). These policies rely on the notion that the 'geographic propinquity' of disadvantaged households produces a social dynamic at the local level that works to compound disadvantage, and which can only—according to the policy rationalisation—be addressed through implementing social-mix redevelopment programs that dilute the concentration of disadvantaged households (Darcy 2010; Ruming et al. 2004). In New South Wales, social mix emerges as a central policy and built-form mechanism to alleviate tenant disadvantage, noting that '[t]enure diversification is part of a number of strategies to reduce the level of disadvantage that can occur in public housing estates' (FACS 2013). Such rationalisations rely on the problematisation of public housing tenants as 'deficient' subjects in need of role-modelling—with this role-modelling to be achieved through locating middle-class owner-occupying households in geographic proximity to disadvantaged social housing tenants (Ziersch et al. 2018).

The mechanism through which these socially mixed redevelopments tend to occur is PPP: 'Through public private partnerships, [the NSW Land and Housing Corporation][2] is capturing the benefit of private sector financing to deliver new assets and create communities with 70 per cent private and 30 per cent social housing' (FACS 2013). In some estates, this results in a loss of social housing onsite, while in others, such as in Waterloo, a major inner-Sydney redevelopment site, the government has promised to retain existing numbers of social housing dwellings. Depending on the time frames and configuration of redevelopments, tenants may be rehoused offsite either permanently or temporarily or may be moved immediately into new housing onsite.

In New South Wales, the pursuit of private financing for estate redevelopment has gained momentum since the launch in 2016 of the Communities Plus program. Communities Plus, the state government's estate regeneration strategy, is described as:

---

2   The state government agency responsible for managing state housing assets.

> a new generation of integrated housing developments working with the private, non-government and community housing sectors, in Sydney and regional NSW. The NSW Government, through Land and Housing Corporation (LAHC) sites will develop new and replacement social housing integrated with affordable and private housing ... Offering an innovative approach to social housing growth, Communities Plus leverages the value of the existing property portfolio to accelerate supply. (FACS 2017: 4)

Under Communities Plus, regeneration is tendered to private sector developers, partnered with community housing providers, to redevelop public housing sites (Johnston and Turnbull 2016). Central to the program is the capacity to maximise the redevelopment opportunities of estates due to, first, the increased value of state-owned public housing land and, second, the ability of the government to reconfigure the planning framework (rezoning) that allows higher densities and greater development yield—that is, increased potential for the number of dwellings onsite, leading to increased profit margins. Both these processes increase the underlying value of land. As Johnston and Turnbull summarise:

> Currently some ... [NSW] public-housing estates and sites are located where value in those sites can be 'unlocked'. The sites can be redeveloped at higher densities (with high-rise or medium-rise buildings); with components of private for-sale dwellings and also with components of social housing and intermediate ('affordable') housing. (2016: 16)

This opportunity to capture the 'benefit of private sector financing' goes some way towards explaining why governments in Australia have pursued social-mix redevelopments 'with vigour' (Darcy 2010: 6) despite limited evidence that they produce improved outcomes for incumbent tenants (Arthurson 2002; Clampet-Lundquist 2004; Darcy 2010; Galster 2007; Keene and Geronimus 2011; Manzo et al. 2008). Rather, social mix—and, in particular, the 70:30 private to public ratio—emerges as an economic condition that underpins the financial viability of urban regeneration schemes that are increasingly transferring funding, planning, development and management responsibility to the private sector (Darcy and Rogers 2016).

Transfer of social housing assets

Internationally, transfers of stock and tenancy management to non-government providers have been enthusiastically embraced by governments seeking to shift public housing off their balance sheets. In the United States, more than 260,000 dwellings have been privatised since the 1990s. This pales in comparison with the United Kingdom, however, which started with a much higher proportion of social housing stock. There, about 3 million dwellings have been privatised since 1981 (Madden and Marcuse 2016: 30), including the transfer of about 1.5 million former council houses to housing associations (Pawson and Mullins 2010).

In recent years, Australia has begun to follow suit, with transfers of stock to community housing providers rapidly increasing in pace and volume. Despite the community housing sector being described as recently as 2006 as 'poorly placed to take over management' of social housing due to its 'small size and lack of financial management skills' (Berry et al. 2006: 309), the rate of transfers has rapidly increased, with state and Commonwealth governments agreeing in 2009 to work towards an aspirational target that would see ownership and/or management of up to 35 per cent of social housing stock transferred to community housing providers by 2014 (DHS 2009). This was a significant increase on the 11 per cent held by community providers at the time of the agreement.

For state governments, the community housing sector is financially attractive as it is treated by the Commonwealth Government as private housing for welfare purposes. That is, community housing tenants—unlike public housing tenants—are eligible for the CRA payment, which provides a federal subsidy for their housing. This provides a revenue boost, increasing the level of rent received by the community housing provider (closer to market rents, rather than the subsidised rent paid by public housing tenants), prompting great enthusiasm for 'management transfer' among state governments.

New South Wales plans to continue this steady pace of transfers, with the Future Directions policy aiming to see management of government-owned dwellings transferred to 'community housing providers and other non-government organisations through a competitive process. Within 10 years, the community housing sector will manage up to 35 per cent of all social housing in NSW' (FACS 2016: 10). This privatisation of public assets has been 'justified largely by the financially-advantaged position' of these organisations (Pawson and Wiesel 2014: 345). Further, state governments assume community housing providers have potential for greater management efficiencies than the large bureaucracies governing public housing (Yates 2014).

Key to the emphasis placed on the non-government sector is its perceived potential to leverage funds unavailable to the public sector—for example, through its ability to raise private debt, attract tax benefits, charge higher rents, cross-subsidise and undertake commercial activities (Yates 2014). Transferring public housing properties to community housing providers is thought to be a contribution to the 'critical mass' needed for community sector operators to reach sufficient size to leverage private finance to fund new construction (Pawson and Gilmour 2010). Governments, as noted by Pawson and Gilmour (2010) and Milligan et al. (2009), appear to be counting on the capacity of community housing providers to use existing stock as leverage to secure loans for further investment.

Whether this private finance opportunity will be realised in a significant way by community providers remains to be seen. Community housing providers were found to be 'viable but unsustainable' (FaHCSIA 2009)—that is, they are likely to continue to break even, but are unlikely to be able to accumulate the cash required to be considered 'sustainable'. This situation is likely to limit the extent to which these organisations will be seen as strong candidates for accessing private finance (Yates 2014), which is expected to prove particularly challenging as ageing housing stock begins to require renewal in the coming years. Hall et al. (2001) identify substantial barriers that will constrain the flow of private finance to community housing providers, including low returns, high risks, high management costs, illiquidity and a lack of market information.

This transfer of public housing in Australia reflects what Christophers (2017) describes as the 'indirect' financialisation of public assets: governments themselves do not necessarily treat land as an asset, which might involve developing, letting, leveraging or speculating; rather, they transfer or sell the asset so the private (or not-for-profit) sector can handle the asset in this way. These transfers of land, housing and tenancies to third-sector providers can, then, be viewed as a form of indirect privatisation, deregulation and financialisation.

Marketising social housing in New South Wales: Privatisation, deregulation and financialisation

Beyond the apparent opportunities to utilise private finance to fund social housing, governments have also embraced the opportunity to create a quasi-market for social housing, reframing social housing tenants as 'consumers' who must be presented with 'choice' regarding their housing. 'Choice' has been a driving rationale for the transfer of social housing to diverse providers both overseas (for a discussion of the UK example, see Cowan and Marsh 2005) and in Australia (Jacobs et al. 2004). Choice, through its associations with 'efficiency through competition', has been a key rationale in the marketisation of major public sector reforms in recent decades (Pollitt and Bouckaert 2004). This emphasis on 'choice' comes as part of the 'quasi-commodification' of social service provision (Cowan and Marsh 2005: 23) that relies on framing tenants as self-regulating 'consumers' making rational decisions about housing in a system that looks something like a market (Jacobs et al. 2004).

Indeed, recent changes in New South Wales under the Future Directions policy place further emphasis on 'choice', with the policy claiming the transfer of tenancy management to community providers will result in 'more competition and diversity in the provision of tenancy management services' (FACS 2016: 6). Choice-based letting has been used to manage tenant relocations in public housing redevelopments in New South Wales (Melo Zurita and Ruming 2018). Further, moves towards a 'choice-based' letting and allocations policy signal an attempt to operationalise 'choice' within the allocation of social housing units. Choice-based letting has been used in other contexts, including the United Kingdom and Europe, to provide the illusion of market-based provision in which 'consumers' bid for a product (Cowan and Marsh 2005). Choice might best be understood here not as an outcome of policy, but as a tool for conditioning tenants into the behaviour of autonomous and responsible citizens active in their consumption habits (Cowan and Marsh 2005), through requiring them to behave as though they were 'customers' exercising choice in the private market.

Pawson and Wiesel (2014: 352) argue the notion of 'competing for customers' that is implied by the choice discourse seems alien in a field where 'demand inherently exceeds supply', as tenants generally have no choice but to accept any tenancy offered. Social tenants, then, are actors 'who cannot exercise market power' but are increasingly 'treated as if they could' (Pawson and Wiesel 2014: 352). Pawson and Wiesel (2014: 352) argue the 'greater choice' provided by a multiprovider system may lie more in expanding the options available to governments for selecting recipients for funding than in tenants selecting suitable accommodation.

The transfer of housing stock and tenancy management (that is, the day-to-day management of tenancy issues and disputes, handling of rent and maintenance of buildings) to non-government housing providers— mostly, community housing organisations which operate as not-for-profit associations—has been another key mechanism in the privatisation of public housing. Though not necessarily framed by governments as a privatisation measure, the tenancy transfer process can be seen as one in which a landlord directly controlled by an elected authority is exchanged for one 'formally constituted as a private entity' and only indirectly accountable to government via regulation (Pawson and Wiesel 2014: 353).

The redeveloped estates being delivered under the Communities Plus program involve social housing managed by community housing providers, rather than state providers as was the case before renewal. Redevelopment, then, becomes a means through which the privatisation of land, housing assets and social housing management are simultaneously transferred to non-government actors. However, these shifts in policy objectives and mechanisms have not seen the withdrawal of the state from housing provision. Governments continue to take on a broad range of new roles within the social (and affordable) housing sectors including facilitative roles relating to tax incentives, regulation, land supply and direct funding of construction of new social and affordable housing (van den Nouwelant et al. 2015), as well as direct subsidies for private rental including the CRA payments.

Beyond the CSHAs, a suite of policies, funding arrangements and taxation conditions works to secure the dominance of the private market as the most appropriate form of housing provision in Australia. Such conditions include a series of first homeowner grants, increasing CRA payments, negative-gearing concessions and capital gains and stamp duty discounts (Groenhart and Gurran 2015).

There is a strong preference from the government's perspective for debt associated with social service and housing provision to be shifted 'off the balance sheet' (Pawson et al. 2019), and an unwillingness to be directly involved in the management of properties or tenancies. This shift towards non-government providers of subsidised housing entails a redirection of welfare provision away from direct payments or subsidies to individuals towards both the commercial and the not-for-profit sectors, with payments, such as CRA, serving as a 'proxy landlord subsidy' (Jacobs 2015: 60).

Yates (2013: 111) characterises changes in the provision of social and affordable housing as a shift from 'supply-based subsidies for construction' to 'individual-based subsidies for consumption'. Although subsidies for construction were given a brief boost through the National Rental Affordability Scheme and the response to the Global Financial Crisis (GFC), there is a clear government preference for a shift towards subsidies for consumption, with construction funded through private contributions or through private finance leveraged through assets now held by not-for-profit providers. Increasingly, the 'reluctant landlords' at both Commonwealth and state levels are turning their attention towards the third and private sectors to fund and manage social housing.

In 2007, the community housing sector managed about 33,500 tenancies nationally (AIHW 2007). By 2018, this figure had risen to 80,000 tenancies nationally (CHIA NSW 2021), including about 35,000 tenancies in New South Wales alone (CHIA NSW 2018). Dwellings built under recent major Commonwealth funding packages have largely been transferred to community providers, such as the Social Housing Initiative (discussed below), which aimed to transfer about 75 per cent of newly built stock to community providers (Yates 2014). The rapid growth of the community housing sector through policy shifts has led to major changes (about 22 per cent of social housing is managed by community housing providers), including the professionalisation of its boards and management, the commercialisation of larger providers and a 're-balancing between social and economic objectives' (Gilmour and Milligan 2012: 478).

Despite a prolonged decline in state funding for social housing, the GFC of 2007–08 emerged as, somewhat ironically, the catalyst for the most significant government investment in social housing in decades (Ruming 2015). In response to the global recession, the Rudd Labor government introduced the Social Housing Initiative (SHI) as part of its fiscal stimulus packages, delivering $5.6 billion to fund new social housing dwellings. The delivery of the SHI was a central element of the wider National Partnership Agreement on Social Housing and the largest investment in social housing construction in Australia since the 1980s, funding the upgrade of 2,500 dwellings and construction of 20,000 new dwellings (Yates 2014; Groenhart and Gurran 2015). While the provision of new social housing helped the Labor government, at least partially, meet its pre-election goal of improving housing affordability, the primary motivator for the form and timing of expenditure under the SHI was the capacity to stimulate construction activity nationwide. Government investment in social housing emerged as a form of stimulus that had a multiplier effect in the economy. A KPMG (2012: 2) report suggested that for every $1 of construction activity spent under the SHI, $1.30 in total turnover was generated in the economy. In short, the investment in social housing was not a response to the undersupply of social housing, but a way of maintaining employment in the construction sector.

For many authors exploring financialisation, the GFC operated as a catalyst for 'financial actors, markets, practices, measures and narratives' (Aalbers 2016: 215) to become involved in housing. While these actors moved into housing in the wake of the collapse of risk-investment mechanisms (the subprime mortgage market), it is also vital to recognise the role of the state in shifting towards financial logic, promoting private sector investment and setting regulatory frameworks that facilitated this growing private and financial sector involvement. In Australia, the housing market was not as financialised as places such as the United States; nonetheless, the Commonwealth Government mobilised the GFC as an opportunity to reconfigure the funding and management of social housing. In particular, the SHI emerged as an opportunity for the state, despite funding construction, to continue to withdraw from management and future funding of social housing. The SHI was positioned as a way of stimulating the community housing sector. As then Commonwealth housing minister Tanya Plibersek (2009: 6) said: 'Over the next five years, I would like to see more large, commercially sophisticated not for profit housing organisations emerge and operate alongside the existing state and territory housing departments.'

The minister went on to argue that community housing providers would offer the 'flexibility and commerciality we need to transform our social housing system' (Plibersek 2009: 6). The goal was for 75 per cent of dwellings constructed under the SHI to be transferred to community housing providers (COAG 2009a, 2009b). The NAHA aimed to have up to 35 per cent of social housing managed by community housing providers by 2014 (FaHCSIA 2010)—a target that was not achieved, with 22 per cent of social housing being managed by community housing providers in 2013–14 (AIHW 2015). Nevertheless, within the context of the NAHA, which removed limits on stock transfer, the SHI, despite not reaching its 75 per cent target, was the largest transfer of state-owned housing assets to the not-for-profit community housing sector in Australia's history. This stock transfer worked to restructure the community housing sector, with 75 per cent of those dwellings that were transferred allocated to large, well-performing providers (Gilmour and Milligan 2012).

The principal justification for the transfer of stock to the—particularly large—community housing sector was the belief these assets would work to facilitate access to private development capital, which, in turn, could deliver affordable housing (Blessing 2012; Ruming 2015). The economic viability of community housing providers as social housing providers also rested on the ability of tenants to access CRA. Thus, community housing was a more financially viable alternative to state-funded models (Pawson and Gilmour 2010). This represents a form of subsidy-shifting, from state governments (reducing the number of subsidised dwellings) to the Commonwealth Government (through increased demand-side subsidies), which partly offsets the decline in direct funding provided under the NAHA. This was actively promoted by the Commonwealth Government, which supported the market-based principles that underpin community housing, both financially and ideologically.

Conclusion: Social housing of the future

The shift towards privatised provision of social housing is taking place despite ample evidence that private market provision of rental housing involves significant problems with affordability and security of tenure for low to moderate-income households (Hall et al. 2001; Karmel 1998; Yates and Wulff 2005). Today, those living in social and public housing are among the most vulnerable households in Australian society. Marketisation and financialisation of housing are likely to result in increasing precarity for these most vulnerable households, as their housing is devalued as infrastructure for living and valued more and more as an instrument for capital accumulation.

The story of the funding, provision and management of social housing in Australia over recent decades is one in which the reduced willingness of the state to provide direct resources has seen SHAs increasingly reconfigure the way in which they view and use land and housing assets. State-owned land and housing are now assets to be leveraged to provide affordable housing—increasingly provided by the private sector. While historical policies have resulted in underinvestment in and the residualisation of social housing, it is this context, along with significant increases in land value and opportunities to increase development potential, which makes private sector–led urban regeneration projects viable. These same characteristics make these redevelopments appealing to the private sector, which seeks to maximise profit through the redevelopment process. Likewise, the direct sale of social housing assets emerges as a response by the state to increasing asset value, despite concerns about the ongoing displacement of disadvantaged communities from certain parts of our cities—a process of gentrification in which previous tenants (poorer and disadvantaged) are evicted as they can no longer secure affordable housing in the same area.

The growing reliance on community housing providers is also a product of the historical underinvestment in public housing by the state. On one level, the increasing reliance on community housing providers for tenancy management emerges as a form of public sector outsourcing, with a belief that the non-government (both not-for-profit and commercial) sector is more efficient. On the other hand, the transfer of stock to community housing providers represents a significant shift in the financial configurations centred on the belief that community housing providers can access private sector capital, via bank lending, to provide new affordable housing stock. Success to date has been questionable, with an observed reluctance of private sector capital to invest in the sector, although a series of government interventions have sought to overcome these barriers.

The marketisation of public housing in New South Wales has, then, not involved a simple transition from state ownership and management to a market operation. It has, rather, involved a series of policy mechanisms intended to replicate market conditions within a sector that remains heavily characterised by state ownership and management of assets. The state, despite placing increasing emphasis on the efficiency of not-for-profit and commercial operators in the housing sector, remains central to the regulation and provision of social housing. Marketisation emerges, then, as a complex process involving regulation and deregulation, financialisation and privatisation; however, it is far from 'complete' in the case of NSW social housing reform.

Epilogue: Prospects for the social housing sector

Australia has an unequitable housing system, 'granting those who manage to ascend the so-called "housing ladder" all sorts of housing and financial freedoms, while punishing those who treat their house as a home rather than as a financial tool' (Rogers and Power 2021: 315–16). The commodification of housing is most apparent in the private housing sector, where relaxed access to mortgage finance, tax subsidies for capital gains and rental losses as well as loosening tenure security have allowed housing to be increasingly treated as a liquid and financialised asset. However, as we have shown throughout this chapter, the social housing sector is far from insulated from these forces of marketisation. Those outside homeownership face challenges and are subject to often paternalistic limits imposed by investor (private rental), government (public housing) and not-for-profit (social housing) landlords. Rogers and Power argue:

> To make matters more complicated, the housing sector itself is a knotty set of intersecting economies and jobs. Governments have long used the housing system as an economic driver, and as a site for the creation of jobs, and in Australia this is true across the public, private and now the not-for-profit housing sectors. (2021: 316)

Economic research shows we cannot simply turn off these economies and jobs, 'but we do need to find new ways of bringing the public, private, and not-for-profit sectors together, because our current system isn't working' (Rogers and Power 2021: 316).

Many of Australia's leading housing scholars broadly agree that systemic rather than piecemeal changes are needed in our housing system. There is increasing recognition that placing an unfettered market and wealth accumulation at the centre of our housing system is failing us, and many believe it is not the future. In fact, we need a massive injection of government (public) and not-for-profit (social) housing supply. It is not enough to provide funding for social and affordable housing construction alone. We will not address our systemic housing 'crisis with a few small policy changes or taxation exceptions around the edges' (Rogers and Power 2021: 317). In policy terms, there are three steps we could take today to begin to remedy the housing crisis. First, we could turn off the policy settings that encourage, promote or inadvertently drive the commodification of housing. Treating the house as a financial asset drives housing inequality. Second, we could build more public and social housing and peg rents to tenants' incomes rather than the free rental market. Third, we need a different way of understanding value in our housing systems, where financial value is simply one of many values we include in our calculations of 'value for money' (McAuliffe and Rogers 2019). For example, we could place care, or how we care for each other through the home, at the centre of how we think about and organise our housing systems (Power and Mee 2020).

References

Aalbers, M.B. (2016). *The Financialisation of Housing*. London: Routledge.

Aalbers, M.B., Loon, J.V. & Fernandez, R. (2017). The financialization of a social housing provider. *International Journal of Urban and Regional Research*, *41*(4): 572–87. doi.org/10.1111/1468-2427.12520.

Adkins, L., Cooper, M. & Konings, M. (2020). *The Asset Economy*. Chichester, UK: John Wiley & Sons.

Allport, C. (1988). The human face of remodelling: Postwar 'slum' clearance in Sydney. *Urban Policy and Research*, *6*(3): 106–18. doi.org/10.1080/08111148808551329.

Arthurson, K. (1998). Redevelopment of public housing estates: The Australian experience. *Urban Policy and Research*, *16*(1): 35–46. doi.org/10.1080/08111149808727746.

Arthurson, K. (2002). Creating inclusive communities through balancing social mix: A critical relationship or tenuous link? *Urban Policy and Research*, *20*(3): 245–61. doi.org/10.1080/0811114022000005898.

Arthurson, K. (2004). From stigma to demolition: Australian debates about housing and social exclusion. *Journal of Housing and the Built Environment*, *19*(3): 255–70. doi.org/10.1007/s10901-004-0692-1.

Arthurson, K. (2010). Questioning the rhetoric of social mix as a tool for planning social inclusion. *Urban Policy and Research, 28*(2): 225–31. doi.org/10.1080/08111141003693117.

Arthurson, K. (2012). *Social Mix and the City: Challenging the mixed communities consensus in housing and urban planning policies.* Melbourne: CSIRO Publishing. doi.org/10.1071/9780643104440.

Atkinson, R.G. & Jacobs, K. (2008). *Public housing in Australia: Stigma, home and opportunity.* Paper No. 01, Housing and Community Research Unit. Hobart: University of Tasmania. Available from: eprints.utas.edu.au/6575/1/public_housingLR.pdf.

Australian Bureau of Statistics (ABS). (2016). *Census of Population and Housing 2016.* Canberra: ABS.

Australian Institute of Health and Welfare (AIHW). (2007). *Community Housing 2006–07.* Commonwealth State Housing Agreement National Data Report. Canberra: AIHW.

Australian Institute of Health and Welfare (AIHW). (2015). *Housing Assistance in Australia 2015.* 29 May. Canberra: AIHW. Available from: www.aihw.gov.au/reports/housing-assistance/housing-assistance-in-australia-2015/contents/summary.

Australian Institute of Health and Welfare (AIHW). (2019). *Housing Assistance in Australia 2019.* 18 July. Canberra: AIHW. Available from: www.aihw.gov.au/reports/hou/housing-assistance-in-australia-2019/housing-assistance-in-australia-2019/contents/social-housing-dwellings.

Berry, M., Whitehead, C., Williams, P. & Yates, J. (2006). Involving the private sector in affordable housing provision: Can Australia learn from the United Kingdom? *Urban Policy and Research, 24*(3): 307–23. doi.org/10.1080/08111140600876851.

Blandy, S. & Hunter, C. (2013). The right to buy: Examination of an exercise in allocating, shifting and re-branding risks. *Critical Social Policy, 33*(1): 17–36. doi.org/10.1177/0261018312457869.

Blessing, A. (2012). Magical or monstrous? Hybridity in social housing governance. *Housing Studies, 27*(2): 189–207. doi.org/10.1080/02673037.2012.649469.

Bryan, D. & Rafferty, M. (2018). *Risking Together: How finance is dominating everyday life in Australia.* Sydney: Sydney University Press. doi.org/10.2307/j.ctv175nt.

Christophers, B. (2015). The limits to financialization. *Dialogues in Human Geography*, 5(2): 183–200. doi.org/10.1177%2F2043820615588153.

Christophers, B. (2017). The state and financialization of public land in the United Kingdom. *Antipode*, 49(1): 62–85. doi.org/10.1111/anti.12267.

Clampet-Lundquist, S. (2004). HOPE VI relocation: Moving to new neighborhoods and building new ties. *Housing Policy Debate*, 15(2): 415–47. doi.org/10.1080/10511482.2004.9521507.

Community Housing Industry Association (CHIA) NSW. (2018). *State of the Industry 2018: Community housing in NSW*. Sydney: CHIA NSW. Available from: communityhousing.org.au/wp-content/uploads/2018/12/Stateofthe Industry-web.pdf.

Community Housing Industry Association (CHIA) NSW. (2021). *NSW Community Housing Data Dashboard*. [Online]. Sydney: CHIA NSW. Available from: communityhousing.org.au/our-impact/data-dashboard/.

Council of Australian Governments (COAG). (2009a). *National Partnership Agreement on the National Partnership and Jobs Plan: Prosperity for the future and supporting jobs now*. Canberra: COAG.

Council of Australian Governments (COAG). (2009b). *Special Council of Australian Governments Meeting: Nation building and jobs plan*. Communiqué, 5 February. Canberra: COAG.

Cowan, D. & Marsh, A. (2005). From need to choice, welfarism to advanced liberalism? Problematics of social housing allocation. *Legal Studies*, 25(1): 22–48. doi.org/10.1111/j.1748-121X.2005.tb00269.x.

Darcy, M. (1999). The discourse of 'community' and the reinvention of social housing policy in Australia. *Urban Studies*, 36(1): 13–26. doi.org/10.1080 %2F0042098993709.

Darcy, M. (2010). De-concentration of disadvantage and mixed income housing: A critical discourse approach. *Housing, Theory and Society*, 27(1): 1–22. doi.org/10.1080/14036090902767516.

Darcy, M. & Rogers, D. (2016). Place, political culture and post–Green Ban resistance: Public housing in Millers Point, Sydney. *Cities*, 57: 47–54. doi.org/10.1016/j.cities.2015.09.008.

Department of Families, Housing, Community Services and Indigenous Affairs (FaHCSIA). (2009). *Achieving a Viable and Sustainable Community Housing Sector*. Canberra: Commonwealth of Australia.

Department of Families, Housing, Community Services and Indigenous Affairs (FaHCSIA). (2010). *Regulation and growth of the not-for-profit housing sector.* Discussion Paper, April. Canberra: Commonwealth of Australia.

Department of Family and Community Services (FACS). (2013). *Family and Community Services Annual Report 2012–13.* Sydney: NSW Government. Available from: www.facs.nsw.gov.au/__data/assets/file/0010/279037/3005_FACS_AR_2012-13_WEB_FACS_R.pdf.

Department of Family and Community Services (FACS). (2014). High cost harbourside assets to be sold for a fairer social housing system. Media release, 19 March, NSW Government, Sydney. Available from: web.archive.org/web/20140620201417/http://www.facs.nsw.gov.au/about_us/media_releases/high_cost_harbourside_assets_to_be_sold_for_a_fairer_social_housing_system.

Department of Family and Community Services (FACS). (2016). *Future Directions for Social Housing in NSW.* Sydney: NSW Government. Available from: www.socialhousing.nsw.gov.au/?a=348442.

Department of Family and Community Services (FACS). (2017). *Future Directions for Social Housing in NSW: Transforming the current social housing system.* Progress update December 2017. Sydney: NSW Government. Available from: www.socialhousing.nsw.gov.au/__data/assets/file/0006/536793/2017_Future_Directions_Evaluation.pdf.

Department of Human Services (DHS). (2009). *Implementing the National Housing Reforms: A progress report to the Council of Australian Governments from Commonwealth, state and territory housing ministers.* Melbourne: Victorian Government Department of Human Services. Available from: web.archive.org/web/20120428123322/http://www.dhs.vic.gov.au/__data/assets/pdf_file/0009/564381/Implementing-national-housing-reforms.pdf.

Farha, L. & Porter, B. (2017). Commodification over community: Financialization of the housing sector and its threat to SDG 11 and the right to housing. Extract from the civil society report: *Spotlight on Sustainable Development, 2017 Civil Society Reflection Group on the 2030 Agenda for Sustainable Development.* Available from: www.2030spotlight.org/sites/default/files/download/Spotlight 2017_2_11_Farha_Porter.pdf.

Fields, D. (2017). Urban struggles with financialization. *Geography Compass, 11*(11): e12334. doi.org/10.1111/gec3.12334.

Fields, D. & Uffer, S. (2014). The financialisation of rental housing: A comparative analysis of New York City and Berlin. *Urban Studies, 53*(7): 1486–502. doi.org/10.1177/0042098014543704.

Fitzpatrick, S. & Pawson, H. (2014). Ending security of tenure for social renters: Transitioning to 'ambulance service' social housing? *Housing Studies*, *29*(5): 597–615. doi.org/10.1080/02673037.2013.803043.

Fraser, J.C., Burns, A.B., Bazuin, J.T. & Oakley, D.A. (2012). HOPE VI, colonization, and the production of difference. *Urban Affairs Review*, *49*(4): 525–56. doi.org/10.1177%2F1078087412465582.

Galster, G. (2007). Should policy makers strive for neighborhood social mix? An analysis of the Western European evidence base. *Housing Studies*, *22*(4): 523–45. doi.org/10.1080/02673030701387630.

Gilmour, T. & Milligan, V. (2012). Let a hundred flowers bloom: Innovation and diversity in Australian not-for-profit housing organisations. *Housing Studies*, *27*(4): 476–94. doi.org/10.1080/02673037.2012.677019.

Groenhart, L. & Gurran, N. (2015). Home security: Marketisation and the changing face of housing assistance in Australia. In G. Meagher & S. Goodwin (eds), *Markets, Rights and Power in Australian Social Policy* (pp. 231–55). Sydney: Sydney University Press. doi.org/10.30722/sup.9781920899950.

Hall, J., Berry, M. & Phibbs, P. (2001). *Policy Options for Stimulating Private Sector Involvement in Affordable Housing across Australia: Operationalising and implementing viable new options ('Stage 5')*. AHURI Final Report No. 36, April. Sydney: Australian Housing and Urban Research Institute Sydney Research Centre. Available from: apo.org.au/sites/default/files/resource-files/2003-03/apo-nid115696.pdf.

Harvey, D. (2008). The right to the city. *New Left Review*, *53*: 23–40.

Harvey, D. (2018). *The Limits to Capital*. London: Verso.

Hayward, D. (1996). The reluctant landlords? A history of public housing in Australia. *Urban Policy and Research*, *14*(1): 5–35. doi.org/10.1080/08111149608551610.

Jacobs, K. (2015). A reverse form of welfarism: Some reflections on Australian housing policy. *Australian Journal of Social Issues*, *50*(1): 53–68. doi.org/10.1002/j.1839-4655.2015.tb00334.x.

Jacobs, K., Hulse, K., Stone, W. & Wiesel, I. (2016). *Individualised Housing Assistance: Findings and policy options*. Final Report No. 269, 30 August. Melbourne: Australian Housing and Urban Research Institute. doi.org/10.18408/ahuri-4105001.

Jacobs, K. & Manzi, T. (2019). Conceptualising 'financialisation': Governance, organisational behaviour and social interaction in UK housing. *International Journal of Housing Policy, 20*(2): 184–202. doi.org/10.1080/19491247.2018. 1540737.

Jacobs, K., Marston, G. & Darcy, M. (2004). 'Changing the mix': Contestation surrounding the public housing stock transfer process in Victoria, New South Wales and Tasmania. *Urban Policy and Research, 22*(3): 249–63. doi.org/ 10.1080/0811114042000269281.

Johnston, C. & Turnbull, G. (2016). Communities Plus: Something old something new. *Inner Sydney Voice, 129*: 16–17.

Jones, A., Phillips, R. & Milligan, V. (2007). *Integration and Social Housing in Australia: Challenges and opportunities.* Brisbane: Australian Housing and Urban Research Institute Queensland Research Centre.

Joseph, M.L. (2006). Is mixed income development an antidote to urban poverty? *Housing Policy Debate, 17*(2): 209–34. doi.org/10.1080/10511482.2006. 9521567.

Karmel, R. (1998). *Some issues in estimating housing needs.* AIHW, Housing Assistance: Reports on Measurement and Data Issues, Welfare Division Working Paper No. 17. Canberra: AIHW.

Keene, D.E. & Geronimus, A.T. (2011). 'Weathering' HOPE VI: The importance of evaluating the population health impact of public housing demolition and displacement. *Journal of Urban Health, 88*(3): 417–35. doi.org/10.1007/ s11524-011-9582-5.

KPMG. (2012). *Housing Ministers' Advisory Committee: Social housing initiative review.* September. Melbourne: KPMG. Available from: www.nwhn.net.au/ admin/file/content101/c6/social_housing_initiative_review.pdf.

Lawson, J., Berry, M., Hamilton, C. & Pawson, H. (2014). *Enhancing Affordable Rental Housing Investment via an Intermediary and Guarantee.* AHURI Final Report No. 220, April. Melbourne: Australian Housing and Urban Research Institute at RMIT University & the University of New South Wales. Available from: www.ahuri.edu.au/sites/default/files/migration/documents/AHURI_ Final_Report_No220_Enhancing-affordable-rental-housing-investment-via- an-intermediary-and-guarantee.pdf.

Madden, D. & Marcuse, P. (2016). *In Defense of Housing: The politics of crisis.* London: Verso.

Manzo, L.C., Kleit, R.G. & Couch, D. (2008). 'Moving three times is like having your house on fire once': The experience of place and impending displacement among public housing residents. *Urban Studies*, *45*(9): 1855–78. doi.org/10.1177/0042098008093381.

McAuliffe, C. & Rogers, D. (2019). The politics of value in urban development: Valuing conflict in agonistic pluralism. *Planning Theory*, *18*(3): 300–18. doi.org/10.1177/1473095219831381.

Melo Zurita, M.D.L. & Ruming, K. (2018). 'From choice to chance': Choice-based letting use in forced tenant relocations in New South Wales, Australia. *Housing Studies*, *34*(8): 1243–62. doi.org/10.1080/02673037.2018.1531112.

Milligan, V., Gurran, N., Lawson, J., Phibbs, P. & Phillips, R. (2009). *Innovation in Affordable Housing in Australia: Bringing policy and practice for not-for-profit housing organisations together.* AHURI Final Report No. 134, 13 July. Melbourne: Australian Housing and Urban Research Institute. Available from: www.ahuri.edu.au/research/final-reports/134.

Morris, A. (2017a). 'It was like leaving your family': Gentrification and the impacts of displacement on public housing tenants in inner-Sydney. *Australian Journal of Social Issues*, *52*(2): 147–62. doi.org/10.1002/ajs4.10.

Morris, A. (2017b). The removal of Millers Point public housing tenants in inner-Sydney by the New South Wales government: Narratives of government and tenants. *Urban Policy and Research*, *35*(4): 459–71. doi.org/10.1080/08111146.2017.1335194.

Murphy, L. (2015). Financialization (un)limited. *Dialogues in Human Geography*, *5*(2): 206–9. doi.org/10.1177%2F2043820615588156.

Pawson, H. & Gilmour, T. (2010). Transforming Australia's social housing: Pointers from the British stock transfer experience. *Urban Policy and Research*, *28*(3): 241–60. doi.org/10.1080/08111146.2010.497135.

Pawson, H., Milligan, V. & Martin, C. (2019). Building Australia's affordable housing industry: Capacity challenges and capacity-enhancing strategies. *International Journal of Housing Policy*, *19*(1): 46–68. doi.org/10.1080/19491247.2018.1469108.

Pawson, H. & Mullins, D. (2010). *After Council Housing: Britain's new social landlords.* Basingstoke, UK: Palgrave.

Pawson, H. & Pinnegar, S. (2018). Regenerating Australia's public housing estates. In K. Ruming (ed.), *Urban Regeneration in Australia: Policies, processes and projects of contemporary urban change* (pp. 311–32). London: Routledge. doi.org/10.4324/9781315548722.

Pawson, H. & Wiesel, I. (2014). Tenant agency in Australia's public housing transfers: A comparative assessment. *International Journal of Housing Policy*, *14*(4): 344–67. doi.org/10.1080/14616718.2014.952957.

Plibersek, T. (2009). Room for more: Boosting providers of social housing. Speech to Sydney Institute, Sydney, 19 March.

Pollitt, C. & Bouckaert, G. (2004). *Public Management Reform: A comparative analysis*. Oxford, UK: Oxford University Press.

Power, E.R. & Mee, K.J. (2020). Housing: An infrastructure of care. *Housing Studies*, *35*(3): 484–505. doi.org/10.1080/02673037.2019.1612038.

Randolph, B. & Judd, B. (2000). Community renewal and large public housing estates. *Urban Policy and Research*, *18*(1): 91–104. doi.org/10.1080/0811114 0008727826.

Rogers, D. & Power, E. (2021). The global pandemic is accelerating housing crises. *International Journal of Housing Policy*, *21*(3): 315–20. doi.org/10.1080/ 19491247.2021.1957564.

Ruming, K.J. (2015). Everyday discourses of support and resistance: The case of the Australian Social Housing Initiative. *Housing, Theory and Society*, *32*(4): 450–71. doi.org/10.1080/14036096.2015.1048896.

Ruming, K.J. (2018). Urban regeneration and the Australian city. In K. Ruming (ed.), *Urban Regeneration in Australia: Policies, processes and projects of contemporary urban change* (pp. 1–24). London: Routledge. doi.org/10.4324/ 9781315548722.

Ruming, K.J., Mee, K.J. & McGuirk, P.M. (2004). Questioning the rhetoric of social mix: Courteous community or hidden hostility? *Australian Geographical Studies*, *42*(2): 234–48. doi.org/10.1111/j.1467-8470.2004.00275.x.

SGS Urban Economics & Planning. (2000). *Public Housing Estate Renewal in Australia*. Australian Housing Research Fund Project No. 212, November. Melbourne: Spiller Gibbins Swan Pty Ltd. Available from: apo.org.au/sites/ default/files/resource-files/2000-11/apo-nid65450.pdf.

Smith, S.J. (2008). Owner-occupation: At home with a hybrid of money and materials. *Environment and Planning A*, *40*(3): 520–35. doi.org/10.1068%2 Fa38423.

Troy, P. (2009). The Commonwealth Housing Commission and national housing policy. Paper delivered to fourth State of Australian Cities National Conference, Perth, 24–27 November.

van den Nouwelant, R., Davison, G., Gurran, N., Pinnegar, S. & Randolph, B. (2015). Delivering affordable housing through the planning system in urban renewal contexts: Converging government roles in Queensland, South Australia and New South Wales. *Australian Planner*, *52*(2): 77–89. doi.org/10.1080/07293682.2014.914044.

Wynne, L. & Rogers, D. (2020). Emplaced displacement and public housing redevelopment: From physical displacement to social, cultural, and economic replacement. *Housing Policy Debate*, *31*(3–5): 395–410. doi.org/10.1080/10511482.2020.1772337.

Yates, J. (2013). Evaluating social and affordable housing reform in Australia: Lessons to be learned from history. *International Journal of Housing Policy*, *13*(2): 111–33. doi.org/10.1080/14616718.2013.785717.

Yates, J. (2014). Protecting housing and mortgage markets in times of crisis: A view from Australia. *Journal of Housing and the Built Environment*, *29*(2): 361–82. doi.org/10.1007/s10901-013-9385-y.

Yates, J. & Wulff, M. (2005). Market provision of affordable rental housing: Lessons from recent trends in Australia. *Urban Policy and Research*, *23*(1): 5–19. doi.org/10.1080/0811114042000335250.

Ziersch, A., Arthurson, K. & Levin, I. (2018). Support for tenure mix by residents local to the Carlton Housing Estate, Melbourne, Australia. *Housing Studies*, *33*(1): 58–76. doi.org/10.1080/02673037.2017.1344201.

8

Designing public subsidies for private markets: Rent-seeking, inequality and childcare policy

Adam Stebbing

Introduction

The 'radical marketisation' of the childcare sector has coincided with its rapid expansion, which has largely been driven by the increased labour force participation of women and the growth of generous public subsidies for private provision in recent decades. The childcare sector includes early childhood education and care (ECEC), outside school hours care and family day care. In 2018, there were 18,699 government-approved service providers catering for almost 1.3 million (31 per cent of) children aged from newborns to 12 years (PC various years). In 1988, it was estimated that government-funded ECEC services assisted only 73,883 (2.3 per cent of) children in the same age group (AIHW 1993: 127, 133). Over a similar period, the sector has been transformed by the shift to for-profit provision, with the proportion of childcare places offered by private for-profit centres surging from 22 per cent in 1991 to around two-thirds in 2020 (ACECQA 2020; Brennan 2007: 216).

The radical marketisation of the childcare sector has been the subject of mixed assessments. The Productivity Commission (2017: 61) enthusiastically promoted the ECEC market as evidence of 'the value that user choice and competition can have in human services'. Yet, mounting evidence supports persistent concerns about limits to the availability and affordability of quality childcare services as profits for providers have soared in the past two decades (Brennan 2014; Hill and Wade 2018). There is wide recognition that the public subsidies for child care—which are the largest source of funding for the sector—have contributed to both inefficiency, by placing few limits on the rent-seeking of for-profit providers, and inequity, through recent reforms that have cut support for some low-income households. While correct as far as it goes, this assessment of public subsidies overlooks important differences between the design of the policy instruments enacted by successive governments to subsidise child care and how these different policies have interacted with the private market.

This chapter examines the subsidies for child care that successive federal governments have enacted since the mid-1980s, comparing and contrasting policy designs. It proceeds in four sections. The first classifies the childcare sector using Gingrich's (2011) typology of social service markets and highlights the role of public subsidies. The second section explains the policy-instruments approach, which recognises the tools of statecraft to be social as well as technical devices, and which underpins my analysis of the different designs for childcare subsidies. The third and major section charts the evolution of public subsidies for child care, highlighting the political choices behind the design of tax expenditure, cash benefit and rebate policy instruments. The fourth section concludes that childcare policies that more closely resemble direct expenditures have been less inefficient and more equitable than those that possess features of tax expenditure. A short Epilogue considers the implications of temporary measures for child care introduced in the initial stages of the Covid-19 pandemic.

A 'private-power' market? Rent-seeking in the childcare market

To provide context for my analysis of public subsidies, this section draws on Gingrich's (2011) typology to classify the structure of the childcare market and discusses how the design of some public subsidies has the potential to exacerbate rent-seeking.

Gingrich (2011) contends that existing social service markets do not resemble the 'free-market' model that animates neoclassical economics and much policy discourse. Instead, she argues that social service markets are institutions that organise behaviour through competitive mechanisms that vary in both structure and outcomes. The structure of this competitive mechanism 'follows from how the "demand" side (users and purchasers) and the "supply" side (producers) interact to both deliver and distribute services' (Gingrich 2011: 19). Her typology differentiates between six ideal welfare market models that vary systematically along both the *allocative* dimension, which entails how costs are shared between service users and the state, and the *productive* dimension, which involves how control over production is distributed between service users, the state and private service providers (non-profit and for-profit) (Gingrich 2011: 9). While the allocative dimension relates to the distributive outcomes of a social service market, the relationship between the two dimensions has a bearing on the quality and efficiency of services produced.

The institutional structure of the Australian childcare market conforms to what Gingrich (2011) terms the 'private-power' model. Consistent with the allocative dimension of this model, the costs of childcare services delivered by private providers (for-profit and non-profit) are shared between service users and the government. Public subsidies cover a substantial proportion but not the full price of child care for most service users, with the rate of benefits for parents and guardians calculated according to family income, the price of childcare services and hours of care (Services Australia 2021). The productive dimension of the childcare market is also consistent with the private-power model because the control private providers have over the design of services and price is subject to little oversight and few constraints from the state and consumers (Hill and Wade 2018). As a result, the quality and efficiency of childcare services are reliant on competition between providers for consumers. Gingrich (2011: 17) argues that private-power markets 'promise innovation but face the risk of rent-seeking and uncontrolled cost-cutting at the expense of efficient or high-quality production'. At the same time, this market model may make it difficult for consumers to access affordable and high-quality services if providers are relatively free to charge additional fees on top of public subsidies.

The vulnerability of private-power markets to rent-seeking is relevant to the childcare sector. Rent-seeking occurs when large private organisations use their market power in political processes to gain advantageous public policy settings that reinforce their economic interests (Stiglitz 2013: 48). As Stiglitz notes, rent-seeking can involve:

hidden and open transfers and subsidies from the government, laws that make the marketplace less competitive, lax enforcement of existing competition laws [and regulations], and statutes that allow corporations to take advantage of others or to pass costs on to the rest of society. (2013: 48)

Not only does rent-seeking further concentrate wealth and economic advantage, it also tends to divert resources away from productive activities and thereby disadvantages other stakeholders (Stiglitz 2013: xxxiii). Rent-seeking benefits private sector providers in social service sectors (such as child care), while the costs are borne by the state, the community and households.

Public subsidies as 'policy instruments'

There are wide concerns that the series of public subsidies for child care enacted by governments of both major persuasions since the mid-1980s have contributed to rapid fee inflation and rent-seeking. Despite these concerns, key differences in policy design have affected the equity of these subsidies and their susceptibility to rent-seeking. What appear at first to be relatively minor differences have had significant impacts, particularly as childcare coverage has expanded and, with it, the cost of public subsidies. To better understand these differences and their impacts, this chapter draws on insights from the policy-instruments approach to classify and analyse patterns in the design of public subsidies over time.

Policy-instrument analysis starts from the proposition that policies can be classified into groupings that have common features that reflect meaningful trends in design. Since there is no consensus on the level(s) of abstraction at which policy instruments should be analysed, it is necessary to define the concept and clarify which of the numerous available frameworks is employed (see Howlett 2019; Salamon 2001; Vedung 1998). A policy instrument is defined here, following Salamon (2001: 1641–42), 'as an identifiable method through which collective action is structured to address a public problem'. Salamon understands policy instruments as 'identifiable methods' of public action that share a set of common design features that are typical of practice but may vary in certain manifestations. Salamon posits that, as methods that structure collective action, policy instruments are institutions that routinise patterns of social behaviour.

And, by highlighting that policy instruments are collective actions that respond to public issues, he acknowledges that they may impact the behaviour of state agencies, private entities and households.

Policy instruments are understood from this perspective to be technical, social and political devices. As technical devices, they establish the parameters of the roles, and the extent of accompanying responsibilities, that various actors and organisations have at all stages of a program, from design to delivery (Salamon 2001: 1627). By establishing these parameters, a policy instrument is also a social device that structures 'specific social relations between the state and those it is addressed to, according to the representations and meanings it carries' (Lascoumes and Le Gales 2007: 4). Lascoumes and Le Gales (2007: 4) contend that policy instruments 'structure policy according to their own logic', regardless of the specific aims stated, because these tools of public action reflect different understandings of policy problems and serve to organise social behaviour. It follows that policy instruments are also political devices because their designs elevate certain interests over others by allocating costs and benefits, expanding or contracting the roles of different policy actors, and reflecting specific ideas related to different viewpoints on the social issue and how to respond to it (Salamon 2001: 1628).

To analyse trends in the policy instrument design of public subsidies for child care, I draw on the tax expenditure – direct expenditure continuum proposed in joint research with Spies-Butcher (see Stebbing and Spies-Butcher 2010). This continuum positions fiscal policy instruments that deliver support for individuals and families according to how directly public expenditure is allocated for public accounting purposes. Direct social expenditures, such as public services and cash transfers, that are funded from general tax revenue and/or involve services delivered by the public sector occupy the left end of the continuum. Tax expenditures, such as tax exemptions and tax rebates, that are selective tax discounts that have similar budgetary effects to direct expenditures, but which channel funding to private provision, occupy the right end (Stebbing and Spies-Butcher 2010: 590). In the middle of the continuum, there are hybrid policies—such as rebates and subsidies—that exhibit features of both direct and indirect policy instruments. This continuum is useful to understand trends in public subsidies for child care, as direct expenditures, tax expenditures and hybrid policies have all been employed.

Direct Expenditures		Hybrid Policies	Tax Expenditures	
Public Services	Cash Transfers	Rebates Subsidies	Tax Rebates	Tax Exemptions
Public policies delivered directly as social services or cash benefits by state bureaucracy to their recipients, typically on a weekly or fortnightly basis.		Public policies exhibiting features of income transfers and tax expenditures. Hybrid policies include those with multiple delivery mechanisms.	Public policies delivered only as tax reductions to their recipients, generally through annual tax returns. Constitute deviations from the tax benchmark.	

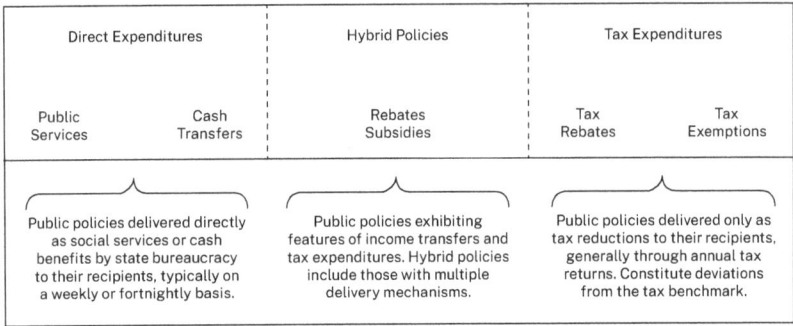

Figure 8.1 The continuum of direct expenditures and tax expenditures

Source: Adapted from Stebbing and Spies-Butcher (2010).

The relative position of a policy on the tax expenditure – direct expenditure continuum affects its visibility and distributive effects (Stebbing and Spies-Butcher 2010: 591). Direct social expenditures are typically framed (in Australia) as redistributive government-funded benefits that target most support to poorer and lower-income households. These policies involve highly visible budget appropriations that are routinely captured in public accounting processes. In contrast, tax expenditures are generally framed as incentives that give taxpayers back their own money to promote certain behaviours or compensate particular groups. These policies may not be redistributive, and often provide flat-rate or regressive benefits (Stebbing and Spies-Butcher 2010). Tax expenditures often lack transaction trails and have low visibility in public accounting processes, thus avoiding regular oversight (ANAO 2008).

In sum, this continuum postulates that policies with designs closer to direct expenditures are both more visible and more equitable than policy designs resembling tax expenditures. Deviations from these trends are not unexpected when analysing recent subsidies for child care, however, since policy instruments are among multiple factors that can influence policy design (Howlett et al. 2018). Other factors that can influence (but not determine) the impact of policy design on equity and service price include both the feedback effects (path dependence) of earlier policy designs, the political appeal of particular frames, and broader changes to the structure of the sector (Hacker 2004). To account for these multiple factors, my analysis of childcare subsidies tracks the impact of policy instrument design alongside the legacy of previous policy settings and the marketisation of the sector.

Subsidising private care: A policy history of public subsidies for child care

This section examines how the different policy instruments selected to subsidise child care since the mid-1980s have affected the equity of social benefits and the potential for rent-seeking in a rapidly changing sector. My account starts with a brief overview of the federal government's childcare policies in the 1970s. However, the main focus is the mid-1980s to the present day, as this period coincides with the shift to the enduring demand-driven policy approach that allocates funding to ECEC services based on the number of children enrolled and the rapid marketisation of the childcare sector.[1] When tracing the reform path of public subsidies over this period, my analysis considers the policy instruments that successive federal governments have selected and the implications of broader changes to what Gingrich (2011) terms the allocative and productive dimensions of the childcare sector. After briefly charting developments before the mid-1980s, the analysis charts the policy instruments recently used to subsidise child care (see Figure 8.2).

Early childcare subsidies

Initially, the policy instruments that subsidised child care had a supply-side design that financed non-profit providers, albeit via the mechanism of block grants to the states, to purchase facilities or reduce fees paid by families (Hill and Wade 2018). In 1972, Commonwealth financial support for centre-based child care was introduced by the McMahon Coalition government to shore up the supply of quality care for children in special need, especially children from low-income families with working mothers. The government allocated $6.5 million to non-profit providers, including services operated by local governments, using the policy instrument of direct grants to fund the building of facilities and recurrent grants to meet staffing costs (SSCCA 1998). In 1974, Commonwealth financial support for non-profit providers was expanded by the Whitlam Labor government, which extended block grants to the states to cover child care in non-profit centre-based services and to other forms of child care such as family day care and outside school hours care (SSCCA 1998). The Fraser

---

1   Despite some overlap, demand-driven funding that is calculated in relation to the number of children enrolled is distinct from demand-side funding that is paid to parents who access child care.

Coalition government targeted funding for child care, reducing overall funding and limiting support for preschools to block grants for the states, while introducing grants to non-profit services for fee relief to cover low-income families (at the discretion of centre managers) (SSCCA 1998). These public subsidies directly supported non-profit childcare providers allocated via block grants to the states and a submission-based approach with community groups requesting support from the Commonwealth Government.

The Hawke Labor government made incremental changes to the childcare subsidies during its first term in office. After its election in 1983, the Hawke government, in partnership with the states and territories, allocated further funding using direct grants for non-profit providers to establish more than 6,000 childcare places (McIntosh and Phillips 2002). At the same time, the government replaced the submission-based approach with a needs-based system that targeted capital and recurrent grants at localities that had a high proportion of working parents, fewer existing childcare services and lower household incomes (SSCCA 1998). This was followed in 1984 by a commitment to establish a further 20,000 childcare places (Brennan 1998: 176). These reforms largely maintained the supply-side policy instruments for existing non-profit providers to assist with staff salaries, despite increasing provision and greater targeting. These reforms also did not change the structure of the childcare sector, which was still dominated by non-profits and did not have features associated with markets.

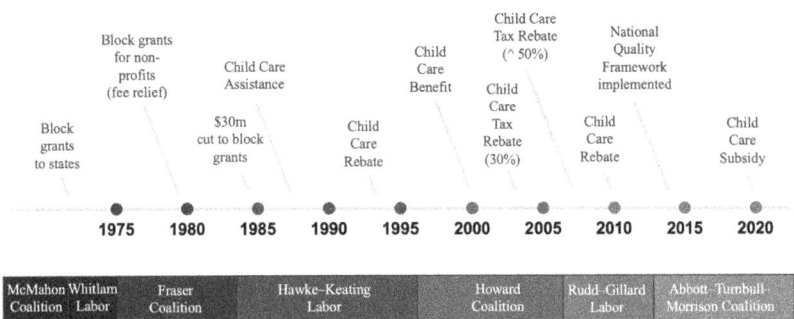

Figure 8.2 Childcare subsidies: A timeline of recent policy instruments
Source: Based on author's research.

Childcare assistance: A targeted industry subsidy for non-profit services

As Labor's ideological position increasingly favoured neoliberal ideas that prioritised marketised policy solutions, the Hawke government overhauled childcare subsidies in the mid-1980s. First, the government cut back subsidies for non-profit services. Later, it introduced a new 'demand-driven' approach to targeting fee relief.

In the May 1985 minibudget, the government tightened fiscal policy as a response to the current account deficit crisis, cutting expenditure on childcare subsidies by $63 billion (a reduction of about 40 per cent) (Brennan 1998: 180; Kelly 1994: 205). This included the retrenchment of block grants to the states that allocated $33 million per year for preschool services and the reduction of subsidies directed to non-profit providers by $30 million (Brennan 1998: 180). Senator Don Grimes, the community services minister, justified these cuts by arguing that existing childcare subsidies were poorly targeted. He claimed eligible families accessing full fee relief in childcare services could receive a benefit 12 times the value of the family allowance,[2] while 90 per cent of children aged under five had no access to the subsidies (Brennan 1998: 182–83).

In 1986, the Hawke government renamed fee relief Child Care Assistance and established a new funding formula that extended support to all non-profit providers and targeted additional fee relief to low-income households. Child Care Assistance was simpler than the previous grant system and more redistributive, as a targeted subsidy that allocated funding to providers based on the number and age of children enrolled from lower-income households (Brennan 1998: 183). Although the government claimed the new formula was both fairer and simpler, controversially, the new funding instrument severed the link between childcare subsidies and staffing profiles. As Brennan (1998: 183–84) documents, previous supply-side funding had subsidised 75 per cent of award wages and had thereby enabled childcare services to retain experienced and qualified staff who received higher wages. Because it no longer automatically covered all children receiving child care in a service nor insulated non-profit providers from wage increases, the new demand-driven instrument effectively halved the recurrent subsidies received by most non-profit

---

2   A modest payment to all parents, usually mothers, which was at that time universal (AIHW 1993: 9).

childcare centres. Childcare services, as the government acknowledged, could address the shortfall by hiring less-qualified staff and/or raising fees. This resulted in many centres substantially increasing fees, which offset the government's increases to fee relief.

The Hawke government's reforms to the childcare subsidies reoriented what Gingrich (2011) terms the allocative and productive dimensions of social service markets. These reforms lowered the ceiling on public financial contributions to some centres because the demand-driven subsidy standardised the support for services with similar profiles of users, regardless of staff qualifications and experience. At the same time, the new demand-driven funding instrument shifted responsibility for meeting the costs of better-qualified and more experienced staff to service users. These reforms also rearranged the productive dimension of the childcare market by reducing government control over service delivery by giving service providers greater scope to reorganise their operations to reduce costs and employ less-qualified staff. The changes to both dimensions of the childcare market had the potential to increase competition among non-profit providers for service users, while removing the financial incentive to retain experienced and qualified staff. This was not lost on unions and childcare professionals, who claimed the reforms put service quality and industrial conditions for staff second to expanding the sector (Brennan 1998: 185).

Towards a two-tier scheme? The industry subsidy and the cash rebate

Despite proposals by senior ministers in the late 1980s to introduce a voucher system paid to parents, the Hawke and Keating Labor governments continued to expand the scale and scope of demand-driven operational subsidies to providers for the remainder of their terms in office. In 1988, the Hawke government established the National Child Care Strategy (NCCS), which committed to creating 30,000 new childcare places at non-profit services (including 20,000 places in outside school hours care) (SSCCA 1998).[3] In the leadup to the 1990 federal election, the government announced the NCCS would create a further 50,000 childcare places over the following six years and, in a break with

---

3   The Hawke government also offered incentives for employers to establish childcare services for their employees in the late 1980s, but this will not receive special attention here as these kinds of services have not accounted for a significant share of the market.

past practice, it extended Child Care Assistance to for-profit service providers (Brennan 1998: 186). And, in 1993, the Keating government introduced the Child Care Rebate, which represented the first childcare benefit paid to service users (families) and announced the New Growth Strategy to support the creation of 354,500 new childcare places in non-profit care by 2001 (SSCCA 1998). While the initial NCCS represented an incremental expansion of state support, the decisions to both extend support to for-profit providers and introduce the rebate shifted the coordinates of childcare policy.

The Hawke government's decision to extend Child Care Assistance to for-profit childcare services was a watershed moment that considerably expanded public funding and underpinned the longer-term transformation of the sector. Overturning decades of bipartisan support for restricting public subsidies to non-profit services, this policy change followed intensive lobbying from commercial industry groups and advocacy from the Australian Council of Trade Unions (which had previously opposed this change) leading up to the 1990 election (Brennan 1998: 200). The government justified this change as necessary due to the ongoing undersupply of child care and so as not to disadvantage families with children placed in for-profit services who would otherwise qualify for Child Care Assistance (Brennan 1998: 201). This change also appealed to the government as it encouraged women's labour force participation and child care was prioritised by women in working-class electorates (Brennan 1998: 196). Senior members of the government were on the record as supporting the extension of subsidies to commercial child care on efficiency grounds, as for-profit services had lower average fees than their non-profit counterparts (Brennan 1998: 90).[4] At the same time as it extended them to for-profit services, the government announced that receipt of the subsidies was conditional on services complying with a new national accreditation system (SSCCA 1998). This was at least partly to assuage non-profit providers' concerns about the policy change prioritising low-cost childcare services at the expense of quality (Brennan 1998: 193).

The Keating government's Child Care Cash Rebate was layered on to Child Care Assistance, meaning it operated alongside the existing policy rather than changing it. The rebate departed from previous subsidies in two main respects, in that it was not means tested and it was delivered

---

4   As Brennan (1998: 191–92) notes, cost comparisons did not take into account the different services provided, or the client groups supported, by for-profit and non-profit child care.

using a policy instrument that disbursed benefits directly to families with children rather than to service providers. The Child Care Cash Rebate provided a flat 30 per cent rebate for a family's work-related childcare expenses for a child aged from newborn to 12 years who paid between $16 and $110 per week, excluding fees covered by Child Care Assistance (AIHW 1995: 122). Annual limits for the cash rebate were set at $1,466 for one child and $3,182 for two or more children (AIHW 1995: 122). The cash rebate was administered via Medicare offices and extended public subsidies to child care delivered by relatives or friends, provided they were registered with the Health Insurance Commission (McIntosh 1997). The cash rebate considerably expanded eligibility for public childcare subsidies to higher-income households; it was less equitable than earlier policies, not only because of its flat-rate benefit, but also because poorer families typically had lower out-of-pocket costs than higher-income earner (SSCCA 1998). Nevertheless, the overall distributive effects of childcare subsidies remained equitable, since almost three-quarters of expenditure was allocated via Child Care Assistance (AIHW 1995: 128).

When establishing the Child Care Cash Rebate, the Keating government reframed child care as a work-related issue concerning families rather than a welfare issue involving support for lower-income groups. Minister for Family Services Rosemary Crowley declared the cash rebate would:

> make child care more affordable and increase the choices for Australian families ... Child care is no longer a welfare issue. It is an economic issue and now an integral part of the government's approach to building a highly skilled and adaptable workforce. (SSCCA 1998)

The design of the cash rebate reinforced this framing of child care in two main ways. On the one hand, the cash rebate was administered via health agencies, which set it apart from social security and Child Care Assistance. Although a tax rebate would also have not been administered via social security, the government favoured a cash rebate because of concerns the former policy would have regressive benefits (SSCCA 1998). On the other hand, the cash rebate reinforced the emphasis the government placed on promoting choice because benefits were delivered to families rather than to childcare services. As Hill and Wade (2018) claim, this is consistent with the government's 1993 National Competition Policy reforms, which sought to activate service users as consumers to encourage competition between childcare services.

The Hawke and Keating government reforms contributed to the rapid transformation of the childcare market from the early 1990s. The reforms modified the allocative dimension of the childcare market by fostering the unprecedented growth of public subsidies due to extensions to a wider array of service providers and users, with state expenditure more than doubling in real terms between 1988 and 1994 (AIHW 1995: 127). Still, there were limits to the subsidies a family could claim each week and no price controls, so the state's expanded financial role did not control families' potential out-of-pocket expenses. The reforms of both Labor governments underpinned changes to the productive dimension of the childcare market by increasing the appeal of commercial child care to families and private investors (Hill and Wade 2018). Although capital grants and operational subsidies were reserved for non-profit providers, commercial child care had fewer barriers to market entry as it was not subject to the planning regime for non-profit services (Brennan 1998: 215). Under these policy settings, for-profit childcare services more than tripled the number of places offered (from 32,000 to 121,600) between 1991 and 1997, whereas non-profit provision stagnated (increasing from 42,000 to 46,300 places) over the same period (Brennan 1998: 214). The rise of commercial child care made the sector increasingly reliant on competition for affordable quality services, but the continuing shortage of child care exposed service users and the government to the risk of rent-seeking.

Entrenching private provision: Two tiers of childcare policy

The Howard Coalition government pursued no fewer than three sets of reform to childcare policy that aligned with its shorter-term fiscal strategies during its 11-year tenure. First, after taking office during 1996 with the budget in deficit and a commitment to reduce public spending, the government reduced public expenditure on child care through increased targeting and reduced subsidies. Second, in 1999, as part of its household compensation package for the new Goods and Services Tax (GST), the government repackaged 12 existing family support policies into three benefits, one of which was the means-tested Child Care Benefit. Third, in 2004, with the budget in surplus during the first phase of the mining boom, the government introduced the Child Care Tax Rebate as a second subsidy to assist families with mounting childcare expenses. Although the distributive effects of each set of reforms varied, the Howard government consistently favoured policy settings that prioritised for-profit provision.

The Howard government's first set of reforms sought to contain expenditure on subsidising child care. Child Care Assistance was targeted by limiting the subsidy to 50 hours of work-related care or 20 hours of care for non-work purposes and by reducing the income thresholds of the means tests applied to families with two or more children (Baxter et al. 2019: 8; McIntosh 1997).[5] The Child Care Cash Rebate was partially means tested by reducing the rebate to 20 per cent for higher-income earners (Baxter et al. 2019: 8). In 1998, the administration of both these public subsidies was transferred from health agencies to the new Commonwealth services delivery agency, Centrelink, and benefits were paid fortnightly in arrears to families (AIHW 1997: 104). At the same time, despite promising to retain them in the 1996 election campaign, the Howard government retrenched the operational subsidies for non-profit services citing the rationale that this measure would increase competition with for-profit services (Brennan 1998: 223; McIntosh 1997). It also dismantled the New Growth Strategy of the Keating government, redirecting $11 million to expand child care in rural locations (McIntosh 1997). The Howard government also capped the growth of private childcare places at 7,000 per year in 1998 and 1999 (Brennan 1998: 223). Shifting the design of the childcare subsidies from the left to the centre of the direct expenditure – tax expenditure continuum (Figure 8.1), these reforms limited the subsidies to payments that partially reimbursed service users, which increased the costs borne by non-profit services and families.

The Howard government's second set of reforms formed part of the rationalisation of family support when introducing the GST in 2000. Both Child Care Assistance and the Child Care Cash Rebate were replaced with a new payment named the Child Care Benefit. Retaining many design features of Child Care Assistance, the Child Care Benefit was a means-tested benefit paid to eligible families with children placed in approved services that subsidised up to 50 hours of work-related care if parents met the activity test of 15 hours per week or 20 hours for other purposes (AIHW 2001: 170). The Child Care Benefit had a progressive structure and was indexed; low-income households earning up to $29,857 received up to the full rate of $129 per week, at which point a taper rate applied until households earned $85,653 and received the minimum rate up to $21.70 per week (AIHW 2001: 170). Although framed as a cash

---

5   It should be noted that although, on paper, 50 hours of child care covers five eight-hour working days a week and one hour on either side of a shift, private services typically charged families for the full operating hours rather than an hourly rate for care.

payment, the Child Care Benefit was a hybrid policy primarily delivered as an upfront reduction of childcare fees (94 per cent of families opted for the payment to go directly to their provider in 2001), but families could also choose to receive it as a lump-sum cash refund at the end of each financial year (AIHW 2001: 170). This benefit increased the amount of financial assistance available to lower-income families than earlier childcare subsidies, as part of the government's compensation package for households aimed at reducing political opposition to the new GST (Brennan 2014: 156; Smith 2004: 149).

The Howard government's third set of reforms introduced the Child Care Tax Rebate, which was announced during the 2004 election campaign by the Coalition parties amid rising out-of-pocket childcare expenses for families with children (Brennan 2007). Reviving many aspects of the Keating government's Child Care Cash Rebate, the Child Care Tax Rebate provided a flat-rate 30 per cent tax rebate on out-of-pocket childcare costs up to $4,000 per year per child (Brennan 2007: 222). Like the earlier cash rebate, the tax rebate offered most benefit to high-income families with the largest out-of-pocket childcare expenses. However, the Child Care Tax Rebate could could only be claimed by one parent on their annual income tax return as a tax offset that reduced the taxes owed (Baxter et al. 2019: 9). The rebate reduced the incentive for services to constrain childcare fees because it was claimed on an annual basis and had no weekly limit. The tax rebate was also more inequitable than the cash rebate because 'low-income families will miss out if [the] amount for which they are eligible is greater than the tax bill' (Brennan 2007: 222). Families thus had to earn a taxable income to receive any benefit. And, while one parent in a couple could transfer the unused balance of the tax rebate to their partner, single parents did not have this option. Recognising this inequity, the government transformed the tax rebate into a hybrid policy in 2007, by allowing families to claim it as a cash payment via the Family Assistance Office at the end of the year, which meant low-income families could receive their full entitlement (AIHW 2007: 37).

By the end of its term, the Howard government restored the two-tier structure of childcare subsidies it had dismantled a mere seven years earlier. After initially requiring higher-income families to take on greater responsibility for financing child care by targeting public subsidies at lower-income groups and reducing the hours to which they applied, the government gradually expanded the allocative role of the state by increasing financial assistance to support lower-income groups via the first tier of the

Child Care Benefit and to families using child care across the income distribution with the second tier of the Child Care Tax Rebate. The overall distributive effects of these subsidies were progressive—estimated to cover 80 per cent of childcare expenses for lower-income earners and around 39 per cent of the costs for higher-income earners (McIntosh 2005). Yet, as with previous subsidies, these policies placed a ceiling on the state's financial contributions to child care without imposing price controls, leaving families ultimately responsible for out-of-pocket expenses from rising fees.

The Howard government's policies are widely recognised to have further entrenched for-profit services as the dominant mode of provision in the childcare market (Sumsion 2012: 209; Newberry and Brennan 2013). The Howard government also reduced the state's limited involvement in the productive aspect of the childcare market by retrenching the capital grants and subsidies for non-profit providers and dismantling the few planning restrictions that remained, thereby leaving the location and size of (for-profit and non-profit) childcare operations 'up to the market' (Baxter et al. 2019: 8). Under these policy settings, the childcare market became more concentrated as it expanded, with large commercial and corporate operators increasing their profitability and market share. This was exemplified by the rise of ABC Learning, which became the largest publicly listed childcare corporation in the world and accounted for more than 20 per cent of childcare places offered across Australia at its peak in the mid-2000s (Sumsion 2012: 209). Press and Woodrow (2009: 236) argue the sheer scale of ABC Learning's operations allowed it (and other corporate providers) to dominate the childcare market, reducing consumer choice because its strategy of saturating services in particular locations meant it effectively became the only provider available. The combination of a market dominated by corporate child care and generous public subsidies left both the government and families highly exposed to the rent-seeking of private service providers.

Renovating the second tier: From a tax rebate to a cash rebate

The Rudd and Gillard Labor governments (2007–13) changed both tiers of childcare funding, aiming to address cost-of-living pressures by reducing the out-of-pocket costs for families accessing care. As part of its election platform targeting voters from middle-income households, Labor promised to increase the Child Care Tax Rebate from 30 to 50 per cent of out-of-pocket childcare fees and to make the rebate payable to families each quarter, to reduce the delay in refunds (Bongiorno 2008: 600). Daniels (2008: 87) claims the tax rebate design and potential to increase women's workforce participation meant it was not framed as 'middle-class welfare' in public debate. The Rudd government delivered on its election commitment in the 2008–09 budget, increasing the rebate to 50 per cent of out-of-pocket expenses and raising the maximum annual payment from $4,354 to $7,500 per child in care (Daniels 2008: 87).[6] The increased generosity of the Child Care Tax Rebate was partially offset by the removal of the Child Care Benefit's minimum payment for higher-income earners. As the design of the Child Care Tax Rebate had the potential to delay receipt of the refund to 18 months, the government made the refund available on a quarterly basis to remove a potential work disincentive for low-income families (Daniels 2008: 88). In 2009–10, the Gillard government converted the tax rebate into a cash rebate that was renamed the Child Care Rebate, due to concerns about the administrative burden for families and services. This made the benefit payable on a fortnightly basis and incorporated the payment into routine budgetary processes.

Leaving the two-tier structure of childcare policy they inherited intact, the Rudd and Gillard governments' incremental reforms increased the state's already significant allocative role by expanding the rate and ceiling of the Child Care (Tax) Rebate and reducing the administrative burden in accessing it. These reforms facilitated the rapid growth of the state's financial commitment to child care, from $3.2 billion in 2007–08 to $7.7 billion in 2015–16—an increase of 137 per cent in real terms (Baxter et al. 2019: 10). By 2016, almost all families accessing child care received some benefit from public subsidies; while 98 per cent of families accessing child care received the Child Care Benefit and/or the Child Care Rebate, 72 per cent of families received both (Brennan and Fenech 2014). However, as the reforms focused on expanding the second-tier rebate, households with middle and high incomes benefited most; households on lower incomes came to pay a larger share of their income for child care than higher-income earners between 2007 and 2015 (Hill and Wade 2018). Like previous public subsidies, the reforms limited the financial obligations of the state without imposing price controls or limiting the

---

6   Initially, the Rudd government announced the Child Care Tax Rebate would be indexed annually, but the $7,500 annual limit was frozen until 2017 (Baxter et al. 2019: 9).

out-of-pocket expenses of households. Brennan (2014: 157) argues the generosity of the Child Care Rebate exacerbated the potential for fee inflation as it effectively guaranteed public funding of half of any increase.

The Rudd and Gillard governments increased state control over the productive aspects of the childcare market but retained the firm commitment of their predecessors to private provision. On the one hand, the government increased the regulation of the childcare sector through the new National Quality Framework (NQF) implemented in 2014. The NQF was linked to accreditation and, without accreditation, providers could not offer care eligible for the Child Care Benefit and rebate (Brennan and Fenech 2014). With the aim of driving quality improvement under the NQF, childcare services are evaluated using standardised assessment items and the results are published on a government website (Brennan and Fenech 2014). The NQF also increased the qualifications required of staff for services with 24 or more childcare places (Brennan and Fenech 2014). Although non-profit services tended to outperform for-profit providers, evidence suggests this oversight has improved quality across the sector (see Cortis et al. Chapter 1, this volume; Hill and Wade 2018). On the other hand, following the collapse of ABC Learning at the height of the GFC in 2008, the Rudd government funnelled $56 million to finance the continued operation of the centres until they were purchased by Goodstart, a non-profit consortium (Sumsion 2012: 211). This affair highlighted the ongoing role of the government in managing the risk of failure in the childcare market, given the broader economic consequences and the government's determination to avoid owning childcare services. It also resulted in the proportion of for-profit long-day childcare centres falling, from 88 to 66 per cent in 2009 (Brennan and Fenech 2014).

Back to the 1980s? The Child Care Subsidy

The Abbott and Turnbull Coalition governments (2013–18) enacted sweeping reforms of childcare subsidies to address persistent problems limiting parents' workforce participation (Beutler and Fenech 2018: 20). Tasked with investigating issues confronting the childcare sector and proposing reform, the Productivity Commission (2014: 19–20) found widespread accessibility and affordability issues (estimating 165,000 parents were unable to work longer hours due to the unavailability of suitable child care) and recommended combining the two public subsidies into one to simplify and better target support. In 2015, the

Abbott government responded with the Child Care Assistance Package. This package had three main components to be implemented in 2017 (Beutler and Fenech 2018: 17). First, it replaced the Child Care Benefit and Child Care Tax Rebate with the Child Care Subsidy (CCS), which was paid directly to childcare providers on the basis of the number of hours accessed by enrolled children. Second, it established the Child Care Safety Net, which targeted support to families with an Additional Child Care Subsidy and a program of grants for services in disadvantaged localities. Third, the Nanny Pilot Program trialled subsidising child care provided by nannies in the home. The Turnbull government revised the Child Care Assistance Package into the Jobs for Families Child Care Package in 2017, reducing the scale of the nanny pilot and delaying the introduction of the first and second components until 2018.

The CCS further expanded public support for child care at a cost of $7.7 billion in 2018–19. The subsidy is paid directly to approved childcare providers (removing the option for families with children to claim the benefit directly) to cover a proportion of the hourly fees for eligible families (Frydenberg and Cormann 2019: 5–10). Compared with the two subsidies it replaces, the CCS covers a higher proportion of fees for all but the highest-income earners, with a taper rate gradually reducing from 85 per cent for households earning less than $68,183 to 0 per cent for those on annual incomes of $352,453 or higher. The CCS has also removed the annual cap on the total benefit subsidised for households with incomes up to $188,163 and increased the cap to $10,373 per child for households earning between this amount and $352,453.

Despite expanding public support for families, the CCS is designed to constrain the state's financial liabilities for each unit (hour) of child care provided. It introduces 'hourly rate caps' indexed to the consumer price index (CPI), which sets the maximum hourly childcare fees to which the subsidy applies. In contrast to previous subsidies that were calculated as a percentage of childcare fees, the hourly fee cap places a clear limit on the subsidy the state will pay per hour of child care regardless of its actual cost. Childcare fee increases above the CPI now need to be absorbed by households as growing out-of-pocket expenses. The CCS retains an income test that reduces the percentage of the hourly rate cap that is subsidised for families with higher combined incomes (see Table 8.1). It also sets an annual cap (per child) when families have a combined annual income of more than $188,163 (Services Australia 2021), and it reduces the childcare hours subsidised for some families by increasing the limits of the activity tests, which are calculated in relation to 'recognised activities' such as paid employment and education. Although these features limit the financial cost to the public purse, the CCS still exposes the childcare market to fee inflation and rent-seeking because it does not impose limits on the user fees private providers charge to families.

While the focus of reforming childcare policy had long been on increasing the workforce participation of parents, the CCS goes further in making receipt of childcare subsidies conditional on parents meeting activity tests.[7] The subsidy halves the amount of subsidised care for parents or primary carers with household incomes of less than $68,163 per annum who undertake less than eight hours per fortnight of approved activities (such as paid or unpaid work, education or training and/or volunteering), from 48 to 24 hours per fortnight. Otherwise, all parents (or primary carers) with household incomes of $68,163 or more are required to undertake at least eight hours of approved activities each fortnight or to fall into a safety-net category to be eligible for between 36 and 100 hours of subsidised child care over the same period.[8] This measure retains the maximum limit of 50 hours of subsidised care per week of the policies it replaces, but this is only available for families in which all parents undertake more than 48 hours (rather than 30 hours) of approved activities each fortnight.

The Abbott and Turnbull governments' reforms continued to expand the state's allocative role in the childcare sector, but the increased conditionality of the CCS has restructured the distributive effects of public support even though most families benefit. The CCS provides most benefit to single-parent families and couples with both parents undertaking more than 48 hours of recognised activities per fortnight in stable employment and with low to medium household incomes, as these groups receive higher discount rates on childcare fees and face no annual cap on benefits (Beutler and Fenech 2018: 18). The CCS has mixed distributive effects for higher-income earners because it increases the annual cap on total benefits and reduces the rate of the fee discount. The CCS reduces the benefits received by families with parents or primary carers that have no

---

7   The CCS is calculated in relation to the hours of approved activity the parent or primary carer with the fewest hours undertakes, the new hourly fee cap that sets the maximum hourly rate that will be subsidised for different types of child care and their household income.

8   In other words, parents with household incomes of at least $68,163 who do not meet the activity test receive no subsidised care (rather than up to 48 hours per fortnight), while those earning above this amount who undertake activities of up to 16 hours per fortnight can access 12 fewer hours of subsidised care per fortnight (36 hours rather than 48 hours).

or low hours of recognised activities. More concerning, however, is the fact the CCS reduces the benefits for disadvantaged families with low incomes and/or insecure employment with variable hours of work who do not meet the activity tests, including Indigenous Australians (Brennan and Adamson 2015: 12).

The Abbott and Turnbull governments' reforms largely retained the state's limited role in the productive aspect of the childcare market. They did increase the involvement of the state at the margins through the establishment of the Community Child Care Fund—a competitive grant scheme to which private providers could apply for assistance when setting up operations in disadvantaged, regional and/or remote locations (Morrison and Cormann 2016). Since the total amount allocated by the fund is $110 million per annum since 2016, its overall impact on the childcare market has been limited. The Coalition governments' reforms continued the trend of increasing the public subsidies for child care by federal governments over the previous three decades, which ensured the sector remained attractive to private investors and shored up financial ratings agencies' classification of child care as a blue-chip investment. So, despite their significant expenditure in the childcare market, governments' main instruments to influence service delivery remain the accreditation process and the NQF.

There is growing evidence to suggest that in shoring up the appeal of childcare services to private investors, the public subsidies are contributing to rent-seeking. On the one hand, the childcare market is both highly consolidated and highly profitable, particularly in centre-based long day care. In this market segment, large organisations that operate 25 or more services make up only 1 per cent of childcare providers but offer 33 per cent of places (ACECQA 2020). As noted above, commercial childcare providers have been rated as blue-chip investments, with substantial property assets and $992 million in profits during 2016–17 (Hill and Wade 2018). On the other hand, growth in childcare fees continues to outstrip inflation, even as public subsidies rapidly increase. Baxter et al. (2019: 15) estimate childcare fees increased by 3.8 per cent, on average, in real terms each year between 2007 and 2017. More recently, as the government financed a further $543 million to reach a total of $8.1 billion in public subsidies during 2018–19, childcare fees increased by an average of 4.9 per cent (while the CPI rose by 1.9 per cent) in the same year (Morrison and Cormann 2018; Frydenberg and Cormann 2019; DESE 2021).

At the same time, the capacity of the NQF to lift service quality is limited by persistent issues with affordability and accessibility. Affordability has been undermined by rapid fee inflation not absorbed by rises in public subsidies (Hill and Wade 2018). The Melbourne Institute estimated median expenditure per hour of child care rose 51 per cent in real terms for families between 2004 and 2017 (Wilkins et al. 2019: 20).[9] Accessibility remains an issue, even though coverage has increased to 53 per cent of couples and 41 per cent of single-parent families (Wilkins et al. 2019: 11). In addition to cost barriers, the availability of child care remains an issue for families—particularly outside school hours (Hill and Wade 2018).[10] The Australian Bureau of Statistics (2018) estimates additional child care was required for about 373,000 (or 9.3 per cent of) children in 2017. Although non-profit and for-profit services have increased NQF ratings recently, childcare quality concerns are supported by research finding that public (state and local government) and non-profit providers consistently offer higher-quality services than for-profit providers (see Brennan 1998, 2014; Hill and Wade 2018). In 2019, 25 per cent of for-profit private providers across the childcare sector were 'working to meet' the NQF, while only about 14 per cent of non-profit and 9 per cent of public providers received a similar rating (ACECQA 2020).

Conclusions: Policy design and public subsidies for the childcare market

Since the 1980s, Labor and Coalition governments have expanded the scale and scope of public subsidies for the private provision of child care to address persistent accessibility and affordability issues as increasing demand has continued to outstrip growth in the sector. Along with the decision to extend public support to for-profit services, the shift from supply-side to demand-driven subsidies initiated by Labor and continued under the Coalition has received bipartisan support for almost three decades. Yet, the policy instruments selected by the various governments—subsidies, cash benefits, cash rebates and/or tax rebates—have coincided with their distinct policy priorities, varied distributive effects and different levels of susceptibility to rent-seeking. Although not reducing every difference to

9   Baxter et al. (2019: 22) show that 57 per cent of families with an employed parent who do not access child care report they do so because of difficulties meeting costs.
10   Baxter et al. (2019: 51) found half of services had difficulties meeting parent requests for child care outside usual operating hours (before 6am and after 6pm).

the choice of policy instrument, there are clear patterns in the distributive effects of these subsidies and their susceptibility to rent-seeking by private providers that underline how instrument choice has had a bearing on policy design.

The distributive effects of the childcare subsidies have varied according to the position of a policy on the tax expenditure – direct expenditure continuum. Direct expenditure programs such as Child Care Assistance, the Child Care Benefit and the Child Care Subsidy that are highly visible in public accounting processes have had the most equitable benefit structures of the demand-driven public subsidies for families with children for whom all parents are in stable and secure employment. The conditionality of the Abbott–Turnbull governments' Child Care Subsidy, and the activity tests enacted by the Howard government for Child Care Assistance and then the Child Care Benefit, have nevertheless been sources of inequality for disadvantaged families on low incomes with casual, insecure and/or irregular work. As the only tax expenditure that has been used to subsidise child care, the Child Care Tax Rebate was less visible in public accounting processes and has been inequitable because it functioned as a second-tier subsidy that provided most benefit to families on middle to higher incomes who had higher out-of-pocket expenses. Because the rebate was administered via the tax system, lower-income households were unlikely to have high enough tax obligations to receive the full benefit and were more likely to find the delay accessing any benefit via annual tax returns difficult. The distributive effects of the two hybrid policies—the Child Care Cash Rebate and Child Care Rebate—were less inequitable than the tax expenditure, but also benefited households with higher incomes as second-tier policies that covered expenses not covered by existing direct expenditure programs.

The susceptibility of the childcare subsidies to rent-seeking by private providers also differed with the position of a policy instrument on the tax – direct expenditure continuum. Direct expenditure programs that were highly visible, including Child Care Assistance and the Child Care Benefit, had limited exposure to rent-seeking, partly because they were targeted at lower-income households with limited capacity to pay high out-of-pocket costs and disincentives to do so, as well as the annual caps on total benefits.[11] The current Child Care Subsidy is more complicated; although

---

11 However, to the extent that families reduced or stopped using child care due to disincentives, it is likely to have had other economic consequences such as decreased economic activity due to lower participation rates, particularly among women, and increased gender inequity by reducing women's choices.

hourly fee caps and lower discounts for higher-income households reduce public liabilities, there are few limits on the out-of-pocket payments required of households in a market with inadequate supply.[12] The hybrid policies, including the Child Care Cash Rebate and Child Care Rebate, had the highest susceptibility to rent-seeking of those examined because there were only annual limits placed on the rebates and they were layered on to existing direct expenditures with which they operated in tandem. As a result, fee increases would be partly absorbed by the rebates until the annual limit was reached and higher-income households that benefited most from these programs could more readily absorb any remaining out-of-pocket expenses.[13] The Child Care Tax Rebate tax expenditure had less visibility and seemed most susceptible to rent-seeking as a policy that benefited higher-income earners who had the greatest capacity to pay.

It should be emphasised that my claim is that policy-instrument choice is a factor that has a bearing on the policy design of childcare subsidies but does not determine their specific features. This is because policy design is a political and social process in which the choice of instrument can reflect as well as shape the political preferences of the governments that deploy them. In other words, my claim is not that policy-instrument choice has a uniform bearing on the specific design features of a policy, such as its distributive effects or the potential for rent-seeking. It follows from this that some policy designs are likely to deviate from the features commonly associated with the policy instrument. What my analysis does show, however, is the childcare subsidies that have been delivered via policy instruments with a more equitable structure do not involve clear trade-offs with service quality or efficiency and may have fewer effects on fee inflation than the less-equitable policy instruments.

The lack of clear economic benefits for the childcare market from the series of public subsidies has coincided with what Newberry and Brennan (2013) term the 'radical marketisation' of the sector and the rapid consolidation of for-profit organisations as the dominant service providers. The marketised childcare sector, which has been classified here as a private-power market, has the potential to foster innovation, but it

---

12 It is too early to assess the longer-term impact of this policy given its recent introduction, particularly as the initial reduction in inflation was followed by substantial fee increases (as noted earlier in the chapter) and the unfolding economic consequences of the Covid-19 pandemic complicate matters.
13 The hourly fee caps that were introduced with the CCS could be incorporated into the design of rebates, but the flat-rate structure of both policies would have less-equitable effects than the CCS.

is also prone to rent-seeking if commercial profit-maximising entities gain too much control over production. Considering the wide range of policy instruments that have been used to subsidise fees in the past three decades, my analysis has provided further evidence of the unsuitability of demand-driven public subsidies to control fees in a market with this structure, especially when the priority has been to constrain the growth of public expenditure rather than ensure service quality or set limits on the out-of-pocket expenses for households that access child care.

Epilogue: Temporary universal child care during a global pandemic

During the writing of this chapter, the temporary measures for child care that were introduced in response to the Covid-19 pandemic both reaffirm the government's central role in the sector and point to potential avenues for reform. The Morrison Coalition government took the unprecedented step of reconfiguring the Child Care Subsidy early in the pandemic, making public financial support to providers during the lockdown conditional on them offering eligible families free child care for three months from April 2020. The reconfigured CCS provided childcare operators with up to half of the fees they received before the pandemic by replacing demand-driven payments with a 'business continuity payment' (Klapdor 2020).[14] At the same time, many private childcare services were also eligible for the temporary JobKeeper benefit that paid $1,500 per fortnight for each eligible employee; to qualify, the turnover of non-profit services had to decline by at least 15 per cent and that for for-profit services had to fall by 30 per cent (Klapdor 2020).

These fiscal stimulus measures reaffirmed the government's central role in managing the risk of failure in the childcare sector. During the early stages of the pandemic, many families unenrolled their children from child care or kept them at home because of health concerns, school closures and/or financial insecurity (Klapdor 2020). Some families who made this choice continued to pay a gap fee to private childcare services to avoid losing their child's place, given the unresolved issues with both accessibility and

---

14   This was calculated as half the fees families paid (up to hourly rate caps) during the fortnight before 2 March 2020. Similar temporary arrangements were put in place for childcare services during subsequent state-level lockdowns in Victoria and New South Wales.

affordability discussed in this chapter. The childcare sector (like many others) was ill equipped to respond to the financial challenges presented by low attendance and high unenrolment rates, with Early Childhood Australia estimating that 650 childcare services (mostly outside school hours care) had closed by April 2020 (Hurst 2020). In these conditions, the Morrison government's policy response averted market failure, in a similar but distinct way to the Rudd government's response to ABC Learning's failure during the GFC. The government's intervention provided greater certainty for families, workers and providers, as well as avoiding the potential economic impacts that the collapse of the childcare sector would have had during the pandemic and the recovery.

Although clearly responding to the unique circumstances presented by the Covid-19 pandemic, the Morrison government's fiscal stimulus measures for the childcare sector point to potentially promising avenues for future reform. In particular, the temporary changes to the CCS meant families using childcare services received free universal child care (provided activity tests were met) for three months. These changes demonstrated how the 'hourly rate caps' of the CCS and regulatory tools could be employed to require private services to meet conditions that improve equity and reduce potential rent-seeking in return for cash subsidies. There are many possible reform paths here, all of which require careful consideration and further public investment. Incremental reform to the CCS could involve placing a ceiling on the out-of-pocket expenses that private services are allowed to charge families to remain eligible for public subsidies, whereas more ambitious reforms could require services to not charge gap payments to lower-income families and provide incentives to reduce or abolish out-of-pocket expenses for all families.

References

Australian Bureau of Statistics. (2018). *Childhood Education and Care, Australia*. Canberra: Australian Bureau of Statistics. Available from: www.abs.gov.au/statistics/people/education/childhood-education-and-care-australia/latest-release.

Australian Children's Education and Care Quality Authority (ACECQA). (2020). *NQF Snapshot Q1 2020*. Canberra: Australian Government.

Australian Institute of Health and Welfare (AIHW). (1993). *Australia's Welfare*. Canberra: AIHW.

Australian Institute of Health and Welfare (AIHW). (1995). *Australia's Welfare*. Canberra: AIHW.

Australian Institute of Health and Welfare (AIHW). (1997). *Australia's Welfare*. Canberra: AIHW.

Australian Institute of Health and Welfare (AIHW). (2001). *Australia's Welfare*. Canberra: AIHW.

Australian Institute of Health and Welfare (AIHW). (2007). *Australia's Welfare*. Canberra: AIHW.

Australian National Audit Office (ANAO). (2008). *Preparation of the Tax Expenditures Statement*. Audit Report No. 32, 2007–08. Canberra: ANAO.

Baxter, J., Bray, J.R., Carroll, M., Hand, K., Gray, M., Katz, I., Budinski, M., Rogers, C., Smart, J., Skattebol, J. & Blaxland, M. (2019). *Child Care Package Evaluation: Early monitoring report*. Melbourne: Australian Institute of Family Studies.

Beutler, D. & Fenech, M. (2018). An analysis of the Australian Government's Jobs for Families Child Care Package: The utility of Bacchi's WPR methodology to identify potential influences on parents' child care choices. *Australasian Journal of Early Childhood*, 43(1): 16–24. doi.org/10.23965%2FAJEC.43.1.02.

Bongiorno, F. (2008). Howard's end: The 2007 Australian election. *The Round Table*, 97(397): 589–603. doi.org/10.1080/00358530802207427.

Brennan, D. (1998). *The Politics of Australian Child Care: Philanthropy to feminism to beyond*. 2nd edn. Melbourne: Cambridge University Press. doi.org/10.1017/CBO9780511597091.

Brennan, D. (2007). The ABC of child care politics. *Australian Journal of Social Issues*, 42(2): 213–25. doi.org/10.1002/j.1839-4655.2007.tb00050.x.

Brennan, D. (2014). The business of care: Australia's experiment with the marketisation of child care. In C. Miller & L. Orchard (eds), *Australian Public Policy: Progressive ideas in the neoliberal ascendency* (pp. 151–68). Bristol, UK: Policy Press. doi.org/10.46692/9781447312697.010.

Brennan, D. & Adamson, E. (2015). *Baby Steps or Giant Strides?* June. Sydney: McKell Institute. Available from: mckellinstitute.org.au/wp-content/uploads/2022/02/The-McKell-Institute-Baby-Steps-or-Giant-Strides-June-2015.pdf.

Brennan, D. & Fenech, M. (2014). Early education and care in Australia: Equity in a mixed market-based system? In L. Gambaro, K. Stewart & J. Waldfogel (eds), *An Equal Start? Providing quality early education and care for disadvantaged children* (pp. 171–92). Bristol, UK: Policy Press. doi.org/10.2307/j.ctt9qgznh.13.

Daniels, D. (2008). Child care. In *Budget review 2008–09*. Australian Parliamentary Library Research Paper No. 31, 2007–08, 26 May (pp. 87–88). Canberra: Department of Parliamentary Services. Available from: www.aph.gov.au/binaries/library/pubs/rp/2007-08/08rp31.pdf.

Department of Education, Skills and Employment (DESE). (2021). *Child Care Data for Financial Year 2018–19*. Canberra: Australian Government. Available from: www.dese.gov.au/early-childhood-data/resources/child-care-data-financial-year-2018-19.

Frydenberg, J. & Cormann, M. (2019). *Budget 2019–20: Budget strategy and outlook*. Budget Paper No. 1, 2 April. Canberra: Commonwealth of Australia. Available from: archive.budget.gov.au/2019-20/bp1/download/bp1.pdf.

Gingrich, J. (2011). *Making Markets in the Welfare State: The politics of varying market reforms*. Cambridge, UK: Cambridge University Press. doi.org/10.1017/CBO9780511791529.

Hacker, J.S. (2004). *The Divided Welfare State: The battle over public and private social benefits in the United States*. Princeton, NJ: Princeton University Press.

Hill, E. & Wade, M. (2018). The radical marketisation of early childhood education and care in Australia. In D. Cahill & P. Toner (eds), *Wrong Way: How privatisation and economic reform backfired*. Melbourne: Black Inc. Books.

Howlett, M. (2019). *Designing Public Policies: Principles and instruments*. 2nd edn. London: Routledge.

Hurst, D. (2020). Australian child care operators fear they will have to close without a government lifeline. *The Guardian*, [Australia], 2 April. Available from: www.theguardian.com/australia-news/2020/apr/02/australian-childcare-operators-fear-they-will-have-to-close-without-a-government-lifeline.

Kelly, P. (1994). *The End of Certainty*. Sydney: Allen & Unwin.

Klapdor, M. (2020). COVID-19 economic response: Free child care. *FlagPost*, [Blog], 6 April, updated 19 May 2020. Canberra: Parliamentary Library. Available from: www.aph.gov.au/About_Parliament/Parliamentary_Departments/Parliamentary_Library/FlagPost/2020/April/Coronavirus_response-Free_child_care.

Lascoumes, P. & Le Gales, P. (2007). Understanding public policy through its instruments: From the nature of instruments to the sociology of public policy instrumentation. *Governance*, 20(1): 1–21. doi.org/10.1111/j.1468-0491.2007.00342.x.

McIntosh, G. (1997). *Child care in Australia: Current provision and recent developments.* Background Paper 9, 1997–98. Canberra: Parliamentary Library. Available from: www.aph.gov.au/About_Parliament/Parliamentary_ Departments/Parliamentary_Library/Publications_Archive/Background_ Papers/bp9798/98bp09.

McIntosh, G. (2005). *The new Child Care Tax Rebate.* Parliamentary Library Research Note, No. 3, 2005–06, 5 August. Canberra: Department of Parliamentary Services. Available from: www.aph.gov.au/binaries/library/ pubs/rn/2005-06/06rn03.pdf.

McIntosh, G. & Phillips, J. (2002). *Commonwealth support for childcare.* Parliamentary Library E-Brief, 26 April, updated 6 July. Canberra: Parliament of Australia. Available from: www.aph.gov.au/About_Parliament/Parliamentary _Departments/Parliamentary_Library/Publications_Archive/archive/childcare support.

Mendes, P. (2017). The Australian welfare state system. In C. Aspalter (ed.), *The Routledge International Handbook to Welfare State Systems* (pp. 75–90). London: Routledge. doi.org/10.4324/9781315613758.

Morrison, S. & Cormann, M. (2016). *Budget 2016–17: Budget strategy and outlook.* Budget Paper No. 1, 3 May. Canberra: Commonwealth of Australia. Available from: archive.budget.gov.au/2016-17/bp1/bp1.pdf.

Morrison, S. & Cormann, M. (2018). *Budget 2018–19: Budget strategy and outlook.* Budget Paper No. 1, 8 May. Canberra: Commonwealth of Australia. Available from: archive.budget.gov.au/2018-19/bp1/bp1.pdf.

Newberry, S. & Brennan, D. (2013). The marketisation of early childhood education and care (ECEC) in Australia: A structured response. *Financial Accountability & Management, 29*(3): 227–45. doi.org/10.1111/faam.12018.

Press, F. & Woodrow, C. (2009). The giant in the playground: Investigating the reach and implications of the corporatisation of child care provision. In D. King & G. Meagher (eds), *Paid Care in Australia: Politics, profits, practices* (pp. 231–52). Sydney: Sydney University Press. doi.org/10.30722/ sup.9781920899295.

Productivity Commission (PC). (2014). *Child Care and Early Childhood Learning.* Inquiry Report No. 73. (2 vols). Canberra: Productivity Commission. Available from: www.pc.gov.au/inquiries/completed/childcare/report.

Productivity Commission (PC). (2017). *Introducing Competition and Informed User Choice into Human Services: Reforms to human services.* Productivity Commission Inquiry Report, 27 October. Canberra: Productivity Commission. Available from: www.pc.gov.au/inquiries/completed/human-services/reforms/report/ human-services-reforms.pdf.

Productivity Commission (PC). (Various years). *Report on Government Services.* Canberra: Productivity Commission. Available from: www.pc.gov.au/research/ongoing/report-on-government-services.

Salamon, L. (2001). The new governance and the tools of public action: An introduction. *Fordham Urban Law Journal, 28*(5): 1611–74.

Senate Standing Committee on Community Affairs (SSCCA). (1998). *Child Care Funding.* December. Canberra: Parliament of Australia. Available from: www.aph.gov.au/parliamentary_business/committees/senate/community_affairs/completed_inquiries/1996-99/childcare2/report/index.

Services Australia. (2021). *Child Care Subsidy.* Canberra: Australian Government. Available from: www.servicesaustralia.gov.au/individuals/services/centrelink/child-care-subsidy.

Smith, J. (2004). *Taxing Popularity: The story of taxation in Australia.* 2nd edn. Sydney: Australian Tax Research Foundation.

Stebbing, A. & Spies-Butcher, B. (2010). Universal welfare by other means? Social tax expenditures and the Australian dual welfare state. *Journal of Social Policy, 39*(4): 585–606. doi.org/10.1017/S0047279410000267.

Stiglitz, J.E. (2013). *The Price of Inequality.* Melbourne: Penguin Books.

Sumsion, J. (2012). ABC Learning and Australian early education and care: A retrospective ethical audit of a radical experiment. In E. Lloyd & H. Penn (eds), *Childcare Markets: Can they deliver an equitable service?* (pp. 209–25). Bristol, UK: Policy Press. doi.org/10.1332/policypress/9781847429339.003.0012.

Vedung, E. (1998). Policy instruments: Typologies and theories. In M.L. Bemelmans-Videc, R.C. Rist & E. Vedung (eds), *Carrots, Sticks & Sermons: Policy instruments and their evaluation.* London: Routledge.

Wilkins, R., Laß, I., Butterworth, P. & Vera-Toscano, E. (2019). *The Household, Income and Labour Dynamics in Australia Survey: Selected findings from waves 1 to 17.* The 14th Annual Statistical Report of the HILDA Survey. Melbourne: Melbourne Institute—Applied Economic & Social Research & The University of Melbourne. Available from: melbourneinstitute.unimelb.edu.au/__data/assets/pdf_file/0011/3127664/HILDA-Statistical-Report-2019.pdf.

Wilson, S., Spies-Butcher, B. & Stebbing, A. (2009). Targets and taxes: Explaining the welfare orientations of the Australian public. *Social Policy & Administration, 43*(5): 508–25. doi.org/10.1111/j.1467-9515.2009.00676.x.

9

Public providers: Making human service markets work

Bob Davidson

Introduction

This book is replete with examples of problems in the operation and outcomes of human service markets. Many of those problems are intrinsic, inevitable and essentially unremovable, given the nature of both markets and human services. Many, though, are the result of the poor design and/ or management of specific markets. Whatever the drivers in each case, the result all too often has been that the net effects of marketisation for many human services have been counterproductive in achieving the key objectives of the services.

This chapter, however, is based on the proposition that this does not have to be so and that markets can be used to consistently improve human services. For that to happen, market mechanisms should only be used in a limited and strategic way, while certain elements that are not part of the neoclassical market model need to be in place. My purpose here is to outline how one such element—namely, a well-functioning public provider (that is, owned and operated by government)—can improve the operation and outcomes of human service markets. While the marketisation of human services is fundamentally directed at moving away from monopoly public providers, ironically, the managed (or quasi) markets thereby created often work best if a well-run public provider participates in the market. Fundamental to enabling this—and indeed the raison d'être for public providers—is government and the boards and senior managers of public providers understanding that a public provider is not simply another competitor in the marketplace, but a *policy instrument that has unique capacities to effect broader systemic and societal change.*

Public providers have historically played an important social role in ensuring that human services are available on a more universal and equal basis across the population and have most commonly been justified in these terms. Here, however, the main focus is on an aspect rarely covered in modern writing, but which was the main reason public providers were used widely in the broader economy throughout the twentieth century—namely, to make the market work better in providing essential goods or services in sectors that have significant intrinsic market failure (Goot 2010).[1] This aspect was of little relevance to human service public providers before the 1980s, but it is now of central importance given the extensive marketisation of these services.

Importantly, the position taken here is based on the recognition that there are no simple prescriptions for the provision of human services, that no service system or approach is perfect and that the optimum system and approach will vary with each situation. The provision of human services and the design of markets for them are constantly a 'choice between imperfect alternatives' (Wolf 1988), in a world where the theory of the second best is ever-present (Lipsey and Lancaster 1956). Public providers have their limitations but are a key element in the good design of human service markets.

While the major focus of the chapter is on human services, much of the discussion also applies to public providers more broadly (for example, in the banking and energy sectors). Similarly, while the focus is on Australia, the issues raised here are relevant to many situations internationally (for example, in the United Kingdom, in relation to changes in the National Health Service and the changing role of local government in aged care over the past four decades).

The chapter, however, must be read with an important caveat in the contemporary context. The decades-long dominance of neoliberalism, exacerbated by long periods of governments philosophically opposed to

---

1   The term 'market failure' as used here is not restricted simply to when existing markets are not working well, but also includes when *no* market—or service—has been established.

and lacking understanding of the role of government, has taken many of the remaining public providers a long way from the principles and possibilities espoused in this chapter. There is much evidence of the remaining public providers being focused mainly on commercial success: senior managers parachuted into jobs without previous experience in any human service sector, let alone the one in which they are now working; large bonuses paid to senior staff simply for doing their job; politicised appointments; and operations ignoring many of the principles outlined later in this chapter. The result has been a loss of capability, performance and public faith in public providers that may take some time to recover even if the political and bureaucratic will to restore them was there. That does not, however, reduce the potential value that public providers have and the validity of the arguments contained in this chapter, even if, for the moment, some of them cannot achieve all the potential benefits.

The next section gives an overview of the historical and contemporary contexts in which public providers of human services have had to operate, focusing on the distinctive intrinsic features of both public providers and human services, and the major impacts of neoliberalism on each of them. Two sections then set out the key issues to be addressed in the design of effective public providers. Most fundamentally, there are preconditions that governments need to put in place in terms of the philosophical and policy frameworks in which public providers must operate and the operational principles that then guide their behaviour. Alongside this, it is necessary to address the common criticisms of public providers, especially in terms of their relative efficiency and cost, and the risk of residualisation. The chapter then moves on to explain how a human service public provider can be a powerful policy instrument, by outlining the broad roles it should play in the market and the specific mechanisms through which it can shape the market in ways that no non-government provider can fully duplicate across a large and complex service system.

The context for the operation of public providers of human services

Three key elements form the context for this chapter: the role of public providers in general (that is, in the wider society as well as human services), the nature and provision of human services (regardless of whether markets are used) and the ever-expanding dominance of neoliberalism in most nations since the early 1980s. More specifically, two major effects of neoliberalism are particularly relevant here: the reduced presence of public providers in general and the growth of human service markets.

Public providers in general: A brief overview

History and diversity

Public providers have played a major role in the development of many nations. In some form, they have existed for millennia, but it was from the nineteenth century that they became an integral part of the society and economy of many nations, including Australia (for example, public schools, hospitals, postal services). The presence of public providers grew substantially in the twentieth century, not just in human services, but also more broadly across the economy, although there were constant reforms at the margin in response to changes in the political complexion of national and state governments (Goot 2010).

Historically, public providers have been used in sectors that both produce essential goods or services and have experienced substantial market failure. This has included sectors in which users pay all or most of the cost (for example, electricity, banking) and sectors in which governments pay all or most of the cost (for example, most human services, public infrastructure). It has included sectors in which public providers have had a monopoly and sectors in which they have been only one of multiple suppliers competing for custom.

There has been—and remains—much diversity among public providers. They differ by the level of jurisdiction (national, state, local), by the type of organisational entity (for example, departmental unit, statutory authority, company limited by guarantee) and by operational factors (for example, form of executive control, employment of staff). There are also variants specific to a sector (as with comprehensive and selective public schools). There is insufficient space here to discuss the nature, features and implications of each of the various forms of public provider in relation to all the issues covered in this chapter. What is important, however, is to note that there will be much variation in how each of these issues plays out in practice in each situation.

The traditional roles of public providers

Where they have been used, public providers have traditionally played *five key roles*. First, a core purpose of public providers has been at the level of individual users, to ensure essential services that are affordable and of reasonable quality are available to everyone who needs them, whatever their personal circumstances or location. A second core role has been to periodically provide a critical policy instrument to facilitate a rapid and effective response to, and recovery from, major social and economic disruption.[2] Both these roles involve directly providing assistance to many individual citizens, but in the course of giving this assistance, public providers have also significantly contributed to developing better overall service *systems* (in terms of the key system objectives outlined later, such as universality, quality, efficiency, equity and stability).

Traditionally, public providers have also been designed and operated to play three further roles that impact primarily at a broader systemic and societal level. These roles are:

- to improve the overall service system for the service being provided through their capacity to have a wider influence on other providers and sectoral norms
- to enhance the contribution of a service to broader social and economic goals (for example, the contribution of education to economic performance) by virtue of the government's capacity to direct a public provider to operate in certain ways
- to improve the operation and outcomes of markets in the sectors in which they operate.

Importantly, the systemic and societal benefits encompassed in all five roles represent the critical and unique contribution of public providers, rather than them simply being providers of services to individuals. It is a key contention of this chapter that the five roles are no less important and relevant today in marketised human service systems, that public providers are still uniquely best-suited to achieving them and that in sectors with significant intrinsic market failure, the overall service system will be more effective, efficient, equitable and stable when a public provider is present. The converse view is that the roles can be carried out as well, if not better

---

2   In Australia, the bushfire, flood and Covid-19 crises since 2020 have strikingly demonstrated this point.

and less problematically, by non-government providers—both non-profit organisations (NPOs) and for-profit organisations (FPOs). This broader debate is at the heart of the chapter, although the primary focus here is on improving the operation and outcomes of the *markets* for human services.

The source of the unique potential contributions of public providers

The unique contribution public providers can make via the five roles outlined above derives primarily from a combination of their public ownership and size.[3] Public ownership enables public providers to draw on the unique legal and moral powers and responsibilities of government. More specifically, this encompasses: 1) the unique legal and coercive powers of government to direct and coordinate individuals, organisations and resources, including fiscal powers to tax and spend; 2) the resulting capacity to marshal (obtain and organise) substantial financial and physical resources that enable the development of organisations with the size needed to adequately address large and complex needs in society; 3) the greater guarantee of stability and continuity of basic services across a jurisdiction given government's longevity (albeit the form of services may change over time); 4) the capacity to maintain and develop linkages with other bodies, given both the longevity of government and its powers to require other bodies to work with its agencies; 5) the moral responsibility of government to use its powers in the public interest and the fact it will be subject to public criticism and possibly electoral consequences if it is seen to do otherwise; 6) the power of government to provide practical and moral leadership through its legal powers and the constant attention it receives; 7) a greater obligation, often based in law, to be more transparent and accountable than non-government bodies; and 8) each of the above factors reinforcing one another, creating synergies that cannot exist independently of public providers that have *all* these features. In summary, public providers have a moral responsibility to operate in the public interest, plus the legal powers and resources to do it in ways and to an extent that cannot be guaranteed by non-government providers.

---

3   In this chapter, the term 'size' for an organisation is used to encompass not just its scale (as measured by dollar turnover, number of employees, and so on), but also the scope of its services and its geographic spread. See Davidson (2015: 115–20) for a discussion of the nature and significance of each of these and other key structural dimensions of service providers.

However, these powers and moral imperatives are of limited value unless they are harnessed to substantial organisational power. Hence, the other important driver of the benefits of a public provider is its size, which also generates two major forms of power. There is the logistical power based on a capacity to operate on a large scale for a wide range of services across a large and diverse geographical area. This enables it, for example, to reach all regions and potential service users in a jurisdiction, to achieve a critical mass and economies of scale and scope in the delivery of services, to absorb major unplanned impacts without threatening its long-term operation or survival, to harness the synergies and interdependencies of a large organisation and to obtain efficiencies that also set up a platform for better services. Coupled with this, there is the power to influence others that comes with size. This can help set public norms, standards and expectations about services. This power to influence becomes market power where services are marketised and—as discussed later—enables a public provider to influence the behaviour of other providers, sectoral norms and government benchmarks for quality, equity, efficiency and price.[4]

Importantly, it is also because of the above factors that there is strong public support for public providers even after governments of both the left and the right have so often chosen to ignore that these are the first-choice providers for many citizens.

The nature and provision of human services

As shown throughout this book, the terms 'human services' or 'social services' encompass a wide range of service types. While there is much diversity between the various service types, they also have a number of common features that distinguish them as a group from other products (goods and other services).[5] These distinctive features are in relation to: 1) demand (limited finances and/or limited personal agency of service users), 2) the production process (the centrality of human skills, attributes and relationships as inputs to production, and the consequent limited scope to increase productivity without reducing quality) and 3) the final

---

4   Size, of course, is a double-edged sword, in that it can lead to overly bureaucratic behaviour and lack of responsiveness to individual users.
5   I have elsewhere set out detailed analyses of human services and human service markets (for example, Davidson 2009, 2012, 2015, 2016). This and later sections briefly note key findings relevant to this chapter.

'product' (limited tangibility, measurability, observability, storability and homogeneity) (Davidson 2015). These features create issues for the provision of the services regardless of markets, but they are also the source of substantial intrinsic (and often unremovable) market failure that is generally deeper and more pervasive than for most other products (Arrow 1963; Le Grand and Bartlett 1993; Blank 2000; Davidson 2015).

A key implication of these distinctive features is that government must play a major role in human services to ensure the quantity and quality of services expected in a modern developed nation. At a minimum, government needs to provide substantial funding and some level of regulation. But it also often must have a role in policy, purchasing and delivery if the services are to be provided effectively, efficiently, equitably and reliably to all the people who need them.

Governments fund human services because of both their importance to the wellbeing of citizens and their contribution to broader social and economic goals (for example, the role of education in economic development). For these two core goals to be achieved, there are several widely agreed objectives for both the services and the systems that provide the services—notably, universality, effectiveness (which primarily derives from the quality, responsiveness and diversity of services), equity, efficiency, choice, stability, innovation, accountability and linkages with other sectors. From the perspective of individuals who need the services, there are three key requirements: availability, affordability and quality. These broad goals and service objectives are logically the criteria with which to assess a service and service system in each specific case, including the impact of both marketisation and public providers. They are a touchstone for the discussion throughout the chapter.

Neoliberalism

The term 'neoliberalism' has been defined and applied in multiple ways by different writers (see the Introduction to this volume). Notwithstanding these differences, there are two points about neoliberalism that would be generally accepted—namely, that it is ostensibly based on a core belief in personal liberty, the power of markets and the need to limit the state (as opposed to collective action and state intervention); and that it is a movement that has been massively successful over the past 40 years in shaping public policy and transforming economic and social life internationally along the lines of those core beliefs. It is primarily regarding these two broad points—its core beliefs and its overall impact—that neoliberalism is relevant to this chapter.

Within these broad parameters, however, neoliberalism has many dimensions. It variously represents, inter alia, a set of ideas; an array of specific changes to legislation, institutions and processes; an approach to statecraft and a set of political strategies to promote these ideas and achieve desired changes; and, perhaps most significantly, it represents a mindset and frame of reference through which to view and interpret the world that have become the default position for many decision-makers. Through all these means—often in *Gestalten* ways—neoliberalism has changed the world over the past four decades. When we speak here of the 'impact of neoliberalism', it refers to the possibility that any one or a combination of the above factors may be relevant in any situation.

Neoliberalism can be critiqued in terms of both the theoretical quality of the analysis and prescriptions emanating from this world view and the extent to which the above forces have promoted ends that are at odds with its stated ideas and goals. While claiming to be driven by objectivity and rationality devoid of special interests, neoliberalism has been driven substantially by ideology, politics and private interests, often without—or even in defiance of—evidence-based studies, while its notion of liberty involves ensuring the powerful can continue to exercise and grow their power (Mirowski and Plehwe 2009; Nik-Khah and Van Horn 2012). For example, drawing on both neoclassical economics and libertarian philosophy, neoliberalism promotes the idea of a minimal state, claiming government action distorts and reduces the preferences and freedoms of individuals (Hayek 2007; Friedman 1962), and the state will inevitably be captured by vested interests (Buchanan 1978). Such a view, however, ignores the positive impacts of much state action, as well as the actual motivation and practice of many public officials and institutions aimed at promoting the public interest and common good (Douglass 1980). Moreover, in practice, neoliberalism has often not reduced state intervention, but simply changed the nature of intervention and who exercises control over it.

There have undoubtedly been major economic and commercial gains from the changes driven by the many faces of neoliberalism, as reflected in the growth of gross domestic product and international trade over the past four decades, but these have not translated into a higher standard of living for many people. Rather, they have led to greater inequality (which in turn has been shown to limit economic growth) and to questions about the adequacy of conventional economic statistics as indicators of national wellbeing (Cingano 2014; Monbiot 2017).

Similarly, markets have also indisputably played a central role in raising living standards over the past two centuries. But markets do not form naturally for some goods and services, and virtually all markets have some level of market failure.[6] While there is general agreement about the broad causes of market failure and the need for government intervention where such failure is extensive, there are major differences of opinion as to the extent and depth of market failure in any situation and the nature and extent of intervention required. Such differences lie at the heart of the central issues of this chapter, which is essentially about how best to address market failure.

We now consider two major effects of neoliberalism in human services that are relevant in this context: the reduced presence of public providers and the growth of human service markets.

The reduced presence of public providers

By the early 1980s, public providers had a substantial presence in Australia. Some sectors had a mixed economy with a large and well-supported public provider as an option for users in a competitive market (for example, the Commonwealth Bank, Qantas); in other sectors, in which users paid their own costs, there was a monopoly public provider (for example, electricity, telecommunications); and in those sectors that were publicly funded, services were largely—sometimes totally—delivered by public providers (for example, many human services). As a result of the growing hegemony of neoliberalism, however, this has been substantially reversed over the past four decades, with a major reduction in the presence of public providers in most sectors via the processes of marketisation, marginalisation and— ultimately, in many cases—privatisation or abolition.

In Australia, *none* of the government research and policy papers in the past 30 years relevant to human services—most of which are very strong in promoting greater marketisation and contestability for public funds—

---

6   Formally, market failure exists where *any* of the conditions of perfect competition are violated.

argues that a public provider is either undesirable or unnecessary.[7] Moreover, when governments decide to downsize or dispose of public providers, it is often done quietly, sometimes with no public announcement beyond informing the users who are affected. The proponents of privatisation know it is not popular with most citizens (Quiggin 2018).

To the extent that reasons are given publicly for the downsizing or elimination of public providers, they have centred on (rarely substantiated) claims about: 1) alleged problems with public providers concerning operational limitations (especially in terms of efficiency, cost and responsiveness to user needs), misuse of monopoly and market power by large government agencies or decisions allegedly driven by the personal interests of politicians and officials;[8] 2) the lack of need for a public provider given non-government bodies can supposedly do the task as well, if not better; and 3) improvements to services that will supposedly be driven by new entrants and competition, such as greater quality, efficiency, diversity and choice for users. While such claims are often poorly based, anecdotal and/or politically driven, there is such a long history of tales of Kafkaesque and other poor behaviour by public agencies that one certainly cannot idealise public providers. In addition, critics claim that ending or reducing public providers will have broader benefits for government, such as: 4) reducing the operational overload on government (Rose 1979; Moran 2018), enabling it to be more strategic and to 'steer not row' (Osborne and Gaebler 1993); 5) reducing financial and operational risk for government; and 6) releasing limited public funds for other programs.

The real reasons for the reduced presence of public providers are more complex. In summary, we can identify six major factors that largely explain their reduced presence over the past four decades.[9] First, it was an inevitable consequence of marketisation that the 'market share' of public providers would fall. Second, and allied to this, government policy in this period commonly supported a greater use of non-government providers. Third, the operational shortcomings of public providers have clearly played a part in some sectors.

---

7   This is the case from Hilmer (1993) through to Harper et al. (2015), the Aged Care Sector Committee (2016) and many Productivity Commission reports concerning human services over the past 25 years (for example, PC 2018).
8   These issues are discussed in more detail under 'Potential problems with the operation of public providers'.
9   Davidson (forthcoming) provides a more extensive discussion of these factors.

Fourth, the reduced presence has been substantially driven by ideology, politics and private interests. Ideologically, public providers have been a major target of the neoliberal goal for smaller government (Berg and Davidson 2018). There have also been more directly political motives to reduce the exposure of government to financial and political risk, to cripple public sector unions and to transfer much of the cost of services to service users—motives that are often opaque because they are considered by policymakers to be in the public interest but likely to be unpopular. Then, increasingly important over time, non-government providers, both FPOs and NPOs, aware of the dollars and power of being a major provider of government-funded services, have come to have substantial influence on policy and program design.[10] This influence commonly accelerates once some critical mass is reached, rising in some cases to such interests now effectively deciding policy in some fields (Gingrich 2011; Edwards 2020).

A closely related fifth factor is that the debate about the appropriate role of public providers is now framed by a set of concepts originally developed by proponents of smaller government—notably, competitive neutrality (Hilmer 1993; OECD 2012), commercial in confidence, soft budget constraints (Kornai 1986; Kornai et al. 2003), stewardship (Hamilton 2016; Carey et al. 2018) and risk. I argue elsewhere (Davidson, forthcoming) that these concepts are conceptually flawed, especially in the ways they have been applied to human service markets.[11] Finally, the cumulative impact of these five factors over time has created a self-perpetuating downward spiral in the capacity of, and public confidence in, government and its agencies.[12] Hence, as noted in the introduction to this chapter, there is now some difficulty in calling for a greater role for public providers because government may be less capable of operating them effectively and in the public interest.

---

10 An important aspect of this is a process that has been described as the 'game of mates' (Murray and Fritjers 2017), which includes, for example, the 'revolving door' for people moving between government and the private sector.

11 For example, competitive neutrality as it has been applied commonly: 1) prevents public agencies from adopting measures that simply reflect the unique and intrinsic advantages of the public sector; 2) prevents payments to public providers for activities aimed at improving the overall service system; and 3) is a one-way street with non-government agencies receiving government funding not being required to service more complex users and more remote or difficult areas, or meeting the same level of public accountability as public providers.

12 Indeed, Mazzucato (2018: 259) argues there has been a deliberate process of 'gaslighting' (or undermining) the public sector, such that the state and its officials have lost their confidence to achieve results.

In general, the reduced presence of public providers has *not* been a result of comprehensive, evidence-based assessments of their performance or outcomes. In fact, there is much evidence of good practice and good outcomes from public providers over many years. Cross-ownership studies consistently show the quality of services from public and NPO providers is likely to be higher than from FPOs (Weisbrod and Schlesinger 1986; Amirkhanyan et al. 2008)[13] and is often highest in public providers (Royal Commission into Aged Care Quality and Safety 2021; Yang et al. 2021). Moreover, public support for public providers remains high—favoured by most people for a number of services (Meagher and Wilson 2015). In summary, while public providers are not perfect, they have a history of achievement and much support from service users.

Human service markets

From the late 1980s, neoliberalism led to the introduction of market mechanisms to varying extents in most human services in most nations. However, one result of the extensive market failure intrinsic in human services is that markets for these services do not form naturally and governments have had to construct managed (or quasi) markets, of which there are many forms (Davidson 2008, 2012, 2015; Gingrich 2011).[14] Then, within each of those managed markets, there is significant market failure, especially arising from the need for a third party to provide much of the purchasing power, the limited personal agency of many users (few of whom are *Homo economicus*) and extensive asymmetries of information.

Market mechanisms thus need to be used in more limited and strategic ways with human services. For example, more contestability should not mean unregulated entry or lower capability standards for providers, competition should be based mainly on the quality of services with limited price competition, choice is complex and may be reduced by too many options, while high co-payments exclude people who need a service (Davidson 2015). However, the many warning signs from theory about

---

13   Such findings are also reported in this volume in relation to the family day care sector (Chapter 1) and aged care (Chapter 6), while Chapter 5 notes the privatisation of public providers of disability services reduced the potential benefits of choice from the NDIS.
14   In Davidson (2008, 2012, 2015), I developed a schema identifying three major types of managed market: single contract, in which government contracts one provider to service a given group of users; quasi-voucher licensing or demand-side funding, in which funding follows the user, who is free to choose any licensed provider; and a hybrid form under which government selects a small number of providers from whom users can then choose.

excessive marketisation and the long empirical international experience of problems have commonly been overlooked by governments as they have tried to substantially replicate conventional markets in human services.

Problems with service providers in human service markets

Consequently, the marketisation of human services has been very controversial, with frequent and recurring problems in service delivery across most service types. There are several problems directly related to service providers:

1. Providers can choose where and whom they service and thus gaps— often substantial—develop in service systems. No services may be available for some areas or people; services for others may be inadequate and some eligible people may in practice be excluded from available services through cream-skimming, parking or high co-payments.

2. There is much potential for poor or opportunistic behaviour by providers, especially through cutting costs by reducing the quality of staff and services under some acceptable minimum in ways that are difficult to detect. As discussed below, there are severe limits to the extent to which regulation and contracts can prevent or control such behaviour.

3. Human service markets are subject to the danger of providers setting prices either too low to cover the cost of quality services or too high to exploit their market power.

4. There are extensive expenditures by providers on items that are not part of delivering the service and exist only because of markets and commercial motives (for example, many transaction costs, marketing, information technology, advisory services, profits for FPOs) and represent an inefficient and wasteful leakage of public and user funds (Davidson 2018).

5. Most non-government providers (including NPOs) must necessarily be ultimately concerned with their own situation and their desire to thrive, or at least survive. Hence, the focus of many has now moved to their financial bottom line rather than the services and broader social goals.

6. All the above problems are especially likely when the large for-profit corporations that are increasingly taking over human services are involved.

A major source of these problems has been the relaxation of regulations constraining the entry of new providers, which has allowed poor and opportunistic providers to be let into most sectors. Nor has marketisation brought the efficiency gains it promised. In many cases, the unit cost of services may be less, but that is far too often a result of cuts to inputs by providers that lead to lower quality—and hence to lesser services.

Moreover, the operation of the markets has been suboptimal and they have commonly failed to deliver better service systems. The above list of problems shows that universality, equity and even efficiency in many respects are intrinsically curtailed by markets. Markets also impact negatively on the stability and continuity of services. While neoclassical theory about competitive markets posits that the process eventually leads to equilibrium, the theory also assumes that, over time, there will be a continuing process of less-efficient providers exiting the market and new providers entering, pointing to the fact that continuing instability is actually a *goal* of competitive markets.

The marketisation of human services has ostensibly been driven by the promise it will improve the outcomes of services for both direct users and society more broadly. What is evident both from theory and from the empirical experience of the past four decades, however, is that marketisation often cannot deliver on these goals, with a core source of the problem being the nature and behaviour of service providers. This is emphasised by the case studies in this book. Indeed, markets, left largely to themselves with relatively open entry for new providers and 'light-touch regulation' of provider behaviour—as is now a common basis for government policy—are most likely to substantially impede achieving the key objectives of human services.

Alternative policy instruments in human service markets

Notwithstanding the problems associated with the marketisation of human services, it is clearly here to stay, at least for the foreseeable future. The value of having some market mechanisms, the current pervasiveness of marketisation in every sector, the current policy frameworks that have emerged from neoliberal perspectives and the realpolitik of powerful interests benefiting from it will ensure that. However, if the goals and objectives of human services are to be achieved and the operation and outcomes of human service markets are to be optimised, there is a need for substantial government intervention in these markets that goes beyond simply providing funds and light-touch regulation.

We have earlier pointed to the powers and responsibilities of government and the way they can be powerfully harnessed by public providers. Of course, governments do not have to use their powers by establishing public providers but have several other policy instruments to try to improve the operation and outcomes of any system or market that provides goods and services.

In summary, there are six other key policy instruments that can be used.

1. The first option in a neoliberal age is to consider measures to *increase competition* in the sector—for example, by reducing barriers to entry for new providers, reducing limits on the mobility of inputs and the spread of technology, improving public information about providers and the market and consumer education.

2. The approach most commonly supported by the critics of marketisation is greater *regulation of the service behaviour of providers* by more closely specifying and enforcing how the services are to be resourced, delivered and monitored.

3. Governments can also more tightly regulate the *initial entry of providers* into the sector and their *commercial behaviour* (for example, pricing, marketing).

4. Rather than invoking their coercive powers via regulation, governments can *influence the incentives* for providers' behaviour (in relation to services and commercially) through financial and nonfinancial incentives and disincentives. Moral suasion and 'nudge economics' can play a role here (Thaler and Sunstein 2008).

5. Governments can also reduce providers' costs by *establishing common infrastructure* that encourages good practice (for example, training programs, innovation clearing houses).

6. In a managed market, government has much scope to control or influence all aspects of the *design and operation of the market*.

Davidson (forthcoming) analyses in detail the roles and limitations of each of these instruments with human services. In summary, each has a role to play in the design and management of human service markets where there is significant market failure, but they are all limited in their effects; they often introduce additional costs for users, providers and governments; and they can even be counterproductive in some situations. It is in this context that a public provider can represent a powerful addition to the policy armoury of government that can uniquely contribute to achieving the objectives of human services in a market environment in the ways outlined below.

Preconditions for the effectiveness of public providers

The core argument of this chapter is that public providers have a unique capacity to improve the operation and outcomes of human service markets in the environment outlined above. This is most likely to happen where certain preconditions are in place in terms of the philosophical and policy frameworks set by government and the operational principles for public providers that guide their behaviour.

The philosophical frameworks: The role of the state

A key tenet of neoliberalism is a belief in the need for a minimal state. This chapter, however, is grounded in a quite different conception of the role of the state—one that takes account of the strengths and limitations of both the state and the market. Hence, it recognises the substantial and demonstrated capacity of the state to play a positive proactive and productive role in improving the lives of its citizens by achieving better economic and social outcomes. This is in the tradition of writers such as Keynes (2004, 1973), Polanyi (2001) and, more recently, Hind (2010), McAuley and Lyons (2015), Raworth (2017) and Mazzucato (2015, 2018, 2021).

The role of the state envisaged here, however, also remains within tight limits, following the guiding dictum of Keynes (2004: 40): 'The important thing for government is not to do things which individuals are doing already, and to do them a little better or a little worse; but to do those things which at present are not done at all.' That is, to do what no-one else can or will do. However, it is also often the case that to do well what no-one else can do, the state may have to do some of what others do (as, for example, if it is to be a cost-efficient provider of last resort, as explained later).

The policy frameworks

At the core of policy, there needs to be a recognition that programs of public funding for human services exist for public interest purposes; they are not business development programs for non-government bodies, as is too often the tenor of contemporary policy documents. Alongside this, it is important that there is some level of contestability for the services of a public provider such that it does not have a monopoly or excessive market power.

More specifically, it was noted earlier that the current policy environment for marketisation discriminates against public providers in terms of key concepts that frame policy. To address this, there needs to be: 1) a more sophisticated interpretation and implementation of the notion of competitive neutrality (for example, such that *all* service providers receiving public funds do their share of servicing more complex, more costly and higher-risk users and areas); 2) more transparency required of all funded bodies rather than them being able to hide behind notions such as commercial in confidence; 3) an acknowledgement of the need for government to have soft budget constraints when they are used in a limited way for clearly defined public interests; 4) an acceptance by government of the need to go beyond mere stewardship of the market to more direct management in setting its parameters; and 5) government accepting greater risk in supporting new developments aimed at enhancing the public interest.[15]

Operating principles for public providers

Central to the case for public providers is the fact they are primarily a policy instrument, rather than simply another competitor in the marketplace. For this to occur, it is essential that public providers establish and adhere to a set of core principles that are based on pursuit of the public interest. These principles will vary with each situation, but they should, at a minimum, encompass: 1) a mission for the organisation that embodies a clear vision of the role of government in creating public value (rather than, for example, setting commercial and financial success as the

---

15 It is important here to distinguish between taking risks to open new areas of knowledge (Mazzucato 2015, 2018, 2021) and the undesirable forms of risk taken by some public agencies in moving into dubious entrepreneurial activities simply to increase their profits and/or market share. The latter occurred, for example, with the state banks of South Australia and Victoria in the 1980s, while Walker and Walker (2000: 71–74) recount Pacific Power's plans in 1998 to invest in offshore activity—plans it then used to try to justify privatising.

key goals); 2) a definition of its scope of activities that acknowledges both the limits of its mission and the range of activities essential to achieve the mission; 3) a core obligation to ensure services are available for all people and areas, with a particular focus on those who would not otherwise receive a service; 4) a core obligation to a minimum level of quality and responsiveness to individual needs for all of its services for all people, while, as far as resources allow, striving for excellence; 5) a preparedness to move into areas and activities where no-one else is willing to go if these have broader public interest benefits; 6) financial self-sufficiency, operating within the revenue obtained from its services, taking account of any additional explicit subsidies from government that would be payable to other providers in the absence of a public provider (for example, to support systemic improvements or 'community social obligations'); 7) a commitment to being a best-practice employer; 8) a commitment to transparency, such that detailed information on the operations, finances and outcomes of the organisation is publicly available;[16] and 9) limited commercial goals (for example, in terms of profit, sales, growth and the approach to service quality and pricing).[17]

Where in this chapter it is stated that a public provider can have various positive effects, this assumes the provider has the mission, structures, resources, personnel and incentives to enable it to operate in the above ways. This does not imply it will be perfect in all respects, but that it fundamentally operates along these lines.

A key issue for a public provider in relation to its role as a participant in the market is its approach to service quality and pricing. The public provider's commitment to the public interest should ensure the quantity, quality and organisation of its staff and other inputs are such as to produce good-quality services that are available to everyone who needs them at an affordable and efficient cost (possibly free, depending on the level of government subsidy). It should be able to produce these quality services relatively efficiently because its size will allow it to achieve the critical mass and economies of scale and scope that enable the most efficient use

---

16   There is a need for some limits on transparency, because of safety, privacy and to limit gaming of the system.
17   These principles are based on my reading of the theoretical and empirical literature on public and non-government providers and my extensive professional experience with providers of all kinds in market and non-market environments across many services. The principles are presented here as being indicative of what is possible and as a stimulus to other researchers, rather than purporting to be a final definitive statement of what is required.

of its inputs. At the same time, it should not be unnecessarily increasing its costs by leakages (such as extensive marketing). Then, its commitment to the public interest should ensure its prices reflect actual costs,[18] as it eschews the opportunity to use its market power for its own interests and ignores the opportunities available to commercial-maximising providers to obtain 'rent' (excess profit) that flows from its market power.[19]

This final principle requires that, as a market participant, a public provider should have limited commercial goals. For example, while it naturally wants to ensure people use it, it should not seek to maximise revenues or actively pursue increased market share per se. High demand may continue to generate substantial growth, but it does not need to actively seek to grow beyond the level necessary for the optimum critical mass and economies of scale and scope. While this does not preclude making users aware of the services available and taking steps to present them positively, it should not involve extensive marketing and use of other 'satellite' services (such as advisors) more than is necessary to operate efficiently and to give users genuine information about its services. Further, the organisation should not be getting into financially risky entrepreneurial activities simply to increase market share and revenue.

While the above principles should be expected of all providers, the fact is commercial and market pressures inevitably divert many non-government providers, both NPOs and FPOs, from these principles. However, with a well-run public provider, it will be the public interest and the wellbeing of citizens, not the wellbeing of the organisation, that are paramount. Notwithstanding this, clearly, there will be some non-government providers that are able to stick to the principles—but, as we shall see, even then the transaction costs of contracting make them more costly and uncertain than an efficient public provider.

As noted earlier, there is much diversity among public providers in the type of organisational entities and management structures that are put in place, and hence, there will be much variation in how these principles apply in individual situations. In all cases, however, the success of public

---

18   Formally, price will be equal to long-run average cost (P=LRAC), where the cost includes an allowance for future investment and unforeseen contingencies.

19   The argument in this paragraph assumes the level of government subsidy available to all providers or users is sufficient to enable the most efficient provider to offer a minimum-quality service. This is not always the case (Cortis et al. 2017). Moreover, it is not unknown for government to allocate a level of funding and other resources to public providers that is inadequate to carry out the additional tasks they have been asked to do.

providers in following these principles is dependent on the *selection of board members and senior managers*. It is imperative the organisations are controlled by people with a keen sense of the potential and responsibilities of public bodies and a motivation primarily focused on achieving better services, rather than simply the survival and/or growth of the organisation. This has been threatened in recent years by the politicisation and de-specialisation of senior management in many public providers.

One result of applying the above principles may be that, in some respects, a public provider may have greater costs (for example, from providing better wages, working conditions and organisational arrangements), but in other respects, it will have lower costs (by minimising marketing and other leakages of the service dollar). It is not evident from theory whether that will mean the total overall costs of a public provider in any specific case are higher or lower. This is an empirical question for each situation. What is clear is the factors that generate the higher cost elements in a well-run public provider are important in improving quality and equity and are socially more beneficial than many of the elements that generate higher costs for commercial maximisers.

Clearly, the model public provider set out above will work most effectively if it is established at the outset of a new managed market (Wilson 1989: 96), although it can still be a powerful force if used by a government wanting to substantially and positively reform a sector.

There will be criticism that the organisation sketched in this section is utopian. The fact, however, is many public providers broadly operated along these lines both before and since the onset of neoliberal dominance.[20] Moreover, the prospect of such an organisation is based much more on realistic assumptions and empirical experience than that propounded by the proponents of the minimal state and perfect competition.

---

20   For examples in Australia and elsewhere, both in and out of human services, see Denhardt and Denhardt (2007), Goot (2010), Hind (2010), McAuley and Lyons (2015), and Sitaraman and Alstott (2019).

Potential problems in the operation of public providers

The previous section painted a positive picture of how a public provider, with adequate resources and good governance and management, can be effective and efficient. This section acknowledges the potential problems that can arise in the design and operation of public providers.

We have earlier noted the alleged operational shortcomings of public providers. The issues relating to risk, control by vested interests and the misuse of market power have all occurred, though nowhere to the extent claimed by promoters of privatisation. Moreover, those issues are largely addressed by the principles set out above. That does not mean such problems will not occur, but they will be much less likely to occur if these principles are established and followed, and then only occur in defiance of explicit rules against them. Of course, governments often see *political risk* in operating public providers, and it has been common for public providers to be eliminated for this reason, regardless of how well they have been working. However, the fact is if government is still paying the cost of a service and/or has regulatory responsibilities, it will not fully escape criticism for poor performance by providers of that service.

There are two major aspects in which there are genuine intrinsic potential problems for public providers: relative efficiency and cost, and the danger of residualisation.

The relative efficiency and cost of public providers

The reason most commonly proffered for removing or downsizing public providers is that they are less efficient and more costly than alternative providers. In fact, it is far from clear that public providers are less efficient or more expensive than non-government providers for providing equivalent services to an equivalent set of users.

There are four major points to consider. The first two relate to the potential for public providers to have higher costs, while the last two relate to the potential for non-government providers to have higher costs. First, government agencies are potentially subject to several intrinsic pressures for *X-inefficiencies* (Leibenstein 1966).[21] These can arise because there is little or no contestability for the goods/services produced by a public provider, more bureaucracy (partly a result of the greater requirements on government agencies for probity and accountability) (Wilson 1989), guaranteed tenure of employment for many public sector staff, a public union wage premium (Hart et al. 1997: 1147) and soft budget constraints that can result in less discipline and urgency. In this context, large size can obviously have negative effects. While these forces indisputably can adversely affect the relative efficiency and cost of public providers, history shows they do not necessarily have to and are substantially avoidable if the above preconditions are in place. It is also the case that many public employees have a strong 'internal motivation' to provide the most effective and efficient services, and that guaranteed employment tenure can both attract better workers and enable them to fully focus on achieving good services.

Second, to the extent that public providers have higher total costs in any service sector, this usually results from higher labour costs of the sort that both: 1) underpin more services (from acting as a provider of last resort) and/or higher-quality services (using staff who are better paid because they are more skilled and experienced);[22] and 2) have broader positive systemic and societal effects (for example, attracting a sufficient supply of quality staff for the sector, ensuring a decent living wage for low-paid workers, helping to stimulate stagnant macroeconomic growth).[23] Empirically, multiple studies of human services by ownership of providers show that in general both unit costs and quality are likely to be lowest in FPOs and highest in public providers.[24]

---

21 X-inefficiencies occur when a firm lacks the incentive to tightly control costs, generally because of a lack of competitive pressures. They are manifested in poor attitudes and practices of managers and employees, especially complacency, lack of responsiveness, poor workplace cultures, overstaffing, poor use of inputs and general organisational 'slack'.
22 The other side of this coin is that contractors may substitute much cheaper (and less-capable) labour.
23 Covid-19 has also shown the public health impact of low wages in human services. One factor in the virus spreading was that many aged care staff worked in a number of facilities because low pay led to them taking more than one job.
24 The lower unit cost is often described as 'higher efficiency' but in such cases 'efficiency' is usually measured simply by lower unit costs with little analysis of whether that reflects better ways of using resources. Indeed, the normally linked finding of lower quality suggests that, to a significant extent, it does not.

Third, some costs of non-government providers are greater than those of public providers. This can occur with both labour costs (for example, at more senior levels and from higher wages in some sectors such as private schools and private hospitals) and non-labour costs (for example, government has lower borrowing costs for upfront investments such as buildings and information technology). More significantly, however, are the multiple leakages of the service dollar in non-government providers (both NPOs and FPOs) for functions that are not part of the actual service. Fourth, many empirical studies over a long period show that, flowing from these extra costs, outsourcing government functions is often much more expensive than using public providers (Walker and Walker 2000; Mazzucato 2021). For Mazzucato (2021: 37–49), the claim that 'outsourcing saves taxpayer money and lowers risk' is one of the major 'myths' about modern government.

In summary, as noted earlier, it is not clear from theory or empirical evidence whether the cost of a public provider following the desirable operating principles in any specific case will have higher or lower total costs than non-government providers.

The danger of residualisation

The other major problem for a public provider is the risk of residualisation. This in large part stems from the fact that in any well-functioning service system, *someone* must be designated as a provider of last resort to handle the more difficult cases, and this should be the role of the public provider. Government can and should absorb more risk and, without a public provider, there is often no provider of last resort.

However, this is a fine line for a public provider. Over time, it can become identified in the minds of users as simply a safety net for 'hard cases' that is unable to provide quality services. In Australia, this has especially occurred with employment services and housing, and is currently a major issue in schooling, where parents avoid some public schools that are seen to be offering a limited curriculum and/or dominated by disadvantaged students. This is reflected on the provider side by the process of cream-skimming, whereby some providers appeal to and disproportionately choose low-cost, low-risk and/or more affluent users, while rejecting the less able and less affluent. It is a given that public providers will have a higher proportion of 'difficult' cases, but it is important they also keep getting a good supply of more capable users, so they can maintain the quality of their services and avoid a downward spiral of 'middle-class opt-outs'.

It is not possible to eliminate cream-skimming by non-government providers, but steps can be taken to minimise it, including: 1) ensuring genuine competitive neutrality whereby all providers that receive government funding (either directly or via subsidies for users) are required to take some of the more complex and higher-cost users (as has occurred with residential aged care in Australia); 2) adjusting the level of subsidies to the user profile of the provider (as in case-mix funding models); 3) means testing of both the user and the provider (in relation to both their income and their assets) in those cases where a user wants to opt out of the public provider and put a public subsidy towards paying for deluxe services (for example, as in private schools and aged care); and 4) reducing other incentives and opportunities for commercial maximisers as part of the design of human service markets.

Improving the operation and outcomes of human service markets

This section explains how well-run public providers can uniquely add to improving the operation and outcomes of human service markets in a context where there are multiple problems with these markets and the desirable preconditions for public providers are in place. We first outline the broad roles public providers should play and then describe some specific mechanisms by which they positively influence markets.

The broad roles of public providers in human service markets

The positive impact of a well-functioning public provider in improving the operation and outcomes of markets substantially flows from the influence it can have on other providers by establishing industry norms and practices.

First, it should seek to operate as an exemplary provider—a model of good behaviour for other providers in both its services and its commercial actions. Far more powerfully, however, its role will be to lead the way in setting standards and benchmarks for the sector, especially in relation to the quality of services, the efficiency and cost of production and the price of services, by generating market pressures of which all providers need to take account. In summary, it means there is a large socially maximising provider with sufficient market power to set norms for the sector that other providers must follow if they are to remain fully competitive. In this way, the case for how a public provider can enhance the operation and outcomes of human service markets is firmly grounded in neoclassical microeconomic market theory. In effect, the public provider acts as competitive market theory claims a provider will act, responding to user needs and preferences and basing its prices on the most efficient long-run average cost. It is financially self-sufficient, without exploiting market power to charge high prices or collect 'rent'. Nor does it cut its costs by reducing the quantity or quality of its resources to such an extent that services are below a minimum acceptable quality.

In these ways, it can willingly act within the market disciplines that competition theoretically should bring, but which are blurred or lost in the imperfections of real-world markets and market power. Then, by the logic of competitive market theory, other providers would need to match the quality and price of the public provider or risk losing business. A public provider can thus both limit the exercise of market power by other providers and use its own market power in the public interest, acting as a powerful countervailing force to the incentives that markets can generate for poor behaviour by providers. In turn, government should have less need to use its coercive powers (regulation), indirect incentives/disincentives or persuasion (all of which have their limitations, as noted earlier).

A well-run public provider will actively adopt an industry and market leadership role in its own practice to advance the public interest. It is a combination of the attributes of its public ownership, including a prime focus on the public interest, and its size that gives public providers a greater potential capacity to have this impact compared with other providers. There is a large body of theoretical and empirical evidence to show that in markets with significant market failure, the presence of a public provider as a competitor in the market, efficiently charging at cost, can be a powerful force to reduce the growth and exploitation of market power by other providers, to maintain quality services and to control prices.[25]

At the same time, the presence of alternative providers is an important constraint on a public provider misusing its market power should there be a change in membership of the board or management to people less committed to the principles outlined earlier. Alternative providers make it less likely the public provider will fall into the natural traps of monopoly power with less responsiveness to user needs and determining output and price in the interest of the provider rather than users and the wider society.

How public providers improve the operation and outcomes of markets

As part of the broad role outlined above, there is a range of specific ways in which a public provider can improve the operation and outcomes of human service markets. This section outlines four of the main possible improvements—limiting the negative effects of marketisation, increasing the efficiency of the market, reducing the total cost of services and facilitating other goals of marketisation—and the key mechanisms that underpin each of them. While these show the major impacts of a public provider in a market, they are indicative rather than exhaustive of all the possible effects.

Limiting the negative effects of markets

We have seen that, notwithstanding the positive effects markets can have on human services, they intrinsically work against achieving objectives such as universality, a minimum-quality service for all, equity, stability, transparency and accountability. In the more volatile managed markets based on demand-side funding, these risks are even greater (Cortis et al. 2013). Some examples follow of how a well-run public provider can limit the negative effects of markets in relation to the universality, stability and quality of services.

A public provider ensures everyone can receive a quality and efficient service by acting as a provider of last resort for people and regions otherwise unable to obtain services. In principle, in any specific case, it should be

---

25 For example, see Evatt Research Centre (1988), Quiggin (2003), Denhardt and Denhardt (2007), and McAuley and Lyons (2015).

possible to obtain some provider at some price to carry out this role, but it is done most effectively and efficiently if there is a single designated provider with a wider presence that can be deployed rapidly, rather than applying successive bandaids for each episodic case.[26] A public provider also ensures a stable and continuous service for all users. In a market, there is likely to be a continuing flux of providers entering and exiting the sector, and the stability of services for any person or area over time cannot be guaranteed if they have to rely on non-government providers.

A further example of how a public provider can limit the negative effects of markets is by its capacity to exert competitive pressure to keep the bar higher for the overall quality of services in the sector, preventing the 'race to the bottom' that has occurred in some sectors. One critical aspect of how this is achieved is by building and maintaining a quality workforce in the face of competitive market pressures to cut costs. The public provider can lead the way in following a 'high road' offering good remuneration and working conditions that stimulate recruitment and retention, rather than a 'low road' on which less able people or migrant workers who are prepared to accept lower pay and conditions are used to fill the gaps (Folbre 2006).

Increasing the efficiency of the market

Public providers, however, can go beyond merely acting as a safety net and bulwark against the negative impacts of marketisation and play a key role in making markets work more efficiently via several mechanisms that promote competition and reduce production costs.

Most fundamentally, a public provider can help create a more efficient market by improving the information available to all participants. The availability of perfect information is central to effective markets, but human service markets are characterised by major asymmetries of information, which are made far worse by the current capacity of providers to claim commercial in confidence about much critical information. However, when one large provider is transparent about its own financial and operational detail, it can have a wider effect in improving the amount and quality of information available more generally in the sector. In turn, this can facilitate the development of a set of detailed benchmarks that can be used by service users (to compare providers), by government funding and

---

26   The next section shows why a public provider can do this more cost-efficiently for government overall than a non-government provider.

regulatory bodies (to assist in the design and management of the market) and by other providers (to guide their behaviour). It also reduces the capacity of commercial-maximising providers to exploit the asymmetries of information. Importantly, it gives funding and regulatory authorities more detailed information to enable industry parameters (for example, subsidies, co-payment rules, mandatory staffing) to be set at levels that generate the best outcomes. It is commonly difficult for authorities to obtain that information from providers at the level of detail needed. The presence of a public provider can enable the detailed insider knowledge to be available to users and to funding and regulatory authorities.

A second major mechanism by which a public provider can increase efficiency across a sector is by contributing to setting a platform for more efficient production costs and prices for services. It can achieve these levels itself but, by being transparent with its own operational and financial data, it can help establish benchmarks for quality and prices to which other providers must respond, driving the cost of and prices for quality services to a more efficient level.

A well-run public provider further contributes to overall efficiency through being the most cost-efficient provider of last resort. Ultimately, in any specific case, it should be possible to obtain some provider at some price to carry out this role, but the price charged by an efficient, socially maximising non-government body is likely to be higher than an efficient public provider. As well as the transaction costs for both sides in establishing and monitoring the contract, the non-government body will reasonably add a risk premium to cover not just possible cost blowouts, but also operational and reputational risks. This is a financially and commercially logical—and almost inevitable—outcome. Moreover, the non-government provider will often have a degree of market power in this situation such that the government agency responsible for the welfare of the person(s) involved has no option but to pay the asking price. As a result, the risk premium can be very large in some instances. Simple market theory suggests competition among possible providers of last resort will compete away (or substantially reduce) the risk premium; but the reality in markets is the high premium rate becomes the 'market rate' below which no potential provider of last resort will go, knowing that over time they will also have opportunities to receive work at this rate.

Finally, an important point from contestability theory (Baumol 1982; Baumol et al. 1982) is that there does not have to be a new entrant to promote more competitive and efficient outcomes from a market, merely that there is the real potential of one. In this way, there can be implicit pressure on incumbent providers in a market to provide more information and to reduce their costs and prices. Hence, it is important that, at the very least, governments signal that a public provider remains an option, even if one may not be established in every case.

Reducing the total cost of services

The discussion thus far has revealed some ways in which public providers can reduce the total cost of quality services for both government and users via the market. First, they can reduce the need for other policy instruments such as regulation, thereby reducing the often-high administration, transaction and compliance costs associated with those instruments. Second, the transparency of a public provider will provide better information about costs to funding and regulatory authorities, which in turn will enable a more accurate assessment of the 'efficient price' for quality services on which the government subsidy paid to all providers should be based. Over time, this should reduce the level of the subsidies government needs to pay all providers for a service over the longer term. This effect will be reinforced by the fact the public provider's own costs are more likely to demonstrate the real costs of providing services, as its expenditure will not include many of the 'leakages' that are present with more commercially focused providers.

Facilitating other goals of marketisation

Public providers can also play a distinctive role in promoting three aspects of improving services and service systems that are particularly important for the proponents of marketisation: choice, innovation and diversity of services.

Choice: There is much evidence that many Australians want their essential services (including human services) to be provided by a public provider. For example, in a 2009 survey across a number of human services, the proportion of people who preferred a public provider ranged from 36 per cent in child care to 87 per cent for health services (Meagher and Wilson

2015).[27] Given that choice has now been established as an overarching policy goal in human services in Australia following the acceptance by the Council of Australian Governments of the recommendation by the Harper Review of competition policy that 'choice should be at the heart [of] human services' (Harper et al. 2015: 247), public providers should logically play a large role in the delivery of most human services. Certainly, removing a public provider means choice for many people will be substantially limited.

Innovation: The proponents of marketisation argue that markets and competitive pressures generate innovation. Two associated arguments are that private enterprise is more 'adventurous' and not stifled by the bureaucracy of government, and that competition allows for the entry of new, smaller enterprises that are engines of innovation. The evidence about each of these claims is, at best, mixed.

While some small organisations are very innovative, most new technological and organisational developments in today's world come from large bodies that have the capability and resources to bring together well-equipped and well-resourced multidisciplinary teams, and to achieve the critical mass, economies of scale and efficiencies necessary for continuing innovation. In these ways, the large size of a public provider can support innovation. Moreover, stringent service standards that limit the entry of new providers to those most capable can reduce the need for regulation of behaviour, thereby enabling more innovation by all providers (Davidson 2017).

It is also important to understand the nature of innovation, which Mazzucato (2018) summarises as being 'cumulative, collective, and uncertain'. In practice, most innovation in organisations involves incremental adaptation, drawing from existing, albeit often newly established, knowledge, rather than new, discrete breakthroughs by unconnected players. Hence, rapid and wide dissemination of new ideas, processes and technology is critical in generating a culture of innovation, but the dominant ethos of commercial in confidence means that, in practice, service providers in a competitive market try to keep new developments to themselves. A public provider, however, should have as part of its remit the responsibility to disseminate innovations, both its

---

27 The preference of many users for public providers is also revealed in international data. In the United Kingdom in 2013, 84 per cent of people believed the National Health Service 'should be run in the public sector' (YouGov survey, cited in Mazzucato 2018: 253).

own and others of which it is aware. There is little or no incentive for non-government providers to do this; on the contrary, there are strong incentives for them not to do so.

Public providers can also play an important role in stimulating and making breakthrough changes, as Mazzucato (2015) has demonstrated. She argues that, historically, public agencies have been prepared to enter areas considered far too risky by non-government bodies, and there is little evidence of 'crowding out' in highly innovative areas where private companies avoid large uncertainties. For Mazzucato, governments should embrace risk, not avoid it, and reducing the role of government can destroy a key dynamic that generates much of the innovation in the wider economy.

Diversity: A popular view of public providers is that they provide rigid, standardised, one-size-fits-all forms of services that are unresponsive to the distinctive needs and preferences of individual users. This can be—and often has been—the case, but equally there are many examples of public providers that provide diverse and responsive services. A well-run public provider with scale has a level of resources that allows greater flexibility to respond to the full range of needs among its users, including services for groups with vital niche needs that are not otherwise viable.[28]

It is often asserted that non-government bodies can be more responsive and diverse in their services. In practice, however, commercial (and survival) considerations mean they must also often focus on achieving economies of scale to lower cost, which leads to greater standardisation of services (Ritzer 2013), institutional isomorphism (Di Maggio and Powell 1983) and mission drift (Weisbrod 2004)—all strong forces to reduce the diversity of providers and services.

---

28 With human services, this particularly occurs at a community level where specialised services for a local subgroup (such as Indigenous people) become embedded in the day-to-day operation of local public schools, public hospitals, TAFE centres, and so on.

The effect of residualisation on the value of public providers

We have looked at how the problem of residualisation can arise for public providers and broad approaches through which it can be best addressed and minimised. We now look at how it can affect the capacity of public providers to achieve their potential contribution.

Increasingly, public providers in many sectors have been marginalised and reduced to the role of a residual safety-net provider for only the most difficult users or regions. The size of a public provider, however, is at the core of the unique contributions it can make, and much of its value is dissipated if it is simply a residual safety-net provider.

First, it means the organisation will be unable to achieve the critical mass and economies of scale and scope that are necessary for maximum effectiveness and efficiency. Second, it can only carry out the safety-net role effectively and efficiently if it has a broader role and presence, and thus is able to respond rapidly in any area. Third, residualisation creates a continuing downward spiral in the appeal and capability of a public provider. Fourth, it can lead to tighter eligibility criteria for using a public provider, resulting in some people with real needs 'falling between the cracks', as is now clearly happening with public housing in Australia. Fifth, and most damagingly in the context of this chapter, it means public providers will be much less influential as a positive force in setting benchmarks for the market and acting as an industry leader to improve the service system and the market.

Can other providers replace a public provider?

While the discussion thus far has been presented largely in terms of a publicly owned and operated provider, it has also made the broader case for there to be a large provider working in the public interest with the authority of government behind it. One implication of the arguments used for marketisation is that a government will better achieve its goals by paying a non-government body to do what its public providers have been doing. This section considers the possibility of government contracting a single social-maximising NPO to carry out the roles and follow the principles expected of a public provider outlined above.[29]

Frameworks for decision-making

A range of frameworks have been developed to guide governments as to whether there should be public providers in specific fields or whether services should be 'externalised'. Despite the simplistic nostrums encouraged by many neoliberal ideas, the reality is that deciding whether a public provider is required is a complex question, where determining what should happen depends very much on the circumstances of each situation.

The framework developed by Alford and O'Flynn (2012) to determine when and how a government-funded service should be externalised is a good example of the approach needed. It is based on three key considerations—namely: 1) the impact of externalisation on the services (for example, in terms of the objectives of human services outlined earlier); 2) the impact of externalisation on the broader strategic goals of government beyond the services; and 3) the relationship(s) between government and the external provider(s) required to effectively monitor an external provider and assess the two sets of impacts. There are, then, various frameworks to assess the three considerations, some examples of which follow.

Central to assessing each of the three considerations is the concept of 'incomplete contracts' whereby it is not possible *ex ante* to specify all the situations that may arise *ex post*. This is almost inevitably the case with human services given their distinctive characteristics. There are three major aspects of incomplete contracts of particular interest here: asymmetries of information, the impact of poor-quality services and the unavoidable incompleteness of such contracts.[30]

---

29 This is the alternative that is most favoured by the critics of public providers. The other major alternatives are to rely on the market, to contract an FPO or to contract multiple NPO and/or FPO bodies to jointly carry out the role of a public provider. Each of these alternatives simply introduces complexities that make the case for using non-government providers less attractive. Charter schools in the United States provide a good example of the multiple problems that can arise where a number of non-government bodies operate the 'public option' (Sitaraman and Alstott 2019: 115–17).

30 The term 'contract' here also applies to the basis for government approvals of providers to operate in quasi-voucher licensing (demand-side funding) systems (see note 14). Indeed, the problems discussed here are likely to be even greater in quasi-voucher licensing systems, which place much greater onus on individual users to detect and rectify problems.

First, asymmetries of information mean a purchaser (whether a user or government) cannot be fully aware of the quality of the production process or the final product. Blank (2000) developed a model to help determine the appropriate level of 'public–private interaction' in social services in any specific case. Essentially, she identifies the major sources of market failure in social services[31] and then argues that the nature and extent of government intervention in each situation should vary with the nature and extent of market failure. This is necessary given the greater the market failure in any situation, the greater are the transaction costs and uncertainty for government in ensuring the objectives of a service are being met by an external provider. Blank concludes that, given the extensive market failure in most social services, a public provider is often the best option, although she does have an important caveat that it is necessary to consider other factors in each situation, especially the efficiency of the current public option.

Hart et al. (1997) point to a second problem with incomplete contracts through the increased risk that a supplier seeking to minimise costs will compromise quality, given that incomplete contracts enable 'an agent with strong incentives to pursue one objective [that is, lower costs] … to shirk on other objectives' (Hart et al. 1997: 1131). The 'shirking', of course, is possible because of the asymmetries of information. Hart et al. (1997: 1130) argue that 'the bigger the adverse consequence of [non-contractable] cost cutting on [non-contractable] quality, the stronger is the case for in-house [government] provision'. In the language of risk-management theory, Blank focuses on the *likelihood* of problems, while Hart et al. focus on the *impact* of those problems.

Third, the uncertainty and risk arising from incomplete contracts can never be totally removed, for, as Williamson (2000: 599) has noted, 'all complex contracts are incomplete', given the intangibility of many of the factors and the extremely high transaction costs of trying to establish the full reality in such cases. Ultimately, this means a government considering outsourcing faces the classic 'make-or-buy' question that confronts any organisation needing to obtain inputs (Coase 1937).

---

31   The sources of market failure that Blank identifies are essentially the same as those derived from the distinctive characteristics of human services set out earlier in the chapter.

The limits of external providers

It is clear many non-government providers can provide services for significant numbers of people that are as good, and sometimes better, than a public provider. However, there are a range of reasons why they cannot achieve the key *systemic* contributions of a well-run public provider, or at least cannot do so without significant extra cost and uncertainty.

First, there are extra costs associated with contracting compared with an efficient public provider. There are transition costs in moving to the external provider—costs that are repeated if the contractor is changed in the future. There are transaction costs in establishing and managing the contract, including disputes over what precisely is required under contracts—something that is very much the norm in such arrangements. Additionally, an NPO will inevitably (and sensibly) add a risk premium to the price given the financial, operational and reputational risks it faces, while government will have limited control over the various leakages of the service dollar (for example, marketing), especially where the contractor has a broader operation. After all these costs, there remains the inevitable uncertainty about the operations and performance of any contractor.

Second, an external provider generally will have less capability and motivation than a public provider to achieve systemic and broader strategic goals. It does not have the same institutional linkages, system leverage and capacity to coordinate resources and other bodies that come with being a government agency. Moreover, in many cases, the contractor will not be able to respond as quickly to urgent and emerging needs, as it must negotiate funding and the conditions of any changes to its contract. Then there is the issue of motivation. An external body, however well intentioned at the outset, will ultimately have to be concerned with its own survival and growth in ways that may conflict with the public interest.

Third, there will be developments during the contract that will generate more issues. Inevitably, there will be changes over time both in the environment in which the provider must work and in the provider itself that will challenge the sustainability and continuance of any initially agreed role and operating principles for the external provider. In addition, a contract to effectively operate as a public provider will enable the NPO to develop and use significant market power, which it can then use in its own interests rather than the public interest. Then, if the outsourcing arrangement does not work out (as inevitably happens in some cases), it can be difficult—and costly—to revert to a public provider, especially given the leverage an incumbent contractor has in such a situation.

Fourth, it is commonly claimed that NPOs have positive features that cannot be replicated by public providers—in particular, that NPOs have greater flexibility because they are free of the restraints of government bureaucracy and closer to the communities they serve. These may or may not be the case in each situation, but there are many examples of public providers having greater flexibility and being closer to their communities than are non-government bodies.[32] Finally, an NPO cannot, by definition, give many people their first choice of a public provider.

This is not to say there is no case in which a non-government body can replace a public provider. After all, the reason for frameworks such as those of Alford and O'Flynn (2012) and Blank (2000) is to examine where that is possible. Rather, the point is that, in general, there are powerful arguments for retaining a public provider in a competitive human service market that are all too often ignored. Moreover, these are not all-or-nothing situations. It may be that after consideration of all the factors, government decides to have a mixed market, making services and funding more contestable, but still retaining a public provider to ensure that all the critical unique roles of public providers set out in this chapter are achieved.

Conclusion

The core proposition in this chapter is that a public provider can be a powerful and unique policy instrument at a systemic level to improve the operation and outcomes of markets in sectors that provide an essential good or service, but which have substantial intrinsic market failure. The need for a public provider is especially strong where government must be a significant source of the purchasing power for the good or service, as with human services.

---

32 See Lyons (2001) and Dollery and Wallis (2003) for discussion of 'voluntary failure' and the problems associated with the delivery of services by NPOs.

Unfortunately, this valuable policy instrument has been progressively devalued and discarded over the past four decades under the weight of ideology, politics and private interests, with the extensive marketisation of human services leading to a major reduction in the presence of public providers in most human services. At the same time, however, marketisation also means that the capacity of public providers to improve the operation and outcomes of markets—of little relevance in human services before the 1980s—assumes some significance, especially in light of the multitude of problems with markets in many human service sectors, as revealed in this book.

Public providers are not perfect, but they have an important role to play, at both an individual and a systemic level, in human service markets. Governments have a range of other instruments with which to address the problems of human service markets, but too often these instruments are limited in their impact, costly and even counterproductive. The revitalisation of public providers is thus an important element in building future social infrastructure. They should not be the only or a privileged player in a market, but they should be used as an essential policy instrument to ensure a basic level of services for all and to assist the broader service systems and markets to work better. Moreover, the option of a public provider is central in considering how best to design a managed market in each situation. Even if the option is not taken up, the analysis can point to the inherent weaknesses of a proposed human service market that need to be addressed.

The benefits of public providers set out in this chapter presuppose a government that wants to optimise the public interest and user outcomes from the market—and not simply outcomes for large non-government providers (both NPOs and FPOs) closely aligned to the government. Critical to the success of public providers are the senior people responsible for them. Ministers, board members and executive staff must be totally committed to the operating principles outlined earlier. If they are not—and ideology, politics and private interests are allowed to dictate the design and management of the markets—it is hard to see *any* human service market working well.

Unfortunately, however, there are now many powerful forces inside or influencing government that are not focused on achieving the best possible public policy outcomes. This may extend to 'state capture', whereby narrow private interests have such access and influence they are able to effectively determine and control policy and the distribution of public resources in a sector.[33] In such cases, one could argue that a public provider represents a worst-case scenario to be avoided.

Notwithstanding these extreme cases, surely if there is a single big lesson from the past two centuries, it is that successful economies and societies are based on the effective blending of markets and government intervention. While there are many possible variations of how this blend can be achieved (Esping-Anderson 1990; Gingrich 2011), neither monopoly public providers nor total reliance on non-government bodies and the market is the best way to provide human services. In this context, strong and active public providers as participants in competitive markets can play an important role.

Some of the above will be derided by some as outdated and ideological, but this is not some utopian view of public providers, nor a proposal to return to the monopoly public providers of the welfare state. Rather, it is a contemporary twenty-first century view that absorbs the lessons and failures of both the welfare state and neoliberalism and builds on the strengths and limits of markets and the state. It acknowledges the limitations and imperfections of public providers, but in a world of choosing between imperfect alternatives where the theory of the second-best is ever-present, the public provider remains an important policy instrument not just to improve human services and service systems, but also to make markets for these services work better.

Ironically, proponents of marketisation have become so fixated on dismantling the influence of the state that they have overlooked the one mechanism that may actually make human service markets work well.[34] In practice, the lack of a substantial socially maximising public provider is a major risk factor for both the operation of markets in human services and the overall provision of these services.

---

33 See Hellman et al. (2000) for a seminal paper by World Bank staff on the concept of state capture, Murray and Fritjers (2017) and Australian Democracy Network (2022) give recent Australian perspectives.
34 This is similar to the argument of Mazzucato (2015) that a reduced role for government in research undermines a core driver of innovation.

Epilogue: Future prospects

This chapter is relevant at two levels for the future: to revitalise existing public providers and to support the establishment of new public providers. Despite a substantially reduced presence, public providers still play a significant role in the delivery of human services in Australia, especially through public schools, hospitals, housing and vocational education, as well as having a presence in fields such as aged care, primary health care, homelessness and child protection. This chapter shows how those services can be revitalised to achieve much more than they have been asked to in recent decades.

Insofar as establishing new public providers (or restoring former ones), this is only likely on a larger scale as part of a turnaround in the broader attitude to and understanding of the role of government. The recognition of the need for this turnaround is certainly occurring on many fronts as the perils of neoliberal ideas and excessive marketisation are revealed. To some extent, it has happened over the past decade with public providers in major new initiatives (such as the National Broadband Network), while the importance of public providers has been reinforced in Australia since 2019 through the bushfire, flood and Covid-19 crises.[35] Notwithstanding these developments, it may be some time before there is a more general revival of the belief in the value of government and the opportunity for a more substantial use of public providers.[36]

References

Aged Care Sector Committee. (2016). *Aged Care Roadmap*. Canberra: Department of Health. Available from: www.health.gov.au/sites/default/files/aged-care-road map_0.pdf.

Alford, J. & O'Flynn, J. (2012). *Rethinking Public Service Delivery: Managing with external providers*. Basingstoke, UK: Palgrave Macmillan.

---

35 The National Broadband Network is responsible for the core infrastructure of open-access data services (including the internet) in Australia.

36 However, even the most pessimistic view of the future for public providers should see the position presented in this chapter in the same light as the apparently dim prospects for success of the neoliberal ideas of the Mont Pelerin Society when it was established in 1947. Those ideas have now ruled the world for the past 40 years.

Amirkhanyan, A.A., Kim, H.J. & Lambright, K.T. (2008). Does the public sector outperform the nonprofit and profit sectors? Evidence from a national panel study on nursing home quality and access. *Journal of Policy Analysis and Management*, *27*(2): 326–53. doi.org/10.1002/pam.20327.

Arrow, K. (1963). Uncertainty and the welfare economics of medical care. *American Economic Review*, *53*(5): 941–73.

Australian Democracy Network. (2022). *Confronting State Capture*. Canberra: Australian Democracy Network. Available from: australiandemocracy.org. au/s/state-capture-report-2022-online.pdf.

Baumol, W.J. (1982). Contestable markets: An uprising in the theory of industrial structure. *American Economic Review*, *72*(1): 1–15.

Baumol, W.J., Panzar, J.C. & Willig, R.D. (1982). *Contestable Markets and the Theory of Industry Structure*. San Diego, CA: Harcourt Brace Jovanovich.

Berg, C. & Davidson, S. (2018). *Against Public Broadcasting*. Brisbane: Connor Court Publishing.

Blank, R.M. (2000). When can public policy makers rely on private markets? The effective provision of social services. *The Economic Journal*, *110*(March): C34–C49. doi.org/10.1111/1468-0297.00519.

Buchanan, J.M. (1978). From private preferences to public philosophy: The development of public choice. In *The Economics of Politics* (pp. 15–25). IEA Readings 18. London: Institute of Economic Affairs.

Carey, G., Dickinson, H., Malbon, E. & Reeders, D. (2018). The vexed question of market stewardship in the public sector: Examining equity and the social contract through the Australian National Disability Insurance Scheme. *Social Policy & Administration*, *52*(1): 387–407. doi.org/10.1111/spol.12321.

Cingano, F. (2014). *Trends in income inequality and its impact on economic growth*. OECD Social, Employment and Migration Working Papers No. 163. Paris: OECD Publishing. Available from: www.oecd.org/els/soc/trends-in-income-inequality-and-its-impact-on-economic-growth-sem-wp163.pdf.

Coase, R.H. (1937). The nature of the firm. *Economica*, *4*(16): 386–405. doi.org/10.1111/j.1468-0335.1937.tb00002.x.

Cortis, N., Macdonald, F., Davidson, B. & Bentham, E. (2017). *Reasonable, Necessary and Valued: Pricing disability services for quality support and decent jobs*. SPRC Report 10/17. Sydney: Social Policy Research Centre, University of New South Wales.

Cortis, N., Meagher, G., Chan, S., Davidson, B. & Fattore, T. (2013). *Building an Industry of Choice: Service quality, workforce capacity and consumer-centred funding in disability care*. Report for United Voice, Australian Services Union & Health and Community Services Union. Sydney: Social Policy Research Centre, University of New South Wales.

Davidson, B. (2008). Non-profit organisations in the human services marketplace: The impact of quasi voucher-licensing systems. Paper presented at the 37th Annual Conference of the Association for Research on Nonprofit Organisations and Voluntary Action, Philadelphia, PA, 20 November.

Davidson, B. (2009). For-profit organisations in managed markets for human services. In G. Meagher & D. King (eds), *Paid Care in Australia: Politics, profits, practices* (pp. 43–79). Sydney: Sydney University Press. doi.org/10.30722/sup.9781920899295.

Davidson, B. (2012). Contestability in human services markets. *Journal of Australian Political Economy*, *68*(Summer): 213–39.

Davidson, B. (2015). Contestability in human services: A case study of community aged care. Unpublished PhD thesis, University of New South Wales, Sydney. Available from: unsworks.unsw.edu.au/fapi/datastream/unsworks:37450/SOURCE02?view=true.

Davidson, B. (2016). Marketisation and human services providers: An industry study. In F.S. Lee & B. Cronin (eds), *Handbook of Research Methods and Applications in Heterodox Economics* (pp. 364–87). Cheltenham, UK: Edward Elgar. doi.org/10.4337/9781782548461.00027.

Davidson, B. (2017). Optimum contestability in human service markets: An alternative to letting a hundred feral cats bloom. Paper presented to the Australian Conference of Economists, Sydney, 21 July.

Davidson, B. (2018). The marketisation of aged care in Australia. In D. Cahill & P. Toner (eds), *Wrong Way: How privatisation and economic reform has backfired* (pp. 101–16). Melbourne: Black Inc. Books.

Davidson, B. (forthcoming). *Public Providers of Human Services in Competitive Markets*.

Denhardt, J.V. & Denhardt, R.B. (2007). *The New Public Service: Serving, not steering*. New York, NY: M.E. Sharpe.

Di Maggio, P. & Powell, W.W. (1983). The iron cage revisited: Institutional isomorphism and collective rationality in organizational fields. *American Sociological Review*, *48*(2): 147–60. doi.org/10.2307/2095101.

Dollery, B.E. & Wallis, J.L. (2003). *The Political Economy of the Voluntary Sector: A reappraisal of the comparative institutional advantage of voluntary organisations.* Cheltenham, UK: Edward Elgar.

Douglass, B. (1980). The common good and the public interest. *Political Theory, 8*(1): 103–17. doi.org/10.1177/009059178000800108.

Edwards, L. (2020). *Corporate Power in Australia: Do the 1% rule?* Melbourne: Monash University Publishing.

Esping-Anderson, G. (1990). *The Three Worlds of Welfare Capitalism.* Cambridge, UK: Polity Press.

Evatt Research Centre. (1998). *The Capital Funding of Public Enterprise in Australia.* Sydney: H.V. Evatt Foundation.

Folbre, N. (2006). Demanding quality: Worker/consumer coalitions and 'high road' strategies in the care sector. *Politics & Society, 34*(1): 11–31. doi.org/10.1177/0032329205284754.

Frank, T. (2016). *Listen, Liberal.* Melbourne: Scribe.

Friedman, M. (1962). *Capitalism and Freedom.* Chicago, IL: Phoenix Books.

Gingrich, J.R. (2011). *Making Markets in the Welfare State: The politics of varying market reforms.* Cambridge, UK: Cambridge University Press. doi.org/10.1017/CBO9780511791529.

Goot, M. (2010). Labor, government business enterprises and competition policy. *Labour History, 98*(May): 77–95. doi.org/10.5263/labourhistory.98.1.77.

Hamilton, P. (2016). 'Stewardship': Buzzword, inkblot, or a new way to deliver human services? *FlagPost*, [Blog], 23 September. Canberra: Parliamentary Library. Available from: www.aph.gov.au/About_Parliament/Parliamentary_Departments/Parliamentary_Library/FlagPost/2016/September/Stewardship_of_human_services_delivery.

Harper, I., Anderson, P., McCluskey, S. & O'Bryan, M. (2015). *Competition Policy Review: Final report.* March. Canberra: The Treasury. Available from: treasury.gov.au/publication/p2015-cpr-final-report.

Hart, O., Shleifer, A. & Vishny, R.W. (1997). The proper scope of government: Theory and an application to prisons. *The Quarterly Journal of Economics, 112*(4): 1127–61. doi.org/10.1162/003355300555448.

Hayek, F.A. (1944 [2007]). *The Road to Serfdom.* Chicago, IL: University of Chicago Press.

Hellman, J.S., Jones, G. & Kaufmann, D. (2000). *Seize the state, seize the day: State capture, corruption, and influence in transition.* Policy Research Working Paper 2444. Washington, DC: World Bank and European Bank of Reconstruction and Development. Available from: openknowledge.worldbank.org/handle/10986/19784.

Hilmer, F.G. (1993). *National Competition Policy.* Report by the Independent Committee of Inquiry. Canberra: AGPS. Available from: ncp.ncc.gov.au/docs/National%20Competition%20Policy%20Review%20report,%20The%20Hilmer%20Report,%20August%201993.pdf.

Hind, D. (2010). *The Return of the Public.* London: Verso.

Keynes, J.M. (1926 [2004]). *The End of Laissez Faire.* New York, NY: Prometheus.

Keynes, J.M. (1936 [1973]). *The General Theory of Employment, Interest and Money.* London: Macmillan.

Kornai, J. (1986). The soft budget constraint. *Kyklos, 39*(1): 3–30. doi.org/10.1111/j.1467-6435.1986.tb01252.x.

Kornai, J., Maskin, E. & Roland, G. (2003). Understanding the soft budget constraint. *Journal of Economic Literature, 41*(4): 1095–136.

Le Grand, J. & Bartlett, W. (eds). 1993. *Quasi-Markets and Social Policy.* London: Macmillan.

Leibenstein, H. (1966). Allocative efficiency vs. x-efficiency. *American Economic Review, 56*(3): 392–415.

Lipsey, R.G. & Lancaster, K. (1956). The general theory of second best. *Review of Economic Studies, 24*(1): 11–32. doi.org/10.2307/2296233.

Lyons, M. (2001). *Third Sector: The contribution of nonprofit and cooperative enterprise in Australia.* Sydney: Allen & Unwin.

Mazzucato, M. (2015). *The Entrepreneurial State.* New York, NY: Public Affairs.

Mazzucato, M. (2018). *The Value of Everything: Making and taking in the global economy.* London: Allen Lane.

Mazzucato, M. (2021). *Mission Economy: A moonshot guide to changing capitalism.* London: Allen Lane.

McAuley, I. & Lyons, M. (2015). *Governomics: Can we afford small government?* Melbourne: Melbourne University Press.

Meagher, G. & Wilson, S. (2015). The politics of market encroachment: Policymaker rationales and voter responses. In G. Meagher & S. Goodwin (eds), *Markets, Rights and Power in Australian Social Policy* (pp. 29–96). Sydney: Sydney University Press. doi.org/10.30722/sup.9781920899950.

Mirowski, P. & Plehwe, D. (2009). *The Making of the Neoliberal Thought Collective.* Cambridge, MA: Harvard University Press.

Monbiot, G. (2017). *Out of the Wreckage.* London: Verso.

Moran, M. (2018). Whatever happened to overloaded government? *The Political Quarterly, 89*(1): 29–37. doi.org/10.1111/1467-923X.12450.

Murray, C.K. & Fritjers, P. (2017). *Game of Mates: How favours bleed a nation.* Currumbin, Qld: Publicious.

Nik-Khah, E. & Van Horn, R. (2012). Inland empire: Economics imperialism as an imperative of Chicago neoliberalism. *Journal of Economic Methodology, 19*(3): 259–82. doi.org/10.1080/1350178X.2012.714147.

Organisation for Economic Co-operation and Development (OECD). (2012). *Competitive Neutrality: Maintaining a level playing field between public and private business.* Paris: OECD.

Osborne, D. & Gaebler, T. (1993). *Reinventing Government: How the entrepreneurial spirit is transforming the public sector.* New York, NY: Plume.

Polanyi, K. (1944 [2001]). *The Great Transformation: The political and economic origins of our time.* Boston, MA: Beacon Press.

Productivity Commission (PC). (2018). *Introducing Competition and Informed User Choice into Human Services: Reforms to human services.* Inquiry Report No. 85, 27 October. Canberra: Productivity Commission. Available from: www.pc.gov.au/inquiries/completed/human-services/reforms/report/human-services-reforms.pdf.

Quiggin, J. (2003). Governance of public corporations: Profits and the public benefit. In M.J. Whincop (ed.), *From Bureaucracy to Business Enterprise: Legal and policy issues in the transformation of government services* (pp. 27–42). Aldershot, UK: Ashgate.

Quiggin, J. (2018). Privatisation is deeply unpopular with voters. Here's how to end it. *The Guardian,* 29 January. Available from: www.theguardian.com/commentisfree/2018/jan/29/privatisation-is-deeply-unpopular-with-voters-heres-how-to-end-it.

Raworth, K. (2017). *Doughnut Economics: Seven ways to think like a 21st-century economist.* London: Penguin Random House.

Ritzer, G. (2013). *The McDonaldization of Society.* Thousand Oaks, CA: Sage.

Rose, R. (1979). *Ungovernability: Is there fire behind the smoke?* Strathclyde Studies in Public Policy No. 16. Glasgow, Scotland: Centre for the Study of Public Policy, University of Strathclyde. doi.org/10.1111/j.1467-9248.1979. tb01209.x.

Royal Commission into Aged Care Quality and Safety. (2021). *Final Report: Care, dignity and respect. Volume 1: Summary and recommendations.* Canberra: Commonwealth of Australia.

Sitaraman, G. & Alstott, A. (2019). *The Public Option: How to expand freedom, increase opportunity, and promote equality.* Cambridge, MA: Harvard University Press. doi.org/10.2307/j.ctv2d8qx28.

Thaler, R.H. & Sunstein, C.R. (2008). *Nudge: Improving decisions about health, wealth, and happiness.* New Haven, CT: Yale University Press.

Walker, B. & Walker, B.C. (2000). *Privatisation: Sell off or sell out?* Sydney: ABC Books.

Weisbrod, B.A. (2004). The pitfalls of profits. *Stanford Social Innovation Review,* *2*(3): 40–47. doi.org/10.48558/82vx-ym41.

Weisbrod, B.A. & Schlesinger, M. (1986). Public, private, nonprofit ownership and the response to asymmetric information: The case of nursing homes. In S. Rose-Ackerman (ed.), *The Economics of Nonprofit Institutions: Studies in structure and policy* (pp. 133–51). New York, NY: Oxford University Press.

Williamson, O. (2000). The new institutional economics: Taking stock, looking ahead. *Journal of Economic Literature,* *38*(3): 595–613. Available from: www. jstor.org/stable/2565421.

Wilson, J.Q. (1989). *Bureaucracy: What government agencies do and why they do it.* New York, NY: Basic Books.

Wolf, Charles, jr. (1988). *Markets or Governments: Choosing between imperfect alternatives.* Cambridge, MA: MIT Press.

Yang, O., Yong, J., Zhang, Y. & Scott, A. (2021). *Competition, prices and quality of residential aged care in Australia.* CEPAR Working Paper 2021/10. Sydney: Centre of Excellence in Population Ageing Research, University of New South Wales.

10

Conclusion: The present and future of social service marketisation

Adam Stebbing and Gabrielle Meagher

Introduction

After decades of change in every major service sector, market instruments can seem destined to organise the delivery and distribution of social services into the foreseeable future. While currently popular with governments across the political spectrum, market instruments are no more or less inevitable than other policy designs. The proliferation of social service markets, which are neither self-constituting nor self-regulating arrangements as anticipated by neoclassical economics, is the culmination of policy choices successive governments have made in favourable political and economic circumstances. Both the prevalence and political expedience of market instruments underscore the importance of understanding how marketisation has reshaped social service provision and contributed to ongoing problems.

The contributions to this volume have shown how inefficiency, low quality and inequality pervade many social service markets. Avoiding simplistic explanations that attribute these issues to either a few 'bad apple' service providers or an amorphous neoliberalism that is the sum of all negative developments in recent years, the chapters recognise the diversity of market models and argue that the specific instruments employed have made social service provision susceptible to these problems and, in some cases, exacerbated them. This final chapter proceeds in three sections. First, to consolidate the contribution of this volume to research on social service marketisation, we reflect on the assembled findings. Second, we point to future research possibilities by providing an overview of aspects of marketisation in Australia that are yet to be fully explored. Third, given its unprecedented impact on society and the economy, we consider the implications of the Covid-19 pandemic for the future of social service marketisation. Complementing contributors' proposals in the chapters of this collection, we conclude by looking beyond marketisation, to discuss some recently articulated possibilities for renewal of the public sector and its ways of working with other social institutions.

Reflections on the proliferation of social service markets

The case studies assembled for this volume provide further evidence that the development and design of publicly subsidised social service markets have resulted from conscious choices made by both Labor and Liberal–National Coalition governments in recent decades. Governments have adapted a wide range of market instruments to subsidise private social services—including contracts, tax expenditures, subsidies, individualised budgets and regulatory devices—in response to rising demand for social provision amid the adoption of New Public Management approaches and the increasing influence of neoliberal ideas. Yet, despite considerable diversity in both the design of market instruments and the structure of service sectors, evidence from the case studies indicates market instruments have not justified policymakers' faith in them and have often exacerbated, rather than resolved, problems of service provision.

Commonwealth Rent Assistance for private renters
replaces public housing as primary subsidy.

Australian National Training Authority established,
opening competitive public funding to private
vocational education.

Compulsory private superannuation introduced.

Childcare subsidies extended to for-profit long-day
childcare centres.

Competitive tendering established in employment
services and opened to private (non-profit and for-
profit) providers.

Aged Care Act introduces user-pays principles,
removes some regulatory oversight of staffing, fees
and financial accountability in residential aged care.

Private Health Insurance Tax Rebate introduced to
promote uptake.

Student loans to cover fees extended to VET,
including weakly regulated private providers.

Living Longer, Living Better reforms introduce
'consumer directed care' into community aged care.

National Disability Insurance Scheme Act enacted.

Keating ALP

Howard LNP Coalition

Rudd–Gillard ALP

1992

1993

1994

1997

1999

2012

2013

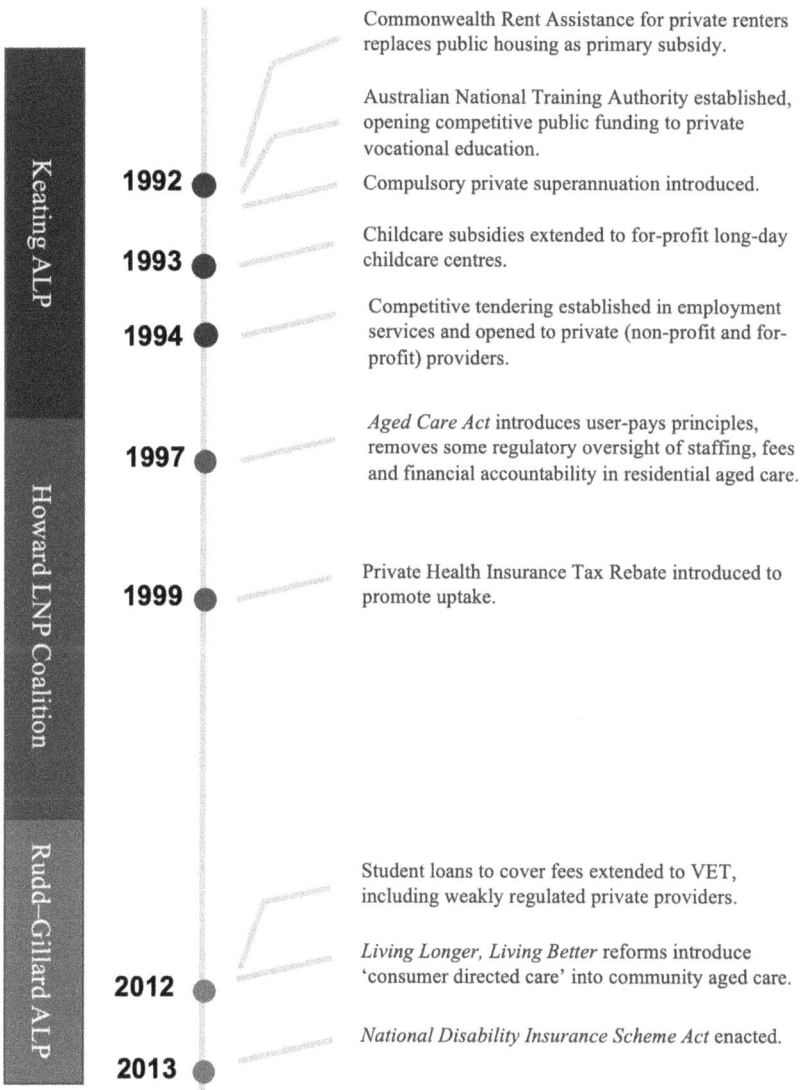

**Figure 10.1 Opening markets into Australian social services: A timeline
of key policies**

Source: Based on authors' research.

The case studies in this and related volumes (Cahill and Toner 2018;
Meagher and Goodwin 2015) are revealing, but a sense of how this
patchwork came to be stitched together is also useful. Figure 10.1
presents a timeline of important 'initiating' moments in the history
of social service marketisation in Australia over the past three decades

(see also Meagher and Wilson 2015). Labor governments made many of these first moves, seeking efficiency and innovation (in employment services) or choosing the path of least resistance to broaden access (to child care and superannuation). Coalition governments have typically extended and deepened markets that Labor opened or have sought to weaken universal benefits or user protections that Labor had established (for health care and aged care). The detail presented in the chapters shows that, in line with Gingrich's (2011) prediction, the parties have often sought to achieve different goals and to (re)distribute costs and benefits to different stakeholders with marketisation policies. While containing public expenditure has often been a shared goal in service system design, the Coalition has tended to reinforce private provider power and Labor has attempted to manage markets for the benefit of service users. Yet, it also seems clear that market ideas have been a bipartisan 'cognitive lock' (Blyth 2001) through which most social service policy problems and their solutions have been framed.

Extending public subsidies to for-profit service providers

The extension of public subsidies to for-profit providers across the social services sector has been a—perhaps *the*—distinctive characteristic of the market instruments that featured as our case studies, when compared with earlier policy instruments. Although acknowledging that the marketisation does not require privatisation, it is noteworthy that market instruments for social services departed from the established practice of reserving public subsidies for non-profit providers. This practice had enjoyed bipartisan support from Federation until the final decades of the twentieth century. When introducing market mechanisms, decision-makers provided three main but often interlinked rationales for subsidising for-profit operators: to address shortages in social service provision, to empower service users as consumers and to improve efficiency through competition. Subsidising for-profit providers has been used to increase access and meet unmet demand for social provision while limiting calls on the public purse. In the case of superannuation, Labor's policy shift to (mandatory) occupational super in the late 1980s was justified as improving the adequacy of retirement income from the pension and avoiding the startup costs of a national super scheme (see Stebbing, Chapter 4). Regulatory reforms designed to advance this retirement policy in the late 1980s extended tax concessions to for-profit funds to enforce operational standards across the sector (see Chapter 4). When granting for-profit childcare and family day care services access to public subsidies in the early 1990s, Labor claimed widespread shortages in subsidised non-profit services restricted assistance to the fortunate few and the non-profit sector had little capacity to meet surging demand (see Chapters 1 and 8). As Laura Wynne and colleagues outline, in housing policy, recent governments at both state and federal levels have shifted investment from public to social housing via asset-transfer schemes and public–private partnerships with the intent of leveraging further private investment (see Chapter 7).

Often, though, public subsidies to for-profit providers have been justified as providing consumers with choices across the social services sector. Gabrielle Meagher and Richard Baldwin (Chapter 6) trace how both the Coalition and Labor have supported subsidising for-profit residential aged care services and regulatory reforms to increase consumer choice in the past two decades. Consumer choice also featured prominently in Labor's justification for extending public subsidies to for-profit childcare services and subsequent reforms (see Chapter 8). Natasha Cortis and colleagues (Chapter 1) chart how the Coalition reformed family day care services in the mid-2000s, repealing regulations that limited the scale of private providers in the name of increasing consumer choice and service supply. In the same period, the Coalition supported increasing the access of for-profit super funds to occupational superannuation in the name of increasing consumer choice. Perhaps more prominently, as Georgia van Toorn shows, advocacy for consumer sovereignty by local and transnational disability rights groups was a major factor in the selection of individualised budgets as the mechanism to distribute funding for the NDIS (Chapter 5).

While increasing consumer choice has been a goal in its own right, public subsidies to private providers have also appealed to policymakers as a means of stimulating competition among those providers to improve efficiency. Demand-driven subsidies rely on consumer choice to stimulate this competition. For example, the rationale for streamlining the policy treatment of private residential aged care providers since the late 1990s has been to achieve competitive neutrality between for-profit and non-profit services (see Chapter 6). In contrast, contracting out relies on competitive tendering for governments to choose between the expressions of interest lodged by private providers. Adèle Garnier (Chapter 2) highlights that the Coalition's introduction of competitive tendering for refugee resettlement services to maximise 'value for money' was framed as a major innovation in the mid-1990s. Diana Perche (Chapter 3) further notes that competitive tendering was the market mechanism relied on to foster the efficiency of employment services in remote Indigenous communities, as consumers could not exercise choice with single providers operating in each of the 60 regions.

The rise and rise of profitable social services

The proliferation of market instruments across the social services sector has been followed by the rapid growth of for-profit social provision. Not only have for-profit providers responded to the incentives from public subsidies by expanding their operations, but also their growth has consistently outpaced that of public and non-profit providers. Table 10.1 presents data for the past 25 years on the market shares of public, non-profit and for-profit organisations in residential aged care, community aged care, child care and employment services. The most striking trends over this period are the increasing market shares of the for-profit service sector and the decline of the public sector. What makes the increasing market share of for-profit providers even more significant is that it has coincided with growth in the social services sector. In child care, the total number of long day care places increased 29 per cent in the five years to 2020. Of these new places, 89 per cent were in for-profit centres. In residential care for older people, Meagher and Baldwin (Chapter 6) note the number of places increased by 50 per cent between 2000 and 2018. Of these new places, 70 per cent were in for-profit facilities. In community care for older people, following the introduction of consumer-directed care in the Home Care Packages program in 2016, the number of providers has increased by 84 per cent, and two-thirds of the new providers are for-profit. In employment services, the share of for-profit providers has fluctuated over time, but has also increased considerably. The pattern appears to be that non-profit providers gain more contracts under Labor government tenders (1995 and 2009–15), while for-profit providers gain more under Coalition government tenders (1998–2009 and 2015–22). The growth of for-profit services has often coincided with consolidation, with larger providers amassing considerable market share in mature social service sectors. The childcare sector exemplifies this trend; the corporate giant ABC Learning was estimated to offer more than one-fifth of long-day childcare places in Australia at its peak in the mid-2000s. Following the collapse of this business, large private organisations that operate 25 or more services make up 1 per cent of service providers and offer one-third of childcare places (Stebbing, Chapter 8). The two largest players in 2019 were Goodstart Early Learning, a non-profit rescued from the ashes of ABC Learning in 2010, with 9 per cent of all places in 646 centres, and G8 Education, a listed company that has grown rapidly by acquisition in recent years, with 7 per cent of places in 500 centres (A. Richardson, 2020b). Superannuation has also been transformed since the 1990s, with the number of private 'institutional' super funds declining in number from 4,734 to 202 between 1996 and 2018 (see Chapter 4). Although over a longer time frame, the residential aged care sector has also experienced consolidation. Large church-run, non-profit providers have long had a place. However, in the past two decades, large for-profit providers have emerged—some listed on the stock exchange, others privately held (see Chapter 6). Some 2 per cent of these businesses operate more than 20 facilities each, and account for more than 25 per cent of all places (A. Richardson, 2020a). The number of employment service providers in the outsourced system has also declined over time, as the program has been redesigned and renamed by successive governments. Contracts were issued to about 300 'Job Network' providers in 1998, to 100 'Job Services Australia' providers in 2009 and to 40 'Jobactive' providers in 2015 (Jobs Australia 2015). In the 2015 tender round, extended to 2022, the largest five providers operated one-third of all service sites.[1] Of these, three were for-profits, operating almost one-quarter of all sites. The largest provider, the for-profit Max Solutions, operates more than 13 per cent of all Jobactive sites.[2] For the CDP providing employment services in remote communities, 20 of the 60 regions are serviced by six for-profit providers, including Max Solutions (Chapter 3). And, in refugee services, market concentration is more pronounced in immigration detention than in resettlement services; as Garnier (Chapter 2) notes, Paladin Holdings and Paladin Solutions were awarded $313 million for two contracts in Papua New Guinea from 2007.

---

1   From July 2022, a new employment services program called Workforce Australia will be in operation. Providers appointed to the national panel and those licensed to provide 'enhanced services' have been selected (see Employment Services Tenders, available from: tenders.employment.gov. au/tenders/b0bb0fc3-23ae-ec11-983f-002248d3b28f). For-profit providers are well-represented among licensees and the larger panel. Shortly after the program began in mid-2022, the new Labor government signalled broad support for the program's design and responded to reports of problems from jobseekers with the promise of possible reforms following a parliamentary review (Young 2022).
2   Authors' calculations based on data in Jobs Australia (2015).

Table 10.1 The growth of for-profit social service provision, 1994–2020

Provider	Residential aged care[a] (operational places, 30 June, %)						
	1994	2000	2005	2010	2015	2020	1994–2020 (% change)
Public	12	10	8	6	5	4	-8
Non-profit	61	63	61	59	57	55	-6
For-profit	28	27	31	35	38	41	13

	Home care packages[b] (service outlets/providers, 30 June, %)						
	1995	2000	2005	2010	2015	2020	2000–20 (% change)
Public	n.a.	16	18	15	18	12	-4
Non-profit	n.a.	78	78	78	69	52	-26
For-profit	n.a.	6	4	7	13	36	30

	Long day care for children[c] (1994–2009, % providers; 2015, 2020, % places)						
	1994	2000	2004–05	2008–09	2015	2020	1994–2020 (% change)
Public	16	10	3	3	5	4	-12
Non-profit	26	24	26	22	33	28	2
For-profit	58	67	71	75	62	68	10

	Employment services[d] (provider organisations' share of services, %)						
	1995*	1998–2000	2000–03	2009–12	2012–15	2015–22	1995–2020 (% change)
Public	80	37	8	0	0	0	-80
Non-profit	20	30	45	61	70	55	~+45
For-profit		33	47	39	30	45	~+35

* Contracted case management services only.

n.a. not available

Notes: This is a revised and updated version of Table 1 in Meagher and Goodwin (2015). Years reported are determined by contracting rounds. The name of the mainstream employment services program has changed several times; it is currently called Jobactive.

Sources: [a] For 1995, AIHW (1995); for 2000, SCRGSP (2001); for 2005, SCRGSP (2006); for 2010, Department of Health (2011); for 2015, Department of Health (2016); for 2020, ACFA (2021). [b] For 2005, AIHW (2006); for 2010, AIHW (2011); for 2015 and 2020, ACFA (2021). [c] For 2004–05 and 2008–09, DEEWR (2010); for 2015, authors' calculations using data from ACECQA (2016); for 2020, ACECQA (2020). [d] For 1995, Senate Employment, Education and Training Legislation Committee (1995); for 1998–2000 and 2000–03, PC (2002: 4.10); for 2009–12, Personal communication, Director, Deed Administration, Business Partnerships Branch, Employment Services and Support Group, Department of Employment, March 2014; for 2012–15 and 2015–22, Jobs Australia (2015).

The growth of publicly subsidised for-profit providers in consolidating social service sectors has increased both their market power and their investment appeal. The market power of for-profit retail super funds has increased as the investments held grew more than tenfold from $60 billion to $622 billion between 1996 and 2018, while less than one-third of the original number of funds still operates after amalgamations and mergers since the beginning of this period (Stebbing, Chapter 4). As well as exerting considerable market power, the private superannuation sector is highly profitable and charged $9 billion in annual fees in 2017. At the same time, the financial risks faced by retail super funds (a majority of which are owned by the four major banks) are mitigated by the dominance of accumulation super accounts in the sector and mandatory employer contributions. The childcare sector is also highly profitable; as Stebbing (Chapter 8) notes, commercial childcare providers have been rated as blue-chip investments because of high profits and substantial assets, primarily in real estate. Aged care, too, has been profitable. At 15.7 per cent, the average return on equity among for-profit providers in 2018 was among the highest of any industry (BDO 2020: Table 4.5).[3] Real estate is also an important revenue source for residential aged care providers, which together hold billions of dollars in accommodation deposits from older people, in addition to income streams from public subsidies and user fees (Meagher and Baldwin, Chapter 6). For-profit providers can use complex business structures to protect their property assets and increase

---

3   BDO prepared this report for the Royal Commission into Aged Care Quality and Safety, before the impact of the pandemic on the sector. A more recent survey has found that declining occupancy and higher costs have reduced profitability (Stewart Brown 2022).

their profits, with regulations making relatively few on their financial accountability (BDO 2020). Employment and other social support services make good private investments, too. Max Solutions, the largest provider in the Jobactive employment services program, is a subsidiary of Maximus, a company listed on the New York Stock Exchange with market capitalisation of $7.27 billion in September 2021.[4] In addition to its Jobactive contracts, Max Solutions has contracts to deliver services across multiple specialised employment support, training and assessment programs in Australia.[5] Maximus recently reported to its shareholders that its Australian revenues over the three years to 2019 exceeded $900 million.[6] Its Australian operations contributed about one-third of the company's non-US income over these years, on which it earned an average gross profit of 15.9 per cent (Maximus 2019).[7]

However, the profitability of large service providers in mature and consolidated social service markets is not the only story here. The case studies in this volume also demonstrate how accepted and uncontroversial market instruments that subsidise for-profit services have become to the allocation, delivery and expansion of social services in Australia. This is evident in both the variety of market instruments policymakers have employed and the range of social services to which they have applied them. Using market instruments, policymakers have extended subsidies to social services that were previously considered the domain of government or the non-profit sector, such as family day care (Cortis et al., Chapter 1) and employment services in remote Indigenous communities (Perche, Chapter 3). Moreover, it would have been unthinkable mere decades ago for the state to enter public–private partnerships with property developers to build and administer social housing (Wynne et al., Chapter 7), let alone contract out the operation of offshore immigration detention facilities (Garnier, Chapter 2). It is also notable that the NDIS—among the largest expansions to social service provision in recent memory—has instituted the hyper-marketised device of individualised budgets to allocate disability services (van Toorn, Chapter 5).

---

4   The value was US$5.39 billion on 7 September, converted to AUD at a rate of 0.741 on the same day.

5   See www.maxsolutions.com.au/our-services. As one clicks through, the wide range of services, from job placement to child welfare assessments, emerges.

6   The total in US dollars was $679,079,000. The AUD value presented here is based on the authors' calculation, using average annual exchange rates for each of the three years 2017, 2018 and 2019.

7   Authors' calculations based on data on pages 26 and 53 of the *Annual Report* (Maximus 2019).

Evaluating the impact of social service marketisation

Despite oft-repeated claims about the benefits of marketisation, the case studies presented in this volume have shown that, in practice, the design of social service markets in Australia has often contributed to rent-seeking, low service quality and/or inequality. Market instruments that subsidise for-profit providers contribute to rent-seeking when their design contains the state's financial commitment without limiting service users' out-of-pocket expenses; this was exacerbated in cases where there was persistent unmet demand or low levels of service competition. Although it is difficult to calculate precisely, Gabrielle Meagher and Richard Baldwin (Chapter 6) note that residential aged care services are susceptible to rent-seeking by for-profit providers from recent reforms to additional service fees and accommodation charges. Adam Stebbing (Chapter 8) traces how childcare fee rises have continued to outstrip inflation in this sector since public subsidies were extended to for-profit services in the early 1990s. And Adèle Garnier (Chapter 2) contrasts the cost inflation of for-profit-dominated immigration detention services that are contracted through restricted tenders, with the cost effectiveness of the non-profit resettlement services subsector.

Market instruments that render social services susceptible to rent-seeking or that stimulate low levels of competition among private providers have been shown in the case studies to be key factors that result in low-quality services, particularly in sectors that are weakly regulated. Cortis and colleagues (Chapter 1) explain that, following the removal of several restrictions on the scale of their operations, for-profit family day care services had an incentive to lower service quality by reforms in the mid-2000s that increased demand-driven public subsidies but withdrew operational funding. They argue these policy settings distorted the ensuing growth in family day care places towards low-quality for-profit services. Diana Perche (Chapter 3) shows that service quality is adversely affected in the CDP by the lack of competition between private providers and the government funding arrangements that rely on providers' reports of attendance metrics instead of measures of the quality of employment services. In residential aged care, removing in 1997 the requirements for providers to acquit the funding they received against funds expended to provide care led to a decline in the amount of care older people receive and in the qualifications of care staff (see Chapter 6). In turn, these changes resulted in the problems exposed in submissions and testimony to, and reports by, the Royal Commission into Aged Care Quality and Safety.

So far, our focus has been on the impact of market designs on the ownership structure and the integrity of social service systems. But there are impacts on social service users, too, as discussed in the Introduction and in various ways throughout the volume. In summary, market designs that rely on consumer choice and provider competition to allocate services and to maintain and improve service quality tend to shift risks and costs to service users. When services to marginalised social groups, such as Indigenous Australians and refugees, are outsourced to for-profit providers, a different set of problems emerges, especially where public oversight is weak or lacking.

Emerging and future directions for research on marketisation in Australian social policy

This volume adds a set of original case studies to existing knowledge about the origins, extent, design and impacts of social service marketisation. Yet, there are marketised services and marketisation practices that are not yet fully understood or are emerging. Even in the policy fields covered in this and other recent collections (Cahill and Toner 2018; Meagher and Goodwin 2015), many unanswered questions remain.

The politics of regulation and the institutional power of private business

In the light of evident problems with service quality raised in the Introduction, and the extent and concentration of private provision across multiple social service sectors discussed above, research on the politics of regulation is needed to understand whether, and to what extent, marketisation has enabled rent-seeking regulatory capture by private providers of social services. As Busemeyer and Thelen (2020: 475) argue, as their dependence on private actors to provide publicly funded services grows, governments face increasingly 'strong incentives to accommodate business interests to keep them committed to the public–private arrangement'. How Australian governments have responded to these incentives, and whether their responses explain the evident weaknesses of oversight in, for example, aged care and disability support, is an open research question.[8]

Another related but under-researched question about the politics of regulation and the power of business is the complex triple game played by the 'big-four' accounting and consulting firms in relation to the public service and the public purse more generally. One lucrative activity in which these firms engage is the provision of contracted policy advice and other services to governments. Table 10.2 gives an overview of the total value of published contracts with federal government agencies for each of the big-four companies. The amounts are large, ranging from just less than $1 billion over the decade to 30 June 2020 for Ernst & Young (EY) to nearly $1.7 billion for KPMG. A rough sense of change over time is gained by measuring the share of total value in tenders published in the five years to 30 June 2020, which, as Table 10.2 shows, was almost two-thirds. This upward tick continues a trend identified by van den Berg and colleagues (2020: 114), who found the value of contracts to the big-four firms increased considerably between the two decades they studied: 1997–2007 and 2007–17.

Other well-known international accounting and/or consulting firms are also contracted by federal government agencies to provide advice and other services. However, the amounts involved, while large, are much lower.[9] One important exception is Accenture—until two decades ago, part of Arthur Andersen, the fifth of the then 'big-five' accounting and consulting firms. In the decade to mid-2020, the total value of Accenture's contracts with federal agencies was more than $3.4 billion, including four contracts

---

8   In a rare quantitative study of the role of consultants in policymaking in Australia, van den Berg and colleagues cautiously discuss the potential policy influence of Serco and Broadspectrum, two international companies whose business is government contracts, and who have had multibillion-dollar contracts to run asylum-seeker detention centres, as discussed in Chapter 2. The authors note: 'While their profile, and those of similar firms, might not suggest "leadership" on substantive policy issues, the scale of their engagements, and the intimate involvement in programme management and delivery these potentially represent, do raise questions about their indirect policy influence and potential political leverage' (van den Berg et al. 2020: 128).
9   For example, for the same 1 July 2010 – 30 June 2020 period shown in Table 10.2, the total value of Grant Thornton's contracts was $7 million; BDO, $8 million; and ACIL Allens, $28 million. The Boston Consulting Group has had total contracts to the value of $184 million over the decade, which is certainly substantial but equal to just 20 per cent of the total value of EY's contracts and 11 per cent of the value of KPMG's. Similarly, McKinsey had contracts with a total value of $172 million. (Authors' analysis of data from the Australian Government's procurement information system AusTender, available from: www.tenders.gov.au.)

for sums exceeding $110 million each. While the largest contracts are for the provision of digital infrastructure—including a single contract (of several) to the value of $572 million, for the My Health Record system—the company also provides more traditional project management and management advisory services.[10]

A second activity in which these companies engage is the production of documents, projects and events that claim to provide 'insight' into the future direction of government and policymaking. Five years ago, the trend was for documents with titles such as *Creating Public Value: Transforming Australia's social services* (EY 2014), *Reimagining Public– Private Partnerships* (PwC 2017) and *Gov2020: A journey into the future of government* (Eggers and Macmillan 2015). More recently, multimedia products including podcasts, such as PwC's 'Government Matters' and Accenture's 'Social Services: From the era of support to the era of empowerment', are available on the companies' websites, along with information about offerings such as Deloitte's GovLab, which is 'designed to support public sector organisations in developing the mindset, skillset and toolkit needed to innovate' (Deloitte 2022).

Part-research, part-advocacy and part-marketing, these materials appear to be directed at governments as potential customers of the companies' services. A casual examination of these materials suggests marketisation is among the taken-for-granted strategies for 'transforming', 'reinvigorating' and 'reimagining' government. There is room for more systematic research into this growing body of multimedia discourse, how it frames the problems of contemporary government and public service and the relationship between how the companies frame the problems of the public sector in their 'freelance' policy advocacy, on one hand, and the substantive policy work they do for governments on the other. Particularly salient to the concerns of this volume is the question of whether these consulting firms act as 'instrument constituencies', chasing problems with (marketising) solutions at the ready (Sturdy 2018).

---

10   Authors' analysis of data from AusTender (available from: www.tenders.gov.au). Note that, for the purposes of this brief overview, these figures relate to a search on the name 'Accenture' only. Accenture is a global company with more than 900 subsidiaries, according to business database D&B. In Australia, Accenture subsidiaries trade under other names, and at least some have a presence as government contractors. Avanade, for example, is a joint venture between Accenture and Microsoft, majority-owned by Accenture, and had federal agency contracts to the value of $17 million for the 10 years to 30 June 2020.

Table 10.2 Overview of contracts between federal agencies and the big four, published 2010–20

	No. of contracts	Total value of contracts ($ million)	Share of total value in contracts published since 1 July 2015 (%)
Deloitte	2,172	1,039	72
EY	2,099	923	54
KPMG	3,360	1,689	67
PwC	2,589	1,386	65
Total	**10,220**	**5,037**	**65**

Source: Authors' analysis of published AusTender data (available from: www.tender. gov.au). Initial searches used company name, followed by checks to identify whether additional subsidiary name and Australian Business Number (ABN) searches would yield more comprehensive results. Search dates were 1 July 2010 – 30 June 2020. Results were sorted by publication date to obtain values for 1 July 2015 – 30 June 2020. The data may be incomplete if additional ABNs or alternative subsidiary titles did not emerge during compilation of the data.

A third activity in which the big-four firms engage is arguably their primary reason for being: accounting, auditing and advice to business clients. There has been considerable controversy about the quality and integrity of their work in this fully private domain, prompting the establishment in Australia in 2019 of a joint parliamentary inquiry into the regulation of auditing in Australia (Parliamentary Joint Committee on Corporations and Financial Services 2020). Our interest here is in the findings of international research that the big four are deeply implicated in assisting their clients with tax evasion (Ajdacic et al. 2021; Jones et al. 2018), which weakens both government capacity and public trust. In Australia, a commissioner of the Australian Taxation Office has called these companies a 'systemic' risk to the integrity of Australia's tax system (Tadros 2019).[11]

Together with the major sums they make from government contracts, their freelance advocacy for public sector reform and their other business and political activities, 'the big four are at the centre of a profoundly troubling web', which, as journalist Bernard Keane (2019) argues:

---

11   And while Accenture is no longer in the business of accounting and auditing, the company has been implicated in reports about multinational tax evasion (Dalby 2019), while also offering advice to others on 'navigating compliance' with international attempts to arrest the practice (Accenture 2018).

links taxpayer funding and the provision of policy advice—often from consultants with no specific sectoral expertise—to millions in political donations to the major parties, the systematic undermining of government tax collection worldwide by companies using the services of the big four and the loss of trust in large companies because of conflicted auditing. These companies help create the problem of governments lacking revenue to properly fund their public sectors, and then offer to fix the problem by offering their own services, while auditing companies with which they have lucrative commercial arrangements.

These problems have been exposed by investigative journalists, including Keane and others (Bagshaw and Gartrell 2018; West 2016, 2018; Whyte 2020a). However, research that more closely and systematically specifies the scale and scope of these activities and the connections between them is needed.

Private exercise of public authority and the rise of the 'private servant' in the public sector

This and other recent collections have focused mainly on social service marketisation organised through contracting or voucher models with explicit, institutional separation of the public authority that funds and regulates services and the private provider that delivers them. Other forms of marketisation are blurring this institutional separation in both directions. In some cases, decisions formerly taken by public officials are now delegated to employees of private organisations, while in other cases, staff working in public sector organisations are employed by private businesses. These arrangements externalise public authority and destabilise lines of accountability, raising questions about the quality of government and the rights of citizens subject to it.

In employment services, for example, decisions about income-support payments that were formerly taken by public officials are now taken by employees of private providers. Researchers have scrutinised these delegated powers over more than two decades since the privatisation of the Commonwealth Employment Service in the 1990s. Indeed, the magisterial longitudinal comparative program of research on the construction and reconstruction of the market for employment services led by Mark Considine over two decades stands as a model for analysis of other social services (Considine 1999, 2001; Considine et al. 2011, 2015, 2020; O'Sullivan et al. 2019).

Yet there are developments in delegated authority in employment services that remain to be studied. An important case is the CDP in remote Indigenous communities (see Perche, Chapter 3). Another is ParentsNext, a 'pre-employment program' for people who receive the Parenting Payment, which offers income support to parents of young children (overwhelmingly, mothers) who lack other means. ParentsNext was rolled out in 2018 through contracts with 53 private providers, of which 12 were for-profit businesses that received nearly one-quarter (23 per cent) of funds allocated, while the remainder were non-profits. Providers have power to exempt a person from the program's requirements and, as with other mutual-obligation programs, can issue sanctions that result in loss of income support. There is emerging evidence from media reports (Burns 2019) and a parliamentary inquiry (Senate Community Affairs References Committee 2019) of problems with ParentsNext arising from conflicting incentives to private providers.

The same vulnerable group of mothers and children may also be affected by decisions outsourced by the former Child Support Agency (now part of Services Australia; on which more below). Data from AusTender show that, for the financial year 2019–20, Services Australia made 65 contracts worth more than $10.3 million to such decision-makers, many of whom were hired year after year. We are not aware of any research examining possible impacts on the quality and integrity of outsourced decision-making, or the implications for the welfare of families involved.

It seems reasonable to ask why contractors hired year after year are not simply employed by the outsourcing public agency and thereby brought under the strong governance structures of public sector employment. This question is at least as relevant for the tens of thousands of privately employed staff across the public sector, including in government departments. These 'private servants' (Mannheim 2020) often work alongside their public servant colleagues carrying out the institutions' normal operations, while formally employed by private labour hire companies. In September 2020, two media reports based on data accessed through freedom-of-information requests sought to quantify the extent of this practice, and to explore the legal status of these murky arrangements (Mannheim 2020; Wilson 2020). According to these reports, the use of labour hire aims to keep down the official headcount in the Commonwealth public service, while managing the workload of public institutions, following the imposition of a staffing cap by the Coalition government in 2015. Many of the external employees in the public service perform routine functions, but higher-level roles, including in the Senior Executive Service, are also outsourced.

Spending on labour hire across the federal public service in 2019–20 exceeded $4.7 billion and amounted to more than 14 per cent of total spending on staff—down from more than $6.2 billion and more than 18 per cent of total spending on staff in 2018–19 (Mannheim 2020). Both reports discuss the risks of nepotism and other forms of corruption in appointments because, under labour hire arrangements, the recruitment of private providers is not governed by the rules and practices of the public service (Mannheim 2020; Wilson 2020). These contracts are often struck with large international corporations, such as Serco, Hays and Adecco.[12]

Growth in the use of contract labour was highlighted in a major review of the public service published in late 2019 (PM&C 2019). The report found the staffing cap and increased use of contractors and consultants contributed to declining capacity in the public service, along with a lack of long-term thinking and poor use of employees' skills (PM&C 2019: 185). The report noted that data on the numbers and costs of contractors were inadequate, so the costs and benefits of private labour were hard to assess.

The use of contract labour and labour hire was scrutinised by the Senate Select Committee on Job Security (2020-2), which was dominated by the ALP, then in opposition. The committee examined job insecurity both in the public service and in publicly funded jobs, such as those in outsourced social services. It recommended that 'the Australian Government introduces a policy stating that an objective of all public funding for employment, or the provision of goods and services, is to protect and

---

12 According to our analysis of data from the official database for public procurement, AusTender, the total value of federal government contracts over the past decade (since January 2011) with Serco is $5.2 billion. Many of the more than 400 contracts over this time appear to be with the Department of Defence for services such as the maintenance of defence materiel, and there are some very large contracts for running detention centres, as Adéle Garnier discusses in Chapter 2. But two contracts for a total of $463 million are to provide staff to the Australian Taxation Office, while three others totalling $250 million are to staff Services Australia (including one of its predecessor organisations, Centrelink) for three years from late 2017. UK-based recruitment company Hays has made nearly 16,000 contracts with federal public organisations in the past decade, with a total value of more than $1.9 billion. Contracts with Adecco number 790, with a total value of $627 million, of which $497 million was tied up in 20 contracts for staffing Services Australia. Many other companies have contracts with total values in the hundreds of millions for labour hire arrangements.

promote secure employment' (Senate Select Committee on Job Security 2021: xiii). Now in government, it remains to be seen if and how Labor will act on the committee's recommendations.

This brief overview is the tip of a rather large iceberg. Yet the consequences of these practices for every aspect of public service operation in social policy fields—including service quality, transparency, privacy, equality and democratic accountability, but also the ethics of (public) office (du Gay 2008)—remain to be fully examined.

New organisations, new forms of private–public integration?

On 1 February 2020, a new 'executive agency', Services Australia, replaced the Department of Human Services, and combined multiple former Commonwealth agencies—including Centrelink, Medicare and the Child Support Agency—which administered Australia's largest social policy programs, including income support and public health insurance. In the same month, the then minister for government services, Stuart Robert, told a business audience about the government's plans for the new agency: 'The private sector is indispensable to developing and delivering the government's service revolution' (Robert 2020). Going beyond outsourcing, the government is seeking 'co-investment' in infrastructure to deliver government programs. The role the private sector plays and how privacy, transparency, equality and democratic accountability are exercised depend on the kinds of commercial 'partnerships' the government enters into in creating this agency, which touches the life of every Australian. There is considerable outsourcing of labour in Services Australia, as noted briefly above, and substantial sums have been spent with large consulting firms McKinsey and KPMG, which have prepared the plans for its rollout, among other roles (Burton 2020).[13] Yet before Minister Robert made his speech, the private sector was already well integrated into the agency, not least in the opaque proprietary software and other technologies that shape the foundations of its new, hybrid public–private digital governance model (Brown 2020).

13   Intriguingly, PwC published one of its freelance policy advocacy documents in 2012, called *Transforming the Citizen Experience: One stop shop for public services* (PwC 2012).

The creation of mega-agencies that have increasingly porous and complex relationships with external business organisations brings new risks. Some arise from staffing practices already discussed. But there are others: in April 2020, a major data breach was discovered at a similar agency at the state level, Service NSW. Public reports, which emerged months after the breach, stated that documents related to more than 100,000 people had been compromised, and the cost of remediation blew out from the early estimate of $5 million to between $25 and $35 million (Bavas 2020; Hendry 2021). More basic are the risks of unaccountability, the invisibility of decision-making and processes hidden by bureaucratic and commercial secrecy (Brown 2020). There is a need for more research on the establishment and evolution over time of such agencies,[14] and a longitudinal study of the building and operation of Services Australia could reveal much.

The Covid-19 pandemic and the future of social service marketisation

The first wave of the Covid-19 pandemic challenged proponents of marketisation as ill-prepared governments and underfunded public institutions struggled to find the skilled staff, medical equipment and consumables to respond to spiking rates of illness. In several countries around the world, as death tolls in nursing homes spiralled, calls to limit for-profit provision and to nationalise nursing homes emerged (Altmann 2020; Gomez 2020; Peterkin 2020; Swadden 2020). In a 'vision statement' delivered in May 2020, the then leader of the Labor opposition, now Prime Minister Anthony Albanese, said:

> The contracting out of essential public services is not in the national interest and must stop. It's time to put human beings and human dignity back into human services. The basics of life such as early childhood education should be nurtured and made affordable. (Albanese 2020)

Further, the pandemic has exposed the limitations of service systems based on consumer choice, individualised funding and market-organised supply. For example, the NDIS, which delegates to myriad private providers responsibility for sourcing, training, screening and managing

---

14   A recent study by David Lloyd Brown (2020) is a very good beginning.

disability care workers, has left governments without the control or even the intelligence they need 'to identify the workforce, train them in infection control, mobilise supplies to all who need these and upscale the workforce in [the] face of shortages in care workers' (Dickinson et al. 2020: 4). Meanwhile, problems with the outsourcing of security services at private 'quarantine hotels' in Melbourne were blamed for the second, mid-2020 wave of infections (Holden 2020; Schneiders 2020), which resulted in the illness of thousands and the death of hundreds of older people living in residential aged care facilities—themselves very poorly prepared for the pandemic. As Kristen Rundle (2020: 3) argues, hotel quarantine is 'a form of civil imprisonment in service of a public health measure'. Yet, 'the human face of quarantine in both its detention and infection control aspects' was delegated to private security guards, who had no legal or political responsibility to the people they were expected to oversee, at best minimal training in infection control and inadequate personal protective equipment (Rundle 2020: 4).

The pandemic has also provided opportunities for rent-seeking by private businesses, as the same ill-prepared governments scrabbled to procure essential goods, including protective equipment and ventilators—often at extortionate prices (ANAO 2021a; Le Grand 2020)—and hastily purchase private staff reinforcements for health and care facilities at a premium (Davies 2020). Virus testing has been a particular boon for pharmaceutical and pathology companies, the longstanding rent-seeking behaviour of some of which has recently been exposed (see, for example, Kiezebrink and van Teeffelen 2020). In May 2020, the largest commercial pathology companies threatened to stop testing for Covid-19 until the Medicare rebate they received was increased. The Coalition government responded by almost quadrupling the rebate to commercial providers (in addition to offering them other contracts and benefits), while granting a much lower increase to public pathology laboratories, which were more likely to serve rural and remote communities (Knaus 2020). By mid-2021, commercial pathology companies were reporting record profits amid problems with slow testing times amid the winter outbreak in New South Wales (Terzon 2021). In early 2022, the testing system collapsed, as growing infection rates undermined pathology companies' 'cavalier' approach to pooling as many as 20 samples to maximise returns (Morton 2022).

Questions about the quality of procurement in Australia have been raised by the Senate Select Committee on COVID-19 (2020) and there have been several media reports about cosy arrangements using 'limited tenders'

(Crikey 2020a). One troubling report documented the government's approach to Mable, a digital platform for matching individuals who need care and support with individual workers who provide it (Crikey 2020a). Mable was contracted without open tender to the value of $5.8 million to provide emergency staff to nursing homes affected by Covid-19, despite being neither a registered NDIS provider nor an aged care provider. The company was initially unable to supply staff when required (Crikey 2020b). Between the striking of this contract and March 2022, it provided no more than 130 staff to fill 2,711 shifts in residential aged care (Department of Health 2022: Table 1).[15] Discovery and reporting of pandemic procurement by the Senate Select Committee were affected by the government's use of 'public interest immunity' to avoid providing all the information the committee requested (Senate Select Committee on COVID-19 2022: 87–94). It remains to be seen whether the full picture will emerge and whether robust evaluations will be possible—for example, through a royal commission into the pandemic response.

As many have noted, the pandemic has exposed weaknesses and fault lines in many of Australia's institutions. In social services, the question could be posed in terms of the compatibility of marketisation and disaster preparedness. In one of the most influential early characterisations of New Public Management, Christopher Hood (1991) identified three families of values in administrative design—'keep it lean and purposeful', 'keep it honest and fair' and 'keep it robust and resilient'—and noted the close alignment between the values of lean and purposeful administration and what we call marketisation. Hood concludes it is not possible to design public management systems that satisfy all three sets of values simultaneously. The desirability of both robustness and resilience on one hand, and honesty and fairness on the other, is pressing as Australia confronts the challenges of the post-Covid, rapidly warming world, in which inequality is likely to become even more stark. The question for Australian governments now and in the future is whether and how equitably these challenges can be met when lean values are prioritised.

---

15   Dividing the total grant by the number of shifts suggests this amounts to more than $2,000 per shift.

Looking beyond marketisation: Time for renewal of the public sector?

The experiment with marketisation has been under way for decades, intensifying in recent years as governments have extended consumer choice models to new service areas. Yet a recent review found there is little research evidence to support policymakers in designing, steering and managing these markets (Carey et al. 2020). The chapters in this book have explored a range of market structures and problems, contributing to a deeper understanding of how marketised social service systems in Australia do—and do not—work. The chapters have also considered ways forward in the various social service domains they consider. Our brief concluding remarks mostly step back from these specific questions to reflect on some bigger themes that have emerged in recent research about the role of government and market mechanisms and actors in providing publicly funded social services.

In her work on 'markets in misery', Janine O'Flynn challenges researchers to move beyond questions about *how* such markets work to ask whether and when it is *right or wrong* for governments to delegate the provision of human services to private actors. It is, she writes, 'time to confront the cumulative effect of long-run privatization' (O'Flynn 2018). States now govern us through a 'worst of both worlds' hybrid of the dehumanising tendency of the bureaucratic machine and the commodifying tendency of the market. The 'accumulation of many smaller decisions' has resulted in complex, opaque arrangements under which private interests take public money to profit from human misery, misfortune and vulnerability. It is time, O'Flynn argues, 'to bring morality back in' to public administration, in a collective, social effort. We might question the (personal) ethics of the owners of childcare and aged care corporations, whose million-dollar remuneration packages and purchases of luxury mansions and cars are reported in the media with an ironic mix of envy and outrage (see, for example, T. Richardson 2020), but they have gained their fortunes within the politically determined rules of the social service markets they increasingly dominate. This means we need to engage together in the *political* process, with the moral questions these rules raise. Anthony Albanese's 2020 statement, noted above, appears to be taking these questions up, but countervailing pressures are strong. While public opinion has never favoured marketisation, political, business and bureaucratic elites have (Meagher and Wilson 2015).

Kenneth Meier and colleagues (2019) also argue for a renewed focus on politics to improve the quality of governance. They point to the familiar representation of inefficient, ineffective, abusive *bureaucracy* as the problem, and note that marketisation (via New Public Management) has been a widely favoured solution. However, New Public Management has reduced the capacity of government and the sustainability of its (now fewer) achievements. Thus, they argue, representing the problem of governance simply as the problem of bureaucracy is misguided. Bureaucracies have some 'competitive advantages' as policymaking and service delivery institutions: they are adaptable, can work over long time frames and are staffed by experts and other personnel guided by the values of public service and professionalism (among other things). Often *political* decisions render bureaucracies unable to do their work effectively, by under-resourcing them, tasking them with 'unclear, ambiguous, and, at times, conflicting goals' (Meier et al. 2019: 1578) and not allowing them sufficient autonomy to use their expertise. In other words, failures of governance are failures of politics, and it is political failure—including the politicisation of public administration—that leads to many contemporary bureaucratic pathologies.[16]

There are many examples from Australia of bureaucratic pathology of political origin, many of which relate to the funding of external actors, and some of which fall within or close to our concerns in this volume— for example, the 'sports rorts' affair, in which federal government funds for the Community Sport Infrastructure Grant Program were allocated, during the 2019 election campaign, overwhelmingly to communities in seats the government held or hoped to gain (ANAO 2020; Remeikis and Karp 2020). The politicisation of the grants program has been the focus of criticism, but Michael Di Francesco (2020) argues the affair raises another problem: the politicisation of the public service, which meant it failed in its duty to safeguard procedural integrity.[17]

---

16 A perhaps even more pessimistic assessment of the causes and consequences of the loss of capacity in public organisations is offered by Ansell et al. (2021).

17 The 'sports rorts' were not an isolated incident. Similar problems have been identified in other recent Commonwealth grants programs, including the Female Facilities and Water Safety Stream of the Community Sport Infrastructure Program (Snape and Probyn 2020), the Commuter Car Park Projects within the Urban Congestion Fund (see ANAO 2021b) and in the NSW Stronger Communities Fund in that state (Thompson 2020).

Political failure also explains weakly resourced and poorly guided regulatory institutions. Both the amount and the character of quality oversight in aged care during the coronavirus pandemic have been questioned, in the absence of a specific pandemic plan for aged care and a presiding minister considered so incompetent as to be formally sanctioned by Parliament (Butler 2020; Murphy 2020). A brief example: by 11 September 2020, at the height of the second wave of Covid-19 infections in Victoria, barely 20 per cent of that state's nursing homes had been visited by the Australian Aged Care Quality and Safety Commission to have their infection-control systems checked. The commission did not start making these compliance visits around the country until August (Caisley 2020). As for aged care homes with coronavirus outbreaks in the first and second waves of the pandemic, the commission had visited only 30 of the 220 by the end of September 2020 (Connolly 2020). The commission has, like other federal agencies, been affected by the staffing cap discussed earlier: it told the Senate Select Committee on COVID-19 that 27 per cent of its staff were contractors.

Australians may also confront bureaucratic indifference, even cruelty, in their interactions with Centrelink in the administration of income support. Alongside the increasingly complex and punishing compliance requirements overseen by private employment service providers discussed above, there have been years of deliberate political decisions to cut and de-professionalise Centrelink staff and to outsource to international service corporations, including Serco (Karp 2019; Jenkins 2020). The resulting bureaucratic inhumanity is evident in millions of unanswered phonecalls every year (Dingwall 2018; Whyte 2020b) and the 'Robodebt' scandal—an automated debt-recovery program aimed at income-support beneficiaries that was ultimately ruled illegal by the Federal Court (Medhora 2019). Valerie Braithwaite (2020) argues the harms of Robodebt go beyond the immediate harm to citizens, to harming trust in government and threatening democracy.

What these failures reinforce is that the problems of marketisation arise from its design and implementation, which are largely under political control. If governments choose to work with market instruments, a range of principles and practices that could drive up both quality and equality in Australian social services has been identified by researchers. One idea is presented by Bob Davidson in Chapter 9: markets for social services should include a public provider, to model good practice and to ensure equitable access for all to high-quality services. A bigger-picture vision for government's relationships with the external organisations it funds is offered in Janine O'Flynn and Gary Sturgess's research paper (2019) for the recent review of the Australian Public Service (APS). O'Flynn and Sturgess argue that the APS needs to shift from outsourcing to a broader conception of contracting within a 'strategic commissioning' approach. This approach requires 'deep and authentic' engagement with the communities and people who use publicly funded services, to gain the knowledge required to anchor commissioning in community needs and aspirations. Governments working with strategic commissioning take a more system-wide approach and enact different kinds of relationships (including transactional and relational) as appropriate to service goals. This approach requires the APS (and, by extension, the public services of the states and territories) to be resourced—indeed, permitted—to develop new organisational capabilities. O'Flynn and Sturgess's vision for deep community engagement is likely to genuinely empower more Australians than the consumer choice models on which governments currently rely to organise social service markets. It may also contribute to rebuilding the trust in government that is essential to well-functioning, democratically steered public institutions.

When governments make markets for social services, and fund new private actors to provide essential social services to their citizens, they change the role of the state in society. As we have stressed, this change is political and is itself subject to political action. Proposals for public providers in social service markets and for commissioning anchored in community engagement are positive, practical ideas for reorienting state–society relations. This volume has focused on problems with social service markets. To solve these problems, one thing we need to do is to look 'beyond the messes and disenchantment' catalogued herein to uncover 'the factors and mechanisms that enable high performing public problem-solving and public service delivery; procedurally and distributively fair processes of tackling societal conflicts; and robust and resilient ways of coping with threats and risks' (Douglas et al. 2021: 441–42). This call to 'walk on the bright side' is salutary, not least to motivate us as citizens and researchers to remain engaged in constructing a well-governed, good society.

References

Accenture. (2018). Arresting tax evasion: A new global standard for enhanced tax controls—Navigating CRS compliance for banks and financial institutions. *FS Perspectives*. Sydney: Accenture. Available from: www.accenture.com/_acnmedia/pdf-79/accenture-arresting-tax-evasion.pdf.

Aged Care Financing Authority (ACFA). (2021). *Ninth Report on the Funding and Financing of the Aged Care Sector—July 2021*. Canberra: Aged Care Financing Authority. Available from: www.health.gov.au/resources/publications/ninth-report-on-the-funding-and-financing-of-the-aged-care-industry-july-2021.

Ajdacic, L., Heemskerk, E. & Garcia-Bernardo, J. (2021). The wealth defence industry: A large-scale study on accountancy firms as profit shifting facilitators. *New Political Economy*, *26*(4): 690–706. doi.org/10.1080/13563467.2020.1816947.

Albanese, A. (2020). Australia beyond the coronavirus: Fifth vision statement. Speech, 11 May, Parliament House, Canberra. Available from: web.archive.org/web/20200608151358/https://anthonyalbanese.com.au/anthony-albanese-speech-australia-beyond-the-coronavirus-canberra-monday-11-may-2020.

Altmann, R. (2020). The lesson of the Covid-19 care homes tragedy: Renationalising is no longer taboo. *The Guardian*, 7 July. Available from: www.theguardian.com/commentisfree/2020/jul/06/covid-19-care-homes-tragedy-renationalise-crisis.

Ansell, C.K., Comfort, L., Keller, A., LaPorte, T. & Schulman, P. (2021). The loss of capacity in public organizations: A public administration challenge. *Perspectives on Public Management and Governance*, *4*(1): 24–29. doi.org/10.1093/ppmgov/gvaa025.

Australian Children's Education and Care Quality Authority (ACECQA). (2016). *NQF Snapshot Q4 2015: A quarterly report from the Australian Children's Education and Care Quality Authority*. February. Sydney: ACECQA. Available from: www.acecqa.gov.au/media/23046.

Australian Children's Education and Care Quality Authority (ACECQA). (2019). *NQF Annual Performance Report: National Quality Framework*. December. Sydney: ACECQA. Available from: www.acecqa.gov.au/sites/default/files/2019-12/NQF-Annual-Performance-Report-2019.pdf.

Australian Children's Education and Care Quality Authority (ACECQA). (2020). *NQF Snapshot Q2 2020: A quarterly report from the Australian Children's Education and Care Quality Authority*. August. Sydney: ACECQA. Available from: www.acecqa.gov.au/media/29791.

Australian Institute of Health and Welfare (AIHW). (1995). *Australia's Welfare*. Canberra: AIHW.

Australian Institute of Health and Welfare (AIHW). (2006). *Community Aged Care Packages in Australia 2004–2005: A statistical overview*. 30 June. Canberra: AIHW. Available from: www.aihw.gov.au/reports/aged-care/community-aged-care-packages-australia-2004-05/contents/table-of-contents.

Australian Institute of Health and Welfare (AIHW). (2011). *Aged Care Packages in the Community 2009–10: A statistical overview*. 31 August. Canberra: AIHW. Available from: www.aihw.gov.au/reports/age/065/aged-care-packages-in-the-community-2009-10-a-sta/contents/table-of-contents.

Australian National Audit Office (ANAO). (2020). *Award of Funding under the Community Sport Infrastructure Program*. Auditor-General Report No. 23 of 2019–20, 15 January. Canberra: ANAO. Available from: www.anao.gov.au/work/performance-audit/award-funding-under-the-community-sport-infrastructure-program.

Australian National Audit Office (ANAO). (2021a). *COVID-19 Procurements and Deployments of the National Medical Stockpile*. Auditor-General Report No. 39 of 2020–21, 27 May. Canberra: ANAO. Available from: www.anao.gov.au/work/performance-audit/covid-19-procurements-and-deployments-the-national-medical-stockpile.

Australian National Audit Office (ANAO). (2021b). *Administration of Commuter Car Park Projects within the Urban Congestion Fund*. Auditor-General Report No. 47 of 2020–21, 28 June. Canberra: ANAO. Available from: www.anao.gov.au/work/performance-audit/administration-commuter-car-park-projects-within-the-urban-congestion-fund.

Bagshaw, E. & Gartrell, A. (2018). Big four consultancy firms cash in while gifting hundreds of thousands to Australia's major parties. *Sydney Morning Herald*, 1 February. Available from: www.smh.com.au/politics/federal/big-four-consultancy-firms-cash-in-while-gifting-hundreds-of-thousands-to-australia-s-major-parties-20180201-p4yz73.html.

Bavas, J. (2020). Service NSW confirms 180,000 customers' personal details exposed in cyber security breach. *ABC News*, 7 September. Available from: www.abc.net.au/news/2020-09-07/service-nsw-customer-personal-details-hacked-in-security-breach/12637502.

BDO. (2020). *Report on the profitability and viability of the Australian aged care industry.* Research Paper 12, 9 September. Canberra: Royal Commission into Aged Care Quality and Safety. Available from: agedcare.royalcommission.gov. au/publications/research-paper-12-report-profitability-and-viability-australian-aged-care-industry.

Blyth, M. (2001). The transformation of the Swedish model: Economic ideas, distributional conflict, and institutional change. *World Politics, 54*(1): 1–26. doi.org/10.1353/wp.2001.0020.

Braithwaite, V. (2020). Beyond the bubble that is Robodebt: How governments that lose integrity threaten democracy. *Australian Journal of Social Issues, 55*(3): 242–59. doi.org/10.1002/ajs4.122.

Brown, D.L. (2020). Digital government: Ideology and new forms of power. Unpublished PhD thesis, Deakin University, Melbourne. Available from: dro. deakin.edu.au/eserv/DU:30151549/brown-digitalgovernment-2021.pdf.

Burns, A. (2019). Whistleblowers say some employment service providers are exploiting the ParentsNext welfare scheme. *Background Briefing*, [ABC Radio National], 2 August. Available from: www.abc.net.au/news/2019-08-02/ whistleblowers-criticise-parentsnext/11363874.

Burton, T. (2020). Services Australia seeks business co-investors. *Australian Financial Review*, 3 March.

Busemeyer, M.R. & Thelen, K. (2020). Institutional sources of business power. *World Politics, 72*(3): 448–80. doi.org/10.1017/S004388712000009X.

Butler, J. (2020). Australia's top health experts weren't consulted about stopping aged-care inspections. *The New Daily*, [Melbourne], 2 September. Available from: thenewdaily.com.au/news/2020/09/02/australias-top-health-experts-werent-consulted-about-stopping-aged-care-inspections/.

Cahill, D. & Toner, P. (eds). (2018). *Wrong Way: How privatisation and economic reform backfired.* Melbourne: La Trobe University Press.

Caisley, O. (2020). Just one in six care homes checked. *The Australian*, 24 September.

Carey, G., Malbon, E., Green, C., Reeders, D. & Marjolin, A. (2020). Quasi-market shaping, stewarding and steering in personalization: The need for practice-orientated empirical evidence. *Policy Design and Practice, 3*(1): 1–15. doi.org/10.1080/25741292.2019.1704985.

Connolly, A. (2020). Grieving families angry at Aged Care Quality and Safety Commission over perceived inaction during coronavirus pandemic. *7.30*, [ABC TV], 28 September. Available from: www.abc.net.au/news/2020-09-29/aged-care-deaths-prompt-family-anger-at-regulator/12693160.

Considine, M. (1999). Markets, networks and the new welfare state: Employment assistance reforms in Australia. *Journal of Social Policy, 28*(2): 183–203. doi.org/10.1017/S0047279499005607.

Considine, M. (2001). *Enterprising States: The public management of welfare-to-work*. Melbourne: Cambridge University Press.

Considine, M., Lewis, J.M. & O'Sullivan, S. (2011). Quasi-markets and service delivery flexibility following a decade of employment assistance reform in Australia. *Journal of Social Policy, 40*(4): 811–33. doi.org/10.1017/S0047279 411000213.

Considine, M., Lewis, J.M., O'Sullivan, S. & Sol, E. (2015). *Getting Welfare to Work: Street-level governance in Australia, the UK, and the Netherlands*. Oxford, UK: Oxford University Press. doi.org/10.1093/acprof:oso/9780198743705. 001.0001.

Considine, M., O'Sullivan, S., McGann, M. & Nguyen, P. (2020). Locked-in or locked-out: Can a public services market really change? *Journal of Social Policy, 49*(4): 850–71. doi.org/10.1017/S0047279419000941.

Crikey. (2020a). The closed-door contracts flourishing in these COVID times. *Crikey*, 21 September 2020.

Crikey. (2020b). Minister supports calls for aged care royal commission to investigate Mable contract. *Crikey*, 24 September.

Dalby, D. (2019). Accenture settles Lux Leaks tax claim for $200m. *Investigations*, 26 February. Washington, DC: International Consortium of Investigative Journalists. Available from: www.icij.org/investigations/luxembourg-leaks/accenture-settles-lux-leaks-tax-claim-for-200m/.

Davies, R. (2020). Concern over 'opaque' Covid-related contracts awarded around world. *The Guardian*, 1 September. Available from: www.theguardian.com/world/2020/sep/01/concern-over-opaque-covid-related-contracts-awarded-around-world.

Deloitte. (2022). *About GovLab: Enabling innovation in the public sector*. [Online]. Canberra: Deloitte Australia. Available from: www2.deloitte.com/au/en/pages/public-sector/solutions/about-gov-lab.html.

Department of Education, Employment and Workplace Relations (DEEWR). (2010). *State of Child Care in Australia April 2010*. Canberra: Australian Government.

Department of Health. (2011). *2010–11 Report on the Operation of the Aged Care Act 1997*. Canberra: Australian Government. Available from: www.gen-aged caredata.gov.au/resources/reports-and-publications/2011/december/2010 %E2%80%9311-report-on-the-operation-of-the-aged-care-a.

Department of Health. (2016). *2015–16 Report on the Operation of the Aged Care Act 1997*. Canberra: Australian Government. Available from: www.gen-aged caredata.gov.au/resources/reports-and-publications/2016/december/2015 %E2%80%9316-report-on-the-operation-of-the-aged-care-a.

Department of Health. (2022). COVID-19 outbreaks in Australian residential aged care facilities. National snapshot, 8 pm, 10 March 2022. Canberra: Australian Government. Available from: www.health.gov.au/sites/default/files/documents/2022/03/covid-19-outbreaks-in-australian-residential-aged-care-facilities-11-march-2022.docx.

Department of the Prime Minister and Cabinet (PM&C). (2019). *Our Public Service, Our Future: Independent review of the Australian Public Service*. Canberra: Australian Government. Available from: pmc.gov.au/resource-centre/government/independent-review-australian-public-service.

Dickinson, H., Carey, G. & Kavanagh, A.M. (2020). Personalisation and pandemic: An unforeseen collision course? *Disability & Society, 35*(6): 1–6. doi.org/10.1080/09687599.2020.1772201.

Di Francesco, M. (2020). A signal failure: Sports grants, public servants, and traffic lights. *Australian Journal of Public Administration, 79*(4): 584–91. doi.org/10.1111/1467-8500.12434.

Dingwall, D. (2018). More than 33 million Centrelink calls unanswered as DHS denies staffing problem. *Sydney Morning Herald*, 7 March. Available from: www.smh.com.au/public-service/more-than-33-million-centrelink-calls-unanswered-as-dhs-denies-staffing-problem-20180307-h0x4up.html.

Douglas, S., Schillemans, T., 't Hart, P., Ansell, C., Bøgh Andersen, L., Flinders, M., Head, B., Moynihan, D., Nabatchi, T., O'Flynn, J., Peters, B. Guy, Raadschelders, J., Sancino, A., Sørensen, E. & Torfing, J. (2021). Rising to Ostrom's challenge: An invitation to walk on the bright side of public governance and public service. *Policy Design and Practice, 4*(4): 441–51. doi.org/10.1080/25741292.2021.1972517.

Du Gay, P. (2008). 'Without affection or enthusiasm': Problems of involvement and attachment in responsive public management. *Organization, 15*(3): 335–53. doi.org/10.1177/1350508408088533.

Eardley, T. (2003). Outsourcing employment services: What have we learned from the Job Network? Paper presented to the Centre for Applied Economic Research Conference on the Economic and Social Impacts of Outsourcing, University of New South Wales, Sydney, 4–5 December.

Eggers, W.D. & Macmillan, P. (2015). *Gov2020: A Journey into the future of government.* London: Deloitte. Available from: www2.deloitte.com/content/dam/Deloitte/au/Documents/public-sector/deloitte-au-ps-gov2020-journey-future-government2-130315.pdf.

Ernst & Young (EY). (2014). *Creating Public Value: Transforming Australia's social services.* Melbourne: EY. Available from: web.archive.org/web/2016 0229195917/www.ey.com/Publication/vwLUAssets/EY_-_Creating_public_value/$FILE/ey-creating-public-value.pdf.

Gingrich, J. (2011). *Making Markets in the Welfare State: The politics of varying market reforms.* Cambridge, UK: Cambridge University Press. doi.org/10.1017/CBO9780511791529.

Gomez, P. (2020). El plan de Iglesias para 'nacionalizar' las residencias costaría 10.000 millones [Iglesias's plan to 'nationalise' nursing homes would cost 10,000 million]. *La Razón*, [Madrid], 12 June. Available from: www.larazon.es/espana/20200612/vtcuoivr3ffurd2lxzct3blu6e.html.

Hendry, J. (2021). Service NSW unable to notify 54,000 customers impacted by cyber attack. *IT News*, 26 March. Available from: www.itnews.com.au/news/service-nsw-unable-to-notify-54000-customers-impacted-by-cyber-attack-562675.

Holden, R. (2020). Vital signs: Victoria's privatised quarantine arrangements were destined to fail. *The Conversation*, 24 July. Available from: theconversation.com/vital-signs-victorias-privatised-quarantine-arrangements-were-destined-to-fail-143169.

Hood, C. (1991). A public management for all seasons? *Public Administration, 69*(1): 3–19. doi.org/10.1111/j.1467-9299.1991.tb00779.x.

Howlett, M. & Migone, A. (2013). Policy advice through the market: The role of external consultants in contemporary policy advisory systems. *Policy and Society, 32*(3): 241–54. doi.org/10.1016/j.polsoc.2013.07.005.

Jenkins, S. (2020). Services Australia to receive extra 5000 workers. *The Mandarin*, 23 March. Available from: www.themandarin.com.au/128192-services-australia-to-receive-extra-5000-workers/.

Jobs Australia. (2015). *State of Play: Jobactive employment services 2015–2020 tender results*. Melbourne: Jobs Australia. Available from: web.archive.org/web/20160321154943/www.ja.com.au/sites/default/files/final_sop_-_es_2015-2020_tender_results.pdf.

Jones, C., Temouri, Y. & Cobham, A. (2018). Tax haven networks and the role of the Big 4 accountancy firms. *Journal of World Business*, *53*(2): 177–93. doi.org/10.1016/j.jwb.2017.10.004.

Karp, P. (2019). Robodebt reviews may be delayed by lack of trained staff, union warns. *The Guardian*, [Australia], 21 December. Available from: www.theguardian.com/australia-news/2019/dec/21/robodebt-reviews-may-be-delayed-by-lack-of-trained-staff-union-warns.

Keane, B. (2019). Greens take a step forward in reining in the big four accounting firms. *Crikey*, 3 May. Available from: www.crikey.com.au/2019/05/03/greens-big-four-accounting-firms-policy/.

Kiezebrink, V. & van Teeffelen, J. (2020). *Profiting from a Pandemic: How COVID-19 test kit producer Qiagen receives public money but avoids taxes*. SOMO Report, October. Amsterdam: Stichting Onderzoek Multinationale Ondernemingen [Centre for Research on Multinational Corporations]. Available from: www.somo.nl/wp-content/uploads/2020/10/Profiting-from-a-pandemic.pdf.

Knaus, C. (2020). Coalition gave private pathology companies lucrative Covid contracts. *The Guardian*, [Australia], 1 June. Available from: www.theguardian.com/australia-news/2020/jun/01/coalition-gave-private-pathology-companies-lucrative-covid-contracts.

Le Grand, C. (2020). 'Carpetbaggers and snake oil sellers' hike prices on COVID-19 essentials. *Sydney Morning Herald*, 26 May. Available from: www.smh.com.au/national/carpetbaggers-and-snake-oil-sellers-hike-prices-on-covid-19-essentials-20200526-p54wgc.html.

Mannheim, M. (2020). Federal Government spending $5 billion per year on contractors as gig economy grows inside public service. *ABC News*, 10 September. Available from: www.abc.net.au/news/2020-09-10/contractors-and-the-public-service-gig-economy/12647956.

Maximus. (2019). *Annual Report*. [Form 10-K]. Reston, VA: Maximus. Available from: investor.maximus.com/sec-filings/annual-reports/content/0001032220-19-000105/0001032220-19-000105.pdf.

Meagher, G. & Goodwin, S. (eds). (2015). *Markets, Rights and Power in Australian Social Policy*. Sydney: Sydney University Press. doi.org/10.30722/sup.9781920899950.

Meagher, G. & Wilson, S. (2015). The politics of market encroachment: Policy-maker rationales and voter responses. In G. Meagher & S. Goodwin (eds), *Markets, Rights and Power in Australian Social Policy* (pp. 29–96). Sydney: Sydney University Press. doi.org/10.30722/sup.9781920899950.

Medhora, S. (2019). Federal Court rules robodebt 'unlawful' in significant court case. *Hack*, [Triple J Radio], 27 November. Available from: www.abc.net.au/triplej/programs/hack/federal-government-loses-major-robodebt-case/11742494.

Meier, K.J., Compton, M., Polga-Hecimovich, J., Song, M. & Wimpy, C. (2019). Bureaucracy and the failure of politics: Challenges to democratic governance. *Administration & Society*, *51*(10): 1576–605. doi.org/10.1177/0095399719874759.

Morton, R. (2022). The sweet-heart deal that caused testing to collapse. *The Saturday Paper*, 22-28 January.

Murphy, K. (2020). Morrison shrugs off censure of aged care minister Richard Colbeck over Covid conduct. *The Guardian*, [Australia], 3 September. Available from: www.theguardian.com/australia-news/2020/sep/03/morrison-shrugs-off-censure-of-aged-care-minister-richard-colbeck-over-covid-conduct.

O'Flynn, J. (2018). Markets in misery. Contribution to workshop Theorising the Dynamics of Social Service Markets: Risk, Regulation and Rent-Seeking, Macquarie University, Sydney, April.

O'Flynn, J. & Sturgess, G.L. (2019). *2030 and beyond: Getting the work of government done*. ANZSOG Research Paper for the Australian Public Service Review Panel, March. Melbourne: Australia and New Zealand School of Government. Available from: www.apsreview.gov.au/sites/default/files/resources/2030-beyond-getting-business-government-done.pdf.

O'Sullivan, S., McGann, M. & Considine, M. (2019). The category game and its impact on street-level bureaucrats and jobseekers: An Australian case study. *Social Policy and Society*, *18*(4): 631–45. doi.org/10.1017/S1474746419000162.

Peterkin, T. (2020). Prospect of nationalised care homes raised as Nicola Sturgeon signals more help for low-paid workers. *The Press and Journal*, [Aberdeen, Scotland], 20 May. Available from: www.pressandjournal.co.uk/fp/news/politics/scottish-politics/2208124/prospect-of-nationalised-care-homes-raised-as-nicola-sturgeon-signals-more-help-for-low-paid-workers/.

Parliamentary Joint Committee on Corporations and Financial Services. (2020). *Regulation of Auditing in Australia: Interim report.* February. Canberra: Parliament of Australia. Available from: www.aph.gov.au/Parliamentary_Business/Committees/Joint/Corporations_and_Financial_Services/Regulation ofAuditing/Interim_Report.

Pricewaterhouse Coopers (PwC). (2012). *Transforming the Citizen Experience: One stop shop for public services.* February. Sydney: PwC Australia. Available from: www.pwc.com.au/pdf/transforming-the-citizen-experience-one-stop-shop-feb12.pdf.

PricewaterhouseCoopers (PwC). (2017). *Reimagining Public–Private Partnerships.* Sydney: PwC Australia. Available from: web.archive.org/web/2018041806 1143/https://www.pwc.com.au/legal/assets/reimagining-ppps-oct17.pdf.

Productivity Commission (PC). (2002). *Independent Review of the Job Network: Inquiry report.* Report No. 21, 3 June. Canberra: Productivity Commission. Available from: www.pc.gov.au/inquiries/completed/job-network/report.

Remeikis, A. & Karp, P. (2020). From novelty cheque to full-blown scandal: A timeline of the sports rorts saga. *The Guardian,* [Australia], 13 March. Available from: www.theguardian.com/australia-news/2020/mar/13/from-novelty-cheque-to-full-blown-scandal-a-timeline-of-the-sports-rorts-saga.

Richardson, A. (2020a). *Australia Industry (ANZSIC) Report Q8601: Aged care residential services in Australia.* Melbourne: IbisWorld.

Richardson, A. (2020b). *Australia Industry (ANZSIC) Report Q8710: Child care services in Australia.* Melbourne: IbisWorld.

Richardson, T. (2020). Peter and Areti Arvanitis deified by aged-care millions. *Australian Financial Review,* 3 August. Available from: www.afr.com/rear-window/peter-and-areti-arvanitis-deified-by-aged-care-millions-20200803-p55hzp.

Robert, S. (2020). Address to Australia Israel Chamber of Commerce by The Hon. Stuart Robert MP, Minister for the National Disability Insurance Scheme and Minister for Government Services, 28 February, Melbourne. Transcript. Available from: web.archive.org/web/20200319211821/https:/minister.servicesaustralia.gov.au/transcripts/2020-02-28-address-australia-israel-chamber-commerce.

Rundle, K. (2020). *Reassessing contracting-out: Lessons from the Victorian Hotel Quarantine Inquiry.* Governing During Crises Policy Brief No. 7, 21 September. Melbourne: Melbourne School of Government, University of Melbourne. Available from: government.unimelb.edu.au/__data/assets/pdf_file/0008/3496607/GDC-Policy-Brief-7_Reassessing-Contracting-Out_21.09.20final pub.pdf.

Schneiders, B. (2020). How hotel quarantine let COVID-19 out of the bag in Victoria. *The Age*, [Melbourne], 3 July. Available from: www.theage.com.au/national/victoria/how-hotel-quarantine-let-covid-19-out-of-the-bag-in-victoria-20200703-p558og.html.

Senate Community Affairs References Committee. (2019). *ParentsNext, Including its Trial and Subsequent Broader Rollout.* March. Canberra: Parliament of Australia. Available from: www.aph.gov.au/Parliamentary_Business/Committees/Senate/Community_Affairs/ParentsNext/Report.

Senate Employment, Education and Training Legislation Committee. (1995). *Hansard: Committee Hearings*, 23 November. Canberra: Parliament of Australia.

Senate Select Committee on COVID-19. (2020). Australian Government's response to the Covid-19 pandemic. *Hansard: Committee Hearings*, 10 September. Canberra: Parliament of Australia. Available from: parlinfo.aph.gov.au/parlInfo/search/display/display.w3p;query=Id%3A%22committees%2Fcommsen%2Fd37dac99-c40f-47ff-be91-2905bdb90c78%2F0001%22.

Senate Select Committee on COVID-19. (2022). *Final Report*. April. Canberra: Parliament of Australia. Available from: www.aph.gov.au/Parliamentary_Business/Committees/Senate/COVID-19/COVID19/Report.

Senate Select Committee on Job Security. (2021). *Second Interim Report: Insecurity in publicly-funded jobs*. October. Canberra: Parliament of Australia. Available from: www.aph.gov.au/Parliamentary_Business/Committees/Senate/Job_Security/JobSecurity/Second_Interim_Report.

Snape, J. & Probyn, A. (2020). Government's $150 million female sports program funnelled into swimming pools for marginal Coalition seats. *ABC News*, 7 February. Available from: www.abc.net.au/news/2020-02-07/government-cash-splash-swimming-pools/11924850.

Steering Committee for the Review of Government Service Provision (SCRGSP). (2001). *Report on Government Services 2000*. Canberra: Productivity Commission.

Steering Committee for the Review of Government Service Provision (SCRGSP). (2006). *Report on Government Services 2005*. Canberra: Productivity Commission.

Stewart Brown. (2022). *Aged Care Financial Performance Survey: December 2021 (Six months) summary results*. Sydney: Stewart Brown.

Sturdy, A. (2018). Promoting solutions and co-constructing problems—Management consultancy and instrument constituencies. *Policy and Society*, *37*(1): 74–89. doi.org/10.1080/14494035.2017.1375247.

Swadden, P. (2020). Most Canadians support federal takeover of long-term care facilities, poll finds. *CityNews Montreal*, 25 May. Available from: montreal. citynews.ca/2020/05/25/support-federal-takeover-long-term-care/.

Tadros, E. (2019). Deloitte, EY, KPMG and PwC a 'systemic' tax risk: ATO. *Australian Financial Review*, 12 September.

Terzon, E. (2021). COVID-19 testing is lining the pockets of pathology companies. Now other firms want in. *ABC News*, 31 August. Available from: www.abc.net.au/news/2021-08-31/covid-testing-pathology-testing-laverty-healius-sonic-rapid/100420032.

Thompson, A. (2020). NSW Premier Gladys Berejiklian embroiled in grant rorting claims. *Sydney Morning Herald*, 3 July. Available from: www.smh. com.au/national/nsw/nsw-premier-gladys-berejiklian-embroiled-in-grant-rorting-claims-20200703-p558py.html.

van den Berg, C., Howlett, M., Migone, A., Howard, M., Pemer, F. & Gunter, H.M. (2020). *Policy Consultancy in Comparative Perspective: Patterns, nuances and implications of the contractor state*. Cambridge, UK: Cambridge University Press. doi.org/10.1017/9781108634724.

West, M. (2016). Oligarchs of the treasure islands. *Michael West Media*, 11 July. Available from: www.michaelwest.com.au/oligarchs-of-the-treasure-islands/.

West, M. (2018). Big Four: Government's binge on consultants goes ballistic. *Michael West Media*, 20 September. Available from: www.michaelwest.com. au/big-four-governments-binge-on-consultants-goes-ballistic/.

Whyte, S. (2020a). Big four consultants KPMG, EY, PWC, Deloitte donations top $1 million. *The Canberra Times*, 24 February.

Whyte, S. (2020b). Almost five million Centrelink calls missed in one week at start of shutdown. *The Canberra Times*, 12 June.

Wilson, G. (2020). Outsourcing government itself: Inside the hidden privatisation of the public service. *Michael West Media*, 8 September. Available from: www. michaelwest.com.au/privatisation-of-the-public-service/.

Young, E. (2022). Government flags possible reform of $7b Workforce Australia jobseeker program a month after launching it. *ABC News*, 2 August. Available from: www.abc.net.au/news/2022-08-02/workforce-australia-faces-possible-overhaul-amid-concerns/101293330.

www.ingramcontent.com/pod-product-compliance
Lightning Source LLC
Chambersburg PA
CBHW051441270326

41932CB00025B/3387